Andrew Taylor

spent five years as a reporter and ~~~~~~
ting articles to *The Times*, the *Spe* ~~~~~~ *...........y Telegraph*
and working for Dubai Television. His first book, *Travelling the
Sands*, was a history of exploration in the Arabian Peninsula. He
now lives in Oxfordshire.

From the reviews of *God's Fugitive*:

'Surely the definitive biography of [a] half-forgotten literary
genius'   JAN MORRIS, *Independent* Books of the Year

'It is as if Taylor has taken *Travels in Arabia Deserta* . . . and decon-
structed it, nail by nail . . . a marvellous tale about a character
whose "absurdity was closely bound up with his creativity"'
ROGER LEWIS, *Spectator*

'Taylor is an intelligent, perceptive biographer who writes with
vigorous felicity and has the unusual quality of sticking to essen-
tials. [He] is able to throw new light and achieve balance by the
judicious use of the surviving notes which Doughty made at the
time'   J. B. PICK, *Scotsman*

'[Doughty's works] have returned to obscurity, but thanks to this
excellent biography their author will be appreciated for what he
was: a man of original intelligence and formidable steadfastness
and integrity'   LAWRENCE JAMES, *Literary Review*

'Splendid'   *New Scientist*

'[Doughty] would have recognised Andrew Taylor's large-scale
portrait, warts and all, as fulfilling his own tenets of uncompromising truthfulness . . . a good and honest book'
JAN MORRIS, *Independent*

'Colourful, lucid, well-researched'   ANDREW RISSIK, *Guardian*

GOD'S
FUGITIVE

The Life of
Charles Montagu Doughty

Andrew Taylor

Flamingo
An Imprint of HarperCollinsPublishers

Flamingo
An Imprint of HarperCollins*Publishers*
77–85 Fulham Palace Road,
Hammersmith, London W6 8JB

The HarperCollins website address is:
www.**fire**and**water**.com

Published by Flamingo 2000
9 8 7 6 5 4 3 2 1

First published in Great Britain
by HarperCollins*Publishers* 1999

Copyright © Andrew Taylor 1999

The Author asserts the moral right to
be identified as the author of this work

ISBN 0 00 638832 9

Set in Postscript Linotype Meridien

Printed and bound in Great Britain by
Omnia Books Limited, Glasgow

Looking in one direction,
this book is dedicated to
HARRY TAYLOR

and in the other
to
SAM, ABIGAIL AND REBECCA

CONTENTS

LIST OF ILLUSTRATIONS   xi

MAP Doughty's Mediterranean Travels
May 1871–April 1873   xii

ACKNOWLEDGEMENTS   xv

AUTHOR'S NOTE   xvii

FOREWORD   xxi

GOD'S FUGITIVE   1

AFTERWORD   317

NOTES   323

BIBLIOGRAPHY   339

INDEX   343

ILLUSTRATIONS

Theberton Hall
St Mary's Church, Martlesham, Suffolk
Martlesham Hall (*Suffolk County Record Office*)
Gonville and Caius College, Cambridge
Gonville Court, Gonville and Caius College
Downing College, Cambridge

A page from Doughty's European notebook (*Reproduced by permission of the Master and Fellows of Gonville and Caius College, Cambridge*)
Doughty in Damascus (*Caroline Barron collection*)
A page from Doughty's Arabian diaries (*By permission of the Syndics of the Fitzwilliam Museum, to whom rights in this publication are assigned*)
Doughty's sketch of the interior of the *kella* from which he explored the ruins of Medain Salih
Doughty's sketch of the first monument at Medain Salih
Doughty's pencil drawing of an encampment of the Sehamma tribe
Doughty's view of the harsh lava plain of the Harra, across which he travelled

Illawarra, 2 Beulah Road, Tunbridge Wells
D.G. Hogarth, sketched by Augustus John (© *Julius E. White*)
T.E. Lawrence, sketched by Augustus John (© *Julius E. White*)
Merriecroft, Kent
Merriecroft
Portrait of CMD by Dorothy Doughty (*Reproduced by permission of Downing College, Cambridge*)
Doughty as an old man, sketched five years before his death
Doughty's memorial at Golder's Green Crematorium

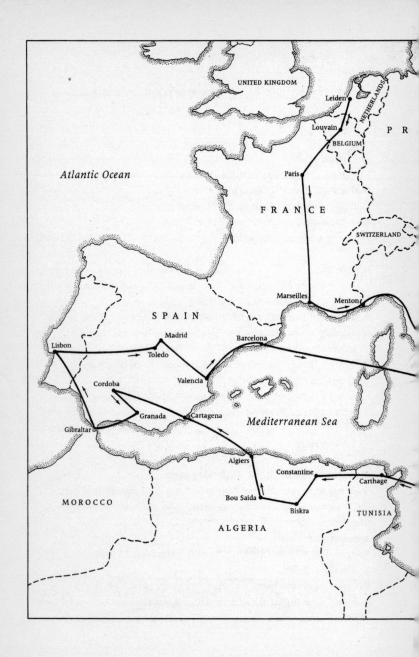

UNITED KINGDOM

Atlantic Ocean

Leiden

Louvain
BELGIUM
NETHERLANDS

P R

Paris

F R A N C E

SWITZERLAND

Marseilles
Menton

S P A I N

Lisbon
Madrid
Toledo
Barcelona

Cordoba
Valencia

Granada
Cartagena
Mediterranean Sea

Gibraltar

MOROCCO

Algiers
Constantine
Carthage

Bou Saida
Biskra
TUNISIA

ALGERIA

Doughty's Mediterranean Travels
MAY 1871–APRIL 1873

RUSSIA

AUSTRO-HUNGARIAN
EMPIRE

Black Sea

ITALY

Naples

OTTOMAN EMPIRE

OTTOMAN EMPIRE

SICILY

Athens

Ephesus

MALTA

Mediterranean Sea

ACKNOWLEDGEMENTS

I have been helped by many individuals and institutions throughout this project. To all of them, I offer my thanks.

Professor John Carey, of Merton College, Oxford, was my teacher many years ago, and is my good friend today. Without his advice and encouragement from the very beginning, the book would never even have been started.

No one can write about Charles Doughty without incurring an immense debt to the work done by his friend David Hogarth, the noted Arabist and former Keeper of Oxford University's Ashmolean Museum. Hogarth's biography, *The Life of Charles M. Doughty*, which gathered together much material which would otherwise have been lost, was published in 1928, soon after the deaths of both its subject and its author. I have tried to acknowledge individual debts in the footnotes.

In addition, I must thank his granddaughter, Dr Caroline Barron, of the History Department, Royal Holloway, University of London, for her cooperation and hospitality in allowing me to consult her collection of Dr Hogarth's letters and papers.

Wilfred Thesiger, last of the line of Arabian explorers of which Charles Doughty was the first, gave me his unique perspective not just on Doughty, but on travelling in the desert in general.

Martin Hotham, of Drinkstone Green, Suffolk, was generous in providing background information about Doughty's mother's family, from which he is descended. I was also fortunate in being able to visit several of the houses in which Doughty lived at various times. Stephen Beaumont, of Theberton Hall, Peter Hatcher, of Martlesham Hall, and Lawrence Brooks, of Merriecroft, Sissinghurst, Kent, all welcomed me, my notebook and my camera to their homes.

In and around the village of Sissinghurst the Doughty family are still remembered. Dr Geoffrey Hattersley-Smith and Mr Edward Ryan were especially helpful with their own memories and their local research.

Various memorabilia of Doughty's travels, his European diary, his word-notes and books from his library are held in the Gonville and Caius College Library in Cambridge, and I am grateful to the Master and Fellows of Gonville and Caius College for their permission to quote from this material. I owe a particular debt to the college Librarian, Mr J. H. Prynne, and his staff, and to the college Archivist, Ms Ellie Clewlow, for their hospitality and assistance during my visits.

Material from Doughty's Arabian diaries and from a number of letters is used by permission of the Syndics of the Fitzwilliam Museum, Cambridge, to whom rights in the publication are assigned. Permission to use other collections of letters and other material was given by the Harry Ransom Humanities Research Center at the University of Texas at Austin; the Royal Geographical Society; and the University of Leiden Library. Extracts from the journal of Frederick Proby Doughty, which is held by the Ipswich Record Office, are used by permission of the Suffolk County Record Office. Material from the BBC is similarly used by permission.

I have received nothing but help, too, from the staff of the Bodleian Library, Oxford; the British Library; the London Library; Oslo University Library; the Public Records Office, Kew; and the National Maritime Museum, Greenwich. Alison Roberts, the Collections Manager at Oxford University's Ashmolean Museum, was particularly cooperative in dealing with my queries about Charles Doughty, stone axes and palaeolithic research.

Mrs Lynne Oualah of Gillotts School, Henley, generously translated Doughty's German articles for me.

I have a particular debt to my friends in Dubai who first opened the door upon the beauties of Arab culture and the Arabic language; and many other friends have helped me directly with preparing this book over the last few months. Julian Bene sat up late into the night, arguing about Doughty and his writing, only to see some of his best ideas slipped silently into the text. To Penny Berry I owe much more than I can ever repay with a book. Other friends and relatives have helped in various ways, among them Tony and Jean Conyers, Alison M. Roberts, Jessica Taylor and Richard Taylor. I have also relied heavily on the professional help and advice of Toby Eady and Michael Fishwick.

Thanks of an entirely different order are due to Dr Tim Littlewood and his team from Oxford's John Radcliffe Hospital. Without their skill and care the last few months, and the next few decades, too, might well have been impossible.

And, of course, my wife Liz, and Sam, Abigail and Rebecca. For the last three years Charles Doughty has been a constant guest at their dinner-table, a frequent sharer in their conversations.

ANDREW TAYLOR
Cholsey
Oxfordshire

AUTHOR'S NOTE

One of the most bitter, if minor, disputes between students
of Arabic has long been over the correct use of the terms
bedu, bedui, beduw, beduin and *bedouin* to describe the
nomadic tribesmen of the Arab world. Doughty, for all his
linguistic pedantry, seems to have used the words more
or less interchangeably, and I have thought it simplest not
to try and change his usage.

In quoting from his poetry, however, I have taken the
liberty of making minor changes to his punctuation in the
interests of clarity. Doughty adopted his own impenetrable
system, as several contemporary critics complained: I can
only apologize to purists who take offence at my attempts
to make the punctuation a help, rather than a hindrance,
to comprehension.

The traveller must be himself in men's eyes, a man worthy to live under the bent of God's heaven, and were it without a religion; he is such who has a clean human heart and longsuffering under his bare shirt: it is enough, and though the way be full of harms, he may travel to the ends of the world.

Travels in Arabia Deserta, i, p. 56

FOREWORD

Charles Montagu Doughty was the foremost Arabian explorer of his or any other age. His two years of wandering with the bedu through the oasis towns and deserts started a tradition of British exploration and discovery by travellers who acknowledged him as their master, and he returned to England to write one of the greatest and most original travel books.

He was that unlikely adventurer for his day, a man who would not kill – and yet he had strength and passion, and could face the threat of his own death without flinching. As a writer, he believed in his writing and in his vision when nobody else did; turning his back on exploration, he dedicated his life to poetry and struggled singlehandedly to change the direction of English literature. He lived through the greatest revolution in thought the world had ever seen, and spent a lifetime wrestling with his conscience over its consequences.

Among his admirers as an artist were George Bernard Shaw, who found *Arabia Deserta* inexhaustible. 'You can open it and dip into it anywhere all the rest of your life,' he declared.[1] There were F. R. Leavis, Edwin Muir, Wyndham Lewis and, most ardent of all, T. E. Lawrence. *Seven Pillars of Wisdom* is, in its way, Lawrence's own homage to Doughty.

And now he is virtually forgotten, his dense and idiosyncratic works valued by antiquarian booksellers and lovers of Arabia, but practically unknown to the readers of a simpler, less painstaking age. The achievement of his travels on foot and by camel seems overshadowed in the days of four-wheel-drive vehicles, helicopters, satellite navigation systems, supply-drops and commercial sponsorship. The great desert journeys are now all in the past. The tradition of Arabian exploration can never be recovered: it is as much a part of history today as the crossing of the Atlantic, or the search for the source of the Nile.

It was Wilfred Thesiger, another great Arabian explorer, who observed that there could never again be a camel-crossing of the desert like his own in the 1940s, or those of the explorers who went before him. 'I was the last of the Arabian explorers, because afterwards, there were the cars,' he said. 'When I made my journeys in Arabia, there was no possibility of travelling in any other way than the way I went. If you could go in a car, it would turn the whole journey into a stunt.'[2]

Thesiger was the last of a line that included Harry St John Philby, father of the Russian spy and the dedicated servant of Ibn Saud, King of Arabia; there was Bertram Thomas, the civil servant who saved up his holidays for his desert expeditions, and became the first European to cross the Empty Quarter; and Gertrude Bell, who travelled to Arabia in the shadow of a disastrous love affair,[3] and demanded that the rulers of Hail treat her like the lady she was and cash her a cheque for £200.

There were the Blunts, Wilfrid and Lady Anne, searching for a romantic Orient which never existed outside the salons of London and Paris; and of course, T. E. Lawrence himself, Lawrence of Arabia, who united the warring tribes just long enough to drive out the Turks and change the face of the Middle East for ever. All of them were passionate, even obsessive, about the desert – and above and before them all stood Charles Montagu Doughty.

The tradition had lasted less than seventy years. Before, there had been adventurers, explorers like Sir Richard Burton or William Gifford Palgrave, who disguised themselves and slipped through Arabia like thieves or spies; after Doughty, with his proud refusal to dissemble, things were never the same again.

Doughty came to Arabia almost by accident, at the end of six years' wandering through Europe and the Middle East. Initially, he intended to investigate reports of a lost city like Petra, close by the pilgrim road to Mecca; but by the time he sailed away from Jedda two years later, he had dug more deeply into Arabia, lived more closely with the wandering bedu, than any explorer before or since. Thesiger was to collect photographs, Philby tiptoed after tiny birds, reptiles and mammals like some ghastly Angel of Death adding to his collection, and all of them gathered fossils, rocks and 'specimens' for the museums at home – but Doughty's vision embraced an entire civilization.

Everything he did was on a grand scale, and the book he eventually wrote about his travels, which appeared some nine years later, covered nearly 1,200 pages. It was written in a style that mingled Elizabethan and Arabian, the rhythms of the Bible with the precision of a scientific text. And apart from being a staggering work of literary ambition, *Travels in Arabia Deserta* was, for many of the explorers who followed him, a first introduction to the Arab world.

'We were in totally different parts of Arabia, so he couldn't give me any information about the country itself, but he could give me a feel for the bedu and their way of life,' said Thesiger, whose own book, *Arabian Sands*, is itself considered a classic.[4] 'It was a massive undertaking. Thomas's books I don't think are worth reading; Philby's are too technical, and I don't find them readable, but there is more in Doughty about the Arabs and their way of life than anywhere else.'

Doughty claimed later that his travelling was no more than a brief distraction in a life dedicated to poetry. But Arabia stayed with him until the day he died – as indeed it did with all the explorers. His obsessions, though, were bigger, more ambitious, than theirs – his book delving at the same time into the soul of a civilization and into the soul of a single tortured human being.

He was born into the maelstrom of the most wide-ranging revolution in the entire history of western thought, and he shared fully in an intellectual upheaval that still reverberates. Scientific disputes are usually remote, abstruse – the bitter argument centuries before, over whether the sun or the earth was at the centre of the universe, had been carried on largely among a small group of committed experts. The vast mass of the people were as unaffected as they were uncomprehending. But the twin shocks of the revolution which hit the mid nineteenth century were to shake the confident world-view of virtually every single thinking person in the western world for decades to come.

Through the early years of the century generations of comfortable certainty were being chipped away by the questing hammers of the new geologists. Not only was the world vastly older than the theologians suggested, the scientists claimed, but the natural forces that had shaped it were still at work. Two books took the argument forward – first Charles Lyell's *Principles of Geology*, and then Charles Darwin's *On the Origin of Species*.

Each was the synthesis of a dispute which had been simmering for decades, but they shifted the ground of the debate irreversibly. First the earth, and now mankind itself, was toppled from its position as the unchanging Creation of a loving God. The reassuring vision of man in the image of his Maker was altered for ever. It was by going to study the work of wind, rain, volcanoes and glaciers, peering through microscopes rather than poring over religious books, that knowledge could be won.

Doughty followed both courses. He was born into a family which, through its generations of conservative Anglican religious ministry and its respect for history and tradition, was likely to be shaken to the core by the revolution. Many people in a similar position struggled to maintain their equanimity by ignoring the scientific arguments, others by relinquishing their religious faith. Doughty, picking over fossils in the Suffolk clay, travelling to Cambridge University to study the dangerous new discipline of Natural Science, struggling with his ice-axe and notebooks over the glaciers of Norway, yet still maintaining his passionate religious sense, was caught in a lifelong dilemma.

After Cambridge, he abandoned science to turn to poetry, abandoned the new fascination with field-study to return to the library. Once again, he was delving back into the past, into the foundations and origins this time of language and literature, a self-taught philologist, linguist and anthropologist. When he set off on his travels, his copies of Chaucer, Spenser and other early English writers in his bags, it was with a closely drawn and wide-ranging intellectual map which could guide his researches in geography, geology, biology, history, anthropology and language.

But he had, too, the deeply introspective determination of a writer and a poet. His wanderings, as far as we can tell, seem to have been largely serendipitous: Doughty was blown by whatever wind took him, first around Europe, then through the Middle East and Sinai, and finally south with the Hadj caravan towards Mecca.

When he returned, it was to a life of unremitting study and contemplation as he embarked first on the story of his travels, and then on a series of epic poems that drew on his experiences, his researches and his uncompromising belief in the corruption and decadence of the English language. He saw himself as a patriot, trying to turn back the clock to a time when language and literature were fresh and pure. He failed, as people who reach back into history always do; but the attempt dominated his life, and the poetry that it created does not deserve merely to be forgotten.

In many ways, he was a man of his times: he felt a Victorian's distaste for industrialization; he joined in the brutal, blustering patriotism of the First World War years; even his fascination with language, with the words and expressions of another age, was shared by other scholars and poets of the period. But, a sort of intellectual Howard Hughes, he read nothing of their work, and virtually nothing of other contemporary writing: the names of the leading poets and writers of his day were completely foreign to him, and he shied nervously away from the onrush of the twentieth century.

He was indeed, in the phrase he was to use many years later, 'God's Fugitive'.

Chapter One

There is nothing in the nature of a biography; nor could there, that I can see, be any utility in it. I was born in '43 and left an orphan when a little child. I am now rather an invalid . . .

Letter to S. C. Cockerell, Christmas Day 1918

The solid, square flint tower of St Mary's Church, Martle-sham, is almost hidden among the Suffolk trees. It stands a couple of miles away from the modern village – easy to miss for the casual visitor.

Inside are the haphazard treasures of thousands of English country churches: a fifteenth-century wall painting of St Christopher, lovingly preserved; an ancient family pew recessed into a wall of the chancel, and now used to store cleaning materials; a stone font from the fifteenth century and a carved oak pulpit from the seventeenth; an ancient chest, and a few pieces of medieval stained glass gathered into a single panel. And along the walls, the carved memorials that say everything and nothing about the long-dead members of a local family – in this case, the Doughtys.

There are George Doughty, died 1798, and his wife Ann; their son Chester, who died in 1802; Major Ernest Christie Doughty, DSO, of the Suffolk Regiment, who died in 1928; his grandfather, Frederic Ernest, Rector of Martlesham for nearly thirty years. Outside, more Doughtys are at rest in the graveyard: Rear-Admiral Frederick Proby Doughty, who died in 1892, and his wife, the former Mary Arnold, with their child Beatrice May, lie there among their relatives.

Of Charles Montagu Doughty, for whom as a child Martlesham was closer to being a home than anywhere else, there is nothing:

his memorial is far away, in a London crematorium. And yet the atmosphere of the simple little church, its unimpeachable, unassuming Englishness and its dignified reserve, reflect one facet of his character. As in churches all over the country, it is the list as a whole, rather than the individual names, which tells the story; of specific characters, particular lives, the memorials are all but silent. There are names, dates, an occasional mention of a life's work, but it is the tradition, the history, not the individual, which counts.

And that, without the slightest doubt, is what Charles Doughty would have thought the proper attitude.

He always backed away from curiosity about his biography or his early life – and indeed, many Victorian children must have shared his experience of childhood as time spent in a foreign and not particularly friendly country. Even for the offspring of a family with lands, traditions and inheritances on each side going back for generations, it could be an unpredictable and precarious existence.

Doughty was born into a world of privilege and high expectations. His father, also Charles Montagu, was a clergyman, the squire of Theberton in Suffolk, and owner of family estates and properties all over the county – but it was only a few months after his birth on 19 August 1843 that the young Charles Doughty suffered the first of a series of devastating blows. His mother, Frederica, never recovered from the strain of childbirth and, at less than a year old, Doughty was motherless. He himself had not been expected to survive. 'It is a long time since I came into the world, and so obviously a dying infant life, that I was christened by my own father almost immediately,' he said later.[1]

But it was the mother, and not the child, who died, and for the rest of his life, the few people who talked to Doughty about his childhood commented on his abiding sense of bereavement. Within a year of his own marriage forty-three years later came a mirror-image of the tragedy, with his own stillborn first child carried off to the churchyard while his invalid wife lay and struggled back to health. Small wonder that later, as he gathered together in his painstaking fashion thousands of word-associations and jottings for use in his writing, among the first under the Latin heading 'Mater' would be 'mother's yearning', 'longing', 'smiling tears' and 'yearning love'.[2]

One of the first and most lasting lessons for the young Charles Doughty was that love was something that was brutally wrenched away – an ache, not a consolation.

At the end of his life, then, his writing drew not just on six decades of dedicated study, not just on the travels through Arabia which had been his formative experience, but also, crucially, upon the sense of loss which had surrounded his earliest memories. The theme repeatedly comes back to haunt him – in his last poem, *Mansoul*, for instance, he describes how he faced his own 'private grief' on his journey around the underworld. 'Death cannot dim thy vision,' he declares at his mother's grave.

> Long cold be those dead lips, that word ne'er spake
> Unworth, unsooth; those dying lips, that kissed,
> Once kisst (thy nature's painful travail past)
> This last new-born on thy dear breast, alas! . . .
> Mother of my life's breath, I living lift
> O'er thee, these prayer-knit hands . . . [3]

And the grief runs deeper than that simple, almost formalized Victorian sentimentality. In *The Dawn in Britain*, the story is told of the baby Cusmon, who was abandoned by his mother, the immortal nymph Agygia, but watched over by her throughout his life. Eventually, after his hundredth birthday, they are reunited at his death.

> She stooped, and dearly kissed
> That bowed down, aged man, and long embraced . . . [4]

When he wrote that, Doughty himself was in his seventies. He is a child again, his lost mother restored, and a lifelong sense of bereavement finds its devoutly longed-for but hollow and insubstantial resolution in an old man's dream. It is significant that he angrily denied suggestions in reviews that this was his own version of an ancient tale: 'There is no such myth, and there is no such version,' he declared. 'The original is that in *The Dawn in Britain* itself.'[5]

The story clearly remained important to him: he could mourn the loss of his mother, but emotionally, he could never quite accept it.

Materially, though, both Doughty and his elder brother Henry were well provided for, their place in society apparently fixed by generations of affluence and family tradition. On both sides, the family were well-to-do, landowning gentry: the census return for Theberton for 1841, just two years before Charles's birth and Frederica's death, shows the Doughtys with the three-month-old Henry and five adult servants. It was a comfortable life in the sheltered and undemanding tradition of the prosperous Church of England.

The Doughtys of Suffolk had built up extensive lands over the centuries, and occupied a succession of livings; Frederica's relatives, the Hothams of East Yorkshire, had produced six admirals, three generals, a bishop, a judge and a colonial governor. It was a family that drank in unquestioning patriotism and the peculiarly restrained devotion of the Established Church with its mother's milk – the sort of family on which the empire had relied for generations.

But it seems, too, to have been a family where the idea of pride and duty replaced any open show of affection. Doughty's cousin, the Rear-Admiral Frederick Proby Doughty who now lies in Martlesham churchyard, wrote a journal in which he recorded his memories of the various members of his family – and on the Doughtys' side at least, there does not seem to have been much obvious emotional closeness. 'We were badly off as children in the matter of relatives – no grandfathers or grandmothers, or relatives that were disposed to do the correct and orthodox "uncle and aunt" business.'[6] The family would perhaps have been scandalized not to be considered 'correct and orthodox', but the message is clear. Of his uncle, the late father of young Charles and Henry, he reminisced: 'I do not recall much connected with him, except on one occasion when walking with my father at Martlesham. I suppose I was rather busy with my tongue – he said to my father, "Why do you allow that boy to go on chattering? Box his ears . . . !"'

And there was more for the young Charles Doughty to contend with than the occasional bad temper of a crusty old Victorian clergyman. For all his wealth, Doughty's father was stretching himself financially, with an ambitious programme of ostentatious building works at Theberton Hall. It seems to have been something of a family failing – only a few years later, after a similar programme of grandiose 'improvements', Doughty's uncle, Frederick Goodwin Doughty, was forced to put his own home of Martlesham Hall, a few miles away, up for sale.

The boys, no doubt, were too young to be aware of the growing problems, but the atmosphere at Theberton Hall cannot have been a happy one. Their father seems to have been shattered by the untimely death of his 'late dear wife', who was only thirty-five when she died. No doubt the young Charles was not the only one to feel a sense of loss and bereavement: his father's own health was not strong, and on 6 April 1850 he put his affairs in order, writing a new will, with an instruction that he should be buried next to Frederica in Theberton Church. Less than three weeks later he was dead, at the age of fifty-two, the doctors giving the cause of death as 'Exhausted nature following a severe bilious attack'. The two boys were now orphans.

Childhood, it must have seemed, was little more than a harsh preparation for a life of loneliness. Theberton Hall was shut up, and within a few weeks the auctioneers moved in. At 11 a.m. on 28 August they started their sale with Lot 1 – two brown bread pans, a strainer and three baking pans – and over the next four days sold off the entire contents of the house. The Reverend Doughty's fine wine cellar and his extensive library were split up and put under the hammer; so were his 'town-built chariot' and his single-horse phaeton. Even more distressing for the two boys, everything in their nursery was sold – brass mounted fender, fire-irons and pictures off the wall. It was a common practice in the mid nineteenth century to sell off the belongings of the dead – but that made it no less heart-rending for the young boys, who had to see what had once been their home broken up and carried off by strangers.

But if the seeds of Doughty's later emotional detachment and determined self-sufficiency can be seen in these bleak years of bereavement, there were other members of his immediate family with a brisker, no-nonsense attitude to death. Frederick Proby

Doughty's detached account of his uncle's financial problems and death seems brutal today, but it probably reflects the severely practical attitude of the family at large.

> He had commenced great alterations to Theberton Hall, building enormous stablings, altering the entrance, building a picture gallery, and other expensive undertakings far beyond his means, and out of character with such an estate. Luckily he died, leaving his sons Henry and Charles ... a long minority before them to recover and pull through the expenses and debts their father had incurred.

In fact, if his will is anything to go by, Charles Doughty senior still had plenty to leave his two sons. For Henry, there were several houses and estates spread over various parishes in Suffolk – among them Theberton Hall itself.

Charles, as the younger son, was less generously provided for, but he still inherited three farms, all his father's government funds and securities, and an unspecified amount of cash, annuities and other investments which derived originally from the Hotham family. His guardian was to be his uncle, Frederick Doughty of Martlesham, father of the journal-keeping Frederick Proby Doughty – but the journal gives little cause to suggest that the move to Martlesham brought any fresh lightheartedness or fun into the little boy's life. The elderly admiral recalled later: 'I never remember a guest staying in the house, and but one or two dinner parties; and visiting friends were few and far distant.' Of his mother – the woman who was to share the job of bringing up the young Charles Doughty – he wrote: 'I fancy she was very delicate – lived mostly when at home stretched out on a sofa. I don't remember her ever entering into any games or sports with us . . .' She had a good education and spoke several languages, but she wasn't known for her friendliness. 'Extreme amiability', her son noted carefully, 'was never one of my mother's vices or virtues.'

Neither Frederick Doughty nor his wife was going to waste much time or affection on their new charge. Within months of his father's death young Charles was packed off to school at Laleham, on the Thames, to come home only for those parts of the holidays for which they could not find another willing relative or friend to take on the burden of his keep.

For Doughty's new guardian was going through his own financial problems, and for much the same reasons that his dead brother had done. He had been pouring money into the rebuilding of Martlesham Hall for nearly ten years when his nephew arrived – perhaps the two brothers were competing in the splendour of their ambitions. If so, they paid a heavy price: only death prevented Charles from crippling himself and his two small sons with debt, while Frederick was eventually forced to sell the Hall which was his pride and joy. 'It was a terrible wrench to all his feelings: the building of the Hall in the Elizabethan style had been the pleasure and the hobby of his life. For years after the sale, the place was never named, or mention made of it,' Frederick's son dutifully recorded. By the time Martlesham was sold, Charles Doughty would have been some ten years old – old enough to sense and recognize the fresh misery that the family was going through. Perhaps there is even a hint in his cousin's journal that the young Charles might have been made to feel some responsibility for the disaster, despite the fact that his father's will had carefully provided for his upkeep and maintenance.

> The sale of the Hall and the estate around it I fancy became inevitable in spite of a hard struggle on the part of my father to make ends meet. The growing up of children and the increasing expense of education in addition to the above sealed its fate . . . The sale was, I have heard on all sides, a terrible blow to my father.

Laleham, with swimming in the river Thames and cricket in a nearby meadow, seemed initially to be an ideal choice of school for a boy who was used to life in the country, and who was already, not surprisingly, showing signs of being shy and withdrawn. The Revd John Buckland had made his career as headmaster there – he had come to Laleham thirty years before with Dr Thomas Arnold, and the two young schoolmasters had set up their own establishments, Arnold preparing older boys for university, and Buckland building up one of the country's first preparatory schools.

Arnold, of course, had moved on to greater things at Rugby School

GOD'S FUGITIVE

after ten years, but Buckland stayed behind. By the time he retired,
three years after Charles Doughty arrived, *The Times* commented
that he was running 'a large and flourishing private school'. The
connection with Arnold was still close, and a letter from his son, the
poet Matthew Arnold, about a visit in 1848 to the man he still called
Uncle Buckland gives an idyllic picture of the establishment as it
then was. 'In the afternoon I went to Penton Hook with Uncle Buckland, Fan, and Martha, and all the school following behind, as I used
to follow along the same river bank eighteen years ago. It changes
less than any place I ever go to.'[7]

But the memories of a man in his mid twenties, however little
the place itself seemed to have changed, were more pleasant than
the day-to-day reality for the thirty or so small boys at the school.
Even Arnold, in a less lyrical mood, described it as 'a really bad
and injurious school', and grumbled about 'that detestable gravel
playground',[8] while 'Uncle Buckland' gloried in a reputation for strict
discipline that was anything but avuncular.

One former pupil – who went on to become a bishop in New
Zealand[9] – recalled how he was summoned from breakfast by Buckland to be asked what religion he was. 'Christian', apparently, was
not a good enough answer, and when the boy stammered nervously
that he did not know 'what sort of Christian' he was, he was sent
off to spend the day locked in the cellar. Eight hours later 'Uncle
Buckland' unlocked the door, and asked him again – and still the
panic-stricken boy had no reply for him. 'The headmaster replied at
last, "Sir, you are a Protestant," and knocked him down. Hardly
a method to encourage Protestantism, the bishop thought, looking
back . . .'

And not one either to encourage a happy atmosphere of learning
and scholarship. Doughty was experiencing early the violent religious
bigotry that he would meet again in the deserts of Arabia: it is hardly
surprising, even though the victim of that attack made his career in
the Church, that many of Buckland's pupils, like Doughty, adopted
an ambiguous attitude to the established religion as they grew up.

But Buckland's no-nonsense attitude would have raised few eyebrows in the mid nineteenth century. The only complaint about the
school that Doughty himself made as he grew older was a much less

8

serious one, his wife wrote in a letter, years afterwards. 'He was six years old, and much resented being made to get out of bed to show visitors what a tall boy he was.'[10]

His guardians positively welcomed the strictness of the regime, and around the time that Buckland retired they moved their young charge away from Laleham and off to the nearby school at Elstree. It was a move from one strict disciplinarian to another, even more overbearing one.

Once again, it was a quiet, country establishment, in a seven-teenth-century mansion at the top of a hill, with a Spanish chestnut tree said to be over a thousand years old outside the front door – the tree, its huge, contorted branches now severely pruned, still stands outside what is now a nursing home. The curriculum was mainly classics, with a few periods a week of mathematics, occasional science lessons, and desultory French from a visiting Frenchman. There was a gravel yard with a fives court, football from time to time, and cricket on the field in front of the house.

Doughty had a slight stammer, which was to stay with him throughout his youth. He was tall for his age, but slim and unassum-ing, although his contemporaries were already finding out that his apparent frailty concealed a deceptive strength and determination. Two of them who met his wife shortly before her marriage told her that, thin and delicate as he was, he had fought and beaten all of them.[11] In another incident, presumably during one of the cricket sessions across the road from the School House, he was hit in the face by the ball. His wife told the story after he died: 'No notice was taken at the time, and he said nothing (so like him!) but the cheek-bone was smashed, which showed all his life.'[12]

On another occasion, he had told her about competing with a group of boys to see who could stand longest on one leg. He was left standing there when they all went off to church – and he was still there on one leg when they came back.

It is probably as well that the Revd Leopold Bernays knew nothing about one of his young charges spending his time in such fruitless vanity when he should have been at prayer. Letters about the head-master 'do not give the impression of a genial or popular man', notes the Elstree School history coyly – and, judging from the sermons

9

that he published during his life, he must have been an awe-inspiring, even terrifying, figure for a young boy. 'Nothing can make life sweet and happy but a constant preparation for death,' was one of his more jovial *bons mots*;[13] in another sermon he stormed at the wide-eyed ranks of small boys before him: 'If we could see the very jaws of hell open to receive us, and ourselves hastening madly down the road, with nothing to arrest our career – how we should pray!' Again, he pondered on how 'one week passed amongst you pains me, with its long catalogue of idleness and carelessness, of disobedience and wilfulness, of harsh and profligate words . . .'[14]

Most of these idle, disobedient and wilful pupils were destined for Harrow School, but Doughty's ambition, even at his young age, was to follow the tradition of his mother's family and enter the navy. His brother Henry had already been at sea for two years, and Charles wanted nothing more than to follow in his footsteps. Some time around 1856, a boy of around thirteen, he was uprooted from school and friends for a second time, and bundled off to Portsmouth, where he was to be prepared for his navy examination at a school called Beach House.

Henry was to leave the navy later for a career as a lawyer. But his future was mapped out for him, as the future squire of Theberton; as the younger son, Charles would have to fend for himself. Life as a naval officer must have seemed to combine excitement with the sense of patriotic duty that had been bred in the young boy's bones – and, too, with the severely practical need for a career.

It was not only the example of his mother's family that had inspired the two Doughty boys with the idea of serving in the navy – for all their seniority, the much-boasted six Hotham admirals would have seemed remote to a small boy, an inspiration to duty rather than passion. But there were other family stories to whet their appetites – most particularly, those of their cousin, the journal-writing Frederick Proby Doughty of Martlesham.

He was only a few years older than they were and had already sailed to Canada, South America, Easter Island and even off to the Baltic to fight against the Russians. Here was a hero with whom they could identify. Though they saw him rarely because he had been away at sea since passing his exams some ten years before, they must have been well aware of his stories and adventures. They did, after all, spend at least some of their holidays with his father, their guardian, Frederick Doughty.

Much of the time, though, the boys were farmed out to a succession of relatives. Theberton Hall, the house where they had been born, and one of the few constant elements in a life that had so far been a series of uprootings and removals, remained locked up. A caretaker and his family lived there, among the gloomy, half-finished building works that were their father's memorial, to look after it until Henry should come of age to take over his inheritance.

Sometimes they stayed with the Newsons, a family who had farmed on the estate for generations, sometimes with their father's sister Harriet Betts and her family, who lived nearby in Suffolk – 'a thoroughly scheming, worldly person', if Frederick Proby Doughty is to be believed – and sometimes, too, with their mother's relatives, the Hothams, who also lived in Suffolk.

Certainly there were happy memories among all the travelling between relatives' houses: in his old age Doughty recalled fondly 'the noble castle ruins and proud church monuments' of Framlingham. 'It is to me one of the memories of childhood, when my mother's father was Rector of Dennington, two miles further on,' he wrote.[15]

Frederick Proby Doughty has left details of one family holiday which he spent with his parents and his cousin and future wife Mary Arnold – with the fourteen-year-old 'Charlie' Doughty acting as unofficial chaperon for the undeclared lovers. Young Charlie at that time was at Beach House and his cousin – who had been at home for several months since his latest voyage – was deputed to collect him from Portsmouth and escort him to North Wales. The long coach journey through Bath and Bristol to Llangollen gave plenty of time for the young man's tales of life at sea – and his teenage cousin would have been an avid listener.

For the two young lovers, it was an ideal family party. The older Doughtys left them to their own devices – they, after all, wanted a quiet, dignified time in a respectable hotel, rather than long walks in the country. And even when their young cousin tagged along, he had better things to do than interfere. 'Charlie was ever alive to the chance of catching a trout . . . Better elements for leaving Mary and myself to our own devices could not have been collected together,' says the journal gleefully.

The young people spent most of their time rambling over the hills – again, little sign of Doughty's supposed frailness. 'Charlie and myself did Beddgelert, and passed over the top down to the pass of Llanberis, and so back to Beddgelert – a walk of over thirty miles. We had been rewarded by a good view from the top of Snowdon.' But if the days were long and energetic, the journal also gives a telling glimpse of what must have seemed to the young people to be equally lengthy but tedious evenings. 'As a family, we are not a festive lot, and, left to ourselves, the sun might travel from its rising to its setting without one observation being made . . . The more genial spirit of my father, as I remember him, seemed by the habitual staidness of his life to have almost died out.'

Frederick's innocent suggestion of a quiet game of cards caused an outburst from his mother: it showed a vicious spirit, and a tendency towards gambling, she stormed. It's a hint of what life at Martlesham must have been like for much of the time – these, after all, were the people who thought the Revd Leopold Bernays a suitable moral guide for their young charge.

As a whole, though, the month in Wales passed happily – the best times, even at this young age, were spent away from wherever happened to be 'home' at the moment. Frederick Doughty recalled it years later as 'a very jolly cruise', and 'Charlie' clearly enjoyed spending time with a cousin who seemed, at twenty-two, to have such a wide and enviable experience of the naval life on which he was himself about to embark.

From Llangollen, at the end of the holiday, he returned to Beach House, and his preparation for his naval examinations – and to a shock and disappointment that was to remain with him all his life. When he was finally entered for the medical test that formed part of the entrance requirement, he was turned down by the examiners, either because of his slight speech impediment, or because his general health was thought not to be strong enough for the rigours of life at sea. More than sixty years later the memory still hurt him. 'My career was to have been in the navy, had I not been regarded at the Medical Examination as not sufficiently robust for the service. My object in life since, as a private person, has been to serve my country so far as my opportunities might enable me.'[16]

His rejection seems to have shocked the staff at Beach House as well. During the following year his maternal aunt, Miss Amelia Hotham of Tunbridge Wells, was assured that he was 'the very best boy that we have met with'. Even allowing for a degree of tact in dealing with pupils' close relatives, it is a verdict that suggests that Doughty's teachers, at least, believed that the navy had missed a good candidate.

Their sympathy, however, must have been of very little consolation to a boy who had seen his ambition snatched away from him, whose elder brother had by now started a career at sea, and who was still all too conscious of his cousin's steady progress in the service. It must have been hard, too, to be surrounded by his contemporaries, who would have been looking forward to their own careers as naval officers. A few months after the examination board's decision he was taken out of the school, and started a course of study with a private tutor.

Clearly, he and his family had decided that if he could not follow one family tradition by joining the navy, he should follow another by going up to his father's old college at Cambridge, Gonville and Caius. Preparation for that involved a degree of formal, structured study, and the records of King's College, London, show the young Doughty lodging in a suitably respectable boarding house in Notting Hill,[17] while he followed a mathematics evening course at the college.

But Doughty remained the prosperous son of a prosperous family, and much of the time between Beach House and Cambridge, his widow said later, was passed in travelling with his tutor through France and Belgium. They were travels that not only gave him his first taste of foreign languages outside the classroom, but also established the connection in his mind between study and the wandering life. Perhaps it was on the roads of northern France that much of the character of the scholar gypsy was formed.

More crucially, though, he returned to the chalk countryside of his home in Suffolk. During his school holidays at his uncle's home in Martlesham or on the Newsons' farm in Theberton, he had amused himself by digging for fossils and stone artefacts – a very fashionable pastime as the revelations of Charles Darwin about evolution were echoing around the world. Now Doughty started geological and archaeological studies in earnest around the village of Hoxne – 'working a good deal with the microscope', he told a correspondent later.[18] In 1862, while still only nineteen years old, he submitted a paper to the Cambridge meeting of the British Association for the Advancement of Science on *Flint Implements from Hoxne*.

It was an ideal place to start. More than sixty years earlier the little Suffolk village, recognized today as one of the most important archaeological sites in Europe, had seen the discovery of some of the first stone axes found in Britain; in 1860 those discoveries were being linked with others made in France, to revolutionize the accepted view of prehistory. Humanity, the researchers demonstrated, had a much longer pedigree than anyone had believed.[19]

It was a controversial, even revolutionary subject, and the decision Doughty made now reflected the self-reliance that had been forced on him by a bleak and lonely childhood, the toughness that the disappointment at Beach House had given him, and the straightforward determination that was already a part of his character. Practically everyone who came into contact with Doughty throughout his life commented on his diffidence – his friends were later to refer to him dismissively as a 'shy dreamer'[20] – but his arrival at Cambridge University showed that his reserved manner hid a rocky determination.

The Admissions Book in the archives of Gonville and Caius College, Cambridge, shows 'Carolus Montagu Doughty' accepted as a new member of the college on 30 September 1861. It was the college that his father and his grandfather had attended before him, but Doughty was determined not simply to follow in their footsteps. It was only two years since Charles Darwin's *Origin of Species* had outraged the certainties of the Established Church with which Doughty had such close family links, and the study of science was still considered barely respectable in the university – and yet it was on the newfangled Natural Science tripos that he decided to concentrate.

His expeditions and diggings in Suffolk had already made him a dedicated geologist and collector of fossils, and he was determined to develop this interest from the start of his Cambridge career. It cannot have been a welcome ambition in a family as steeped as his in the reassuring traditions of Church and countryside.

It is Darwin who is chiefly remembered today as the man who shivered the comfortable theology of the Church of England to its foundations, but more than twenty-five years before *On the Origin of Species* appeared, Charles Lyell had dealt another blow with his *Principles of Geology*. It is hard to overstate the impact of the new science on the intellectual life of the time: Lyell's contention that the earth was still changing and developing after hundreds of thousands of years had broken upon a world where eminent churchmen referred to ancient texts and confidently named 23 October 4004 BC as the precise date of Creation, while Darwin's challenge to the story of Adam and Eve seemed to strike at the very basis of Christianity.

People struggled to hold onto their faith, and John Ruskin spoke for many of them when he declared, 'If only the geologists would let me alone, I could do very well – but those dreadful hammers! I hear the clink of them at the end of every cadence of the Bible verses!'[21] And the geologists themselves felt the draught of their studies upon their own beliefs. In a letter to Darwin, written in the mid 1860s, Lyell said wistfully: 'I had been forced to give up my old faith without thoroughly seeing my way to a new one.'[22] It was a common dilemma, and one which struck particularly hard at a young man like Doughty, passionate in his sense of tradition, yet unswerving in his search for truth.

Doughty had grown up with the rhythms of the Authorized Version echoing in his mind, and his whole instinct was to look back, not forward, for reassurance – but it was in that dreadful clink of the geologist's hammer that he found inspiration. The whole discipline of geology, and the study of natural science itself, was unsettling, revolutionary, and frequently in direct conflict with the teaching of the Church – but it fascinated Doughty.

15

As a child, he had been gripped by the idea of the navy and his family tradition of military service. Later, it would be Arabia, and then the story of the Roman conquest of Britain. Doughty would continue to focus his attention upon some particular subject and, over a period of years, would immerse himself in it, teasing out every last detail, before passing on, his attitude to life altered and enriched by the experience, to some new study. Time was not significant – the writing alone of *The Dawn in Britain* took almost ten years of his life, and the research beforehand at least as long again – but while the fascination was upon him, his obsession would be virtually total.

The shy and diffident young Doughty seems to have made little impression in his early days at Cambridge. He found it hard to make friends with his fellow students – and at the same time he showed no sign of incipient brilliance as a scholar. The Caius examination records show him stumbling uneasily through his first examinations – 27th out of 32 in Classics, 19th of 34 in Theology and, despite his efforts at King's College, London, 30th of 35 in Mathematics. But from the very start there was no doubt where his greatest interest lay.[23]

He clearly enjoyed passing on his geological passion: he dragged one of the junior fellows of the college, Henry Thomas Francis, off to inspect the Kimmeridge clay at Ely and the gravel pits in Barnwell ('When', Francis recalled wryly later, 'I caught a severe cold . . .'). Another friendship was with the future Professor John Buckley Bradbury, with whom he shared a staircase in Caius overlooking Trinity Street – Doughty's old room, which has since been redeveloped, was above the college library where, decades later, the main collection of his private books and papers was held. The two men used to take long walks into the country, visiting the chalk pits and coprolite diggings just outside Cambridge.

Another contemporary at Cambridge, Edwin Ray Lankester, later to become a Fellow of the Royal Society and one of the country's leading zoologists, also recalled Doughty's application and enthusiasm. For a time Doughty had rooms opposite his, and Lankester remembered him, three years his senior, as 'rather shy and quiet, but very kind and anxious to help me'.[24] The unassertive, awkward young man still spent much of his time and money digging at Hoxne.

'Doughty did not take part in such things as rowing, but was always reading geology and philosophy,' he said.

But before he could specialize in his chosen subject, Doughty had to pass the Cambridge first-year examination, the so-called Littlego. The Greek and Latin which had to be dealt with he treated with a certain amount of disdain, doing the work that was necessary without, apparently, much enthusiasm. Sixty years later his colleague of the gravel pits and the Kimmeridge clay, Henry Thomas Francis, remembered teaching him Classics.

> Doughty as an undergraduate was shy, nervous, and very polite. He had no sense of humour, and I cannot remember that he had any literary tastes or leanings whatever. He read Classics with me for his Littlego. He knew very little Greek. When he came up, he was devoted to Natural Science generally. He had made a large collection of Suffolk fossils, and was rather combative in favour of the new studies. He did not like attending lectures.[25]

Francis also recalled a visit from another undergraduate who announced that he was no longer going to take lessons in Classics from him.

> I said, 'Very well, but what are you going to do?' and after a little hesitation he replied, 'The fact is, my friend Doughty tells me you bother one with grammar and all that sort of thing, and that it is far easier to get up the whole business by heart.' My answer was, 'Then we are right to part, for I can't teach Latin or Greek on those conditions.'

The young Doughty simply had no time for literature, and certainly no time for the detailed study of language: those passions would come later. For now, with his characteristic singleminded determination, he wanted to concentrate only on his scientific studies.

He had no time, either, for the religious requirements of his college. Even at Caius, which was not among the most dogmatic or conservative of Cambridge institutions, there was a strict rule demanding daily appearances at religious services, and the college's Chapel Attendance Book shows the young Doughty cautioned twice, and punished once, for his irregular appearances. Maybe unsurprisingly, for a young man who as a boy had been forced to sit through the Revd Bernays's thunderous sermons, he was less than enthusiastic all his life about organized worship: after his death, his widow observed in a letter, 'He never (or hardly ever) entered a church during service, but he loved to sit in any church or cathedral for hours. He was truly religious, in spite of never going to church in the orthodox way . . .'[26]

But Doughty's studies in geology were already chipping away at the foundations of his own belief in much the same way as similar research had done for Lyell. His Christianity was too closely bound up with his sense of family, of tradition, and of Englishness for him ever to disavow it; but there can be little question that poring over the fossils gathered from the Suffolk chalkland must have sown the first seeds of religious doubt in his mind.

Failing to turn up for chapel was not a grave offence, and not likely to have incurred a serious penalty – probably a small fine or a period restricted to the college grounds – but, for a young man as careful of his dignity as Doughty, any punishment would have been a humiliating experience. It was almost certainly one reason for his decision to 'migrate' from Caius to Downing in 1863, two years after coming up to the university – years later, *The Times* said that the move came 'after a difference with the head of his original college'[27] – but there were others.

Cambridge University as a whole was gaining a growing reputation in botany and geology – although it would be several years before anything as dangerous or innovative as a scientific laboratory would be opened – and the relatively new Downing College, anxious to improve its academic standing in the university, was offering a number of Foundation Scholarships in Natural Sciences. Doughty's friend Bradbury had already been accepted for one of these, and although Doughty did not need the £50 a year the scholarship offered, he would have relished the academic standing it would confer.

He was disappointed, because he entered Downing without a scholarship. But simply making the transition from the quiet, enclosed courts of Caius to the wide open spaces of Downing was significant: apart from the lack of enthusiasm at Caius for the new-fangled study of science, there was the rigid insistence on the need to attend not only chapel, but also lectures. Doughty wanted to study on his own, and the more easygoing atmosphere at Downing attracted him. His own explanation was straightforward: 'They bothered me so much at Caius with lectures and chapels and things, and I knew that at Downing I could do just as I liked . . .'[28] Certainly, Bradbury boasted later that *he* never attended a single lecture as an undergraduate at Downing – and, as an additional incentive, the college buildings did not yet boast a chapel.

There was no lasting rift with his former college – on the contrary, Doughty remained on cordial terms with Caius, took his Master of Arts there, presented the college with gifts and paintings, and even used it as a forwarding address later in his life. But for someone who felt less than enthusiastic about the entire ambience of the university, Downing was a more congenial place to live than the more staid and ancient Caius. It was a new college, a college for the modern age, and one which seemed to delight in being almost semi-detached from the university as a whole. Doughty walked away from the college where his father and his grandfather had studied without a backward glance. The young man who was to prove himself in so many ways obsessed by tradition and antiquity was showing in his choice of college, as he had in his choice of subject, that he had a strong and determined mind of his own.

There is no doubting the seriousness with which he approached his chosen field of study at Downing – but it was to be several months before he could resume his formal studies.

Throughout his life Doughty complained of weak health – and throughout his life, when it let him down, he would set off at a tangent to 'convalesce' in some extravagantly physical and energetic enterprise which would have taxed an athlete in the peak of condition. So it was as he started his first term at Downing: he was granted leave to postpone his final exams, and announced his intention of spending some eight or nine months surveying the fiords and glaciers of Norway.

*   *   *

19

The declared aim of his journey was the observation of the ice-flows of the Jostedal-Brae glacier field, and he fulfilled it completely enough to produce his second paper for the British Association when he returned. But those studies took only a couple of months, and much of the rest of his time was spent wandering more or less at random, in much the same way as he did later through Europe and Arabia. Before he travelled north-west to the Jostedal-Brae, he had spent some time at the university in Christiana, as Oslo was then called. The earnest young Englishman, diligently jotting down words and phrases of Danish as he struggled to build up a working vocabulary, must have been an unusual sight in the small university, which had only been founded fifty years before. Norway was a poor country: it was more customary for their students to travel abroad than for foreigners to come there.

Doughty's priorities remained scientific, but his interests extended far beyond the university. This was not the quiet, studious life he had enjoyed at Cambridge: instead, he set off into the hills, lodging with farmers and gamekeepers, sometimes sleeping rough in log huts, and trekking for days at a time on shooting expeditions that took him and his guides miles into the remote mountain slopes.

It was a time that he remembered in Arabia years later when, near the end of his travels, he struggled from the interior towards Mecca 'in a stony valley-bed betwixt black plutonic mountains, and half a mile wide: it is a vast seyl-bottom of grit and rolling stones, with a few acacia trees. This landscape brought the Scandinavian fjelde, earlier well-known to me, to my remembrance.'[29]

That description gives some idea of the Norwegian countryside to which he had travelled, supposedly for the sake of his frail health, and when, in mid 1864, he arrived at the sixty-mile-long ridge of the Jostedal-Brae, it was to find an environment and a lifestyle that were certainly no easier. 'Here is an arctic climate, and we found the lakes covered with ice in the middle of August, still thick enough to bear some wild reindeer, which we disturbed. We slept under a stone, while it froze outside, according to a minimum thermometer.'[30]

Five separate glaciers descended from the ridge into a gorge below, which was so deep and sheer that the sun hardly reached it during the winter months. It was remote, unfriendly country, with just a few scattered farms and a rough bridle path between the rounded boulders which the glaciers had brought inching down with them from the mountains.

But it was a magical land as well, and it was not just Doughty the geologist scrambling with his guide over the rocks, ice and broken ground. As he wrote his report later, his descriptive enthusiasm struggled against a determined scientific detachment. The Nigaard glacier, he wrote,

> seems to flow down in elegant curves; though in reality this is due to the tossing up of the surface by some sub-merged knees of the mountains, and it passes through nearly a straight channel. No stones or earth soil its glittering surface, which appears capping the cliffs and creeping down every depression and pouring out its water in picturesque threads down the rocks.[31]

At the foot of Lodal's glacier, meanwhile, water came gushing out from an arched cavern in the ice some thirty feet high. The name of the lake, Styggevaten, meant 'horrid-water', he jotted carefully in his notebook – names and their meanings would carry a fascination for him throughout his travels, landscape and language inextricably linked in his mind. Between the detached response and the imaginative, he saw little distinction: at times, the Jostedal-Brae sounds almost like the setting for a mystical scene from Ibsen: 'Loud peals are heard booming among the heights when some new ice-shoot takes place and seems to smoke in the distance,' he wrote.

It was also a landscape that encouraged thoughts about the continuity between the present and the far past – the ice offering the imaginative possibility of a direct link with the most distant history. That was the sort of speculation that appealed instinctively to Doughty, and he noted that the glaciers were continually engulfing plants and animals, preserving them virtually for eternity. Humans, too, he said, must occasionally be entombed. 'Very early traces of the human race may some day be dug out from the deposits of the later glacial period, if man was then in existence and inhabited those parts of the globe . . .'

21

But his primary task was the more prosaic one of measuring the speed of the glaciers' movement. He had been loaned a theodolite by the Royal Geographical Association to help him with the detailed surveying – his first contact with that august body, later relations with which were to prove volatile. For the rest, he had a rope, an iron-tipped stick, a set of metal spikes to help him stand on the ice, and the aid of a local guide, one Rasmus Rasmussen.

With this rudimentary equipment, by driving stakes into the ice of the glacier as markers, and building matching stone cairns off to one side, he produced a series of tables for the different glaciers to show the varying speed of the flow. They were, he noted with pardonable pride, the first measurements ever obtained of the seasonal motions of Scandinavian ice streams.

It was a subject of some current scientific interest. Geologists were arguing about exactly what caused glaciers to flow, and Lyell himself was enquiring into the subject for the new edition of his *Principles*. But though there can be no doubting the enthusiasm and determination of the twenty-one-year-old Doughty, his figures leave something to be desired. The distances between his markers, he admits, were little more than estimates; on one glacier, presumably having forgotten to use his theodolite, he has guessed the gradient; and one complete set of figures, setting out the lengths of the different glaciers, he has simply lost, replacing them with estimates.

Later, he was to claim that, in preparing the last edition of his *Principles of Geology*, Lyell called on the young undergraduate to ask for details of his observations.[32] It is certainly likely that Doughty made the great man's acquaintance: the first thing he did when he returned from Norway was prepare a paper for the annual meeting of the British Association for the Advancement of Science on his observations. Lyell, then president of the association, was speaking about glaciation in his inaugural address: what more natural than that he should exchange a few words with the shy, gangling youth who had just returned from Norway? That, though, is as far as it went: the *Principles* includes little about Norwegian glaciers, nothing at all about the Jostedal-Brae, and certainly no acknowledgement of assistance from Charles M. Doughty and his lackadaisical measurements.

But the expedition had given him at least the beginnings of a scientific career. He had become a life member of the British Association earlier that year; now, the misspelled name of C. Montague Doughty was printed in the list of members – albeit with his address, too, wrongly listed as *Dallus* College, Cambridge. While the paper he had produced after his diggings at Hoxne had been only briefly noted by its title in the annual report, the account of this latest one, which was presented to the association's Bath meeting, ran to 350 words. He had also, though still an undergraduate, been making the social contacts necessary for a career in science. He had cultivated not just the acquaintance of Sir Charles Lyell himself, but also that of several other worthies of the British Association and the Royal Geographical Society. And, most important of all, if he had been disappointed not to be given a scholarship by Downing, he was still confidently expected to gain a first-class degree.

But in December 1865 those expectations were dashed. Doughty found himself near the top of the second class in the Cambridge Tripos examinations – although it seems that his examiners were at least as disappointed as he was with the result. More than fifty years later Professor Thomas George Bonney, then Professor of Geology at London University, said of his distinguished pupil: 'I was very sorry not to be able to give him a First, as he had such a dishevelled mind. If you asked him for a collar, he upset his whole wardrobe at your feet.'[33] It would not be the last time in his life that Doughty would be criticized for hurling facts at his readers by the handful.

But while such an examination result would have been a setback, it would not necessarily have prevented him from following a career as a scientist, particularly as he still enjoyed the financial support of his father's legacy. Doughty, though, seems to have changed his priorities during that final year at Cambridge: although he prepared his report on Jostedal-Brae for its full publication, he had abandoned any thought of making his name through science.

A letter written to him shortly before his final examinations by the Revd Henry Hardinge, the rector of Theberton, seems to confirm that he still had grandiose plans – the adolescent boy who had been turned down by the navy clearly still thought in the same patriotic terms of serving his country. Hardinge refers to Doughty's 'researches and noble ambition as regards this earth', and goes on to praise his determination to 'soar above the vanities of this world and take a place among the worthies who have lived for its adornment and the real glory of God'.[34] But the researches and noble ambition would be directed at literature: though science and geology would remain among his interests, his life, he had decided, would be devoted to writing. He left the university with his second-class degree, no firm plans for a career, and a brief formal note of introduction from Bonney.

Doughty, after all, could afford high-flown ambition: there was no pressing need to find a way of earning his living. His education had not been designed to fit him for a career, unless perhaps, like his father, as a parson in one of the Suffolk livings. His inheritance should have enabled him to live a life of comfortable scholarship. For fifteen years his financial affairs had been cautiously managed, with his father's old friend, Henry Southwell of Saxmundham, and his own uncle and guardian, Frederick Goodwin Doughty, acting as trustees. Now, with his studies behind him, he could take up the rights that had passed to him on his twenty-first birthday. He had both the power and the leisure to handle his wealth himself.

What he does not seem to have had was luck or shrewdness: over the next three or four years his inheritance simply withered away. He was never to show the remotest financial acumen, and it is significant that the collapse of his financial affairs should have come just after he took over the active management of his investments from his father's trustees.

Neither Doughty nor anyone else in his family would ever say exactly what happened. Fifty years later the memory of the collapse clearly still hurt: asked about stories of his past involvement in the printing industry, he replied shortly, 'Printing I conceived of in my early inexperience as an adjunct to literature, but I was deceived in that matter, and was somewhat of a victim. Therefore it would not be kind to mention it.'[35]

His widow would only speak generally of 'depreciation of investments' – but the overall effect was that the rest of Doughty's life was passed in a state of genteel poverty. Years after his death she turned

down the offer of financial help for herself and her daughters from
her husband's friends: 'Really we are much better off than a good
many people . . . I think Rubber will recover in time; I have put up
half the grounds for sale; if a small bungalow is built it won't hurt
us, but so far, I've had no success there. I sold 5 dozen spoons and
forks for £17 . . .'[36] Her husband's books, respected as they were,
made little money: financially, he simply never recovered from the
crushing blow of his early twenties.

Doughty's response at the time was to bury himself in his books.
The letter of recommendation he had taken with him from Cambridge had been addressed to the Library of Winchester College,
probably because of some personal connection of Bonney's; but he
used it, and his standing as a graduate, to gain entrance to the Bodleian Library in Oxford.

His name first appears in the Bodleian's records on 1 December
1868; and for the next fourteen months he was an assiduous reader
there. He was, he said later, a solitary man, and entirely dependent
now on his own resources to direct his studies – but a glance down
the list of books he was reading at the time demonstrates that he
had already established where his primary interests lay. There is
nothing of modern science – and precious little as late as the seventeenth century.

There is Gavin Douglas's translation of *The Aeneid*, published in
1553; several books of medieval songs and ballads; a number of
Anglo-Saxon grammars and dictionaries; commentaries on the Bible,
catechisms and sermons. Doughty was immersing himself in the distant past. Above all, he was reading Spenser and Chaucer, the two
poets he believed all his life had reached the uncontested summit of
English literature. It was they, he told an interviewer not long before
he died,[37] who finally decided him upon a life dedicated to poetry.

When, at the end of his life, he completed *Mansoul*, which he
firmly believed to be his greatest work, he declared: 'I have not
borrowed from any former writer; save I hope something of the
breath of my beloved, Master Edmund Spenser, with a reverend
glance backward to good old Dan Chaucer . . .'[38] It was at the Bodleian, as he threw himself wholeheartedly into the new life of a poor
scholar, that he first made their acquaintance.

But there is one book among the volumes of ancient history and literature which seems slightly out of place. Of the works of the seventeenth-century writer George Sandys Doughty chose neither his translations of Ovid, nor his poems based on the Psalms and the Passion, but his travel writing, *A Relation of His Journey to the Levant*.[39]

Possibly he was struck by the similarities between his own position and that of his Jacobean predecessor, who came, like him, from a background of well-connected country gentlefolk with naval antecedents. Sandys, too, had been a literary man and an academic – and in 1610, at the age of thirty-two, he had set off on a journey that took him through Europe and into the Middle East.

The two years of wanderings described in Sandys's book took him through France, Italy, Egypt, the Middle East and Malta. He gazed with a slightly bilious eye on the ancient wonders of the pyramids and of the city of Troy; he was robbed and manhandled by angry Muslims in the towns of Palestine and as he journeyed by caravan across the desert; he was fascinated by the habits and beliefs of the common people who were his companions.

There were moral and religious lessons to be drawn from his travels. The naturally rich lands of the Middle East, he wrote, were now waste, overgrown with bushes, and full of wild beasts, thieves and murderers. It was a country in which Christianity – 'true religion' – was discountenanced and oppressed: 'Which calamities of theirs, so greatly deserved, are to the rest of the world as threatening instructions . . . thence to draw a right image of the frailty of man, and the mutability of whatever is worldly.' The thought, and its expression, could almost have come from the pages of *Travels in Arabia Deserta* two and a half centuries later.

Doughty still hoped to achieve some great literary success, but in the meantime, he could no longer afford the leisured scholastic career he had anticipated: he would have to find some way of supporting himself on his greatly reduced means. Travel, and the life of a wandering scholar, might offer one solution.

Chapter Two

The next year, out of a reverence for the memory of Erasmus, Jos. Scaliger, etc., I passed in Holland learning Hollandish . . . I spent some months also at Louvain and the winter at Mentone (I had always rather poor health). I travelled then in Italy and passed the next winter in Spain, and most of the next year at Athens; and that winter went forward to the Bible lands . . .

Letter to D. G. Hogarth, August 1913

The Charles Doughty who left England for the continent in 1870 was a man who had been emotionally battered almost to submission – shy, retiring, and without a shred of emotional self-confidence. At twenty-seven, he was a Master of Arts, a scholar widely read in medieval literature and with some knowledge of geology and science, a man filled with literary and academic ambition, but without any obvious means of earning a living. His studies provided one safe retreat from the daunting world of human relationships; the lonely life of a solitary wanderer would be another.

There was no need to reach back to the sixteenth century for explanations for his decision to travel. The idea of paying homage to Scaliger[1] and Erasmus,[2] the one looking back from his own time to ancient history, the other rejecting the calling of a churchman and then leaving Cambridge to wander Europe as a peripatetic scholar, was appealing to his intellectual self-esteem, but it did little to explain his real motives.

One manifestation of his chronic lack of confidence was his constant wittering concern about his health. It had already led him to abandon his studies at Cambridge for a year, and he would claim later in his life[3] that his hard work in the Bodleian had left him

27

weak, ill, and in need of a change of climate. It was a common predilection: the hotels and sanatoria of Menton and the other Mediterranean resorts were full of sickly Englishmen taking the air, although few of them would have undertaken travels as extensive or as energetic as Doughty himself was embarking upon.

Like some of them, he had a pressing financial motive for leaving Britain. He had neither possessions nor prospects to keep him in England, and contemporary guidebooks estimated that something under ten shillings a day[4] should be sufficient for walking tours in remote areas of Europe. Life could be lived much more cheaply travelling the streets of the continent than at home; the future would have to look after itself.

So to save his money and to preserve his health, he decided to go abroad. But the letter to Hogarth more than forty years later puts his supposed weak constitution into context: the hardships and discomforts he was to endure over the next eight years would have killed a less hardy individual. He was a man dedicated to living his life through his books and scholarship – and yet, at this time of personal crisis, Doughty the diffident intellectual was determinedly pitting himself against a series of physical challenges. It would not be the last time.

It was not exactly a Grand Tour that he undertook: Europe was in ferment, with either open fighting or sullen, smouldering peace in France, North Africa, Spain and the Balkans. Doughty faced the prospect not just with courage but with all the insouciance of an English gentleman as he picked his way from troublespot to troublespot, peering superciliously past the shattered landscapes and the weary people to jot down his reflections about the ancient ruins he had come to see.

For his first few months out of England, though – 'a long year', he called it later[5] – he stayed in Leiden and the nearby Dutch towns, following his lonely studies and applying himself to learning the language.

He had a vague idea of investigating the historical background of the English civilization which fascinated him – but when he left Holland, he had, like Sandys before him, no plan for where his travels or his studies would lead him. The opportunity to observe the life of the travelling Arabs at first hand – the opportunity which was to provide him with the raw material for his greatest literary work – came to him by chance rather than by intent. One of his greatest talents was in allowing his life to be taken over by such chances and in seizing the benefit of them.

The next two years are the first period of Doughty's life for which his own detailed and contemporary records exist. His diary, painstakingly written in his neat, precise hand, with its occasional pen and ink or pencil diagrams and sketches of landscapes, archaeological remains, or whatever else caught his attention, is far from exhaustive: some vital moments are casually skipped, there are occasional long gaps with no entries at all, and the whole account ends in March 1873, with Doughty still in Italy. His later travels around Greece, Egypt, Sinai and the Middle East can only be pieced together from letters, later memories and other patchy records. Even more frustrating, for much of the time as he wandered around Europe, his imagination seemed infuriatingly disengaged. But the hardback notebook which is now kept in the library of Caius College, Cambridge, faded and battered at the edges, gives an intimate picture of his intellectual and emotional development over a crucial spell of his young adulthood.

It starts as he leaves Leiden for Louvain, with a distaste for his surroundings which was to become familiar over the next few months: Doughty's impressions of northern Europe were less than enthusiastic. In Louvain – a 'very filthy and unwholesome' town – he noted 'the obscene manners of the people who piddle openly in every place', although the observation was carefully crossed out in the diary. Presumably it was a little too crude even for a personal notebook. It remains legible, though, behind Doughty's pencil scribble, as his fastidious indictment of the Belgian people.

He presents much the same litany of dissatisfaction that any middle-class traveller from Britain at that time might have recited. The people, being foreign, were grubby, unhealthy and – worst of all – Catholic.

As he toured the small towns of Holland and Belgium, Doughty displayed an almost comically fastidious obsession with cleanliness:

the details that do excite his imagination are those that arouse his
distaste – the people of Louvain piddling in the street, or the 'slack,
ill complexions' of the Belgian women. But what is noticeable
throughout the young Doughty's notes of his travels in Europe is
how conventional, dismissive and simply unobservant they generally
are. For the most part, the man who would later tease out the most
intimate, most significant details of life among the Arabs appeared
to take only the most cursory interest in the places and people he
met. It was the primitiveness and frequent brutality of Arabia which
would excite his imagination; travel in Europe was often little more
than inconvenient, uncomfortable, and not notably relieved, for him
at least, by any architectural beauty.

His courage is already evident; but though there is no note of
fear or nervousness as he describes his journey through northern
France, there is no sense of personal involvement either. His interest
was never engaged by politics, even though he was travelling through
a Europe that was in political turmoil. Only a few months before,
Bismarck had swept aside the French army and the government of
Napoleon III: France was buzzing with ideas and arguments, alive
with revolutionary and anarchist institutions. While Doughty was in
Louvain, observing with distaste the ill-manners and grubby habits
of the Belgians, some 25,000 people were being massacred in Paris
as the French troops of the government of Adolphe Thiers crushed
the Commune[6] – but his only response, as he reached the frontier
town of Tourcoing a few weeks later, was to note the inconvenience
that such political activity caused the independent traveller. 'Stayed
there that night having no passport, as I had not heard it was become
necessary. Thiers elected President the day before . . .'

Paris itself, a city which had in the last few months experienced
defeat at the hands of the Prussian forces, which had seen tens of
thousands of its citizens flee as the revolutionary Commune was
established, and thousands more killed or arrested as it was put down,
he described as 'brown, cold, humid, deserted, uncheerful looking'.

After such a political cataclysm any city could perhaps be excused
for being slightly less than cheerful. Doughty's undoubted patriotism
and sense of civic pride took little account of what he perhaps saw
as the mere passing fads of a moment, like revolutions; his mind

was set on a longer, greater timescale. And anyway, he might have thought, this was not England.

But he was not staying in Paris. It was now early autumn and, planning to take lodgings for the winter in one of the small towns dotted along the Mediterranean coast, he set off hopefully in the late summer sun, trudging from settlement to settlement.

For a man who complained frequently of his frail physical condition and his lack of robustness, a journey by foot of over 150 miles eastwards from Marseilles, through Cassis, Cannes and Nice, must have been a painful struggle anyway – and one after another they fell short of his exacting standards of comfort and cleanliness. There would be many more times in Doughty's life when he would complain of his weakness and demonstrate his hardihood.

But at length he arrived in the town of Menton, where he seems to have felt at once that he could happily pass the winter. His room at the Pension Trenca, Beau Rivage, looked south over the sea, the mountains towering behind, and here he stayed for several months. For the first time a note of real enthusiasm comes into Doughty's writing as he describes

> happy long family voyages and hungry, beautiful, and aromatic wanderings in the mountains . . . The vineyards, the orchards of oranges and odoriferous lemons, everywhere open to be traversed by a thousand paths; the hundred happy and sheltered valleys, smiling with every gift of nature . . .

He was still complaining querulously of his ill-health and his weak constitution, but according to his diary, he was also deep in his studies throughout the winter. When he left his books, he would tramp along the mountain paths to see the tiny villages, the meadow flowers, the tumbling rivers and, most of all, 'the antique caverns and relics of human habitation'. Doughty already had in mind the outline of the epic poem he saw as his greatest work, which would deal in part with the struggle of the ancient Gauls for conquest in northern Italy.[7]

In his wanderings during his five months in Menton Doughty built up such an affection for the region that, twenty years later, he would return to live just a few miles up the coast. But once the winter was over, he set out on foot again through the mountains.

It was a solitary time: the occasional references to family outings from Menton, to some 'agreeable Germans' he met later in Pisa, or to the 'many excellent and agreeable persons, the librarian Dr Snell-aert and others' he remembered from Ghent, only serve to emphasize how lonely his travelling generally was. Solitude, after all, was what he was searching for.

Doughty pressed on with his hard and energetic journey: thirty miles or so up into the Piedmontese uplands one day, another forty miles the next, a brief day's rest in the cool of the mountain valleys, and then another thirty miles down a river valley to the coastal town of Ventimiglia. It was the country plantations, the flowers and the oranges, the twisting mountain paths overlooking the sea, that caught his imagination; when he reached the cities of Genoa, Livorno, Pisa and Florence, the treasures of the Italian Renaissance were jotted down in his diary with more of a sense of duty than of enjoyment.

But when Doughty arrived in Naples sometime in April, it was to witness a more terrifying example of the forces of nature than he had ever seen before. The nearby Mount Vesuvius had already been rumbling ominously for several months, with occasional minor explosions of rocks and stones, and trickling rivulets of lava bubbling from its crater. It was not at first a cause for great consternation in the surrounding countryside – the last time lava streams had run down the mountainside, four years earlier, joyful local villagers had celebrated the onrush of visitors they confidently expected in their restaurants, cafés and boarding houses.

But this time was different. On the night of 26 April Professor Paride Palmieri, a scientist who had made a career out of observing Vesuvius, was settled in his observatory near the summit. Shortly after midnight he observed a small group of curious tourists passing by with an inexperienced guide on their way up the mountainside – and then, some three hours later, the summit of Vesuvius exploded. A cloud of smoke and a hail of flaming rocks and stones enveloped the unfortunate tourists, who were close to the lava torrent. Some were engulfed in it, and disappeared for ever; two dead bodies were found later, but at least eight people, and probably more, are known to have died.

Doughty, though, was even closer than Professor Palmieri, although it was another fifteen years before he was to write down his description.[8]

> In the year 1872 I was a witness of the great eruption of Vesuvius. Standing that day from the morning alone upon the top of the mountain, that day in which the great outbreak began, I waded ankle deep in flour of sulphur upon a burning hollow soil of lava ... I approached the dreadful ferment, and watched that fiery pool heaving in the sides and welling over, and swimming in the midst as a fount of metal – and marked how there was cooled at the air a film, like that floating web on hot milk, a soft drossy scum, which endured but for a moment, – in the next, with terrific blast as of a steam gun, by the furious breaking in wind of the pent vapours rising from the infernal magma beneath, this pan was shot up sheetwise in the air, where, whirling as it rose with rushing sound, the slaggy sheet parted diversely, and I saw it slung out into many greater and lesser shreds ...

It is the writing of a man spellbound by both the beauty and the mechanics of what he sees – but Doughty was clearly also aware of the danger.

> Upon some unhappy persons who approached there fell a spattered fiery shower of volcanic powder, which in that fearful moment burned through their clothing and, scorched to death, they lived hardly an hour after. A young man was circumvented and swallowed up in torments by the pursuing foot of lava, whose current was very soon as large as the Thames at London Bridge ...

The account is an impressive *tour de force* – the more so as it came so long after the event. Doughty's vivid, awestruck description, with its everyday similes and references, such as the skin on boiling milk,

33

the shredded sheet, or the width of the river Thames, could almost have been written as he watched the eruption.

His fascination is clear: it overcomes any attempt at scientific detachment. And yet there is something disquieting about the writing – something beyond either his infectious enthusiasm or his undoubted physical courage. For all the perfunctory sympathy of his expressions, there is a gloating quality about the way he dwells on the 'spattered fiery shower' and its terrible effects; his attitude towards the suffering and dying tourists seems disturbingly cold, almost like a biologist focusing his microscope on the death-throes of a beetle. Not for the first time or the last, the need of the shy, retiring man to keep his distance had left his emotional responses seeming suspect, his human sympathy oddly lacking.

The eruption continued through the day, with the whole region plunged into darkness by the clouds of smoke and ashes that were hurled some four or five thousand feet into the air. By now, any gleeful anticipation of a minor tourist boom in the surrounding towns was forgotten. The prospect of further eruptions had brought panic to the local people, and on the volcano itself the scene was even more frightening. 'It seemed completely perforated, and the lava oozed, as it were, through its whole surface. I cannot better express this phenomenon than by saying that Vesuvius *sweated fire*,' wrote Professor Palmieri.[9]

That Doughty's diaries, for all the detail of his later description, make no mention of the eruption might lead cynics to doubt whether he had ever been on the mountain at all. But among the collection of Doughty memorabilia at Caius College, Cambridge, is a small sealed glass phial containing a few grams of a light grey powder. A carefully written label on the side reveals the contents to be 'Vesuvius Ashes – Ashes which fell on us in descending 28 April 1872, 3 a.m.'. If his own account is to be believed – and there is no reason why it should not be – he had spent the best part of twenty-four hours on the slopes of a volcano as it erupted beneath him.

His diary is silent, too, about the scenes of devastation which he must have witnessed over the next few days. The worst of the eruptions ended on 1 May, the day Doughty set off for Castagneto, but the lava flows had by then engulfed several settlements on the western slopes of the mountain. Fields, gardens and houses were buried under a flood of molten rock, and whole villages laid waste. If human disaster on this scale troubled or even interested him, he said nothing.

Fifty years later, as he worked on a new edition of *Mansoul*, the memory of the eruption was still fresh. In the poem it is Mount Etna that explodes in smoke and flame, but the experience is clearly that on the slopes of Vesuvius.

> Flowed down an horrid molten-footed flood –
> Inevitable creeping lava-tide,
> That licketh all up, before his withering course.
> Nor builded work, nor rampire cast in haste
> Of thousand men's hands might, and they were helped
> Of unborn Angels, suffice to hold back
> That devastating, soulless, impious march
> Of molten dross . . . [10]

As an old man, he can look back, too, on the suffering of the local people, leaping in a panic from 'tottering bedsteads' to watch the eruption.

> Men gaze on, with cold and fainting hearts,
> Folding their hands, with trembling lips, to Heaven;
> Not few lament their toilful years undone –
> Those fields o'erwhelmed, wherein their livelihood.
> Others inquire, if this were that last fire
> Divine, whose wrath, is writ, should end the world?[11]

A couple of years from the end of his life, he looked back in horror and awe at what he had seen; for now, though, he was silent.

As a geologist, Doughty must have found the eruption fascinating – fascinating enough to risk his life clambering up the trembling mountainside to observe it – and yet, in the record of his journey, it is completely ignored. Four months later, indeed, he inspected the nearby ruins of Pompeii, scene of an earlier and even more disastrous eruption, and then made a second expedition up the now dormant volcano. This time he climbed during the day, taking his leisure to study and make notes on the crater – 'immense and terrific gulf, horridly rent' – and also on the smaller vents left behind by another eruption four years earlier. 'These have the appearance of antiquity, though of but few years,' notes Doughty the geologist and scientific observer – and he then adds, with a calm and chilling detachment: 'Found there a quantity of wild figs and refreshed myself with them. On foot to the Torre del Greco, and returned by railway to Pompeii.'

Clearly, Doughty's preoccupations were not those of an ordinary traveller: his diary treats the eruption of Vesuvius with the same lack of interest as it does the political cataclysm in France. Indeed, it is hard to find anything in the countries through which he passed in these early months of his travels that truly awakened his enthusiasm. With him, though, he had several cases of books and, on the roads of southern Europe as much as in the calmer atmosphere of Oxford's Bodleian Library, it was his studies that preoccupied him.

When the diary resumes on 1 May, after its eventful break, it is to record that Doughty is moving on from Naples to the nearby resort of Castagneto, and another small guesthouse. 'A worthy family – good entertainment,' he notes – and, more importantly, a place where he could be alone with his books.

In his manner, he was still the archetypal crusty English gentleman abroad, complaining in his diary and no doubt to his host about the water, the weather and the scenery – but it was agreeable enough for him to spend some four months there, concentrating on his books and enjoying the home comforts of the lodging house. He left a case and a portmanteau of books with his landlord, Signor Cavalieri, and his family, to be picked up on his way home – which, he now suggested for the first time, might be after another two or three years.

It marks a significant change in his travelling: Castagneto is the last place at which the diary mentions either books or studies until Doughty embarked on his Arabic lessons in Damascus three years later. Whatever his plans had been when he left England, from now on he devoted more time to the places he was visiting, and to the various languages with which he came into contact. The focus of his attention had shifted. For the rest of his travels he is more gypsy –

his own word – than travelling scholar, more an observer of the world around him than a student poring over his books.

From Castagneto he returned to Vesuvius, presumably to see the after-effects of the eruption, and then, after a couple of days' wanderings among the ruins of Pompeii, he took the ferry to Sicily. It was an evening journey, the sea calm, 'the night starry but vaporous, the eye looking . . . into a depth or thickness of stars . . .' Alone on the deck, as the ferry left its luminous trail across the dark sea, he could relax.

It was, predictably, not the people of Sicily who had attracted him – 'the lower sort dull, unintelligent, and half savage manners' – but the volcano. After his experiences on Vesuvius, Doughty wanted to see Etna, which was also rumbling ominously.

It was a starry, moonlit night, with a chill wind blowing clouds of smoke down from the volcano upon Doughty and his guide as they struggled up towards the crater, their breath catching with the reek of sulphur. For someone who had already witnessed the flaming rocks and molten lava of Vesuvius, it must have been a terrifying experience. There were occasional muffled explosions deep within the mountain, and sudden belches of smoke and gas from the summit, while a layer of new-fallen sand which covered everything around the crater seemed to suggest that a new eruption was imminent – but the same detachment which left Doughty immune to the beauty of many of the places through which he passed quashed any fear for his own safety, leaving him as calm and aloof as if he had been in a laboratory, rather than on the summit of a rumbling volcano.

> Edge of crater a soft, moist mould, wet with sulphurous
> vapours which rise everywhere. Saw no yellow colour,
> or gathering of sulphur, but everywhere the like brown
> mould; the walls of the crater of the same – no ribs of
> rocks, nor horrible rendings as at present in Vesuvius, but
> terraced and easy to be descended into on a cord . . .

The last temptation, that of being lowered into the smoking crater of a rumbling volcano, he resisted – but he set off down the mountainside calmly and at his own pace. On the way, indeed, he stopped to admire the dawn, sketching the edge of the sun and its 'deep ruddy and heavenly hues' as it peeped above the horizon out at sea – and, as the sun rose, so another Doughty, a sensitive, appreciative observer, took over.

> Many miles of thick white clouds, much like some Arctic
> sea with towering icebergs – a strange spectacle . . . Oppo-
> site the arising sun, the immense shadow of the mountain,
> as it were another Etna raised into the air in a perfect
> sharpened pyramid, presently with the increasing light
> seemed to spread along the ground,

he wrote, finishing his sketch. That image of the volcano's shadow stayed with him for over fifty years, until, in the revised edition of *Mansoul*, he described 'a summer night of stars', and a journey up the mountainside. The plan, he says, was to

> reach, ere day, his cragged utmost crest,
> And from those horrid cliffs, surview far out
> Trinacria, and great Italia's mighty foot,
> And Etna's immense shadow on the Dawn-mist
> That sunrising should cast . . . [12]

The journey downhill took him some four hours, including stops to inspect an old smoking fissure in the mountainside near the foot of the cone, and then the Roman ruins of the Torre del Filosofo.

> The circular foundations remain – the bottom of a pillar,
> or stonework cemented in the midst of the passage of so
> many centuries – not buried under falling sand, but
> remains as at the first!!! Desert of black sand and water
> – 4 or 5 poor plants. The way all a waste of sand and lavas
> – with many wild craters on either hand . . .

Like the rest of the notebook, they are, of course, merely rough jottings. But, especially when compared with the bland, conventional judgements Doughty makes about towns and architecture, it is impossible to miss the enthusiasm with which he turns to the immensity either of time or of open spaces – the huge shadow of Etna or the centuries of history of the stone foundations. As a writer and as a traveller, his mental horizons are vast, his sense of time almost geological in its scope. It is the sight of human creativity and endeavour set against a background of desolation which suddenly brings his imagination to life.

His enthusiasm is sparked by ruins and remains, by the thought that buildings – or, for that matter, languages or peoples – may still bear some relation to the way they were hundreds of years ago. It is a conventional enough romantic response – half a century before, Shelley had described how 'Two vast and trunkless legs of stone / Stand in the desert' – all that remained of the magnificent statue of the proud King Ozymandias. Had Doughty been the 'traveller from an antique land' in Shelley's poem, his description of the statue might have stressed the same sense of hubris in the dead king, and the same all-pervading bleakness in the landscape. But there is nothing to suggest that Doughty had ever paid any attention to Shelley or any other romantic writers; this is his own emotional response. Conventional as it may be, it is one of the first signs of genuine interest or involvement in his travelling.

In his observation of the people whom he met, his broader judgements and generalizations are often almost comical in their smug dismissiveness. But occasionally, his notes pick out the minutiae of habits or behaviour with a precision that can bring individuals to life like the detail of a Brueghel painting. 'The countryman's salutation "Benedici", their feet in sandals or unshod. The Sicilian curiously daubed carts, with saints and Bible stories. The Sicilians ride on a pack saddle without stirrups (staffe).' The eye roves over the peasants as they go by, registering specific points apparently at random, seeming to note their friendliness and devout Christianity almost in passing. But each individual item is significant – the religious greeting, the biblical paintings on their wagons, their humble way of travelling around. And while Doughty determinedly remains an outsider – the carts are 'curiously' daubed – the pedantic little Italian translation shows how his appreciation of the people will grow through his observations, and also through an understanding of their language. It was the same painstaking, word-by-word linguistic technique which had led him to pore over Latin and Anglo-Saxon grammars in the Bodleian, and which would later see him quizzing his Arab companions about the exact distinctions between different Arabic expressions.

By now the winter was drawing in, the weather 'rough and uncertain', and Doughty was giving up hope of finding suitable accommodation on the island to see him through the winter. His initial plan had been to take a passage to Spain, but, failing to find a direct service, he decided to explore Malta instead, travelling by boat to Syracuse, where he would join the ferry for Valetta. For a gentleman traveller, the winter storms were a nuisance; for the impoverished local fishermen, they could be disastrous. 'Took up two fishermen and a boy whose boat was overturned after a storm of rain and wind one hour before. They were sitting in their boat which was full of water ten miles from the shore. Syracuse at 3.30 p.m. . . . '

Once again, the casual telling of the story seems disturbingly uninvolved. It is Doughty at his most detached, as apparently uncaring about the plight of the fishermen as he had been about the villagers on the slopes of Mount Vesuvius. In the descriptions he wrote of Vesuvius, he had at least the excuse that he was looking back from a distance of several years on the disaster; here, his notes written down almost as the three bedraggled sailors were taken aboard show merely the curiosity of a tourist looking at a picture. There is not a spark of human sympathy. It is almost as if Doughty feels he has mentally set off for the next stage of his travels, and wants nothing more to do with Sicily or its people: 'Rowed on board at 10 p.m. in a storm of rain and lightning. Thick weather. Steamed out of harbour towards midnight . . .'

Presumably there was still no passage to be had to Spain, because what Doughty found in Malta was a ferry to North Africa, a small Glasgow steamship that would take him to the Tunisian port of Goletta. His initial impressions here were as bad as those of Valetta had been encouraging. 'A large filthy village' was his brisk summary of Goletta itself, while Sidi bu Said, where the nearby site of ancient Carthage might have been more to his taste, was dealt with even more contemptuously. 'A confused, rank, open, unprofitable, uncultivated and miserable territorium, scarcely credible ever to have been any good site, or that ever any great city was built there – much less Carthage . . .'

There is a surprising casualness about Doughty's dismissal of the scene of one of the great cities of the ancient world – though the Romans, of course, had left little of Carthage standing for future archaeologists. But in a sense, this is a fitting farewell to the culture of Europe and the Mediterranean: he had left Europe, at least for a short while, and here in North Africa he was to find not only his introduction to the Arab world, but also the real impetus to his imagination.

It was in the French colonial town of Constantine, a four-and-a-half-hour train journey from the coast, that Doughty had his first direct encounter with the Muslim religion. It was Ramadan, but there seems to have been no difficulty in gaining entrance to the main mosque – and no sign, either, of the antipathy Doughty would show later for Islam and all its works.

> A basilica with 4 or 5 rows of pillars, roof flat, floor covered with Brussels carpets . . . Lighted with candles in handsome chandeliers, with worshippers sitting against the columns reading the prayers and service on certain leaves of parchment. Others prostrated themselves on the earth, with their foreheads touching the ground.

For a traveller leaving Europe for the first time, even for one as determinedly unimpressed as Doughty, it was an irresistibly exotic tableau – but it was also an image of a native Arab culture that was, in Algeria in the year 1872, struggling to survive. For several years the *fellahin* had faced a succession of natural disasters – epidemics, crop failures and infestations of locusts – but in 1871, heartened by the defeat of the French armies in Europe, some 800,000 of them had joined a holy war aimed at driving out the colonists who ruled them. It had been a savage but hopeless fight, with farms and villages laid waste by rebels and French soldiers in turn. The end was never in doubt. The leaders of the insurrection were killed or captured, and many of them put on trial as criminals before juries packed with French immigrants.

Elsewhere in the Middle East French, English and Russians nurtured their own ambitions as the moribund Ottoman empire faltered, And in another sense, too, North Africa, Arabia and the Islamic world were under attack.[13] Whatever the ambitions of the politicians, Europe's writers, poets and artists had effectively colonized the Orient for themselves already, and the scene Doughty saw in the Constantine mosque would have been familiar to Victorian England from the paintings and writings about the East that had been fashionable for years. There had been a flood of poems, paintings, novels and fantasies set in a self-consciously Middle Eastern and desert world. By mid century travellers to Arabia were visiting a land and a culture that was fascinatingly strange and different from their own – but one that must at least have seemed, to anyone with even a nodding acquaintance with contemporary thought, reassuringly familiar.

And yet the Orient of the imagination, the Orient of Flaubert, of Edward Fitzgerald, of Shelley, Byron, and of Beckford, was to a great extent a glorious construction of the artistic community itself – an exuberant celebration of ignorance. The day-to-day contemporary reality of Arabia and the rest of the Middle East was of less importance to the writers and artists than the European tradition of the mystic Orient, of the simple nobility of the desert peoples, the romantic despotism of the sheikhs and rulers, the sexual frisson of the harem. It was that tradition, fitting in perfectly with the romantic imagination to create a deliciously frightening picture of the Arab world, that made Arabia superficially familiar to the travellers.

But alongside this romantic vision of the East was a vast and rapidly growing body of scholarly knowledge about the languages, the civilizations and the history of the Orient. The first part of the century saw an explosion of learned societies, of university professorships and periodicals all concentrating on the new and fascinating field of oriental studies. But even that supposedly dispassionate academic work was often based on literature rather than direct observation, and seems to a modern eye to be suspiciously supportive of the imperial and economic objectives of the western powers. Even Sir Richard Burton, not the most reliable of friends of the British political establishment, commented in his account of his travels in Arabia: 'Egypt is a treasure to be won . . . the most tempting prize which the east holds out to the ambition of Europe.'[14]

If anyone could have remained uncorrupted by both romantic myth and imperial dream, it would have been the twenty-nine-year-old Charles Montagu Doughty, with his cantankerous disregard for anything even remotely modern. He avoided both camps: he had no contact with the seductive world of literary orientalism, and precious little with that of the scholastic Arabists,[15] and as a result, his observations were essentially his own. If he later seemed prickly, that was because his view of Arabia had been forced into no literary or scholastic preconceptions. He found among the Arabs an ancient world which was foreign to anything he had seen elsewhere – one which appeared to mirror his own sense of antiquity.

The fighting in Algeria had finished barely five months before Doughty's arrival, leaving behind a bitterness and unrest that even Doughty, temperamentally blind as he was to political upheaval, could not avoid. The trials and the rounding up of suspected militants were going on around him as he travelled slowly south into the heartland of the revolt.

As he pushed inland on a stagecoach drawn by seven horses towards the oasis town of Biskra, the romantic potential of the shadowy scene in the mosque left him unmoved. Instead, as the coach rocked on through the moonlight, he was still concentrating on the landscape – 'stony, arid, and even all bare and naked . . . Icy chillness devouring. Crests of the mountains powdered with snow.'

The first stage of the journey took them thirteen hours, rattling over the stony ground in the moonlight, and they pulled into the oasis of Batna at eight in the morning. Even though the reason for travelling through the night had been to avoid the desert sun, noon found Doughty setting off on a four-hour excursion to view the remains of a nearby Roman colony. If his interest had often been lukewarm in Europe, here in Africa it was passionate. He was clearly not sparing himself – and at four o'clock the next morning, as the moon sank low over the Atlas Mountains to the west, he was on his way again.

Doughty was wide awake throughout the long, hot journey,

43

noticing the landscapes, the occasional caravans and the few local people along the road – a knot of French soldiers surveying the route, Arab women with looped earrings of wire, a farmer ploughing the 'dry dead country'. And then, almost like a lingering shot from a film, came his first authentic image of the harshness, the implacability he would come to know of Arabia. 'Passed on the way an Arab dead, wrapped in his burnous, bound upon poles, and laid across an ass or mule. No distinct road, but only the wheelruts' traces across the country . . .'

It is a vivid sketch, like his earlier one of the Sicilian peasants. Here, though, Doughty focuses upon the movement of the dead man, not that of the living Arabs who were presumably taking him for burial. But where Shelley saw only the 'boundless and bare' sands of the desert, Doughty saw the wheel-tracks threading their way towards the horizon. With the scene there before him, he transcends the conventional response; while Shelley had no imaginative answer to the overwhelming power of the desert, Doughty sees the continu-ing, ageless struggle for survival of the Arabs. Looking around him, he was struck by the awesome barrenness of the sands, white with an efflorescence of salt, and the surrounding bare mountains. But life struggled on imperturbably, with a blank serenity which matched his own matter-of-fact approach. In that contrast, between the vul-nerability of human achievement and the permanence of human endeavour, Doughty was to find a lifelong inspiration, which he maintained with a religious force and passion.

It is a breadth of vision, a sense of history, which gradually comes to accommodate not only his unemotional response to the sufferings of others, such as the shipwrecked fishermen of Giardini or the hap-less tourists on Vesuvius, but also the dogged courage with which he faces his own dangers.

The little party crossed over an ancient bridge built by the Romans, who had struggled to colonize this harsh country – 'still strong and good after so many centuries', Doughty noted approvingly – but for the most part, what signs of man remained were desolate and all but smothered in the blown sand of the desert. He had left far behind him the well-trodden roads and pathways of Victorian Europe, and with them, the ancient and reassuringly familiar civilization they represented. But in the North African desert, with the stolid march of a small group of Arabs along a route marked only by wheel-tracks in the sand, he was discovering a different but equally ancient stability.

It was 22 November when they finally set out from the desert settlement of Biskra, a caravan of ten men with mules and asses loaded with dates, threading their way through the mountains to the west on their way to the oasis of Bou Saida. Perhaps some of the French garrison had warned Doughty of the danger he might be running in such lonely and unsettled country, so soon after a major insurrection; perhaps he instinctively felt the uncertainty of his new position – but an unaccustomed note of caution enters his diary as he leaves on his trek across the mountains. For the first time he was carrying a weapon – a revolver he had borrowed, presumably from one of the soldiers.

He should not approach the Arabs' tents pitched near their own camp, he was told that evening, in case they were hostile to a travelling European. This, he was warned, was dangerous country. In the circumstances, perhaps it is not surprising that he slept little. 'We lay upon the ground; the night cold and still . . . Light cloud covered the ground, foreboding rain. Howling of dogs all the night long.'

It took four more days' hard travelling before they reached the oasis of Bou Saida, deep in the heartland of the revolt. They were lonely days and hard nights, with the travellers seeking what shelter they could from the driving rain by piling up their baggage and huddling around a smoky fire that guttered in the wind. And yet Doughty, the same man who had grumbled his way across Europe, complaining about the weather, the foreigners, the food and his own health, had clearly enjoyed the hundred-mile trek.

Some of the villages they passed had been friendly, and Doughty had even experienced his first taste of Arab hospitality with a group of wandering bedu – hot griddle cakes, boiled eggs and dates, and a night's shelter, side by side with a score of newborn kids and lambs in the nomads' tent. He had, like most Victorian travellers, squirrelled away a collection of notes and 'specimens' – plants, a few snail shells and jottings about the birds he had seen and about the landscape and the occasional stone cairns he had passed.

Where his comments about his European travels had frequently been dismissive and critical, the diary of his five-day trek to Bou Saida trembles with the excitement of the unfamiliar. In Europe there was practically nowhere clean or comfortable enough for him; here in the desert, after a night spent on the hard earth with a mattress of dried sods, kept awake by the bleating of farm animals, the barking of dogs and the pounding of rain upon the rough black sacking of the tent, he was content. 'I had the happiness to pass the Sunday day of rest in cheerfulness and in some hospitality and quiet . . . There I lay in security, and put away my pistol.'

Notable, too, was his first impression of the Arabs with whom he had come into contact. They had reassured him that they thought the English better at least than the French – faint praise, perhaps, in the aftermath of the revolt. And for his part, despite the earlier fears which had left him quaking by the camp fire and clutching his revolver through the night, he could only note now the continual cheerfulness which they showed despite their hard and unforgiving life – that and their 'quavered, drawling songs'.

For those of his own party he had nothing but praise. 'I have taken no hurt, thank God, nor am any the weaker. With the friendly complaisance, gentleness, and hearty kindness of my party of Arabs (three men and a boy) I was very pleased and contented,' he wrote.

But he set off almost immediately for the coast – a three-day trek out of the mountains, to the first public stagecoach that would take him to Algiers. It was an ironic return to civilization. 'We were tossed and tumbled enough to break the last bone in our body,' he wrote after he had disembarked from the diligence. '5 p.m., at Algiers. We have made in 21 hours 50 miles, or a little above!' From there, as there was no ferry for Spain, Doughty took the train to the port of Oran and a steamer to Cartagena. His first Arabian adventure was over.

Chapter Three

In what so land thou comest,
Observe their customs and that people's laws . . .

Mansoul, p. 72

D oughty must have been well aware as his ferry sailed
serenely into Cartagena that Spain was being torn apart
by civil war. When he was travelling in North Africa, part
of the country at least was firmly under the control of the French
troops; here, there was no unchallenged power to enforce order.

When Doughty arrived, the Italian nobleman who had finally
been prevailed upon to accept the crown as King Amadeus had been
on the throne for three years, in the place of Queen Isabella, who
had been driven out in the so-called 'Glorious Revolution' of September 1868. But there was barely a pause in the political chaos,
with republicans and royalist Carlists savaging each other in a whole
series of confrontations, reverses and political about-turns.

Only a year later Amadeus himself would be dethroned in his turn.
It was a time of ferment; and yet, except for the occasional petulant
complaint of trains held up by gangs of armed men, Doughty let it pass
him by, just as he had the aftermath of the convulsions in France. He
had a straightforward, unimaginative physical courage: he was apparently undaunted – and indeed uninterested – by the very real dangers
posed by the wandering bands of partisans and militias.

Traces of the Arab world he had left behind on the other side of
the Mediterranean were still all about him: the cultures of Christianity and Islam, of Europe and North Africa, the Spanish and the Arabs,
had touched each other in Spain over the centuries, and left their
mark. There was the architecture left behind by the Moors, and a

47

whole range of Spanish customs and words that were clearly derived from the Arabic. Local peasants wore a kerchief wound around their heads, he noticed – a *hakis*, virtually the same word as the Arab *harki*. The villages, with their walls built of baked mud bricks, their houses furnished only with mats spread upon the floor, could have been plucked from the North African landscape of the Maghreb; many of the names of the people could equally well be Arabic as Spanish.

This mingling of the two civilizations, he found later, was a source of continual fascination to the educated townsmen of Arabia. Following their arrival in Gibraltar in 711 the Arabs played a leading role in the life and culture of southern Spain for over 700 years, and although it was nearly four centuries since they had finally been expelled, the legends and tales of Muslim Spain were still current in the coffee houses of the oasis towns.

In Arabia such knowledge would prove an effective way for Doughty to establish friendly relations with the people he met. Here in Spain, it seemed to tie together his interest in language with the great scientific movements of the day. If biological species had evolved gradually over the centuries, if geology and landscape were the products of imperceptible change, so too were language and the day-to-day culture of common men. It was the sort of living archaeology that he loved, laying bare the ancient roots of words and habits alike – even if the final similarity between the two cultures which he jotted down wryly in his notebook, remembering his long hours in the Arab caravan of North Africa, was the 'drawling, insupportable singing'!

His grasp of the political turmoil of the present remained rudimentary; but, with his books still safely in storage, Doughty the observer was waking up to his surroundings, responding more enthusiastically to the people he met.

On his way to Gibraltar, for instance, he paused in Málaga – 'a large, uncheerful seatown, without any good streets'. There, he took an interest in the civil strife only when he met a republican *gran carabinero* who gripped him with his description of the conflict that had engulfed the town just a few weeks before. Forty-five people had been killed in the street-fighting between republicans and Carlists –

reason enough, perhaps, in Málaga as in Paris, to wipe any cheerful smile off the face of the town.

The soldier had four or five musket balls still lodged in his body, and he was on the way for treatment in the relative peace of Gibraltar. The excitement is almost audible as Doughty hurriedly jots down what his expansive new friend has told him.

> He said that if he had the opportunity, he would cut the king in pieces with his knife! That the Italians were a people of fiddlers, and that the king was chosen by 150 men only. That all Andalucia was Republican, that all the *paysants* were *méchants*, and that in time of any trouble, they would sally from their houses, and kill any person they might find of the opposite party.

The *gran carabinero*, all moustache-twirling braggadocio, may sound like a character from an opera, with his loud-mouthed and one-dimensional political analysis – but Doughty does at least take a lively interest in what he has to say about the troubles.

Earlier in his travels, the people he met seem often to have drifted through his diaries half-noticed, like extras on a film-set; now, as he gets more deeply involved in his journeying, the characters come increasingly alive under his more focused gaze.

Over the next few weeks he travelled to and fro across southern Spain, peering slightly wistfully, as a would-be naval officer, at the big artillery pieces which loomed threateningly from the fortified galleries of Gibraltar, searching for Phoenician ruins in Cadiz, jotting down revolutionary slogans from the walls of Seville, and muttering tetchily all the while about his personal discomfort: gnats and crudely executed religious oil paintings in Seville, and another 'night of purgatory in the diligence' on the roads through the mountains of the Santa Morena – everything, it seemed, was designed for his irritation.

He arrived in Lisbon on 19 March after another fifteen-hour train journey. The life of a poor wanderer was beginning to pall, and he planned to spend some time in the Portuguese capital gathering his strength and throwing himself with more enthusiasm, at least for a while, into the role of middle-class traveller. He spent sixteen days there, staying at the English-run Barnards Hotel, drawing more funds from home, and meeting fellow travellers and a few compatriots who lived in the city. 'The banker introduced me to the Gremio, an admirable club . . . which was immediately opposite,' he noted. This, perhaps, was more the sort of life that his relatives in Suffolk would have envisaged – although there is still no suggestion that he might resume the studies which had enjoyed such all-consuming importance only a few months before.

He needed the rest because his health was failing – just as the travelling was about to get even more wearing. 'Two long nights and a day' in a stagecoach took him to Toledo, and on to Madrid, where he rested for another week. 'Thence by the night mail 16 hours to Valencia – a journey almost too great for me, being now full of weakness and with a terrible bronchitis, but I trust nearly the last.'

This, perhaps, was the moment he was referring to years later, when he confessed he had been tempted to end his travelling and return home; or maybe he was looking forward to a longer rest in Italy. In any case, there were more hardships to come before he left Spain.

He set off early in the morning for Barcelona, where he hoped to find a ferry out of Spain. But the civil wars were still raging around him, sometimes dangerously close, with the counter-revolutionary Carlist movement mounting a running guerrilla campaign against the liberal and republican forces. For all their Catholicism and dislike of foreigners, and however exciting a character he had found his *gran carabinero* republican, Doughty might have been expected to feel some sympathy for the arch-traditionalists of the Carlist movement; what troubled him, though, was the disruption of his travel plans rather than the politics or the physical danger. The whole region was 'infested by assassins, Carlists', but personal safety never seems to have been a great concern of Doughty's – not on the slopes of Vesuvius, not in North Africa, not in his later travels in Arabia, and not here either. 'At Tarragona, we were compelled to halt. Half the distance from there to Barcelona, they occupy the way, having fired upon the train the previous evening, and threatening the lives of the engine drivers if they conducted trains. For this, the traffic is at a stand.'

And, with Barcelona now completely cut off from the landward side, at a stand it continued for three days. Doughty was stuck in the port of Tarragona. The only way past the surrounding Carlists was by sea, and late on the Sunday evening he embarked on a little schooner for the brief run down the coast.

In Barcelona a ship was in port, about to set out for France, and in less than twenty-four hours he was on board. Two nights in Marseilles were spent sleeping under the stars before he found a passage on to Naples, from where he had now decided – his health apparently no longer giving him trouble – to travel on to Greece. 'The morning of the second day, we cast anchor in the Bay of Naples, a good passage and a fair wind.'

There are four brief lines in his diary noting that he spent some time in the Pension Guidotti, that he climbed Vesuvius again, that he visited the ruins at Herculaneum, and that he spent two or three days on the nearby island of Ischia; but there, abruptly, his own account ends.

With all its infuriating gaps, and with all the obvious limitations of notes scribbled briefly in a traveller's spare moments, the diary is practically the only clue there is to how the bland, conventional twenty-seven-year-old young man who had left for Holland three years before could develop into the acute observer who would later write the *Travels in Arabia Deserta*. Although we know from occasional mentions in the diary that he wrote lengthy and descriptive letters home – he refers, for example, to accounts of Madrid and a great bullfight he witnessed there – hardly any of them survive.

That is not an accident: Doughty had throughout his life a passionate sense of his own privacy, and was never a friend to biography. Personal enquiries were answered tersely, if more or less accurately. Almost all his letters home were burned, according to his wife – and after his death she herself carefully destroyed those he had written later to her,[1] while Doughty himself replied with horror to an apparently harmless request for a picture of himself for a book on Arabian travel. 'I have not such a photograph in the world. I may be allowed to say it would be rather contrary to my perhaps now old-fashioned ideas to see a portrait of myself, a private person, in a published book.'[2]

It is another dimension of his loneliness, the desire for privacy stretching beyond his immediate surroundings. For all its short-comings, and often despite Doughty himself, the diary offers a rare first-hand, contemporaneous account of three formative years of the life of this determinedly 'private person'.

It is often little more than a collection of jottings, much like the notebooks he later filled as he wandered through the Arabian desert, with words repeated, sentences unfinished, and judgements half-formed – and yet it still shows the first stirrings of his own writing style, with its incisive, familiar images, its occasional pomposities, and its striving for a proper, judicious scientific detachment.

For the next three and a half years, following his travels is a matter of picking up snippets from letters which were often written years afterwards, references in his later works, grudging notes of his memories in old age. Not until he sets off into the Arabian desert with the Hadj caravan and begins once again to keep a detailed notebook will there be so precise a record of the growth of the writer's mind.

In the spring and summer of 1873 he based himself in Athens, 'gypsy-ing' around the countryside, as he put it – staying at lodging houses or occasionally sleeping under the stars.

A few memories from those days surfaced later as vivid markers in his writings. In *The Dawn in Britain*, for example, he would describe how the Gauls, in their ill-fated assault on Delphi, were led through the mountains above the Oracle by Thracian guides until they reached the

> . . . parting of two ways, from the cliff-steeps,
> Where, of some antique hero, shines white tomb.[3]

The aching cold of the lonely mountain wanderer is remembered in Doughty's description of the Gauls encamped on the inhospitable Greek hillside as the snow begins to fall.

Brennus and few lords with him, founden hath
Uncertain shelter, the wild eaves of craigs;
Whereunder, hunger-starved, when fallen this night,
And without fire, they daze, with stiffened joints . . . [4]

He was alone, travelling light, and still without most of his books.
The passionate devotion to his 'studies' was now firmly behind him;
his priority the ruins on the ground rather than the words on the
page.

On the other side of the Bosphorus the archaeologist J. T. Wood
showed him how those ruins could be brought to life. At the ancient
Greek site of Ephesus, Wood was painstakingly revealing the remains
of the Temple of Artemis. Doughty was spellbound: the history of
Ephesus itself formed an imaginative bridge between his own various
interests. The temple linked it with the sites of ancient Greece he
had just been visiting; there was the Christian foundation of St Paul
to involve his sense of religious history, and the story of the destruction of the city by the Goths in the third century to excite his interest
as a student of the tribes of northern Europe.

Stone by stone, the temple was emerging from the ground. Wood,
standing with his wife in the middle of the excavation, and sketching
out on a sheet of *The Times* possible designs and elevations of the
way it might once have looked, readily rebuilt it in his imagination
for his fascinated guest.

Doughty's earlier experiences at Hoxne had hardly prepared him
for anything like this. The diggings had been going on for ten years
already, and he had never seen work on such a scale before. It was
a foretaste of the imposing ruins he would see over the next few
months and years.

Having reached Ephesus, on the Asian side of the Aegean, his
taste for archaeology fired by Wood, he must have thought it would
be as easy to go on towards the Holy Land as to go back towards
Europe. After all, England held few attractions for a thirty-one-year-
old scholar of uncertain expectations – no home, no close family ties,
no career, and only the uninviting prospect of a slightly shabby and
threadbare life of genteel poverty.

He described himself later as 'interested in all that pertains to

Biblical research',[5] and it would have been very like Doughty to want to be able to place the books of the Old and New Testaments in a physical context for himself. But he was still not planning any extensive journeys among the Arabs: his taste of Islamic culture in North Africa and Spain remained just another element in the general experience of his travelling.

On he went, towards the Promised Land. Years later, he sketched out an itinerary for his wife – Latakia, Tripoli, Beirut, Sidon, Tyre and Acre, the route of scores of tramp steamers carrying freight and passengers from port to port. At Sidon and Tyre he collected some Roman mosaic tiles, later presented to the Ashmolean Museum at Oxford – but it seems likely that Doughty abandoned his 'gypsying' at least for a while to travel by sea. From Acre, though, he told his wife that he set out on foot again, on the slow journey to Jerusalem. Now he was travelling along roads he had read about and been told about since his infancy, through a landscape where the place-names rang with the sounds and rhythms of the Authorized Version.

But the only brief glimpses of Doughty coming face to face with the realities of the traditions he had drunk in so avidly come through occasional references written down years later in *Travels in Arabia Deserta*. As he set out with the Hadj the following year on his way south to Medain Salih, for instance, his attention was drawn to the devout Persian pilgrims just starting their journey.

> These men, often red-bearded and red dye-beards, of a gentle behaviour, much resemble, in another religion, the Muscovite Easter pilgrims to Jerusalem. And these likewise lay up devoutly of their slender thrift for many years before, that they may once weary their lives in this great religious voyage . . . [6]

It is easy to picture the tall, retiring Doughty, red-bearded himself, watching intently from a distance as the Russian Christians arrived in the narrow streets of Jerusalem, amazed at their fanaticism and yet admiring their devoutness. Their great voyage was over; his was yet to begin.

Doughty's travels during the next two and a half years took him through Gaza to Egypt, from where he struck out into the Sinai peninsula on a three-month expedition, before making his way back north towards Damascus.

> With Bedouin guides, I wandered on through most of that vast mountainous labyrinthine solitude of rainless valleys, with their sand-wind burnished rocks and stones, and in some of them, often strangely-scribbled Nabataean cliff inscriptions – the names, the saws, the salutations of ancient wayfarers.[7]

In Europe he had been a man alone, travelling through a landscape and a cultural environment that were often well-known, but which did not engage his imagination. Here, paradoxically, the strangeness and unfamiliarity of the desert brought him a new sense of fellowship. The man who found human society so hard to deal with felt himself one with a small and select band of travellers, their 'names, saws, and salutations' passed down to him over the centuries.

It was a crucial time, bringing together his studies of geology, of language, and of the people of the region. The formation of the landscape, the development of words, the derivation of names and the roots of a popular culture could all be seen more starkly and clearly in this unchanging world than had been the case in Europe.

While Doughty notes occasional Roman remains in Jerash and Amman, and finds echoes of Greek tradition in the Nabataean carvings,[8] he is moving all the time deeper into an unknown world, a culture whose roots were neither Greek nor Roman. But there was one ever-present link. The Bible, which he carried with him both in his pack and in his head, provided him with a constant reference point, a textbook of how the region had been centuries before. There is clear delight in the *Travels* whenever he manages to relate the ruins or the landscapes he found to the stories of the Old Testament, like the carved stone water-tanks he saw around Hebron and the Dead Sea – where King Uzziah was said to have 'built towers in the desert and digged many wells' for his cattle.[9]

Sometimes, the bland censoriousness of the young man who had left Belgium shows through: he can show the petulance of any traveller disappointed by what he sees, with a bad-tempered and contemptuous belief that the world and the people have degenerated, that the buildings he finds are monuments to a long-past golden age beyond the reach of 'these squalid Arabs'. There was often a wry contrast between the lush poetic beauty of the ancient verses and the everyday reality of the present. In Hesban, for instance, he came upon the ruins of the biblical city of Heshbon – the same place that the poet of the Song of Solomon had seen before him. 'There . . . is a torrent-bed and pits, no more those fish-pools as the eyes of love, cisterns of the doves of Heshbon, but cattle-ponds of noisome standing water.'[10]

The poetry, evidently, had seeped away over the centuries. Now, his imagination was fired by the links between past and present – the continuity imposed by the lives of the people on ruins which seemed to speak only of mortality.

The thread was often personal, like the carvings of Sinai which seemed to be addressed to him as one of a small band of desert travellers. Or it could be linguistic – he wondered, for instance, whether the ruins of Lejun, 'a four-square limestone-built walled town' in the desert, could be all that was left of an outlying Roman military station, with its name a corruption of the Latin *legio*. But there is, crucially, an introduction for Doughty to the unchanging nature of nomad life, a sense that while buildings may crumble, human life goes on: at the same broken-down walls and arches of Lejun, he saw a small Arab encampment.

> Beduin booths were pitched in the waste outside the walls;
> the sun was setting and the camels wandered in of them-
> selves over the desert, the housewives of the tents milked
> their small cattle. By the ruins of a city of stone they
> received me, in the eternity of the poor nomad tents, with
> a kind hospitality.[11]

It is the tents, not the stone walls, that achieve immortality. One of the first things he notices later, when he reaches the ruins of Medain Salih, is the way that the stones lining the well, still used by the travelling Arabs, are scored by the ropes of generations of beduin, hauling up their water. 'Who', he asks, 'may look upon the like without emotion?'

56

His search for ancient remains was almost obsessive: the Arabs, he said impatiently, were 'too supine and rude' to work out how many ruins there were, but in two days' riding near the town of Kerak he claimed to have visited about forty separate sites. There were disappointments, of course – sites with carvings and inscriptions that he was unable to find, and others that he decided were not worth the visit – but it was among these ruins that he began to form his views of the Semitic culture and the Semitic people.

These travels also helped, incidentally, in forming his estimate of the value of oral evidence: some stories, like some sites, were worth more than others. At the Roman site of Jerash, he was told, there was the grave of the Islamic prophet Hud – who, he added tartly, 'lies buried in more places in Arabia'. There was the now-sanctified Alexander the Great, whose body was to be found – 'if you will believe them' – under a heap of stones at Rabbath Moab; and at Kerak he was shown the sepulchre of Noah – 'who is, notwithstanding buried, at great length, in other places'. Later, as he travelled through Arabia, he was to hear stories of the miracles he was supposed to have performed himself, lifting huge boulders with a single touch of his fingers – 'and yet at such times I was sleeping, encamped with the *Aarab*,* nearly half a mile distant . . .'[12]

But it was not only old wives' tales about famous graves that aroused Doughty's scepticism. Travelling around the Holy Land was further undermining the foundations of his belief, which had already been so dangerously chipped away by his scientific studies. Everywhere, he saw the impossibility of accepting much that he had read for years in his Bible.

He liked to use the Bible as a historical guide, and he was not afraid to test its assertions against science and logic. His own slow progress across the desert set him thinking about the exodus of the Jews from Egypt – two and a half million people, six million camels and seven million cattle. When he asked whether even the whole of Sinai, the worst pasture in the world, could have kept them alive, it was no more than the sort of question that scientists had already started asking of the Scriptures – but Doughty's presence there in

* Arabic plural.

the desert lent it a new point and strength. On all sides, his religion was under attack.

He saw, too, the frequent gulf between faith and human kindness, and the way that religious fanaticism could actually shrivel up ordinary, decent humanity. The man whose faith had already been shaken by his studies in libraries and laboratories was now seeing it put under further strain by his own experience in the world.

There was little enough emotional support from the Greek Christians who lived among the Arabs – a 'lickdish peasant priest' at Kerak and his congregation, for instance, among whom Doughty found no evidence of sanctity or a Christian life. 'To the stronger Muslims I would sooner resort, who are of frank mind and, more than the other, fortified with the Arabian virtues,' he commented.[13] It was a telling condemnation from a man who was later to be criticized for his unbending attitude towards the faith of his Muslim hosts.

But he had no illusions about the generosity and humanity of the devout Muslims either. Later, when he set off with the Hadj, he would see a dying beggar by the wayside, ignored by the passing pilgrims, but then picked up and helped by one of Doughty's own servants, 'a valiant outlaw, no holy-tongue man, but of human deeds'.[14] In another bitter moment, he exploded: 'Religion is a promise of good things to come, to poor folk, and many among them are half-destitute persons. Oh what contempt in religions of the human reason!'[15]

In both comments he was speaking specifically about Islam, 'the dreadful-faced harpy of their religion' – but his choice of words is significant. It was not only Islam, but religion as a whole, that seemed to have failed.

His quarrel, in fact, was with neither Islam nor Christianity, but with the rigidity of both; his respect, then as always, for the relation between the individual and God. The Hadj might be, as he suggested, a cruel deception practised on the guileless pilgrims; perhaps there was nothing but contempt due to the more ostentatiously devout among them and their 'loathsome washings'. But their patience, their determination, their religious stamina, could only impress him. 'There are very few who faint: the Semitic nature, weak and quick metal, is also of a wonderful temper and longsuffering in God,' he wrote.[16]

For the first time in his travels his interests started to encompass the welfare and the day-to-day life of the people among whom he was living. Where before he showed no interest in the politics of the countries through which he was travelling, he now noticed indignantly the debilitating effect of the incompetence, inefficiency and corruption of the tottering Ottoman empire. 'The name of the Sultan's government is a band of robbers,' he wrote.[17]

At least some of the barren land, he suggested, could be reclaimed for crops, much as the Arabs ploughed the soil around their villages to eke out a scanty living. Towns and villages, deserted for centuries, might easily be reoccupied: in the ruined city of Umm Jemal he walked through narrow streets and courts choked with giant weeds, his sandals soft on the basalt slabs underfoot. The stone-built houses still had their roofs and walls intact; only the people were missing. 'The "old desolate places" are not heaps and ruins, but carcases which might return to be inhabited under a better government: perhaps thus outlying, they were forsaken in the Mohammedan decay of Syria, for the fear of the Beduins,' he wrote, with a touching faith in the power of strong government.[18] It was, he said, only the lack of such strength and determination that stood in the way: the impoverished Ottoman empire was unable even to pay the wages of its soldiers, or to repair the roads and bridges which were falling into ruin.

The European powers, of course, were only too anxious to make what profit they could from the Ottoman empire. For several decades would-be entrepreneurs had cast a greedy eye on the underdeveloped Ottoman wastes: the historian Sir Edward Creasy was only one voice among many when he predicted, 'With improved internal government, European capital will be poured into Turkey, and will enrich the land where it is employed . . . the busy hum of European industry will increase and find innumerable echoes . . .'[19] That was the optimistic prediction of the 1850s; what had happened in fact was that heavy borrowing and spending in European markets had bankrupted the empire by the mid 1870s.

But while Doughty was a fervent patriot and a dedicated nationalist, he was never an imperialist. He had little interest in the growth of empire for its own sake, and none of the exaggerated estimation of many empire-builders of the abilities of his countrymen. He for one saw little prospect of wealth for either side in talk of western settlers taking over the land. There was, he said, no reason to suppose that the first generation of European settlers would be any more successful than the Arabs in tilling the desert, while succeeding generations would be moulded by the environment in which they lived. 'Were not the sending of such colonists to Syria, as the giving of poor men beds to lie on, in which others had died of the pestilence?'[20]

As word of his wandering spread, Doughty was becoming something of a legend among the Arabs: a European Christian traveller, with an unaccountable interest in unregarded ruins and old carvings, and an insatiable appetite for anything fellow-travellers, villagers or wanderers on the road could tell him about their life. The Arabs with whom he travelled told him that the region had hardly been seen by Europeans, despite its moderate climate and plentiful water; if he encountered occasional suspicion and hostility, he appears to have been treated much of the time with a sort of amused acceptance. Mohammed Aly, later to be his unpredictable host at Medain Salih, was one of a number of people whom he met during this period; so too was Mohammed Said, the Kurdish pasha who was in charge of the Hadj caravan which Doughty eventually joined. The latter, Doughty boasted, had 'known me a traveller in the lands beyond Jordan, and took me for a well-affected man that did nothing covertly'.[21] It was to prove a useful, as well as a creditable, reputation.

In Sinai he found a naked country, its rocky mountains camouflaged by neither vegetation nor soil, and the memory stayed with him through his life, to surface in his last years, in the poem *Mansoul*.

> An austere soil is that . . .
> Whose bald, sun-bleached, gaunt untrod mountain rocks
> Stand, like some bone-work of a former earth . . . [22]

The memory is geological in its scale, and there is also a sense of a lost, disappeared world – a sense that is reinforced by the few mysterious traces of human life.

Doughty was on a lonely track south of Suez, heading for an old

Greek Christian monastery, when he saw what seemed to be a strange stone cottage, its doorway blocked up with rocks and brushwood. An ageing Arab camel-driver barred his way. 'I would have removed some sticks to look in, but the old Beduin cameleer made signs with the hand . . . that men lay therein, stark upon their backs with closed eyes, and with the other, he stopped his nostrils . . .'[23]

His curiosity had taken him to the doorway of a bedu burial chamber, one of dozens of round, stone-built huts he found huddled together in little groups in the most barren and secluded parts of the region.

Later he described them as 'mosquito huts', supposedly built by the former inhabitants of Sinai for protection through the night from swarms of insects. In reality, neither he nor the Arabs who were travelling with him had any idea of their original purpose, their age, or who had built them, but they caught his imagination as unchanged remnants of a distant past. 'They could easily have been in existence for just a few years, or even a few centuries. I have a conjecture they could have been the huts of immigrants who had spread out across the entire Egyptian stretches of desert since the time of Antonius . . .'[24] As the bones of the landscape were naked to the eye, so too were the rare marks of man – not buried or ruined, not needing reconstruction like the buildings at Ephesus, but simply left behind on a barren landscape, among the

> Inhuman silent solitude of sharp dust;
> Wind-burnished stones and rocks.[25]

And the feeling that nothing changed was reflected, too, in the few people who scratched a meagre living in Sinai. They lived along the Red Sea coast as they had done for centuries. Neither the lush imaginations of the Victorian orientalists nor even the poverty he had seen himself in North Africa can have prepared Doughty for this glimpse of timeless Arab hardship. 'These people had neither clothing nor a roof for protection: in the main they live miserably from the food which they can fish or gather from along the shore. The Arabs rightly put down their dark skin colour to their perpetual hunger and nakedness.'[26]

Even in the grim hierarchy of suffering that Arab life represented, these nomadic fishermen must have been near the bottom. Later, as he travelled with the bedu tribesmen, Doughty would focus upon the life and the culture that could lie behind hardship; here, no doubt still feeling himself to be the detached European traveller studying a strange and savage people, he saw no further than their grinding poverty.

It was here in Sinai that his search for the roots of humanity really began. The landscape, the mysterious buildings, even the people themselves, showed little sign of having been changed by the centuries: here for the first time he could see the perspective that his travels would offer of the origins of human life. The search for the distant history of Arabia, he believed, would help to supply an answer to the question which Isaiah had posed in the Bible, and which rang in his mind: 'What was that old human kindred which inhabited the land so long before the Semitic race? Does not the word of Isaiah come to our hearts concerning them? . . . "What was the rock whence ye were hewn, and the hole of the pit whence ye were digged?"'[27]

Most of his notes from Sinai deal with the geology and the structure of the region: to an even greater extent than elsewhere on his travels, this was a land where history could be read in the rocks and stones, and picked up from the occasional ruins of human habitation. But that history was clear, the links between past and present undisguised. Within this bare, forgotten and cruel land could be found not only the ancient soul of Arabia, but also the first clues to the origins of human civilization.

In the spring of 1875 Doughty left Sinai, apparently without much regret, making his way north through the complex system of wadis and granite cliffs towards Aqaba and on through the biblical land of Edom to Damascus. With him were an Egyptian and a bedu guide, fellow-travellers on a journey where every encounter with the tribesmen could mean either mortal danger, or the warmest of welcomes.

The town of Maan,[28] which was their first destination, lay at the edge of a desolate plain, covered with flints and stones, with no shelter from the wind or the beating sun. Here, in a dip in the ground, they waited nervously until nightfall before setting out across the open country to the town. His two companions, more alive to the dangers of the route than Doughty was, warned that any passing group of nomads might now be a threat: their only safety lay in hiding until dusk. It was midnight before they arrived at the town. 'The place lay all silent in the night. We rode in at the ruinous open gateway and passed the inner gate, likewise open, to the suk: there we found benches of clay and spread our carpets upon them, to lodge in the street.'[29] Doughty's plan now was to travel on to Petra, the Nabataean city which had been made famous by the young Swiss explorer Johann Ludwig Burckhardt[30] more than sixty years before. This, surely, would be the climax of his painstaking studies of ruined settlements and inscriptions. 'I had then no other intention than to see Petra. I could speak very little Arabic, not having before studied the history of those countries,' he wrote later.[31]

The ancient rock city was only five hours' ride away, and he set off eagerly, past another ruined site, long stripped of its white marble pavements by the rich traders of Damascus, and on through the outlying cornfields of Maan – fields where the desert met the sown, in Gertrude Bell's later phrase, and where the farmers had no choice but to offer half their crops to the bedu as a bribe for an untroubled life.

How would the local Arabs react to the arrival of this mysterious red-bearded European, riding a mule and wearing an Ottoman-style red tarboosh, who demanded to see the ancient sites that they still treated with a degree of near-religious respect? At first the tribesmen at the village of Eljy demanded money to let him through to the ruins; then he was treated with suspicion as a possible spy, and finally entertained to a meal of mutton boiled in buttermilk. The meal, as Doughty was to discover later, was significant: once he had been entertained to food and drink by the tribesmen, once he had shared their 'bread and salt', he was protected by the laws of hospitality.

The track down to the monuments, he noted with an English country gentleman's fine sense of bathos, ran though 'limestone downs and coombs . . . like the country about Bath'; but from there, among the red sandstone cliffs, he could make out the palatial columns and cornices of the Nabataean city. Burckhardt must have been faced with the same intriguing panorama when he scrambled over the track years before.

At closer quarters it was a world of contradictions: grandiose two-storey facades which fronted nothing but plain, uncarved caves, hacked out of the rock face; a town where the houses had vanished and only the empty tombs in the rock remained.

It was initially courage, resourcefulness and good luck that had brought Burckhardt there; then learning and intelligence that made him realize that the ruins were indeed those of the fabled city of Petra. He had been alerted to their existence in the Wadi Mousa by the casual talk of local people, as he travelled south towards Maan and, disguised as a Muslim traveller from India, he had decided to risk his life by trying to see them for himself. It was much the same decision as Doughty would have taken – except that Burckhardt had his disguise and a story he had concocted about a vow to sacrifice a goat at the nearby Tomb of Aaron to explain his presence. Doughty made no pretences: he simply told the curious, occasionally hostile villagers that he wanted to see the ruins.

Perhaps it was the red tarboosh that persuaded the Arabs to let him through: despite its crumbling power, the Ottoman empire still wielded considerable influence in the region, and the hat may have reinforced Doughty's own claim to have powerful friends. However vehemently the villagers protested their independence, they would have been unwilling to try to outface the authority of the *Dowla*, the Ottoman government. But, after a night spent in caves in the rocky face on the outskirts of Petra, there were still other locals to stand in the way: one group of four with a gun grabbed the bridle of Doughty's mule, and refused to let him through unless they were given money; another goatherd, looking after his flocks with his wife, warned him to keep off the mountain slopes, for fear of attack. Fifty armed men, the Arab warned, would not be enough to protect him against the angry villagers if he tried to climb out of the valley.

In the valley-bottom, though, they found the long, deep cleft through the rocks known as the Siq, a natural passage-way through groves of wild olives to the carvings – and at the end of it, the Khasneh, the so-called Treasure House of the Pharaoh, the most perfect of the monuments. It was no disappointment: its 'sculptured

64

columns and cornices are pure lines of a crystalline beauty without blemish, whereupon the golden sun looks from above, and Nature has painted that sand-rock ruddy with iron-rust'.[32]

Ignoring the villagers' warnings, they climbed out of the valley to the cold mountainside, and found a place to stay for the night in a bedu encampment, where they were entertained with music and singing (enough, said Doughty ungratefully, to 'move our yawning or laughter') before spending another day at the monuments. Leaving his mule at the Treasure House, Doughty set off with another local guide to explore the carvings and inscriptions until, as the sun set, the anxious young Arab urged him to leave. It was not clear whether he was more afraid of the marauding bedu or of the angry spirits of Petra. His plan was to spend the night back at his own village, where Doughty had been entertained three nights before – but when the villagers there heard the sound of the mule's hoofs on the rocky track, they poured out of their houses to drive them away. No unbeliever should enter the place, they shouted – and the man who had tried to bring him was reviled as 'Abu Nasrany', father of Christians. They were forced back up into the hills, back to the bedu encampment they had left earlier.

Doughty did not seem to care what happened to his guide. For him, the attack by the villagers was little more than an exciting interlude, an introduction to the unpredictable hostility of the tribesmen. But the visit to Petra had given a fresh dimension to his travels. While the mosquito huts of Sinai spoke of a primitive people struggling to survive, these grandiose carvings – reduced now to 'night-stalls of the nomads' flocks and blackened with the herdsmen's fires'[33] – were the remnants of a long-vanished prosperous race of builders, traders and merchants. It was there, in the shadows of 'that wild abysmal place which is desolate Petra',[34] that Doughty's dreams of discovering another civilization were born.

During the long nights on the mountainside above Petra the villagers had let slip details of just such another civilization. There were, they said, similar sites further south down the Hadj road, on the way to Mecca. It was the first mention Doughty had heard of a second Petra

– and it had come to him in much the same casual way as had
Burckhardt's initial information about the first one. At first the villagers were unwilling to talk about the sites, particularly to a curious
European Christian, but they assumed that Doughty had arrived
from the south, and must already know about them.

There were several separate sites, known as Medain Salih – the
cities of Salih, a Muslim prophet, who was said to have destroyed
them and their inhabitants because of their wickedness. Each one
was hewn from the solid rock like Petra. Doughty's immediate
thought was that he might be the first European to document those
remains.

And in Maan there was more to be learned: a secretary named
Mahmud – 'a literate person who had been there oftentimes' – told
him about the inscriptions and the carved birds on the massive stone
facades. 'With those words, Mahmud was the father of my painful
travels in Arabia,' he noted later.[35]

The cities were well within the reach of a determined traveller –
some ten days' travel, according to the people whom Doughty asked.
He wanted to set off south at once to see whether the stories he had
heard were accurate – attracted, initially at least, by the possibility
that the ruined cities might be connected with the stories of the Old
Testament. 'I mused at that time it would be some wonder of Moses'
Beduish nation [of] Midian,' he wrote some years later. 'For those
inscriptions which might yield fruit to our Biblical studies, I thought
it not too much to adventure my life.'[36]

Other stories of the Arabian hinterland that may well have been
intended to warn him off simply increased his fascination – stories
of a cruel and powerful prince, who ruled over his desert kingdom
as both tyrant and lawgiver. 'All the next land of wilderness was
ruled by one Ibn Rashid, a mighty prince of Beduin blood, who
lorded it over the tribes . . . I thought I had as lief see his Beduin
court, and visit some new David or Robin Hood, as come threading
these months past all the horrid mountain mass of Sinai,' he said
later.[37] Here, surely, there would be more to fire his imagination
than he had found in Europe.

But his first attempts to join the pilgrimage that might start his
journey there were rebuffed: the Ottoman governor of Maan, well

aware that he might be held responsible if anything were to happen to this headstrong European in the harsh country of the desert bedu, forbade townsmen and travellers alike to help him find a way down the Pilgrim Road.

The only way of reaching Medain Salih, the governor said, would be to accompany the Hadj caravan from Damascus – a suggestion which was clearly a way of fobbing off this importunate Christian.

The governor's caution was understandable: from his point of view, it was the worst possible time to have a European Christian who claimed the highest political connections setting out on such a dangerous and unpredictable venture. Within the past few months tension had been growing throughout the Ottomans' Balkan possessions, and both the Russian Tsar and the western powers were making threatening noises about the need to protect the Sultan's non-Muslim subjects from the excesses of their masters.

In Constantinople Sultan Abdul Aziz was clinging to power by anxiously playing off Russians against Europeans. Allowing Doughty to wander through the wilder corners of the empire would risk demonstrating how feeble was the Sultan's grasp on the extremities of his dominions – and if he were to come to harm, it might provoke an anti-Ottoman *cause célèbre* in the West. Any provincial governor who caused such a diplomatic disaster merely to oblige an eccentric traveller with a penchant for ancient inscriptions would surely attract the unwelcome attentions of the Sultan's stranglers.

So Doughty spent twenty frustrating days in Maan, becoming well known in the streets and coffee houses, as he tried to glean more information about the monuments of Medain Salih. He also took to wandering through the flint beds just outside the tumbledown clay wall around the town, where he found traces of still earlier inhabitants than those of Petra. Lying near the surface, to his astonishment, were seven flint tools, chipped to a sharp edge. It was a tribute to Doughty's own powers of observation, sharpened at the archaeological site of Hoxne all those years before, that he recognized them. They were another imaginative link with people from centuries before. 'We must suppose them of rational, that is an human labour. But what was that old human kindred which inhabited the land so long before the Semitic race?'[38]

They were, indeed, from long before the Semitic race, some of them dating back to Lower Palaeolithic times, hundreds of thousands of years before the appearance of modern man. Forty years later Doughty presented the axes, amongst other trophies, to Oxford University's Ashmolean Museum – and along with them, incidentally, his own clumsy effort to copy the craftsmen of prehistory.

Today they shine dully in shades of green, brown, and grey, still fitting snugly into the palm of the hand, still sharp along the chipped edges, but each one now carrying a precise little note, in Doughty's schoolmasterly hand, to say where it was found.

'They were certainly a significant find – they wouldn't have seen many pieces like this in Britain in 1915,' says Alison Roberts, the collections manager in the museum's Department of Antiquities. 'Not much was known about the Palaeolithic era in Syria or the Near East at that time, and most European archaeologists would have been as excited as Doughty himself to see them. The writing on them is interesting too – it shows Doughty was a very careful, conscientious collector. A lot of people weren't, in those days.'

When he found them, though, Doughty's attention was fixed on Medain Salih. Everything he heard simply whetted his appetite more keenly: the cities lay close together near the pilgrim trail, about halfway between Maan and Medina, their rock chambers like those he had already seen at Petra, but bigger – and every doorway had an inscription and the figure of a falcon or an eagle, wings outspread, carved over it. However close the links with Petra, he believed there was every chance that he might find the remains of a previously unknown desert civilization.

He used all his powers of persuasion with the governor. Although the journey would be difficult and dangerous, he argued, it would not take him into the area of the two Holy Cities which were forbidden to non-Muslims on pain of death. But it was useless: the governor had clearly decided not to take the responsibility of allowing him to make the journey. He would have to travel north to Damascus and try to find more powerful backing.

So, after failing to get permission in Maan, he set off for Damascus. Eager as he was, he does not seem to have hurried on his journey.[39] He spent several months wandering through the countryside, adding to his collection of inscriptions and stories of the region's biblical past. It was hard travelling, often with nothing more than a night under the stars in the shelter of a few rocks at the end of the day – but it took Doughty deep into the history of the ancient land. He found a chain of old watch-towers and fortresses stretching a hundred miles or so into the desert, each one with its own story – one was 'a kasr of the old Yehud', a castle of the ancient Jews; another was reported to be a palace, and a third, scattered with broken columns, and with a massive marble stairway leading from the deserted entrance hall, now no more than the den of some wild beast.

There were silent piles of stones still standing where they had been painstakingly gathered in long-abandoned fields; entire towns and villages, ruined and deserted, which seemed to date back hundreds of years.

> The ruins . . . are built without mortar, with the uncanny natural blocks of flintstone and limestone. There are even, in several of the remains of the regular buildings, foundation walls, vaults, and round arches made of square carved stones which on appearance might have been made by Roman hands – column pieces, marble fragments, etc . . .[40]

The villages that were still inhabited bore a striking resemblance to the ruins in their design and construction: in the past, Doughty's guides told him, this had been a thriving farming region, which had been laid waste years before by a bedu sheikh. Myth, history, or a combination of the two, the awestruck stories told by the Arab farmers bore witness to the dread they still felt of the half-savage nomadic tribes who could descend upon them so suddenly and so brutally. Fear, too, could survive almost unchanged down the generations.

Sometimes, Doughty paid an Arab guide to accompany him on his way; where he had to, he travelled alone, trusting to his luck and his ability to talk his way out of trouble. But whenever possible he fell in with other travellers going on the same track: there were stories to be heard along the way, and some safety to be found in numbers. As he left Maan, for instance, he joined the military captain of the Hadj road and twenty or so of his peasant soldiers, on their way to Nablus. They were well enough armed to frighten off any casual groups of bedu tribesmen they might meet – but he still had to rely on his own wits rather than on the loyalty of his companions. On one occasion, threatened by a group of nomads, he resorted to a straightforward bluff, and shouted orders to the men to arrest them, as if he were a military commander. The soldiers, of course, who had anyway not been paid for nearly a year and a half, were even less likely to obey him than their own captain – but the Arabs didn't know that, and they rode off in panic from the scruffy little troop and their guns.

It was now June, and the countryside was blooming. Doughty had reflected as he left Maan on how the land must indeed have seemed to flow with milk to the Israelites as they trekked wearily out of the wastes of Sinai. Now he found rose-laurel and rushes growing in profusion around the cattle pools, swollen with the spring rain; the grass was a yard high, and the corn growing fat. The bedu he met were turning their cattle loose on some of the richest pasture of the year, and, unpredictable as ever, they were happy to slaughter a sheep for dinner in honour of their guest.

He paused briefly in the town of Kerak, a rough settlement with a bloody history of wars and conquests, which had the air of a frontier town, where criminals and murderers could seek refuge from the stern justice of the Ottoman empire. The countryside round about was dotted with ruined forts, towers and villages, but he did not linger. It was still June when he was a good hundred miles further north, wading up to his waist in the tepid waters of Wadi Zerka, as they tumbled towards the river Jordan.

The biblical land of Gilead, through which he passed on the way to Jerash and Damascus, sounds like a paradise, 'full of the balm-smelling pines, and the tree laurel sounding with the sobbing sweetness and the amorous wings of doves! In all paths are blissful fountains; the valley heads flow down healing to the eyes with veins of purest water'.[41] For all that, though, it remained outside the law. The people, 'uncivil and brutish, not subject to any government', slashed and burned the woodland as if they were living in some remote rainforest: it was a grim and primitive land.

All the time, he was becoming more familiar with the Arab way

70

Theberton Hall: 'Childhood, it must have seemed, was little more than a harsh preparation for a life of loneliness. Theberton Hall was shut up, and within a few weeks the auctioneers moved in.'

St Mary's Church, Martlesham, Suffolk: 'The atmosphere of the simple little church, its unimpeachable, unassuming Englishness and its dignified reserve, reflect one facet of his character.'

Martlesham Hall. This nineteenth-century photograph shows the house much as it was when Frederick Doughty was forced to sell it. His son recorded: 'It was a terrible wrench to all his feelings: the building of the Hall in the Elizabethan style had been the pleasure and the hobby of his life. For years after the sale, the place was never named, nor mention made of it.'

Above Gonville and Caius College, Cambridge: 'The Admissions Book in the archives of Gonville and Caius College, Cambridge, shows "Carolus Montagu Doughty" accepted as a new member of the college on 30 September 1861. It was the college that his father and his grandfather had attended before him.'

Right Gonville Court, Gonville and Caius College, from which Doughty would have ascended to his rooms.

Downing College, Cambridge: 'Simply making the transition from the quiet, enclosed courts of Caius to the wide open spaces of Downing was significant: apart from the lack of enthusiasm at Caius for the newfangled study of science, there was the rigid insistence on the need to attend not only chapel, but also lectures.'

of life and culture, even though he had yet to learn more than a smattering of the language. The wild bedu, still largely unknown and untrusted, seemed to people an uncivilized world in which they made their own law, while on the desert fringes the hard-working farmers and traders eked out a living that seemed to have been unchanged for centuries. 'These desert men lean to the civil life, and are such yeomen perhaps as Esau was. Other of their tribesmen I have seen, which are settled in tents, earing* the desert sand near Gaza; their plough is a sharpened stake, shod with iron, and one plough-camel draught . . .'[42]

But these industrious farmers, too, could turn on him in a moment. They distrusted foreigners and particularly those who, prying into ancient ruins, might prove to be spies. A European and a Christian in a strange land, either alone or with few companions, he was an easy target either for religious bigotry or simple banditry by farmers and nomads alike – the more so when he steadfastly refused to adopt a disguise or make up stories to justify his presence.

There had been his brush with the villagers around Petra; and there had been another incident south of Wadi Zerka when Doughty, sick and weak with his long travelling, was abandoned by his guide at a bedu encampment. At first he was well enough treated: the Arabs made at least a pretence of trying to find the guide who had deserted him, and gave him food and shelter. But they were moving on, they said, and after one night they delivered him to a second encampment.

There, Doughty found only women – and when the men returned later in the day, it was to threaten him, and demand a ransom in return for letting him go. It was a gross abuse of the laws of hospitality – but Doughty was becoming more skilled in the ways of handling the nomad tribesmen. First he protested that he had been given milk to drink by the women of the tribe, and should therefore be treated as a guest; and when that failed, he suggested that the leader of the group, Sheikh Faiz, should give him his horse in return for the ransom – one gift for another.

When Faiz's mare was brought forward, though, he looked at it

* Ploughing; tilling.

in disgust, and told the sheikh it was not even good enough to accept as a present. Faiz, presumably, was not particularly popular among the tribesmen; at any rate, they took Doughty's side, and laughed at their leader's discomfiture. Winning support with a pointed joke and a pained expression remained one of his favourite survival techniques.

He arrived in Damascus weary and sore. His six months in the deserts, the mountains and the wadis had been a completely different experience from anything that had gone before. Physically, it had been an exhausting and draining ordeal, struggling by camel and mule over some of the most inhospitable country in the world – but, more than that, he had been more alone, more exposed, than at any time in his life.

As well as his excitement at the prospect of finding the ruins of Medain Salih, he was finding aspects of daily life and culture among the Arabs that inspired his deep and lasting respect; but, for all his occasional sense of kinship with travellers who had gone before him, it was knowledge won against a background of remoteness and fear. In Europe, after all, he had been surrounded on his travels by the comforts and reassurances of a familiar way of life: even when he slept under the stars, it was within reach of people who shared his standards and values, people with whom he might enjoy a mutual understanding. When he trekked out into the desert of North Africa, it had been a brief excursion into a foreign land – and an excursion made still under a recognizable framework of European colonial law and authority.

Doughty may have lived as a poor traveller before, but it had been in a sympathetic world. His poverty, too, had been at least partly assumed – there had been times, as in Lisbon, where he could briefly drop back into the comfortable lifestyle of an Englishman of a certain class.

Here in the Bible lands he was isolated under the arbitrary and uncertain law of a cruel and largely hostile country, and travelling always on the fringes of what appeared to be a wasteland of lawless savagery. The familiarity which his biblical knowledge might have brought to the terrain often served simply to emphasize the gulf between the magnificence of the past and the squalid meanness of the reality. Physically and emotionally, Doughty remained a man alone.

There were, of course, occasions when he had been welcomed into the Arab tents, fed and entertained. The sheikhs who had killed sheep for him to eat and brought milk for him to drink might seem approachable, even welcoming. In the desert, though, and occasionally crossing his path threateningly, were the wandering bedu. He would learn more about them later – but for now they seemed to represent the very heart of darkness.

But if Doughty's travels had revealed how terrifying life could become without the reassurance of the rule of law, Damascus showed how frustrating the rules and restrictions of officialdom could be. Doughty had been told in Maan that the Hadj caravan might lead him to Medain Salih; but in Damascus, when he asked the Wali, the Ottoman governor of Syria, for permission to accompany the pilgrims, he was fobbed off. The Wali asked the British consul, a career diplomat and Middle East specialist named Thomas Sampson Jago, for his advice, but the consul wanted nothing to do with Doughty or his impetuous plans. 'He had as much regard of me, would I take such dangerous ways, as of his old hat. He . . . told me it was his duty to take no cognisance of my Arabian journey, lest he might hear any word of blame, if I miscarried.'[43]

The governor in Maan had refused to take responsibility; the Wali in Damascus had refused to take responsibility; and now the British consul was refusing to take responsibility. They hoped that this foolish and importunate Englishman would go away and forget his dangerous obsession with Medain Salih, but Doughty kept on pestering them. In what was no doubt another effort to brush him aside, the Wali told him that only an official *firman* or permit from the Sultan himself would gain him acceptance with the pilgrim train.

But the British consulate, through which he would normally have applied for such a document, had washed its hands of him: Doughty would have to find another mediator and, with barely two months to go before the pilgrims would be gathering to depart, there was no time to be lost.

He had already written to the British Association seeking support; now he would approach the Royal Geographical Society to make representations on his behalf. There were also pressing reasons to leave Damascus for a while – there had been an outbreak of cholera in the city, and the troubles of the Ottoman empire had led to rumblings of anti-Christian feeling among the Muslim population. In addition, Doughty had given his brother Henry an address in Vienna where a letter might be left for him to collect. By travelling back into Europe, he might at the same time gather welcome news from home, speed his own message to London on its way, and also avoid a disease-ridden and unfriendly city. Tired as he was, he set off through the north gate of the city, turning his back at least for a while on the Arab world.

It was another hard journey, and Doughty gives a full account of it in one of the few letters from him that have survived. Writing to his brother from the Hotel Wandl after he arrived in Vienna, he described the inhumanity shown by the Turks in the Balkans. 'I saw all their tithes of corn rotting in the fields – the barbarous paschas will have money, and the poor wretches have none to give, and offer them in kind as usual,' he wrote. Hundreds of miles of good land were untilled: 'The Bulgarians are a people of cultivators; but they have not dared hitherto to occupy the land, afraid of the ferocity of the old Turks.'[44]

What he saw awakened Doughty's passionate interest in the social and political situation around him, both now and when he returned to Damascus. The Ottoman empire, the 'disorderly Turkish domination', was dying on its feet around him, with what he dismissed contemptuously as 'a handful of degenerate Turks' uneasily maintaining their rule over some five million Slavs. There was a tense, suspicious mood, with the poverty-stricken Muslims being forcibly conscripted to put down a revolt by Slav peasants in Bosnia and Herzegovina. Doughty himself, wandering through the countryside alone and on foot, was almost picked up as a suspected spy.

Instead of the camel and mule he had relied on to travel in Sinai and up the Jordan valley, he now enjoyed the relative luxury of steamships and, at least as far as the end of the line in Bulgaria, the railway. Elsewhere, rustic horse-drawn carts without springs kept up a brisk eighty miles a day, but offered little comfort over the bumpy roads: 'The bridges only were bad, and often broken through in more than one or two places, but it was rough work ... Sometimes I thought I should have vomited my heart as we dashed at some terrible stone. I stayed at the towns to recover a little,' he wrote to Henry, far away in the remembered comforts of Theberton Hall.

But he was back in Europe, and there was a clear sense of relief. Restless and threatening as the atmosphere might be, it was still recognizably more like home than the foreign lands he had been travelling through. 'The aspect of the country is wholly European – it is green and northern. The houses are built *a la Franca* with pitched roofs and chimneys, the populations mostly Christian,' he wrote. And when he arrived in the then Hungarian capital of Pest on the Danube, he marvelled at the palatial buildings, the wide streets and the tramways. 'I was surprised and astonished and pleased at such a new and advanced world,' he said: eighteen months away had clearly sharpened his appetite for the more relaxed, familiar culture of the west.

They had also sharpened his memories of Theberton. There are few signs of homesickness in his journals, but the letter from home that was waiting for him at the post office in Vienna left him thinking wistfully of the life he had left behind. The renovations had apparently restarted in Theberton Hall, and Henry told him of a garden party and ball he was planning to hold there on 13 September – the very day that his brother collected the letter on the other side of Europe. 'I calculated the hour an hundred times to think what you ought to be then doing. How could you have got on in the old Pict. Gallery, with a floor of earth and mortar! Finally I am settled here, my limbs ache, I am so weary, and my head also,' Doughty wrote as he sat alone in his room at the Wandl. In a man who usually appeared so dignified and controlled, it is an appealing human moment of excited nostalgia.

But 13 September 1875 was too busy a day for him to spend much time moping over Theberton and the familiar social excitements of village life. In the same post as his letter home to Theberton he sent off a more formal message to the Royal Geographical Society in London, asking not only for the society's help in obtaining an official pass from the Ottoman authorities, but also for a grant towards the cost of the expedition. Eight years later he would sit before the members of the society to hear its president, Sir Henry Rawlinson, describe him as being 'in the front ranks of Asiatic travellers' after his 'adventurous and perilous journey';[45] however, as he hurried hopefully to the Vienna post office, he was no more than an unknown supplicant, using every means he could think of to attract Sir Henry's favourable attention.

He detailed the journey he had already made through Sinai and north to Damascus: already, he said, 'without resources and with great fatigue', he had established that the Sinai peninsula had been only recently raised from the sea; he had found more than 300 ruined cities and villages scattered across the region between Maan and Kerak; and he had personally gathered several specimens of ancient flint tools on the gravel plains to the east of Petra. Doughty, a continent away from London, had no way of finding out what were the special interests of the members of the society's council: he was at pains to cast his net as widely as he could in order to catch at least somebody's attention.

Most urgently of all, he told them what he had heard so far of Medain Salih, and what he could hope to find there.

> Here are the traces of an unknown people, of inscriptions unknown. Of what interest they are, I think it is manifest. I wish shortly to go down with the pilgrims – they are jealous of that country, where they say no Frank has set foot. I have trusted to the R Geogr Society to obtain the firman necessary ... My desire is to return immediately to go with the pilgrims to the discovery of these unknown cities and inscriptions.[46]

He had, he said, worked with the society's cooperation before, and he described his expedition to Norway.

> I borrowed from the Socy. at the instance of Sir Rod. Murchison, President, a theodolite with which I measured the daily motions of several Norwegian glaciers, at which time I made other observations of interest to geologists

76

that Sir Chas. Lyell, then preparing the last ed of his Principles, spontaneously visited me to make a number of
enquiries and used my assistance largely in that part of
his labours . . .

The word 'largely' is something of an exaggeration: whatever help
the young graduate was to the eminent Lyell in his ground-breaking
study was at best peripheral. But Doughty's anxiety to impress and
his desperation are clear in every hurried line and every dropped
name. At last he had found a focus for his study which might win
him recognition: as he travelled to Vienna from Damascus, he must
have gone over and over the tempting prospect of Medain Salih in
his mind. The hardships and the threat of disease he could cope with,
but to get permission to set out at all he needed help – and he
believed that he deserved it.

If the society could be persuaded to act quickly, a letter of recommendation might be obtained through the embassy at Constantinople
within three weeks or so – thus neatly avoiding the unenthusiastic
Mr Jago in Damascus. But after five years on the road Doughty was
seeking more concrete help.

The cost of the expedition is too much for a man of slender
income. I have hitherto lived as a traveller with the Arabs
at a small expenditure, but the results are always less than
they might have been with sufficient means, added to
fatigues which might have been spared in that penetrating
climate, a country now ravaged by cholera . . .

He had, he said, already asked the British Association for a contribution of £100, but his letter might have gone astray; would the
Royal Geographical Society support him with one of its grants?

He signed the letter as formally, and as graciously, as he could –
'I am Sir, hoping at some future time I may have the pleasure to know
you, your obedt. servant, Charles M. Doughty, MA, Cambridge, of
Theberton Hall, Suffolk.' After his gruelling time as a despised, homeless wanderer, it was clearly time to play once again the part of a
country gentleman of standing.

He submitted a report on his wanderings in Sinai, and on his hopes from Medain Salih, for the Viennese Geographical Society.[47] He wrote knowledgeably of the topography and geology of the region: the whole peninsula, he believed, had only recently been thrust up out of the sea, a parched land that had been formed by the buffeting and erosion of long-dried-up torrents of water and retreating tides.

But his real interest was in the mysterious 'mosquito huts', the ruins scattered through the mountains of Edom, and, best of all, the stories he had heard of the lost cave cities of Medain Salih. Doughty described with enthusiasm the discoveries he had already made about them at second-hand, through the tales of the Arabs he had met, and was frank about the urgency with which he wanted to set off to see them for himself. 'I don't doubt the existence of such towns; I've heard about them from about a hundred people, who . . . all report in the same fashion. They resemble the former cliff town Petra, and are of the same ilk, as if they had been built by the same master builders . . .'[48]

He had been continuing his investigations into the lost settlements since he left Maan. In Damascus itself, and in the towns and villages along the way, he had heard the same stories – some fifteen or sixteen towns, some in the mountains and others hidden nearby in the desert, known only to the wandering Arabs.

He had, he claimed, 'certain evidence' – though it can have been little more than the hearsay of other travellers – that the carvings to be found there would prove to be ancient inscriptions, similar to those he had already sketched at Petra.

Doughty must have known that his chances of getting permission in time to join that year's pilgrimage were slim. Even if the Royal Geographical Society had replied at once, with all the influence such an august body could muster, there would barely be time for the Ottoman functionaries in Constantinople to go through the formalities – and he had already discovered in Damascus how the official talent for prevarication could eat into the days and weeks.

But neither the Royal Geographical Society nor the British Association was interested in sponsoring his journey. Much of the area he was travelling had already been studied, and the rest was due to be surveyed during the next couple of years, they noted. And there was no urgency about their deliberations: Doughty never heard from the British Association at all, and by the time the RGS considered his letter in November, he was on his way back to Damascus.

He had already sampled the bureaucratic obstacles that could be thrown up by the combined efforts of the Turkish authorities and the British consulate, and he had some experience of the sheer physical danger the expedition would involve. Now, as he left Vienna, he recognized the simple lack of interest of the English scientific establishment as well. But Doughty remained certain that the danger and the difficulty would be worth it. 'The discovery of these towns and their inscriptions may throw a new light on the Bible story. Who knows when they were left by their former inhabitants? What this unknown people was called, and what language they had?'[49]

By now, he was too late to make the journey that year: as he made his way back to Damascus by sea, travelling via Trieste and Alexandria, the Hadj caravan was already on its way south without him. If he were to carry through his plan of going south with the pilgrims to explore the remains at Medain Salih, he would have to fill his time in Damascus, living as cheaply as he could.

He had almost certainly collected more funds from the bank in Vienna to enable him to stay at the Wandl in conditions which, compared with the hard life he was used to, must have seemed like the lap of luxury. Instead of 'gypsying' his way back to Damascus, he took the steamer across the Mediterranean. Clearly, even if his resources were stretched, he had not yet quite run out of money.

The practicalities were fairly simple: one reason for going abroad in the first place had been that a gentleman might live more cheaply as a traveller than he could at home, and he had discovered in Sinai that life in the Arab world would cost even less money than on the roads of Europe. Despite his plea of poverty to the RGS panjandrums in London, he might well be able to stretch his dwindling funds as far as Medain Salih and back.

The trek through Sinai had convinced him that he could withstand the discomfort and physical pain of a long expedition through the desert to the sites. If he had plans beyond that, they were very vague: perhaps he might make his way across Arabia to pick up a steamer at one of the Gulf ports; maybe, even at this early stage, he was calculating that a longer stay among the Arabs could save him still more money. Probably the disease and ill-health he had already encountered on his travels had given him the idea that a little study and a small supply of drugs might even enable him to make a small income. He would not need much in the desert.

Throughout his life Doughty was a man driven by the urge to prove himself. If the navy wouldn't take him because of his weak constitution, then the world should see how much he could endure; if Cambridge denied the first-class quality of his intellect, then he would prove Cambridge wrong; and if the geographical establishment rejected his plans for exploring Arabia, then he would go without their aid.

Damascus, 'this goodly Oriental city', enticed him. A few months had seen the immediate threat of cholera past, and he hired rooms from a Lebanese Christian on the upper floor of a back-street building near the Greek Orthodox cathedral. It was a thriving, cosmopolitan city, where itinerant traders from all over the Middle East, Arabia and even further afield brought their wares to the bazaars. There were tent-makers, carpenters, merchants who bought the skins and feathers of ostriches from the wandering bedu – the skins selling for the price of a good camel, and the feathers alone worth more than their weight in silver, Doughty exclaimed in astonishment; there were Persians, Moors and North Africans in their gleaming white robes who had fled the French rule in Algeria, pompous Ottoman officials in their fashionable red caps with swinging blue silk tassels, and lean, dark-skinned beduin carriers.

In the bazaar he found itinerant doctors, and Christian cloth-merchants who, as a sideline, travelled around the region offering vaccinations to the tribesmen. He seems to have had little time for the practitioners themselves, but he was not too proud to watch them at work, or to buy supplies of his own. Not only might his new-found skill earn him a little money in the desert, but it might also find him friends among the bedu.

It was a relaxing year that he spent in the streets and orchards of one of the Arab world's busiest cities, wandering on his regular afternoon walks through the crowded markets and outlying villages, exploring the groves of oaks just outside the city, where credulous peasants left offerings to make their wishes come true, and striding around the great cathedral mosque of the more conventionally faithful. He met several Arabs on his travels who remembered him there, a tall, bearded European, pacing solemnly along the city streets. Compared with his later experiences in Arabia, it was a tolerant, welcoming place; Damascus, which had been completely closed to Europeans only a few years before, left him with his fondest impressions of the Muslim world. 'How sober, and peaceably full of their not excessive homely toil is the life of such a Mohammedan city of 130,000 souls. And doubtless we exceed them in passionate disorders, much as we excel them in arts and learning . . .'[50]

He was to remember it wistfully from the harshness of the desert – the wide open streets of the city, the roads and hedges, the ripening apricots and the foot-high plantations of vetch grown as food for the camels – but everything now was geared towards his planned expedition south with the next year's pilgrimage.

His main priority was to learn Arabic, and he settled down with a teacher to follow the same method he had used before – picking painstakingly over individual words, worrying out meanings and derivations, and gradually piecing sentences together. But where before he had studied languages almost casually, as a pastime, now he bent his whole mind to the task. His teacher, a Christian named Abdu Kahil, described how Doughty would sit in his room, his watch open on the table, and devour the Arabic texts before him. Doughty himself was always dismissive about his command of Arabic, but over a period of eight months, according to Abdu Kahil, he picked up the language faster than any of his other pupils.

He also adopted an Arabic name, Khalil – maybe the first sign that this project was more central to him than any of the studies he had taken up before. It was not a disguise, and it would greatly annoy him in his old age when newspaper accounts of his travels suggested that it was. Khalil, he explained, is as close a transliteration of his own name, Charles – or Carlo, in the Italian – as he could find. As far as he could, he avoided people who spoke English or other European languages: he had plunged into an Arab way of life, wearing Arab dress and seeking out Arab friends and contacts.

After his time with the nomads of Sinai and Jordan, the city's genial hospitality mixed with a threatening undercurrent of religious bigotry must have been familiar. Certainly, he felt at home enough in Damascus to immerse himself in its day-to-day life. With maybe more passion than shrewdness, he claimed angrily that members of the diplomatic community were involved in a thriving moneylending racket which frequently reduced the Muslim peasants to the status of debt-ridden share-croppers. He had no hesitation in speaking his mind, whether it alienated the diplomats or not: they were nothing better than extortionists, he complained.

Less controversially, perhaps, he searched for partners in a scheme to provide cheap corn for poor families, who suffered cruelly because of the rising prices as winter came to an end. His own business acumen, of course, had already failed to prove its worth at home: perhaps it was just as well that the 'prudent and honest persons' whom he consulted lacked the courage to support his project.

But his main enterprise remained the journey south to Medain Salih, and he knew only too well, from his wandering through Sinai, the sheer physical challenge it would present. As the time for the Hadj drew closer, he set off on expeditions outside the city, settling into a tough regime of irregular sleep and meals of raisins, dates and rock-hard bread, in order to prepare himself. He spent some time hunting bears with Arab companions in the mountains north-west of Damascus, and also, bones aching with rheumatism from the autumn cold and damp, visited several of the ascetic monasteries and hermitages in the region. To the monks, labourers and holy men he must have cut a grotesque figure, this tall, shambling, bearded man, who was prepared to treat his body every bit as harshly as they did themselves, and who seemed to know even more than they did about the Old Testament scriptures and the history of their faith.

His overriding aim, all the time, was to prepare body and mind for the hardships of desert life that he hoped he would soon be undergoing. But when he returned to Damascus just a few short weeks before the caravan was due to leave, all his preparations, his anxious enquiries and requests for help seemed to have brought him no nearer to his goal.

He had made it his business to meet the influential individuals in Damascus who might be useful to him – among them, the Algerian war leader Abdul Kadir, who had led the violent opposition to the French in his native land more than thirty years before. He now lived in splendid exile in Damascus as the unchallenged head of the Moorish community there. His friendship left Doughty in a quandary: a word from him would bring a welcome from all the Moorish soldiers who manned the Hadj forts on the road to Medain Salih, but his disapproval could make the journey impossible. Safer, Doughty decided, not to approach the 'noble Algerian prince' for help at all, but simply to use his name whenever it might be useful.

From officials of the Ottoman *Dowla* and the British consulate alike he continued to receive nothing but discouragement. Perhaps, faced with Doughty's allegations about moneylending, the consulate was unwilling to go out of its way to help. But in any case, there remained the delicate international situation between the Ottomans and the Christian powers: why should either side encourage a journey that could bring them no benefit, and might cause more trouble?

But Mohammed Said Pasha, whose acquaintance he had made while travelling through Jordan two years before, was more encouraging – and he was the leader of the Hadj caravan. He was also an independent man, wealthy in his own right, and he had been impressed by Doughty's honesty and plain-spokenness. Unlike the British consul and the Ottoman officials, he did not turn down Doughty's appeals flat: he could not join the caravan itself, but perhaps he might travel later with the *jurdy*, the military train that was sent out to meet the returning pilgrims, he suggested. Such a proposal gave him a much-needed chink of encouragement, even though, allowing him only three days at most at the ruins, it was in practice little better than an outright refusal.

The pilgrims were gathering for another year's Hadj, caravan drivers with their 'silent great shuffle-footed beasts', servants stuffing cushions and padding under pack-saddles, and pilgrims anxiously equipping themselves with leather water bottles, tents and litters. Almost every Muslim household had someone in the great caravan, and the city was packed with strangers waiting to start. It was a time of busy, excited anticipation; but for Doughty, his preparations complete but with apparently no prospect of joining the great adventure, there was nothing but disappointment.

He could only watch as the pilgrims left to gather some two days' journey outside the city. The streets that had been thronged with camels, swaying litters and shouting merchants were empty and silent again. He was, it seemed, fated not to travel to Arabia.

But there were those among his new Muslim friends who advised him to ignore the official opposition – Christian or not, no one could forbid him to join the caravan, they urged, as long as he had no intention of travelling on to the holy cities of Mecca and Medina. Maybe it was the sudden realization that his opportunity was slipping away; possibly he had planned all along to wait until the pasha and the main body of the pilgrims had left the city; maybe he had picked up some hint that Mohammed Said might turn a blind eye to his presence in the camel train – but whatever the cause, he decided to take this advice and press ahead regardless of the rebuffs he had received. A Persian camel-master, Mohammed Aga, was riding after the caravan to join his servants at the camp outside Damascus, and, after a hurried discussion, a formal agreement between the two of them was drawn up, stamped and officially registered at the Persian consulate. From his dwindling reserves Doughty handed over 1,000 piastres;[51] in return, the Persian promised to provide the *Nasrany** with a camel and take him as far as Medain Salih.

It was afternoon when they left, riding down the long street – the 'Street called Straight', in which the Bible says St Paul was found – towards the Boabat-Ullah, the great southern gate of the city. Doughty's intention not to pretend to be anything other than a Christian if challenged remained firm, but perhaps, dressed as he was as a simple Syrian traveller, 'a stranger amongst foreigners, not much observed, and clad in the Arab manner'[52] he might slip through without being challenged.

It was too late for such calculations, though: Doughty's journey into Arabia had begun.

---

* A contemptuous name for a Christian, or follower of the Nazarene.

Chapter Four

As for me who write, I pray that nothing be looked for in
this book but the seeing of an hungry man and the telling
of a most weary man . . .

Travels in Arabia Deserta, i, p. 56

When Doughty set off in disguise from Damascus, it was
neither hunger nor weariness that preoccupied him, but
the constant fear of discovery. Since he would not pretend to be anything other than what he was, his only safety would
lie in avoiding attention. In his diary already was a reminder to
himself, dated that same Thursday, 10 November 1876, when he
rode down the Street called Straight at the start of his journey: 'To
be circumspect.' But any hope that simple watchful prudence,
coupled with his Syrian dress and his presence among the Persian
pilgrims, might prevent casual acquaintances from identifying him
as a *Nasrany* was short-lived. Even as he rode through the outskirts
of Damascus, there was some good-humoured abuse from passers-by
– it was rapidly clear just *how* circumspect he was going to have to
be.

He was not a likely pilgrim. Within a few hours of leaving the
city his interest in the ruined sites by which they passed aroused the
notice of some of his companions, and the next day there were more
anxious moments when soldiers and merchants challenged him. 'Is
this one who should go with the Hadj?' they shouted; it was clear
that disguise and pretence would be useless anyway. His only hope
was to avoid being noticed as far as possible – and to trust to luck
that word of his presence did not reach Mohammed Said and the
other officers of the Hadj.

Mohammed Aga, the Persian camel-driver, urged the little group on anxiously, heading for the pilgrims' rallying-ground at the village of Muzeyrib. The caravan would be leaving in two days' time at the most, and they would not wait for stragglers. Despite the hurry, it was a good-tempered and optimistic group, the poor pilgrims on foot following cheerfully behind those on camels. 'Like awakening birds, they began to warble the sweet bird-like Persian airs. Marching with most alacrity was a yellow-haired young derwish, the best minstrel of them all; with the rest of his breath he laughed and cracked, and would hail me cheerfully in the best Arabic that he could.'[1]

In two bags, slung beneath him across the back of his camel, Doughty was carrying supplies for a journey which he knew could last for years. One plan he had mentioned in Damascus was that he might make his way across Arabia, through the desert kingdom of Ibn Rashid, to the Gulf coast and on to India; perhaps he might be taken up by bedu travellers; perhaps, on the other hand, the Hadj officials would find him and send him back to Damascus within a few days. He simply had no way of knowing.

With him he had the rudimentary medical supplies which he hoped would gain him friends, respect and even a little money in the desert as a travelling *hakim*, or doctor – a small supply of the Victorians' favourite cure-all, laudanum, a little quinine, a few other medicines and vaccines bought from the despised practitioners in the Damascus bazaar, and also, just as exotic to many of his potential customers, a small tin of tea. He had, of course, his books – two German studies of Arabia, and a seventeenth-century edition of his beloved Chaucer among others. There were bundles of paper, brushes and sponges, with which he planned to take his *papier-mâché* impressions of the inscriptions he was so anxious to find in the ruins of Medain Salih, and notebooks in which to record his diary and his various observations and measurements.

Also, hidden away from prying eyes, he was carrying the instruments on which those detailed observations would rely: a brass aneroid barometer, a thermometer, a pocket sextant and a delicate set of scales in a leather case. Doughty saw himself as a scientist: he had no wish to be just another of the foreign adventurers who had tricked and deceived their way through Arabia. Even deeper in his bags were hidden a few Turkish gold coins and – a mark of the physical dangers he knew he was likely to face – a cavalry carbine and a revolver. He was well aware that if he ever had to use his weapons in a hostile country, his own life would almost certainly be forfeit, and in fact he gave away the carbine within a couple of months of the start of his journey – but the revolver he kept hidden, often hung around his neck beneath his robes. He never fired it, although he drew it several times to demonstrate that he would sell his life dearly if he had to. It was a source of comfort and reassurance as much as a means of defence.

For the conventional traveller of the nineteenth century, with his boxes and portmanteaux, it would have seemed a quixotic and scanty collection of luggage. But in the desert it was different: even these bags were too heavy and bulky for him to manage on his own, and the Persian camel-driver grumbled constantly that the load would break his beast's back. To the travelling bedu, of course, for whom privation was a daily way of life, he seemed to be carrying far too much for one man, and even most of the townsmen who made up the body of the pilgrimage had far less with them than he had. But according to their different standards, both Doughty and the pilgrims were almost bare of possessions, exercising a self-denial which was a part of a religious experience for them, a matter of practicality for him.

At the end of the first day they paused briefly in a little village by the wayside, settling down uncomfortably for a few hours' fitful rest as a steady rain fell on them in the open fields. It was only three in the morning when they were on their way again, heading always south towards the snow-covered peak of Mount Hermon, but even so, it was dark before they finally caught up with the pilgrim gathering.

Doughty had already started the copious jottings that were eventually to form the raw material of *Travels in Arabia Deserta*. They are even more terse and hurried than the notes about his earlier travels and, written as they were in snatched moments of privacy, often as he rode on his swaying camel, they are frequently barely legible. But it was only by referring to them that Doughty was able, years after he returned from Arabia, to write such a precise account of his journeying. His intention from the start was to recreate the atmosphere as well as the physical details of his travels. 'If the words, written all day from their mouths, were rehearsed to them in Arabic, there might every one, whose life is remembered therein, hear, as it were, his proper voice; and many a rude bystander, smiting his thigh, should bear witness and cry, "Ay, *Wellah*,* the sooth indeed!"'[2]

And yet *Travels in Arabia Deserta* was conceived from the start as a literary work, structured, pored over, and prepared for publication. The archaisms, the twisting sentences, the biblical rhythms and cadences are a challenge to a modern reader, but they are also the result of an infinitely painstaking artistry. Most of the conversations, far from being 'written all day from their mouths', do not figure in the diaries at all, but were remembered and set down years later. The book is written throughout with both the disadvantage of distance and the benefit of hindsight, and occasionally, no doubt, with a sense of self-justification; to that extent, it has obviously to be treated with caution as an account of its author's life and of his developing interests and opinions.

Once arrived at Muzeyrib, there was a day for rest and preparation before the caravan started out in earnest. Ahead of the pilgrims were ten marches through the northern highlands – country with which Doughty was already familiar from his earlier journey out of Sinai – before they reached Arabia. For him, though, the pause in camp held more terrors than the march itself. Once on the way, his fellow-travellers might have too much to do to notice him; sitting around in camp, he would be all too conspicuous. The fear of discovery stayed with him all the way to Medain Salih – but to be found and sent back at the very start of the journey would be a disappointment indeed.

All he could do was wait nervously, skulking in his tent among the Persians, as the rest of the pilgrims gathered their strength for the long march ahead. At dawn the camp was dismantled, and they stood ready by the heads of their laden camels until finally, at ten in the morning, the signal gun was fired and the long train – 6,000

* By God!

people and 10,000 or more cattle and pack animals – began to unfold itself laboriously from the campsite. Mount Hermon was now behind them; it would be many weeks before the pilgrims would see it again as they struggled back to Damascus.

The Persian contingent, some 700 strong, was isolated at the back of the long caravan. As Shia Muslims, strangers and schismatics as far as the Sunni majority was concerned, they were kept well away from the main body of the pilgrims to avoid any possible confrontation. Before them stretched a train of pilgrims, servants, camels, pack mules and cattle that might stretch out to two miles in length as it meandered across the plains. For Doughty, such isolation was welcome: the Persians were unlikely to mingle much with the Arabs, and even their Syrian servants – among whom word rapidly spread that there was a Christian in their party – were less likely to gossip when separated from their countrymen by a crowd of foreigners.

Doughty had hired one of the camel-drivers, a disreputable but genial Damascus bandit called El Eswad, to ride out ahead each day with the light baggage train as his servant. His job was to put up his master's tent and cook his supper – and also, more importantly, to sleep at his side as protection through the night. Keeping out of sight among such a mixed throng held its own dangers: for many of the pilgrims, there would be no sin in killing a Christian, an infidel apparently on his way to the holy places. There were too many people already who knew Doughty's secret for him to be able to sleep peacefully alone at night.

As darkness fell, the sound of flutes and singing from the tents mingled with the chanting of the more devout among the pilgrims, the atmosphere of cheerful fellowship contrasting sadly with Doughty's nervous isolation. Perhaps there might have been some comfort in the detachment of Ottoman troopers strung out around the encampment to keep any marauding bedu at bay, but the real danger to the lone Christian among the pilgrims would come from inside the camp, not from the desert. And anyway, what security there was seemed casual and sporadic. At the beginning of the night paper lanterns burned in front of each military tent, and the nervous soldiers occasionally fired off shots into the dark of the surrounding desert, calling to each other from tent to tent for reassurance. By midnight, though, the keenness began to abate, and the lights gradually went out. Some of the soldiers, Doughty guessed, were simply saving their candles; others, not paid by the Ottoman government from one month to the next, would sell them off for profit in the Hadj market.

But in any case, it was not a long night: by 5.30 in the morning the signal gun had sounded, and the pilgrims were on their way again, lit by flares burning in iron baskets at the end of long poles.

Doughty, hunched silently on the back of his swaying camel, settled stolidly into the daily march as the long column wound its way through the dreary, monotonous landscape. He rocked backwards and forwards on the great beast, 'bowing at each long stalking pace upon the necks of our camels, making fifty prostrations in every minute whether we would or no, towards Mecca'.[3] To pass the time, he tried counting the regularity of their paces, hoping to find a way to calculate the distance they were travelling. But the camels, uncooperative in this as in everything, took different strides at different times; in the end he was reduced to working out distances in terms of camel journeys, allowing around two and a half miles an hour as an average speed.

The diary demonstrates the tedium of the landscape: 'Hideous stony desert', 'Vast undulated brown plain', 'Sameness of the weary desert land'. The weather, too, was dull and dispiriting. Setting off generally well before dawn, they marched through the cold and wet of the early morning, their bedding often soaked through by the overnight rain.

Occasionally, they passed ruined and deserted villages and forts, but the need for discretion prevented Doughty from making any detailed notes; when he did see a two-line inscription on a rock face at the wayside later in the journey, it almost led to disaster. Curious pilgrims crowded around him suspiciously as he tried to copy it into his book, some of them almost riding him down and cursing him as he stood in the narrow track. The danger of discovery was ever-present.

His self-imposed 'circumspection' had already faltered. Shouts and cries of pain from a big tent in the Persian camp had led him to break his rule of avoiding company, and he had pushed his way inside to find a man accused of theft stretched out on the ground and being beaten by a succession of assailants. The punishment itself is described in the diary – but in *Travels in Arabia Deserta* Doughty writes at some length about his own intervention. 'It was perilous for me to tempt so many strangers' eyes, but, as humanity required, I called to them, "Sirs, I am an *hakim*; this man may not bear more; hold, or he may die under your handling!" – words which, besides their looking upon the speaker, were not regarded.'[4]

About that part of the incident the diary is silent. Perhaps Doughty was simply writing from memory, having for whatever reason omitted mention of his own courageous appeal from his contemporaneous account; perhaps he was exaggerating his own bravery. It seems unlikely, though, that his intervention was a complete fabrication, if only because of the way it is woven into the fabric of the book. Later in the evening Mohammed Aga chided him for attracting attention. 'What is this meddling with the man's punishment? Wouldst thou to Medain Salih or no? This may be told tomorrow in the ears of the Pasha; then they will know you, and you will be turned back. Come no more forth in the public view.'[5]

And again, some time afterwards, he met an old man, riding on a donkey among the crowd of pilgrims, who seemed to recognize him.

> He would pleasantly greet me, saying, 'How fare you, Khalil Effendi?' and looking upon me, the old eyes twinkled under his shaggy brows as stars on a frosty night. He rode somewhat bowed down with a stiff back upon his beast, and his face might well be less known to me, for it was he who had been so extremely beaten days before at Wadi Zerka.[6]

Whatever happened in detail, it seems clear that there was a beating in the tent, which Doughty witnessed and described in his diary – while the later account of his own intervention, even allowing for the possible exaggeration of a man describing his own courage, chimes in both with the outspoken nature he had already displayed and with the separate mentions of incidents connected with the beating.

Despite that confrontation, as far as he could tell there had still been no gossip about his presence to the Arabs in the main body of the caravan, but each day's journey took them closer to Maan, a town where he knew he might well be recognized. The three weeks he had spent there on his way north out of Sinai, pestering the town's officials for their permission to set off to Medain Salih, might now, ironically, put his whole enterprise in danger – and in any case, the Pasha and the other Hadj leaders might take advantage of their brief leisure there to have him searched for and turned back.

There was a day to sit and wait at Maan, and Doughty stayed anxiously in his tent. The Persian aga, he heard, was summoned to appear before the Hadj council to explain the rumours that had in fact spread among the caravan about a Christian hiding in his party. Mohammed Aga, though, at least by his own account, said nothing. He 'played the merchant', said Doughty, and denied all knowledge of any such fugitive.

But perhaps, in fact, it was at Maan that the Pasha's suspicions were confirmed, and he was told that Doughty had sneaked his way in among the pilgrims. There was little show of surprise when he finally revealed himself at Medain Salih, and there were so many occasions when he drew attention to himself on the road that it is difficult to believe that the authorities were unaware of his presence. The Pasha could well have decided that turning a blind eye to the unwanted pilgrim, and making sure that he ventured no further than the ruined cities, would be the best way of avoiding any trouble.

If so, maintaining the pretence of secrecy was in everybody's interests – but it was only the next day that a moment's indiscretion nearly ended the whole pantomime. Perhaps it was the relief of hearing the signal gun go off at eight o'clock the following morning, and seeing the long train of the caravan begin to unwind on its way out of Maan – but Doughty almost rode into the middle of a little knot of townsmen watching the pilgrims depart. He was normally desperately careful to keep the reading of his instruments or the writing of his notes secret, but this time his aneroid was out in his hand as he checked a reading – and worse still, the group of bystanders included the governor of the town, who had been so adamant before that he should not travel south to Medain Salih, and the secretary Mahmud, whom he had pumped so diligently for information about the ruined cities.

> Perchance they were come out, by order, to look for me. I perceived, I felt rather, that they noted me, but held on unmoved, not regarding them, and came by them also unhindered. They could not easily know me again, one of the multitude, thus riding poorly and openly, clad in their guise, and with none other than their own wares about me ... [7]

Whatever the truth of the situation, Doughty certainly believed he had had a lucky escape – but there was more to come. They marched on for eight hours over black, flinty soil, with no sign of any track to follow, until they came to their next camp site – the last before they began the descent into Arabia itself.

At noon the next day the Pasha and his officers set themselves up on a rock overlooking the way, under a white parasol, to watch the pilgrims wind their way past them. The caravan, which often spread out on the plains until it was a hundred yards or more from side to side, was threading its way two by two through a narrow cleft in the rocks, with the pilgrims leading the unwieldy beasts by their head ropes down a steep slope. If Mohammed Said Pasha had been searching for a vantage point from which to spot any unwelcome intruder, he could hardly have done better.

Doughty did his best to remain inconspicuous as he passed in front of the Pasha, a man whom he had made such efforts to get to know in Damascus. This time it was his camel that was nearly responsible for giving him away. In Maan Doughty had been tricked into giving up the docile mount he had ridden from Damascus, and had been provided with a new, half-trained beast which was still unused to the rigours of the Hadj. As he made his way nervously past the Pasha and his companions, she bolted and snapped her leading rope right in front of them, forcing Doughty to run and get her under control again. He was a tall man, towering over most of the other pilgrims, and with his long, reddish beard he must have been a difficult figure to miss. Once again, he was lucky: if the Pasha did recognize the man who had been so importunate in pleading for a place among the pilgrims, he kept his counsel.

Ten days into the pilgrimage, with the sand and stones of Arabia ahead, the real suffering was beginning. Zealots who had set out without enough supplies, relying on the power of God and the generosity of their fellow-pilgrims, were tasting the implacable cruelty of the desert. And religious passion was no guarantee of human feeling: the pilgrims' humanity withered with their bellies. Last in the train as they were, Doughty and his comrades saw a beggar crawling in the sand at the side of the way, desperately imploring the passing caravan for help. It was the poor servants, rather than the pilgrims, who bundled him onto a camel in the faint hope of saving his life.

There were deaths every day among the old, the weak and the ill-prepared. Neither pilgrims, nor bedu tribesmen, nor soldiers had time or inclination for pity. The more fortunate sick might be helped into brightly painted camel-litters, nodding with ostrich feathers and jingling with bells: for the payment of 100 piastres[8] they might live out the final few hours of their lives in luxury. The end, though, was much the same – dragged from the litter, their heels bumping along the ground, and bundled into a shallow grave in the sand. Doughty's adventure was taking on a horrific reality.

> The lonely indigent man, and without succour, who falls in the empty wilderness, he is desolate indeed. When the great convoy is passed from him, and he is forsaken of all mankind, if any Beduw find him fainting, it is but likely they will strip him, seeing he is not yet dead. The dead corses unburied are devoured by hyenas which follow the ill odour of the caravan. There is little mercy in those *Ageyl** which ride after; none upon the road will do a gentle deed but for silver.[9]

That, at least, was the account Doughty wrote several years later; but while the diaries jotted down at the time reflect the same suffering, they do offer at least a taste of compassion. 'Have died some 20 persons of the Hadj from Damascus. Hitherto, they are washed,

* Soldiers.

shrouded, and buried by the wayside ... The sick and dying were bound down upon a canvas, or they must have fallen at every step ...' The pilgrims may have been powerless to do much, but they did what little they could. The contrast between the two accounts demonstrates how Doughty's own experiences over the following months fuelled his contempt for religious zealotry.

The caravan was moving steadily away from the country which he knew, leaving behind the well-marked track it had followed as far as Maan and striking out into the desert. The weather got hotter and the travelling harder – the sun which had earlier been welcome after the cold of the early morning now began to beat down relentlessly, reflecting back off the hot sand, and the further they marched into Arabia, the less water there was to be found. What there was might taste of sulphur, or possibly be infested with worms, even at the established camping sites.

For the more devout among the pilgrims, the suffering might be self-denial, a worthy part of the pilgrimage itself; for Doughty, though, the sense of isolation that was his worst torture was growing greater with every step into the desert – the man who had so often found his own company sufficient was discovering how much he relied upon a sense of shared culture and experience. Alone among people who shared neither his interests, his beliefs, nor his background, people who cast stones at rocks in the ground in the angry conviction that they were the petrified bodies of idolaters and unbelievers, he was leaving behind everything with which he was familiar, travelling further and further into an unknown world.

He struggled still with the repeated blows which science and rationalism had dealt to his religion, but he remembered nostalgically the old days of certainty and consolation.

> The moon lightened our march this third Sunday night; which name to the heart born in the land of Christians, in the most rumble, weariness and peril of the world is rest and silence. Near behind me, there drove a Persian *akkam*, who all night long chanted to teach his rude fellow, now approaching the holy places, to say his canonical prayer, the Arabic sounding sweet upon his Persian

95

tongue . . . 'Unto God be all glory, the Lord of worlds' –
this lullaby they chanted ever among them till the morning light.[10]

It was an unusual moment of gentleness and tolerance: the lines
from the Koran might be no more meaningful than a 'lullaby', but
they clearly brought tranquillity to a man who felt increasingly
removed by doubt and by sheer physical distance from the comfort
of his own religion.

The pressure caused by Doughty's fear of discovery was beginning
to have its effect. The camel which had so nearly caused disaster
under the eyes of the Pasha as they left Maan had continued to
disrupt the caravan, snapping her ropes and sometimes kneeling
down in the midst of the moving crowd of pilgrims. Her antics not
only drew attention to Doughty, but also stirred up anger and resentment among his weary companions, who stumbled over him in the
dark. Some of them began to torment him, refusing to help him load
her with his bags, and occasionally threatening to leave him behind
to die in the desert.

On one occasion, tired and frightened, he snapped and pulled his
pistol out from under his robes. In one sense, it was a foolish act,
the worst breach so far of his self-imposed call for circumspection.
The threatening gesture alone could have turned the crowd against
him, and letting people know that he had the weapon could only
increase the chance that it would be stolen while he slept. But
throughout his time in the desert Doughty had to strike a difficult
balance between the appearance of weakness and that of strength:
while vulnerability might generally disarm aggression, it was important occasionally to show that there were limits beyond which he
would not be pushed. Had he continued meekly to give ground, the
Persians who were tormenting him might have been tempted to goad
him further; as it was, they backed off in the face of his determination.
After a few days they got bored with their victim, and the danger
passed.

It was not a time of unalloyed hostility from the other pilgrims.
Even though many of them clearly knew his secret, the Persians
among whom he was travelling held Doughty in awe because of his

learning as a *hakim*. Some of them relied on him for medical treatment, although both now and later he found it easier to dispense his medicines and cures than it was to collect payment for them. Others ran to him like children, clutching fragments of bright crystal they had picked up by the wayside, in the hope that they had found handfuls of diamonds.

But the fear of discovery remained. As the caravan approached the little town of Tebuk, a suspicious group of soldiers quizzed him about who he was – so while the Persians enjoyed their day's rest amid the welcoming palm-groves and cornfields, drinking sweet tea, smoking the heavily perfumed *nargilies* or hookahs, and preparing themselves for the next stage of the pilgrimage, Doughty lingered nervously in his tent, awaiting the dreaded summons to the Pasha.

Once again, though, there was no call to the Pasha's tent: if the guards were keeping an eye on him, there was apparently no intention of precipitating a crisis. The signal shot was fired as usual a few hours before dawn, and the caravan moved slowly off through the thorns and tamarisk bushes, across a land scattered with black volcanic pebbles.

The last stage was as hard as any so far, with long marches across rough and uneven sandstone crags and through deep sand that sapped the camels' strength, brief, chilly nights with little rest, and the constant torment of the shortage of water. The diary records the final day: 'Weather mild . . . Approach to Hedjr* through mountains of fantastic rocks . . . they said . . . Tomorrow, you will see wonders – houses in the rocks, and all overturned, and standing above downwards.'

It was the fourth Sunday of the pilgrimage, the weather warm and hazy, and the valley he had travelled so far to find was spread out below him, scattered with desert bushes and surrounded by lowering mountain crags. He had, he thought, completed his journey.

As the caravan approached the rows of white tents already pitched in front of the little Hadj fort, it was greeted by a series of rounds

---

* The ancient name for the area where Medain Salih stood.

blasted off into the desert from the military escort's field guns. The pilgrims had reached the halfway stage on their way to Mecca, and it was not only Doughty who had cause for celebration. The local beduin tribesmen, too, had travelled in from miles around to welcome them – not from any religious fervour, but in the keen expectation of making money. There were tribesmen with joints of mutton for sale, women offering ostrich feathers, and others offering pennyworths of dates spread out in piles on their robes, while for those wanting to make easier money, there was every opportunity to steal from the weary pilgrims.

Doughty's Persian camel-driver, though, had no interest in the celebrations. He was only too anxious to end his risky involvement with the Christian traveller, and as they clambered down from their camels, he was already demanding a signed paper to confirm that he had fulfilled his side of the bargain and delivered his charge safely to Medain Salih. It was only after a lengthy argument that he could be persuaded even to lend Doughty a mule to carry his heavy bags into the fort.

The soldiers of the *kella* were pleased to greet the Hadj, and the supplies that had come down with it, but hardly anyone even noticed their unexpected guest. Mohammed Aly, the *kellaji*, or chief keeper of the fort, was busy receiving the food and stores from the soldiers of the caravan, and he simply waved Doughty inside. He had met him briefly in Damascus, but if he was surprised to see him, and dismayed to hear that he was intending to take up his incautious offer of accommodation, he gave no sign of it. A few minutes later he came inside to find Doughty sitting wearily by his baggage, and showed him the little stone cell in which he could sleep. It was not a warm greeting, but apart from a degree of surliness on the part of his soldiers, there was no sign of any trouble to come.

But after nightfall, just before the pilgrims were due to set off again on their way south, Doughty's man Eswad found him in the *kella*. He had been not only his servant, but also his only constant friend on the journey from Damascus, and now he brought a brief but troubling warning. The garrison of the fort, like the rest of the Hadj service, had the reputation of being men of violence; Doughty should take care, he said. With that, he was gone, and a few minutes later the sound of a gunshot from the camp, the jingle of bells on the camel litters, the grumbling of the camels and the cursing of their drivers announced that the caravan was on the move again. Doughty had achieved his aim; now he was trapped in the desert, surrounded by men who, for all he knew, might simply kill him out of hand.

In fact, he was safer than he knew. He only found out later that the Pasha had summoned Mohammed Aly just before leaving. Whether or not he had known before about the Christian interloper, he certainly knew all about him now. If Doughty tried to take a single step towards Mecca and Medina, said the Emir El Hadj, the Pasha's right-hand man, Mohammed Aly was to bring them his head – but then a warning came from the Pasha: 'Look to it, that no evil befall this man: for wellah, we will require his life at thy hand.' And in case that was not clear enough, the Emir added: 'By Almighty God, except we find him alive at our coming again, we will hang thee, Mohammed Aly, above the door of thine own *kella*.' They were holding the *kellaji* personally responsible for his guest's life.

It was the influential word of protection that Doughty had sought in vain from the British consul in Damascus. Mohammed Aly offered to bring Doughty to answer for himself, but the Pasha, declaring that he had his dignity to maintain, refused. He was determined that Doughty should not proceed towards the Harameyn, the two forbidden cities, but keeping him safe was his priority: he, like the consul, had no wish to be responsible for a new international incident that might embarrass the Sultan's government.

That secret conversation was probably responsible for saving Doughty's life in the *kella*, and also for the tight restrictions that were placed on his movements outside. Mohammed Aly had heard in Damascus that the British consul there had washed his hands of Doughty, but the direct instructions of the two most senior officers of the Hadj could not be ignored. From their point of view, it was a most satisfactory solution of the problem: whatever happened, whether Doughty lived or died, whether he tried to reach Mecca and Medina or not, they could now pass the blame on to the captain of the *kella* where they had left him. Mohammed Aly certainly realized what they were doing. He maintained an attitude of robust independence to their faces – but he knew they were well capable of carrying out their threats. Doughty's life would be safe from the garrison, and he would be protected from danger at the hands of the marauding bedu.

All that, though, was unknown to Doughty himself all the time he stayed at Medain Salih. All he knew was that the *kella* was surrounded by bedu tribesmen who might murder him without a second thought – the first day he was there, they virtually overran the building, brushing the guards aside – and his only protection was a group of mainly Moorish soldiers, 'all of them old manslayers', as he said later,[11] about whose violent characters he had already been warned.

For a full week he stayed shut in the *kella*, slowly recovering from the exertions of the journey. Mohammed Aly – understandably as worried about his own skin when the Hadj returned as about Doughty's well-being – would not allow him out on his own to look at the deserted city. He promised that Zeyd, a leading bedu sheikh, would come in a few days to guide him over the ruins. But the *kellaji* also had designs of his own on the Christian who had arrived with such intriguingly heavy luggage, and carrying a carbine that Mohammed Aly would dearly love to have for himself. In Syria he had been amazed at how much Europeans would pay for old carvings and other antiquities, and he hoped to share with Zeyd a fat profit out of his unexpected guest.

But Doughty, anxious as he was to see the monuments, was in no hurry to reach a deal. The first suggestion was that he should pay Zeyd £10 to take him around the site – a high price, he thought, when none of the ruins was more than two miles from the *kella*. On the other hand, Zeyd had taken the shrewd precaution of warning all the other Arabs not to help him, so he had no choice but to reach some sort of agreement. It was a stalemate, and so it remained for another week, with Doughty kicking his heels inside the fort, while Zeyd and the five fellow tribesmen who were with him enjoyed its hospitality.

It was Mohammed Aly, seeing his profit slipping away as the six Arabs ate at his expense, who broke the deadlock by suggesting that Zeyd should take Doughty for an initial look at the ruins, and then try to reach an agreement. The first group of caves they visited, something like half a mile from the *kella*, was everything Doughty had hoped for: first, there were the stone-lined wells that had been dug out centuries before by the original inhabitants, and then the carved rock surrounds of the caves themselves. Mahmud, the secretary of Maan, had not exaggerated: this, it seemed, was to be Doughty's Petra.

> In the face I saw a table and inscription, and a bird! which are proper to the Hejr frontispiece; the width of sculptured architecture with cornices and columns is twenty-two feet. I mused what might be the sleeping riddle of those strange crawling letters which I had come so far to seek! The whole is wrought in the rock; a bay has been quarried in the soft cliff, and in the midst is sculptured the temple-like monument.[12]

The weather was hot, sultry and enervating, and there were swarms of flies buzzing around them. Doughty clambered eagerly up some rough-hewn steps in the cliff to examine the various monuments, but almost before he had begun, Zeyd was complaining of the heat, and demanding to set off back. He had, of course, no interest at all in seeing his companion make too close a study of the site before they had agreed on a price for his hire: all he wanted was to whet his appetite, and that he had already achieved.

As he made his way unwillingly back towards the valley, Doughty paused to inspect the interior of several other caves. It was a sombre scene, like stepping into an ancient charnel-house: there were grave-pits filled with human bones, and more bones scattered over the sandy floor. Carved into the rock walls were shallow shelves, some obviously measured out for adults and other, smaller ones, for their children.

> A loathsome mummy odour, in certain monuments, is heavy in the nostrils; we thought our cloaks smelled vil-

> lainously when we had stayed within but a few minutes.
> In another of these monuments, Beyt es-Sheykh, I saw
> the sand floor full of rotten clouts, shivering in every
> wind, and taking them up, I found them to be those dry
> bones' grave-clothes![13]

That feeling of disgust, though, was drowned in the excitement of the scientist and the collector. For the moment, at least, there was little to be done but wonder at the mysterious inscriptions carved in the stone, but he swooped eagerly on the shards of glass, fragments of pottery and pieces of cloth and leather that were scattered over the floor, stuffing them into his bag. Today, along with the flint axes from Maan, and a few coins picked out of the sand, they are at the Ashmolean Museum.

Excited or not, Doughty was still well able to drive a hard bargain. Zeyd wanted a thousand piastres for his day's work – as much as it had cost to hire a camel and make the entire journey from Damascus to the *kella* – and even Mohammed Aly was suggesting a payment of 300. The piastres themselves were important enough – the money Doughty had with him would have to last until he returned to Damascus, or some other big city from which he could contact his bank – but there were other factors to be considered as well. Had he paid over what they asked for, the rumour would have gone round that he was carrying huge amounts of money, and was willing to part with it. He would have been the target of every robber and vagabond in the country.

But there was also the tantalizing possibility that Zeyd might take Doughty with him to join his wandering tribe, and maybe set him on his way across Arabia towards the Gulf. There was no point in making an enemy of him. 'I put a little earnest gold into his hand, that he might not return home scorned,' said Doughty shrewdly.[14] But Mohammed Aly was now suggesting that he might visit the caves more cheaply: in return for the carbine he had spotted on Doughty's first day, he said, he would send some of the *kella* garrison with him day by day until he had seen all he wanted. It was enough, and Zeyd rode off to rejoin his people, happy enough with his 'earnest gold', and promising to return when the Hadj came back and take

Doughty off into the interior. After all, there might be money to be made for himself from the Christian's medical skills.

Over the following days Doughty immersed himself in the ancient remains. They were similar to the carved facades he had seen at Petra, with huge pillars rearing up beside ornate doorways into the rock face. Carved birds stretched their massive wings proudly above the entrances, and often there were tablets high on the walls, either inscribed with epitaphs or still waiting for the long-dead mason to do his work. Inside, as at Petra, the caves were generally simple chambers, roughly hewn out of the rock – but the Arabs from the *kella* brought them to life with fantastic stories of their history. The bones scattered around one burial chamber, he was told, marked the scene where men had fallen down dead centuries before in a fight over a dishonoured daughter. High on a wall was the blood of a blacksmith, slain by the girl's jealous father – blood which closer examination showed was no more than the stain of iron rust on the rock face.

The houses of the old caravan city, built from less durable materials than the carved monuments, had long since vanished. '[The] clay-built streets are again the blown dust in the wilderness ... the doors of the desolate mansions ... doubtless have been long since consumed at the cheerful watch-fires of the nomads ...'[15]

Over many of the carved facades had been scratched the tribal marks of generations of nomads which had passed by since the city was abandoned; there were signs left on the walls by shepherds and, in other places, the names of old Muslim travellers who had stopped to look. Like the scars of the nomads' ropes in the soft rock around the wells, these were the marks left by the passing centuries – more evidence of the way the traces of the humblest of the human race might outlast the most grandiose constructions of their masters.

But Doughty's companions, fiddling anxiously with their long matchlocks, were less philosophical. Where he saw the work of ancient craftsmen, intriguing carvings and inscriptions, and possible clues to long-gone civilizations, they saw only likely danger. 'It is more than thou canst think a perilous neighbourhood; from any of

these rocks and chambers there might start upon us hostile beduins,'
they warned him, as they hurried him from one site to the next.[16]

There was no doubting their anxiety, although it was almost
certainly as much for themselves as for the *Nasrany* in their charge.
One of the soldiers at least had killed a tribesman some years before,
and was constantly nervous of being caught outside the fort, where
the bedu might take their revenge. All the garrison were aghast at
the plan Doughty now spelled out to them – that he would travel
east with the nomads, rather than return to Damascus with the Hadj.
'Is it to such wild wretches that thou wilt another day trust thy life?
. . . The beduins are *sheyatin*, of demon-kind; what will thy life be
like amongst them, which, wellah, we ourselves of the city could
not endure?'[17]

That was the reaction of Mohammed Aly as well. Although he
had been friendly enough with Zeyd, he would slam shut the iron
door of the *kella* at the slightest sign of unknown Arabs on the plain,
and would only allow them inside under the strictest supervision,
while the garrison stood by with their weapons in their hands. Like
the Hadj pilgrims, the soldiers who had guarded the camps, and the
townsmen and farmers of Sinai and Edom, the Arabs of the *kella* felt
only fear and mistrust for the beduin.

But it was a fear that seems not to have been passed on to
Doughty. He had been understandably nervous when accosted by
groups of nomads when he was travelling through Sinai, or on
the rare occasions when he allowed himself to be separated from the
Hadj caravan, but for all the hysterical stories he had heard of the
half-wild tribesmen and their savagery, he was ready to reach his
own judgements based on his own experience. About Zeyd, for
instance, the first bedu he had talked to for any length of time, he
was realistic: while he was unyielding when he thought he was being
cheated over the question of payment for visiting the monuments,
he could appreciate the Arab's easy-going nature. 'In him I have not
seen any spark of fanatical ill-humour. He could speak with me
smilingly of his intolerant countrymen; for himself, he could well
imagine that sufficient is Ullah to the governance of the world, without fond man's meddling.'[18]

This was his considered verdict, written down later in *Travels in*

Arabia Deserta, after he had known and travelled with Zeyd in the desert for several months – but his readiness to trust himself to the Fukara sheikh and his fellow-tribesmen shows that it reflects his feelings at the time. It was a considerable act of faith – but Doughty had known his own suffering at the hands of the bigoted Muslim zealots he had met. As an outsider himself, he recognized the prejudice with which the nomads were spoken of and treated by the fearful townsmen.

A letter which he sent back to Europe a few weeks after he had met Zeyd set out his intention of joining up either with Zeyd's Fukara Arabs or with another tribe, the Weled Aly, and winning their confidence with his medicines and vaccines. 'In that way I hope to be among them with a great deal of security to visit Kheybar and to make my way towards the sea eastwards,' he said.[19]

The idea of a visit to the oasis settlement of Kheybar followed on from stories he had heard on the Hadj about its fabled Jewish population. The people there, he had been told, though outwardly Muslim, were in secret 'cruel Jews' who would allow no stranger into their fortified town, and who had almost magical powers in fighting with outsiders. When he did finally visit Kheybar the following year, he found the stories to have as little basis in fact as most of the tales of strange and malevolent tribes in Arabia – although his experiences there bore out all too convincingly the suggestions of their cruelty to outsiders.

Another letter, written at the same time to his aunt Amelia Hotham in Tunbridge Wells – the same Aunt Hotham who had been so reassured about his progress as a young schoolboy at Beach House fifteen years before – gives a similar message.

> From hence I go probably to visit the neighbouring Arabs now in a few days – making various excursions as I may be able. I hope at length to arrive at the Persian Gulf. I do not speak more particularly. Without some special acquaintance with Arabia and an excellent map in your hand you would not follow the routes. I am some 130

miles N. of Medina. I have not even the smallest intention
to visit Mecca ... I am upon the eve of departing upon
an adventurous journey.[20]

Mohammed Aly, though, was unmoving in his distrust of the
nomads. It was many days before he would allow Doughty to travel
the short distance to the Medain Salih remains without an armed
guard from the *kella* – even though on the one occasion when there
was the vaguest report of strange riders spotted on the plain, the
guards had deserted their charge, and hurried willy-nilly to find
safety for themselves. No doubt the *kellaji* had the dire warning of
the Emir El Hadj and the Pasha on his mind – and when he did
finally permit Doughty to visit the sites alone, it was only after he
had made him check from a nearby vantage point that there was no
movement anywhere in the plain.

Doughty himself seems to have had little fear of the nomads, and
he spent days picking over the monuments, the carvings and whatever remnants of a long-gone civilization could be sifted from the
desert sand. He collected more pieces of glass and pottery, and
numbers of roughly struck copper coins, which experts at the British
Museum later said appeared to have been made in imitation of Greek
money around the time of Christ. Medain Salih, clearly, had been a
prosperous Nabataean trading centre on the caravan route along
which frankincense was brought to the Middle East and Europe out
of Yemen, the region known to the Romans as Arabia Felix.

There were also huge rock pictures of animals, some of them
twenty-five feet high, millstones and stone vessels lying discarded in
the sand, and scores of inscriptions which Doughty carefully copied
down into his notebooks.

Medain Salih had lived up to his most optimistic expectations, but
there were reports of yet more ruined towns to be found nearby,
and when the opportunity came to join a group travelling to market
in the nearby town of El Ally, he grasped it enthusiastically. Apart
from enabling him to add to his growing collection of inscriptions,
he thought it would give him the chance to see an oasis town, and

possibly replenish his dwindling resources by selling some of his medicines. Perhaps it might also give him some idea of how he might be received in the desert towns through which his planned journeys with the bedu would take him.

There were a couple of itinerant tinkers at the *kella* who were travelling on to El Ally, and several of the Arabs camped outside and two of the garrison decided to join them. Doughty, Mohammed Aly probably assumed, would be well enough protected.

It was not a friendly journey – while the tinkers and the women from the Arab encampment strode on ahead, Doughty and the two soldiers squabbled bitterly about who should ride the *kella*'s mule – and as they approached El Ally, Doughty's old nervousness returned. For several weeks he had been living openly in the *kella* as a non-Muslim; now, as on the Hadj, he would once more have to try and avoid unwelcome attention. And El Ally, it seemed, was not a welcoming place: when Doughty asked the tinkers where he might find lodging there, he was told: 'Where we are going, there is no hospitality: the people of El Ally are hounds.'[21]

Even before the walls of the town were visible, the frenzied drumming and gunshots of a Muslim festival could be heard. The two soldiers turned and asked him malevolently whether he was not nervous to be going to such a place – and Doughty knew that, with the guns on the streets and the people inflamed by the festival, it would only take one rash shot to kill him. 'I answered in their manner, that I left all unto God.' He had learned already that a little religious-sounding fatalism would go a long way in disarming prejudice.

He slipped unnoticed through the darkening streets to the house of the sheikh of the town, Dahir, who offered him a supper of rice and the use of an upstairs room. Dahir knew his secret within minutes – when Doughty refused to respond to the *muezzin*'s cry from the nearby mosque, the sheikh asked him straight out whether he was a Muslim or not. The reply, to a man who wore the scarlet mantle which had been given him by the Ottoman authorities as a mark of his authority, was a masterpiece of diplomacy. 'I hope it may seem nothing hard to you, that I am of the Engleys, which are allies of the Sultan, as you have heard, and they are Nasara; and I am a

Nasrany, does this displease you? So many Christians are in the Sultan's country that Stamboul is half full of them.'[22]

Dahir himself, who had been warned that the officers of the Hadj were taking a personal interest in Doughty's safety, was welcoming enough – but it was clear the next morning that the children and street urchins of the town were another matter. Doughty's companions of the day before had evidently been gossiping, and the children shouted insults at him from the rooftops as he walked down the street.

Finding that his colleagues from the *kella* had set off back without him, he had no choice but to stay until other companions could be found to accompany him on the dangerous road. Despite the children, it might have been no hardship to linger a while in the plantations and lemon groves. After all, most of the people seemed friendly enough, and scolded the children who shouted after him. One frequently repeated and reassuring phrase was *'Kul wahed aly din-hu'*, 'Everyone to his own religion' – a sentiment that was only too rare as he travelled through Arabia. Doughty, though, was anxious to get back to work on his inscriptions. He had hopes of using a wooden beam from the well as a makeshift ladder, from which precarious perch he might be able to make *papier-mâché* impressions of the actual carvings.

By now, it seems he had firmly decided that he would send his impressions or 'squeezes' back to Damascus with the returning Hadj caravan rather than join it himself: despite the earnest invitations of Sheikh Dahir and other senior figures in El Ally to return there when he left the *kella*, he was settled on starting his travels with the nomads as soon as his work at Medain Salih was finished.

The friendly atmosphere which had led to Dahir's invitations, however, lasted only a few days. Soon he began to notice that the children who mocked him, and stamped contemptuously on crosses they had drawn in the sand, were less rigorously chastised by their elders; then that some of the adults were actually joining in the abuse. His welcome, obviously, would not last indefinitely.

There was disappointment, too, over his hopes for selling his vaccines and medicines. He set up his stall optimistically in the market, but no one brought him their children to be treated, and the few desperately sick people who did come to him for help went away grumbling as soon as they realized they were expected to pay. He had found a similar reluctance to hand over money among his patients on the pilgrimage – but in El Ally, for the first time, Doughty was faced also by a blank religious fatalism in the face of the threat of disease. What he called 'the supine nature of Arabs, that negligence of themselves'[23] was to bedevil his attempts at doctoring throughout Arabia.

He busied himself in the ruins outside the town, where there were more carvings and more inscriptions – and, while the ones at Medain Salih, less than four hours' journey away, were in the Nabataean language of northern Arabia, these, he noted excitedly, were exclusively in Himyaric, the language of the south.[24] But this was all a pastime: Doughty was as anxious now to get back to his main task at Medain Salih as the townsmen were to get rid of him.

Several times Dahir persuaded bedu tribesmen to escort him back, and several times they let him down at the last minute. Finally, on 6 January 1877, the sheikh gathered together his own Negro servant and a group of six armed men from among his followers and, putting his son in charge, he sent Doughty off with them.

The soldiers accompanied them through the most dangerous part of the journey, and then Doughty and the Negro servant made their way alone. Within three hours the familiar crags of Mount Ethlib were visible, then the cliffs near the *kella*, and finally the little fort itself.

It was only later that he heard how narrow an escape he had had at El Ally. People in the town, he was told, had planned to poison him as a spy: 'Wot you, Khalil, what they all say in this country: It is lawful to kill the *Nasrany*, that were a deed well pleasing unto Ullah; he is God's adversary,' he was told. Only the fear of repercussions from the Ottoman authorities saved his life. Stories like that, of course, may or may not have been true; the plot, if it ever existed, may not have been a serious attempt to kill him, and the Arabs telling him the story may have been trying either to frighten him or impress him with their own loyalty. But that the stories should be told at all says much about the atmosphere in the town before Doughty left to return to the *kella*. Whether or not they seriously plotted his death, the local people certainly wanted to see the back of him.

But if Doughty had expected a friendly welcome back at the *kella* where he had made his temporary home, he was disappointed. He was always proud of his outspokenness and his direct manner, and this time he was probably too forthright. When he handed over his carbine to Mohammed Aly, he reasoned, it had been in return for the promise of help in getting to Medain Salih; now, as he kicked his heels in the *kella*, he demanded that the promise be kept, and that an escort be provided for him to visit the ruins.

Mohammed Aly turned on his heel and stamped off, returning a few moments later to hand back without a word the carbine he had earlier eyed so covetously. Doughty, like many people who take a pride in speaking their mind, probably had no idea what he had said to cause offence, and he tried to persuade Mohammed Aly to take the gun back. The response was dramatic.

The *kellaji*, still strong and wiry despite his advancing years, leapt on him, grabbing him by the collar, and suddenly slapped him in the face with all the strength he could muster, almost knocking him off the platform into the yard below. Doughty's appeal to the rest of the garrison for support only infuriated him further: he hit him again, struggling violently as Doughty seized his two wrists.

'By God, I will slay thee now!' he screamed, struggling free and searching in his belt for a knife or a pistol. It was lucky there was no weapon handy; instead, he grabbed hold of Doughty's long, ginger beard, and shook his head this way and that, shouting abuse at him all the time. It was the most dire insult he could inflict in the Arab world, especially as the soldiers and several passing Arabs were watching. That, in fact, seemed to bring him back to his senses and, 'somewhat abashed by the sober looks of those about him, and surprised that I had borne all villainy with unalterable indifference',[25] he stormed off, leaving Doughty angry, bleeding and completely at a loss.

But the angry *kellaji* had not finished. First he ordered Doughty to leave his cell, and move to a cold open archway on the exposed north side of the fort, looking out over a cesspool; then, a few moments later, he sent one of the soldiers to demand the return of the carbine which seemed in some way to have sparked off his sudden outburst. There was no point in letting anger deprive him of such a valuable prize – and anyway, he said, it would be a pledge of Doughty's good behaviour.

To all these indignities Doughty submitted quietly: stranded as he was in the *kella*, he had little choice. He could expect no support from the rest of the garrison, even though they seemed sympathetic: Mohammed Aly, after all, was a fellow-Muslim, a Moorish soldier like themselves and, most important of all, the man who paid their wages.

> I could not ever escape from the place if I fought them with pistol to pistol, life to life . . . Far better to make nothing of this murderous attack, and indeed my only present course . . . Otherwise my labour, expense, and all my fatigues of the present long journey would be spent quite in vain.[26]

He could go back to El Ally, or bring forward his plan to join the bedu tribesmen, but each course of action had its own risks; and each one would mean the end of his hopes of carrying out further research at Medain Salih.

His main hope was that Mohammed Aly, prompted by the others, might have remembered his fear of the Hadj officers, and of the Ottoman authorities in Damascus. Doughty had written letters back to the city, and he was known to be in the *kella*; even though he was unaware at that stage of the specific threats the Pasha of the Hadj had made, he knew there would be awkward explanations called for if he were not alive and well when the caravan returned in a few short weeks. For the time being, though, it was best to avoid any further confrontation: it was several hours before he left his room and went down to the coffee-chamber.

Mohammed Aly and the soldiers were sitting around the fire drinking coffee, and within a few minutes it was clear that the real danger was past, despite the *kellaji*'s continuing angry words. Doughty's *firman* from Damascus was brushed aside – 'I have thirty such firmans at home!' – as were all the powerful friends he claimed there. But although the story of the British consul's dismissive remarks had obviously been passed around the city while Mohammed Aly was there, there was still concern that his presence in the *kella* was known, and that any harm that came to him would have to be explained.

But whether it was fear of the consequences or simply the change of heart of a man who was evidently unbalanced – Doughty himself, though admittedly not an unbiased observer, described the *kellaji* as 'a diseased senile body . . . full of ulcers, and past the middle age . . . his visage much like a fiend, dim with the leprosy of the soul, and half-fond' – after a few defiant threats and blusterings Mohammed Aly was embracing his Christian guest as his *habib*, or beloved. Doughty was relieved, if not fully convinced. 'We drank round, and parted in the form of friends,' he wrote later, with a distinct lack of enthusiasm.[27]

The next day, anxious to put the quarrel behind them, and probably also hoping that the expedition might lead to the discovery of buried treasure in the mysterious rocky caverns, practically the entire garrison of the *kella* accompanied him on a long day's excursion to the ruins, Mohammed Aly riding alongside them. Doughty had succeeded in buying a long beam of tamarisk wood, in which one of the soldiers had hacked a few crude footholds – enough to enable him to climb up to all but the highest of the inscriptions and press his mess of soaking paper into them.

Altogether, he counted about a hundred of the magnificent funeral chambers, which he guessed might represent a town of some 8,000 people. The drying paper hung like butterflies on the face of the ancient carvings, which had been neglected for centuries, apart from the occasional shepherds who had taken shelter there. Some of the inscriptions were all but worn away by the wind and blown sand, but others seemed almost as clear as the day they were carved. Each letter, each grain of sand on the face of the tablet, was preserved in the *papier-mâché* as it set hard under the sun; over the next few days Doughty worked steadily from one monument to the next, clinging uneasily to the top of his makeshift ladder eighteen feet in the air, while squeezing his blotting-paper compress into the carved letters.

At the same time he was preparing to move on. It was almost time for the returning Hadj caravan to arrive at the *kella* to meet the *jurdy*, the military escort, which had come down from Damascus – and in any case, despite the new joviality of Mohammed Aly and his colleagues, the fight in the *kella* had shown that Doughty could not remain there indefinitely.

As the bedu tribesmen from miles around started to gather, ready to offer their wares to the pilgrims, Doughty busily quizzed them about the names of the various wadi systems of the region, and the way they were linked together. This information he later considered one of the main achievements of his travelling: his motives were still primarily scientific, rather than literary. About the maps drawn before his own exploration he remained contemptuous throughout his life: 'The work of the cartographers in construing many unintelligible names of which no man in that country had ever heard, I found when it came to the proof to be commonly of little worth.'[28] His daily effort in putting together a sketch map of the area based on the reports of the travelling bedu, he said, was one of the most important parts of his work. It was only by going over the ground on foot, and by winnowing out details from the people who spent their lives travelling from place to place, that he could gather reliable information.

For Mohammed Aly, though, the gathering of the bedu ready to meet the returning pilgrims represented more of a threat than an opportunity. The atmosphere in the little fort was tense: matchlocks were hidden in the cells ready for any surprise attack, the gates were locked and barred against the hordes of tribesmen who clamoured outside. There were occasional midnight panics, when the garrison rushed to their posts only to find that it was nothing but a false alarm, and one raid carried off much of the *kella*'s herd of sheep.

Behind the walls of his fort, though, the *kellaji* felt secure enough to sing Doughty's praises not only to the visiting bedu sheikhs, but also to the envoys of Mohammed Ibn Rashid, the brutal and feared ruler of the central Arabian city of Hail. Perhaps the 'diseased, senile body' was genuinely trying to make up for the quarrel with his cantankerous Christian guest – the diary notes a 'long and friendly conversation' between the two men a few days later – or perhaps he was simply worried about what report would be passed on to the Pasha on his return. Whatever his motives, his good report was undoubtedly helpful for Doughty's future travels.

At the same time, though, Mohammed Aly's fear for his guest's safety made him limit the excursions to the monuments while the unpredictable bedu were swarming over the plain. When Doughty did get out of the *kella*, the tribesmen gathered to watch him at work, but they did him no harm: despite the dire warnings of the townsmen and the soldiers, the supposed fiends of the desert seemed to bear him no ill-will. He now heard for the first time of the plots against him among the townsfolk of El Ally: even while they had been warning him against the savage nomads, they themselves had been planning his murder. Out in the desert, he could hardly find worse duplicity.

Doughty had to decide where to go next. Early in February the *jurdy* arrived from Damascus, a group of traders escorted by forty troopers with a single brass cannon, to escort the caravan home. This was the expedition which Mohammed Pasha had suggested Doughty might join, but the few days they spent at the *kella* would never have enabled him to gather the collection of specimens he now had to send back. They had a fresh supply of vaccine for him, along with a book he had requested from the British consulate in Damascus – Taverner's *Practice of Medicine*.

The book is now in Cambridge University's Fitzwilliam Museum, with Doughty's note on the title page: 'I carried this little book through Arabia'. But, although its spine is broken, and the book itself almost falling to pieces, there is no evidence that it was ever much used – no thumbed pages or pencil notes. Doughty's medicine relied more on common sense and laxatives than on medical texts.

The returning pilgrims offered the opportunity to send letters back to Damascus. The one to his Aunt Hotham, in which he set out his plan to travel east to the Gulf, was later returned to him because she had died before she received it. It was still among his papers after his own death – a moving record of the start of his journey through Arabia.

> Medain Salih, Hejr, NW Arabia, 2 Feb., 1877: The pilgrims return in their upward journey in two more days, with whom I send you these lines. Here was a considerable place. The antiquities are tombs hewn in the rocks, with inscriptions. It was a market upon the road by which they fetched the incense from South Arabia to Palestine; thence dispersed to all quarters, burned in the temple at Jerusalem and in the heathen temples of the western world, and is only obscurely mentioned in ancient authors. I have transcribed the inscriptions.

He was moving on now with the Arabs, he told her, intending to make 'various excursions' as the opportunity presented itself.

> This small paper will show you at least that I am alive. I am in health, thanks to the warm climate, without other food than corn or rice in this prison. My hands are busy and my head also. The Arabs arrive at every moment now, and press in upon me talking and shouting, greeting, questioning, begging tobacco. I am upon the eve of departing upon an adventurous journey. My love to such as love me that enquire of me,
> Your affect. nephew, Charles M. Doughty.

Doughty wanted to spare his elderly aunt any unnecessary anxiety: there is excitement in the letter, but no sense of foreboding. But a rough draft of another letter sent back to Damascus at the same time shows how well aware he was of the dangers he was courting. It sets out in detail the archaeological, anthropological, geological and political observations he had made. If he failed to return, he wanted to see that what he had discovered would survive.

He described the monuments and inscriptions of Medain Salih and El Ally, and also included what he had learned about the different tribes and the topography. Some of the detailed barometric readings he had taken were set down – and he mentioned in passing the personal danger he had already been in.

> Hardly any few days pass that we not alarmed by a *garru* (raid). Thus out of sight of the *kella*, one is in danger to be cut off from all sides. My life has been variously menaced . . . but only the fear of the Dowlat has restrained the shrews, or as I heard truly at Damascus, every one that met me had killed me . . . [29]

His position, he said, had been made no easier by the attitude of Mr Jago in Damascus – 'afterwards a principal cause I believe of my nearly being slaughtered in the *kella*' – but he had judged it 'unworthy' to travel in disguise.

This document appears almost to be Doughty's will, conceived and written down as he was about to venture into the unknown desert. He had few material possessions to bequeath, but he was anxious that his adventures and achievements should not go unrecognized.

There was also money for Doughty with the *jurdy* – 14 Napoleons and 80 piastres,[30] forwarded to him from the British consulate, some of which he spent at once on equipping himself with a camel ready for his journey. He had evidently had detailed discussions with Zeyd about his plans, which he set out in a letter to the dragoman at the consulate, one Selim Meshaka.

> I . . . go from hence with Zaid [sic], Sheykh of the Fukara Arabs of this district (Anneyzy), to stay sometime with him near Teyma vaccinating and with medicines. Then to Teyma. Then returned he will consign me to the Sheykh of the Ibn Shamer, Bely, Arabs, who will forward me to Wejh on the coast; then returning consign me to Motlog, Sheykh of the Welad Aly Arabs, with whom I may visit Kheybar. From Kheybar to Ibn Rashid and to Bagdad or Bosra, and much more if I am able to descend south to Wady Dawasir and ascend thence to Ibn Saoud, Sultan of E. Nejd,* and to Bagdad.

* The north Arabian highlands.

The outline is understandably imprecise, but there is much more detail there than the vague 'hope at length to arrive at the Persian Gulf', which was all he had told his aunt. Despite his earlier dismissal by Mr Jago himself – who was rather curtly offered his 'compliments' – he was evidently setting out his travel plans as completely as possible so that the British authorities might be able to offer him some help or support if he should need it. It was unlikely that they would be able to do much in any case – but apart from his own resources they would be the only protection he could look to.

With the letter he enclosed 'the fruit of my fatigues, a large round parcel in oilcloth containing impressions of inscriptions, and a packet of drawings and other papers', which he was sending for their safekeeping until he could come and collect them in person. He begged Mr Meshaka to take good care of them – 'Inscriptions so long desired of a country so obscure, which I obtained at the daily adventure of my life ... That which will spoil and ruin them is *pressure* and damp.'

Aware though he was of the dangers, he seems to have had little idea of the sheer magnitude of the adventure on which he was setting out. An optimistic postscript to the letter expresses the hope that he will be back in Damascus sometime later in the year – a deadline he was hardly likely to meet if he followed the itinerary he had already set out. In fact, it was twenty-one months before he finally arrived in Jedda, and two years before he was able to make the journey to Damascus and collect his precious 'squeezes'.

The soldiers of the garrison, the officers of the *jurdy*, even the bedu sheikhs themselves, all urged him to abandon his plans. 'Why cast your life away? You know them not, but we know them: the beduins are fiends,' warned one of the *jurdy*; a bedu sheikh, camped outside the fort, declared: 'If one go to the Aarab, he should carry his shroud under his arm with him.'

The desert, they said, was a lawless country, where even Muslim Arabs dared not venture; how much less should a Christian and a foreigner hope to survive? And for what was he running such risks? There could be no profit in committing himself to the desert and the bedu.

Perhaps there is a clue to Doughty's deepest motivation in the words he quotes of an old, blind Arab sheikh. He, like the others, repeated the advice that the *Nasrany* should return with the Hadj to the comforts of Damascus. But, unlike them, he added a note of encouragement. 'Wilt thou needs adventure, the Aarab are good folk, and thou wilt feel thy heart to be free amongst them.'

If Doughty had any lingering doubts, news that the pilgrims were bringing smallpox with them must have dispelled them. In any case, the Persian camel-driver who had brought him south was nowhere to be found – he had travelled on to Baghdad by sea, his friends said, after suffering stringent questioning in Medina about Doughty's presence in the caravan.

There was one more task to be accomplished before he could set off. The Pasha of the Hadj had been trying to dissuade Zeyd from taking Doughty into the desert, but the avaricious bedu was too fixed on the prospect of earning silver from Doughty to listen. However, the Pasha's approval for the adventure might carry weight among the nomads and the townspeople of the interior, so Doughty would have to brave his anger and seek him out.

When the signal gun went early the following morning, Doughty followed behind with Zeyd, waiting for a chance to speak to the great man. He knew that his illicit journey south had angered the Pasha, so he had to find a propitious moment. It was night-time before he found the billowing green silk tent, and the Pasha was already asleep, so it was only after the caravan had set off the next day that they managed to approach him.

The Pasha, though, could hardly have been more helpful. Without even waiting to be asked, he told Zeyd: 'I commit him to thee, and have thou a care of him as of my own eye.'[31]

It was all Doughty wanted. The Pasha's friendly enquiries about his work at Medain Salih, and his doubts about the wisdom of visiting Kheybar, mattered little: Zeyd's account of the great man's approval, passed on and lavishly embroidered around the nomad fires, would give him at least a measure of protection. Leaving the caravan and riding away to the east, they found wild leeks and potato-like tubers growing in the ground, salad leaves and wild sorrel. As they looked out over the sand, gravel and sandstone outcrops, Zeyd took out a piece of barley-cake to share with him.

'This is of our *surra*;* canst thou eat beduins' bread, Khalil?' he asked. It was a question that only the following months would answer.

* Payment made to the beduin by the Hadj authorities to allow the pilgrims free passage.

Chapter Five

I was living at Damascus and am a Saiehh; is not the saiehh a walker about the world? And who will say him nay! also I wander wilfully . . .

Travels in Arabia Deserta, i, p. 272

Describing himself as a *saiehh* was partly Doughty's audacious way of avoiding the question of why he had come to the desert in the first place. A *saiehh* was God's Wanderer, an itinerant mystic and a devout Muslim, not a Christian and an unbeliever like himself. But it was the title Doughty chose as he shared the hardships of Zeyd's small group of Arabs over the following months – that of a pilgrim committed to a life of blameless contemplation, a homeless man for whom the whole world is home, a man without possessions whose treasure is the whole of creation. It is a self-image of mystical simplicity, and, apart from simply fobbing off unwelcome enquiries, it provides a clue as to how he saw himself and what he felt to be the motivation of his travelling.

It provides, too, an insight into his character. During his months in the desert he was insulted, humiliated and treated with contempt and disdain, and, for the most part, accepted it meekly, although without changing course. More aggressive, piratical travellers like Sir Richard Burton took this submissiveness almost as an insult to their imperial race. 'I cannot, for the life of me, see how the honoured name of England can gain aught by the travel of an Englishman who at all times and in all places is compelled to stand the buffet from knaves that smell of sweat,' Burton stormed, when he read *Travels in Arabia Deserta*.[1]

But Doughty, too, had no shortage of racial pride. Claiming for

himself not just the self-control of a bedu, but the asceticism of a
Muslim holy man was one way of measuring his own worth against
the standards of the desert; but he was able to do that, he had no
doubt, because of the strength imparted to him by generations of
breeding as an English gentleman. His apparent humility was a mark
of strength, not weakness, a sense of the worth and dignity of a
scholar, a Christian and an Englishman never far below the surface.

As they left the lumbering caravan behind them, Zeyd was watching Doughty narrowly to assess his reaction to the harshness of the
landscape into which they were riding. Finally he spoke. If Khalil
would come and live permanently in the desert, he would give him
a camel, the Arabs would find him a wife, and, when he did eventually return to his own people, any children he might leave behind
would be brought up as members of the tribe.

On the face of it, it was an astonishing offer, based on the few
weeks' acquaintance they had had – although perhaps there is a hint
of Zeyd's real motivation in his casual observation that Doughty's
silver could conveniently be sent down for him, year by year, with
the Hadj caravan. There was, after all, no reason why the eccentric
Nasrany should not be a lasting source of income. It is also likely,
especially bearing in mind Zeyd's later behaviour, that the offer was
one of the expansive gestures to which he was prone, owing more
to his enjoyment of the sound of his own magnanimity than to any
real generous intent. Little was valued more highly in the tribe than
the reputation of unstinting generosity. 'The Arabs', Doughty
observed drily in a different context, 'are full of great words.'[2] But
even so, the fact that the offer was made at all shows how serious
Zeyd was in welcoming Doughty into his tribe, and how sure he was
that the *Nasrany* would prove equal in the end to the trials of the
desert.

The first of those trials concerned his camel, bought on his behalf
by Zeyd, just before they left the *kella*, for thirty reals, or something
over half the funds that the Hadj caravan had brought him from
Damascus. It was the first of a series of sick and suffering animals to
be unloaded by the shrewd Arab traders onto the naive and unsus-
pecting Doughty, and before he rode away with Zeyd he appealed
to the Pasha of the Hadj that the seller should be ordered to give

him his money back. Mohammed Said agreed readily to issue the command – but as he vanished into the distance, it was clear that little would be done to enforce it. Law in the desert often depended on the power that backed it up, and for weeks to come Doughty's ailing camel remained a trial to him, and a source of amusement to the Arabs with whom he travelled.

At the end of a long day's walking and riding by turn, with the useless camel shambling along beside them, they reached the *menzel* or camp of Zeyd's Fukara. To his surprise, Doughty was introduced straight away in the women's section of his host's tent – the nomads, he noted later, had no suspicion of Christians, whom they had heard 'reputed honest folk, more than the Moslemin'. 'Khalil, here is thy new aunt . . . and Hirfa, this is Khalil; and see thou take good care of him,' Zeyd said. From that moment, for the next two and a half months, Doughty was part of his household, sharing their wanderings, their meals and, more embarrassingly, their increasingly frequent marital arguments.

They were heading for the oasis town of Teyma, but they moved slowly, usually around five hours' travelling in a day, with an occasional pause of a day or two during which Doughty tried to while away the long, hot hours with the books that were still packed away in his bags. His main study during these weeks, though, was the beduin tribesmen themselves: he was living now cheek by jowl with the supposed devils and demons, the half-savage robbers and marauders, about whom townsmen, soldiers and pilgrims alike had warned him.

The life was certainly hard – thin camel milk to drink, and scanty supplies of water liberally polluted with camel's urine – but notes in the diary show how he was welcomed, and how quickly he was accepted into the tribe. An entry on 16 February, for instance, just three days after he had left the Hadj caravan, reads: 'Zeyd fetched me a drink of fresh camel milk. We roasted locusts while the women set up the tent . . .'

The tribesmen themselves, and more particularly their hardworking wives, were most solicitous about their guest. A first taste of the milk, they warned anxiously, would often give strangers indigestion as it turned to hard curds in the stomach. The women would bake cakes of bread specially for him in the ashes of the cooking fire; the water, which they kept jealously for drinking, was poured out sparingly each morning for Doughty, so that he could wash 'as the townspeople'.

The women's affection for their guest was based at least partly on his unexpected sympathy for them. In a letter written some twenty years later he paid tribute to their easygoing good-humour. 'In the ingenuous freedom of the desert tribal life, where all are each other's cousins . . . [the women] can speak their minds freely, and the good spirits among them, which are many, can and not seldom do sympathise with any who is . . . suffering or oppressed.'[3] But even so, he added, they were 'an oppressed sex'. It was the women, Doughty noticed, who set up the camp in the evening, and who took it down again in the morning, the women who milked the ewes and goats, the women who prepared the dates and milk or sweet butter which was their usual diet. The men of the tribe would look on impassively as they smoked their tobacco pipes and drank their coffee – much, it must be said, as the Victorian heads of households back in England might have done – but Doughty left no doubt that he thought their wives were being shamefully treated. 'The woman's lot is here unequal concubinage, and in this necessitous life, a weary servitude . . . Few then are the nomad wives whose years can be long happy in marriage!'[4]

And housework, of course, was not the end of their duties. How on earth, Doughty asked one of the women one day, did the men of the tribe while away the long hours of the afternoon heat, sweltering in the shadows of their tents, until the evening? After all, the dedicated student may have reasoned sympathetically, they did not have the collection of books which helped him to pass the time. 'And she answered, demurely smiling, "How, sir, but in solace with the hareem!"'[5]

Certainly the happy years of Hirfa's marriage to Zeyd were past. She was, Doughty wrote bluntly but not unaffectionately, 'an undergrown thick Beduin lass, her age might be twenty; the golden youth was faded almost to autumn in her childish face, but not unpleasing; there was a merry wooden laughter always in her mouth, which ended commonly, for the unsatisfied heart, in sighing'.[6] The

constant bickering between her and her husband, which often ended
in Zeyd beating her with his camel-stick in the long hours of the
night, had become a running joke around the campfires; and while
Hirfa, for her part, was not above flirting with the younger men of
the tribe, Zeyd spent night after night with another wife, a young
Bishr woman.

When Hirfa eventually ran off to take refuge in her aunt's tent,
it was Doughty who was pressed to go and persuade her to come
back. Even with the sympathy he had with the women of the tribe,
even with his standing as a guest who might act as intermediary
between husband and wife, it was an oddly sensitive task for such
a constitutionally undiplomatic character – and yet, handing around
pipefuls of tobacco to Hirfa, her aunt and all the old women who
sat around, he carried it off with aplomb. 'Said her aunt, "Well, go
over, Khalil; Hirfa follows, and all we (the bevy of old women)
accompany her" (to bring her home honourably). Soon after, arriving before my tent door, they called me out to pay them another
dole of tobbaco: – and Hirfa sat again in her own *beyt*.'*[7]

Whatever twinges of nostalgia Doughty may have felt for the
well-remembered sounds of the Suffolk countryside, much of this
early time in the desert sounds idyllic:

> No sweet chittering of birds greets the coming of the desert
> light, besides man there is no voice in this waste drought.
> The Beduins, that lay down in their cloaks upon the sandy
> mother-earth in the open tents, hardly before the middle
> night, are already up and bestirring themselves. In every
> coffee-sheikh's tent, there is new fire blown in the hearth,
> and he sets on his coffee pots ... [8]

This familiarity with the way of life of the bedu tribes – the daily
struggle to erect their black worsted tents and bind their possessions
in bundles for the journey, the decisiveness with which the leader
of the group would plunge his spear into the sand to fix the day's
camping place, the way they washed their babies in camel urine to
protect them from insects – this matter-of-fact closeness to their daily

* Home.

existence was something that no other *Frenjy** had ever experienced
and written about.

It was, in fact, a relatively gentle introduction to the life of the
desert, sitting down cheerfully in the long evenings with his bedu
companions to warm themselves at the flickering campfire as the
roasting locusts sizzled in the fire for their night-time snack.

But over the next weeks Doughty would also see the sheer grinding poverty of their life – the black, stinking water they sometimes
had to drink ('sooner than drink their water I very often suffered
thirst, and very oft passed the nights half sleepless'),[9] the diseases
and infections from which they suffered, and the casual and brutal
violence to which they might be prey. It was neither the life of the
noble savage that the European orientalists described, nor that of
unrelieved barbarity that the Arab townsmen would have had him
believe, but rather one of hardship eased by an overwhelming sense
of tribal loyalty.

For the most part he was treated kindly by the Arabs with whom
he stayed, welcomed as a *thaif Ullah*, a guest of God. And yet cruelty
and savagery were part of the self-image of the nomads as well.
Lying around the campfire at night-time, in the midst of the tribesmen, Zeyd would remind Doughty that it was only he who stood
between him and 'the murderous wildness of the Beduins'. Sometimes they would describe themselves as devils, brute beasts and
lunatics; 'There is not, Khalil, a man of us all which sit here, that
meeting thee abroad in the *khala*,† had not slain thee,' he was told
one night – and if these gibes might have been meant ironically,
there were many other times over the following months when fanatic
bedu Muslims threatened the life of the wandering *Nasrany*. One
group said they would throw him and his feared books together on
a fire, and burn him alive; on another occasion he woke to find an
Arab holding a heavy stone over his head, ready to dash out his
brains; and on a third, a nomad sheikh was dissuaded with difficulty
from plunging his dagger theatrically into the Christian's chest.

He had hoped that his vaccinations would win him friends, but

* A Frank, or European.
† The empty desert.

125

as soon as he began to try to use the vaccines, it was clear that they had lost whatever potency they had had. It was a disaster: his expectations at first had been meagre enough, but now, a despised outsider and an infidel, he had no way of earning either money or respect.

> For the benefit of vaccination, the Beduw would almost have pardoned my misbelief; and I might have lived thereby competently in a country where it is peril of death to be accounted the bearer of a little silver. No more than a sick camel now remained to me, and little gold in my purse, and I began to think of quitting this tedious soil . . . [10]

It was a brief spell of weakness – the first of several occasions on which his determination began to fail him.

Despite the friendliness of his companions, he was constantly questioned about why he had come to the desert at all. With the mixture of simplicity and suspicion that he would come to recognize as characteristic of the desert tribes, the Arabs could see no reason but that he was acting as a spy for some foreign enemy. His interest in the countryside, his constant fretting over names and measurements, his obsessive scribbling in his diary, and the mysterious books he spent so long consulting – all these things told against him. 'Tell us by Ullah, Khalil, art thou not come to spy out the country? . . . Khalil loves well the Moslemin, and yet these books of his be what? Also, is he not "writing" the country as he has "written up" el-Hejr and el-Ally?'[11]

But that question of why he was in the desert was one he always avoided, never answered – probably because he did not have a simple answer himself. 'To take the air,' he once snapped rudely; questioned by a group of women in an oasis, and clearly in a more gallant mood, he replied: 'It were enough if only to see you, my sisters.' At different times he described himself as a *saiehh*, as a man who sought out ancient inscriptions for the pleasure of the learned, and as a philosopher. Each answer gives a part, but only a part, of the truth.

His original journey to Medain Salih was certainly prompted by the desire to investigate the ruins he had heard of there, and to take copies of the carvings and inscriptions. There was a genuine fascination with the Arab people, their ancestry, their links with the Bible tales of his childhood, and their own stories and mythologies; as he heard the legends of the mysterious Jews of Kheybar, for instance, he felt a growing determination to visit that town as well. But none of that wholly explains his continued wandering through the desert.

The real impetus behind his journeying was part religious, part literary, and largely psychological. Much of Doughty's life had been that of an outsider – the orphan shunted off to his uncle's family, the shy, diffident youth with the stammer, the would-be officer turned down by the navy, the academic with the second-class degree, the prosperous country squire whose wealth had been allowed to dribble away. Here in Muslim Arabia, the Christian Doughty was in much the same position, but this time there was a difference: he had *chosen* to be an outcast. Every time he responded to a challenge by proclaiming himself to be a Christian English gentleman, he was not only affirming his inclusion within those groups, but at the same time emphasizing his control, his power of choice – a power that had so often been denied him in the past.

In any case, the bedu themselves, with their Spartan lifestyle and their bleak individuality, attracted and fascinated him. In the horrified contempt with which they were described by the Arabs of Damascus, the farmers of the settled lands, the soldiers and the pilgrims on the Hadj, he recognized his own uneasy status as social misfit. Their self-reliance, their strict adherence to an almost knightly code of hospitality and honour, even their quixotic belief in the arbitrary powers of djinns and spirits, carried him back into the long-remembered and deeply loved world of Chaucer and Spenser.

And, while he might protest vehemently against the religious bigotry he found among the fanatic Muslims of the oasis towns, he frequently found himself responding with respect and understanding to the nomads' own personal and undogmatic faith. They would admit shamefacedly to their shortcomings in the detailed observance of prayer times, or the rules of what they might or might not eat; they would even confess ironically that entertaining a Christian at their campfire was a cause for shame to any truly devout believer –

but they still maintained that their unremitting hospitality to the guest and stranger made them better Muslims than the more conventionally pious townsmen. It was an instinctive humanity and fellow-feeling that went beyond the bounds of religious dogma, and one with which Doughty, for all his social awkwardness and prickliness, could readily identify.

Their religion, he said, was inextricably bound up with their own national pride, 'a kind of national envy or Semitic patriotism'. In anyone but Doughty, such an observation might have been a criticism of their lack of conventional devotion – but it precisely reflects his developing attitude to his own religious belief. The critic Anne Treneer writes:

> There is no evidence that he considered the Christian revelation any more capable of withstanding what he called 'the salt of science' than the Mohammedan. His Christianity is not faith in a revelation, but a proud adherence to something beautiful in itself, and formative in the history of his people.[12]

Among the bedu tribesmen of Arabia he found the Islamic mirror of the deeply personal faith towards which he was feeling his own painful way.

But by March, with the summer heat already starting to build up, Doughty's determination to stay in Arabia was beginning to crack. It was not just the constant suspicion among his companions that was sapping his enthusiasm. The failure of his vaccines had crippled his hopes of supporting himself in the oasis towns, and what little doctoring he was able to do was not making him any money. He had to work in the gusting wind, weighing out powders in his portable brass balance as he squatted in the sand. (The balance itself, with its flat pans and delicate strings, is now in the possession of Gonville and Caius College, Cambridge.) There was no pure water with which to mix his potions, and even if there had been, most of his customers had no phials or containers in which to put them. More than all that, though, he was competing with a powerful sense of fatalism among his patients, a feeling that it was almost impious to seek to ease by medicaments a sickness that had obviously been

brought on by the will of God – and, even more critical, an unwillingness to hand over hard cash for treatments that might or might not
work. It was not unalloyed piety: some of them even stole the little
cups in which he had mixed his preparations.

To his bedu companions, who prided themselves on their shrewdness in business dealings, his efforts were a cause of some mirth, a
further demonstration of the foreigner's lack of business sense. 'The
people come to Khalil's tent for medicines; and Khalil, not distinguishing them, will give to all of them in trust; the people . . . go
their ways, and he sees them no more, wellah! Khalil, there is no
wit in thee at all for buying and selling!'[13]

But the failure of his vaccines was only the first of a series of
misfortunes. His ailing camel injured its jaw, leaving the beast virtually useless, while at the same time giving the pragmatic beduins still
more amusement. They named the suffering beast '*ayun bila sinun*',
or 'Eyes-Without-Teeth'. At the same time the watch which he had
been using to work out for his diary the distances he had travelled
suddenly stopped working, probably choked with the same blowing
sand that bedevilled his attempts to mix his medicines.

It was indeed time to leave, he decided – to travel back to El Ally,
and there find a rice caravan on its way down to the Red Sea port
of Wejh, from which he could sail to Egypt, all his plans to cross
Arabia and travel on to India abandoned.

These vacillations and moments of weakness came upon him period-
ically during his eighteen months travelling through Arabia; this
time, it was Zeyd and the other Arabs who changed his mind. If he
would only wait until after the spring, they said, they would be
travelling back towards El Ally, and would be able to help him on
his way; for now, they were within a few days' march of the town
of Teyma.

Doughty had been struck already by the similarities between the
tribesmen whose life he was sharing and those of the Old Testament
who peopled his imagination. The tents of the Arabs, he declared,
were like the 'adorned house' built by Moses in the wilderness;
the nomads with whom he was travelling would swear solemn and

binding oaths in the same terms as Joseph and even Jehovah himself. And now he was approaching Teyma, a city mentioned by Job, Jeremiah and Isaiah. The Arabs accompanying him might see the town as no more than a place where they could replenish their dwindling supplies of food, but for Doughty, the first sight of the long clay walls, the watch-towers and the nodding date palms was a glimpse of biblical history. He reached out to it like a superstitious man touching a talisman.

But the inhabitants of the place were as little interested in what he had to tell them as the bedu frequently were in his insistent questioning about place-names and topography – and indeed, it must have been annoying for the Muslim townsmen to hear this opinionated foreigner, an unbeliever to boot, lecture them about the antecedents in the Christian Bible and the Jewish Torah of their own town. 'Teyma is intended in Isaiah, from whence the caravaners of Dedan, scattered before the bow and the sword of the Beduw, are relieved with bread and water,' he told them enthusiastically. His hearers were unimpressed and unconvinced. 'But the old name was Toma,' they replied stolidly.[14]

He was not the first European to visit Teyma – George Augustus Wallin, a Swedish-born spy working for the Egyptians, had won that honour in the 1840s, and another secret agent, the Italian Carlo Guarmani, employed this time by the French Emperor Napoleon III, had been there disguised as a horse-dealer in 1864. Albrecht Zehme's *Arabien Zeit Hundert Jahren*, one of the books Doughty carried around Arabia, included an account of the Italian's view of the town, which Doughty read while he was there, and evidently found unsatisfactory. 'His visit may have been a flying one and too short to leave much impression on his mind, nor is it likely he would see or hear much if he travelled with valuable horses much by night-time, on account of the heat.'[15] Guarmani did notice the massive town well which was to cause Doughty such problems on a later visit – 'some forty metres in circumference, with forty-eight camels drawing water all the time' – but neither he nor Wallin had shown much interest in the history of Teyma, or in the inscriptions that Doughty was still so anxious to copy down.

The Arabs were making only a brief visit, but while Zeyd bought his provisions, Doughty was free to wander around the prosperous little settlement, noting the flourishing orchards and plantations behind their fortified clay walls, the open, spacious houses, and the imposing stone fortifications which surrounded the ancient city. He had friendly greetings from everyone – even from Ibn Rashid's official representative, a man 'walking stately, upon his long tipstaff, and ruffling in glorious garments', and standing so determinedly on his dignity that he 'seemed to have swallowed a stake'.[16] Despite an earnest and tactless lecture from Doughty on the evils of slavery, and on the principled determination of the *Engleys* to rid the world of slave traders and slave ships, he invited the *Nasrany* back to his own home, to show him ancient inscriptions in the stones there. At the same time, of course, he could build up a more complete picture for his master of what this outlandish foreign traveller was doing in Arabia.

Doughty, though, had eyes only for the inscriptions. Excitingly, after the Nabataean of Medain Salih and the Himyaric of El Ally, these were in a third and unrecognized script. Elsewhere he found the great ruined pillars of some ancient temple lying in the sand near the mosque, and the ruins of a long-abandoned stronghold. The story of ancient Teyma was there to be read in its stones.

But Doughty's studies had to be broken off. The Fukara were unwilling to stay longer in the town because they owed Ibn Rashid five years' taxes. Zeyd and Doughty were called back to the camp with news that the others were already setting off back into the desert.

It was no longer the easygoing wandering of their earlier travels. Whether because of some rumour of approaching forces, or simply from a sudden lack of nerve, the Arabs were anxious to get as far as possible from Teyma, and they set out on a series of forced marches, sleeping under the stars, without tents, and driving their flocks and cattle before them through the day. A single march took them forty miles from the town, hurrying on past ruined buildings in the sand which Doughty would dearly have loved to inspect at greater length. But the Arabs, always dismissive of the ruins which so fascinated him, urged him onwards impatiently.

When Doughty had left the Hadj caravan only six weeks before, he had shocked Mohammed Said by declaring his intention to travel not just to Teyma, but on to Hail and Kheybar, planning months, if not years, in the desert. That, too, was the plan he had spelled out in his letters home from the *kella* – but it was all abandoned. Now, as they had promised, the Fukara were ready to help him on his way back to the coast. Defeated by the desert, he was heading once more towards the fort he had left with such high hopes.

But the weakening of his resolve had not lessened his determination to winnow out what information he could about the ancient history of the land through which he was travelling. With the first panic over, Zeyd took him on a diversion to visit the image of a former sheikh, carved in the rock with dozens of inscriptions around it. These, 'the names doubtless, the saws, the salaams, of many passengers and cameleers of antique generations',[17] were written in the same Himyaric script he had found at El Ally. They told no stories of civic pride, solemn monuments, or the rise and fall of nations, but, like the collections of stones he occasionally found carefully arranged in a triangle to support pots upon a fire, or like the sad little ovals of rocks set in the ground to mark the graves of young children dead by the wayside, they seemed to speak across the centuries in the familiar language of the common people.

Doughty was still especially alive to the links of language from one generation to the next, and the very words on the lips of his companions seemed to bring to life the world of the Old Testament. Clouds of locusts flying overhead were described by the Arabs as *am'dan*, or pillars – 'It is the same word we read in Exodus,' he noted excitedly, ' – the *ammud* of cloud and fire.' He saw, too, how the huge insects were thrown around in the wind, and remembered the Psalmist's line, 'I am thrown up and down as the locust.'[18] The language and stories of the Bible were in any case a familiar part of the day-to-day intellectual furniture of Englishmen of his time and class, but they had always had a particular vividness in his imagination; now they were taking on new meaning in the real world around him.

Even though he was living so closely among them, this combination of an intellectual and an emotional response separated him from his companions. For them, the clouds of locusts meant only two things, as they saw them drifting southwards: the likelihood that the dates of Kheybar would be lost, and the corresponding possibility of toasting the fattened bodies of the insects over their campfires. Even in that, incidentally, Doughty found a biblical echo – they were, he said, like the children of Jacob in Leviticus, who ate the different kinds of locust[19] – but it is the response of a visitor, a man who, whatever the hardships he may be suffering, has another world to return to. For all his pride in living the life of the Arabs whom he accompanied, he remained at heart a scholar, not a bedu.

But the summer was approaching. The whimsical nostalgia with which he had noticed the lack of birdsong in the dawn a month or so earlier was replaced now by real suffering as the desert heat built up.

> The sun, entering as a tyrant upon the waste landscape, darts upon us a torment of fiery beams, not to be remitted till the far-off evening. – No matins here of birds; not a rock partridge-cock, calling with blithesome chuckle over the extreme waterless desolation. Grave is that giddy heat upon the crown of the head; the ears tingle with a flickering shrillness, a subtle crepitation it seems, in the glassiness of this sun-stricken nature: the hot sand-blink is in the eyes, and there is little refreshment to find in the tent's shelter; the worsted booths leak to this fiery rain of sunny light ... [20]

As the heat bore him down, so he recorded it in his diary: 95 degrees in the shade of his tent, at an altitude of 4,000 feet on 15 April, for example. To the end of his journey he would maintain the meticulousness of his note-taking to the best of his ability – one way of imposing his own sense of order on a world and a society that constantly threatened to overwhelm him; but he remained convinced that he should leave. On 8 April he noted curtly: 'My wish was not to make longer stay with the Arabs. Upon this we had some words' – the first mention of his increasingly tetchy relations with Zeyd. The heat was eating away at his patience and his enthusiasm as it sapped his health. 'The harvest was past, and I desired to be gone. The *Aarab* languished lying in the tents; we seemed to breathe flames. All day

I gasped, and hardly remained alive, since I was breathless, and could not eat.'[21]

Tempers were frayed by the enervating weather and by the short-age of food which the locusts had caused, and the situation was not eased by Doughty's habitual outspokenness when he believed he had been unfairly treated. He was not to end his time with the Fukara on a friendly note.

Settled now in his decision to leave the desert, he decided to tackle Zeyd once and for all over the question of his ailing camel. Without a reliable mount he knew he would find it difficult to join one of the rice caravans which made the journey to Wejh – and in any case, it was no more than his right. When they left the Hadj, Mohammed Pasha had told Zeyd to demand Doughty's money back from the man who had sold the beast to him. On top of that, it was one of Zeyd's own animals that had broken the camel's jaw, and the law of the desert said that he was entitled to some compensation.

There was clearly some sympathy for his plight among the other Arabs – the diary notes, for instance, that one of them gave him the friendly advice that he should speak to Motlog, the senior sheikh, about the camel – but he had little hope of satisfaction. After all, he reasoned bitterly, 'Who would give evidence against a sheikh of his tribe, for the Nasrany? Amongst Mohammedans, and though they be the Beduins of the wilderness, there is equity only between them-selves.'[22]

The angry words spoken between Doughty and Zeyd in the course of the dispute were remembered for a long time. Other resentments came bubbling to the surface: Zeyd demanded recompense for the cost of feeding his guest, while Doughty accused his friend of rum-maging through his bags, and scandalized him by calling him *hablus*, a robber. Long after the quarrel was supposedly made up, with the unlikely explanation that the Englishman did not fully understand the meaning of the word, that gibe in particular festered with Zeyd for months to come.

To settle the matter, Doughty swapped his suffering mount for another one, handing over ten reals into the bargain, and demon-strating yet again his lack of shrewdness in the matter of camel-dealing. 'I bought thus upon their trust, a dizzy camel, old, and nearly past labour, and having lost her front teeth, that was of no more value, in the sight of the nomads, than my wounded camel.'[23]

It was clear not only that Doughty would get no further satisfaction from Zeyd, but also that his welcome among the Fukara was running out. Preparing to leave with Zeyd and a small group of Arabs who were making their way down to the *kella* at El Hejr, he gave out presents from amongst his luggage, including much of his clothing. He was still determined on making his way to the coast.

Toothless and aged as it was, his new camel was fit enough for his present purpose, and at dawn the little group set off on a long day's journey towards El Hejr. For the Arabs, it was simply a trip to the *kella* to pick up supplies of rice and coffee they had stored there; for Doughty, a final visit on his way out of Arabia to a garrison he remembered with very mixed feelings. It must have been with some trepidation that he hammered on the door of the fort in the darkness.

Maybe it was lucky that Mohammed Aly himself was away – but in fact the welcome from the rest of the garrison could hardly have been more friendly. 'We were kindly received, and welcomed to a good supper of bread and *samn*** set before us,' notes the diary on 1 May. They drank coffee late into the night, all Doughty's quarrels with their commander and, more recently, with Zeyd too, apparently forgotten.

Zeyd and his men quickly loaded up their supplies and departed, but Doughty's main intention was still to find some way of travelling the 150 miles or so on to Wejh and taking a ship up the Red Sea to Egypt. While he waited for the caravan that would carry him there and on to the coast, he made a trip north to the engraved rocks of Mabrak En Naga, the pass into the plain which he had first seen briefly months before as the Hadj caravan approached the *kella*.

The inscriptions, like those Zeyd had shown him on the way from Teyma, were mostly the brief, casual scrawlings of passing cameldrivers on the ancient frankincense route. The hurriedly inscribed names, dates, blessings, and memorials, chipped out in Himyaric script, Nabataean, even Greek, gave his busy imagination something to work on. 'Here the old ascending passengers might look back a

---

* Clarified butter.

last time to the Nabataean plain, and those arriving from the north had their first sight of Hejra city: all perhaps alighted in this place, and there might one and another take up a stone . . . to beat out his own remembrance . . .'[24]

Despite the increasing heat, he spent as much time as he could when he returned away from the *kella*, poring over the rocks around Medain Salih for more inscriptions, even the occasional copper coin for his collection. Quarrels and disagreements there among the garrison made for a fraught, tense time, and he looked back with more and more affection to his life among the 'freeborn Aarab'.

In short, he was wavering: the decision he had made to set out for home was becoming less fixed. Perhaps he might join a tribe of Moahib Arabs, he thought, up in the relative cool of the Harra* mountains; in any case, three weeks in the *kella* had still brought no firm word of caravans travelling down to the coast. He was caught, as he so often was, in a morass of indecision, turning this way and that, and waiting for something to happen to make up his mind for him. And then, as he searched around for a companion to escort him back to the mountains, came the news that he had been waiting for – a group of Arabs about to set off to Wejh to collect supplies of rice. The only problem was that they were Fukara, leaving in two days' time from the very camp which Doughty had left to make his way down to the plain. If events were making up his mind for him, they were also sending him backwards and forwards across the desert.

There was no time to be lost: it was a hard ride through the night back to the camp, and Doughty arrived there only to find that the Arabs were already leaving. If he wanted to join them, he had no choice but to stay on his camel and ride on with them. So on he went, tired and hungry, but in his haste to leave the camp, he took neither water nor food. The Arabs with whom he was travelling were hurrying to meet the rest of the caravan to the coast, and the next twenty-four hours were a savage test of his determination and stamina, as he struggled not only to keep up with the rest, but simply to stay in the saddle at all.

* Lava-field.

When they paused for water, he would make up a little ground – but no sooner had he caught up with them than they would be off again, their camels rested and watered while his floundered on in the heat. Some of them treated him with contempt as a Christian, and many refused even to let him drink water from their buckets at the various wells; even among the women were those who urged them to slit his throat and have done with it.

The diary tells the story: 'The heat was intolerable – 42°C – and I heard they would not alight till they reached the far-off Harra, thus I suffered many long hours . . . Promised milk on the morrow,' reads a note on Sunday 19 May. The next day, though: 'The Arabs broke up before sunrise. They laughed when I reminded them of the milk, and I responded sharply . . .'

They had no time for sympathy. But it was the heat and the exertion that tortured Doughty most, his skin blistered and peeling in the relentless sun – 'a long dying without death', he called it.[25] The forced march lasted for two whole days, up into the highlands of the Harra, and then stumbling over the sharp flints that were scattered over the mountain tracks. They had to rendezvous with a sheikh of the Billi Arabs named Mahanna, who was to be their escort through the unfriendly country on the way to Wejh, and it was late on the second day before they arrived at his camp. Doughty was crushed both by the journey and by the harshness of his companions. 'I alighted with another at Mahanna's tent, and lay down suffering; they marking this, with a kind inquietude, brought me *leban** to drink, and I slept as the dead . . .'[26]

He was faint with fatigue and hunger, his head spinning and every muscle in his body aching, but his welcome now the frantic journey was over was as generous as the Arabs' limited resources would allow. There was no more mention of the threats or religious fanaticism he had endured. But the last two days had shattered his health and his determination. The difference between him and the Arabs with whom he had travelled was the difference between a man for whom camel-riding and desert travel under any conditions could only be a trial and a test of endurance, and men who had lived

* Sour milk, buttermilk.

137

most of their lives in the saddle. As other Arabian explorers after him were to find, the desert was the beduin's home; there were few Europeans who could survive in a forced march alongside them.

Before the caravan now lay more than a hundred miles of hard riding across the Tehama plain, in the sultry, unforgiving heat: when Mahanna and the Arabs prepared to leave as the sun rose next day, Doughty declared that he could go no further.

> With what anguish must I cross the rest of that rugged lowland country, frying in the sun, with the slow-footed camels, to fall perhaps from the saddle, or give the last breath before the *kufl** should enter el-Wejh ... Might I breathe again upon the mountain, and find there a little milk, I should recover health.[27]

The diary makes no mention of his decision to stay behind. He had no way of knowing at the time that he had effectively committed himself to staying in Arabia for another whole year, and in any case, he was too weak and ill to write more than the briefest of entries. Sickness and fatigue had forced his hand.

The man who had so often in the past complained of his failing health before setting out on arduous journeys was now genuinely sick. For the next week the entries in his diary were terse and hurried as he gradually gathered his strength, left alone among the women of Mahanna's Billi. It was clear, when the sheikh returned, that Doughty's decision to stay behind had been a wise one. The Arabs had hurried through their business in the town, declaring the heat there, alongside what they called 'the Salt Sea', to be intolerable even for them: if they were suffering, it is unlikely that Doughty, sick as he was, would have survived the journey.

And he was still dithering about what to do next. A trading caravan carrying rice up into the Harra passed through the camp on its way from the coast, and the merchant promised to return for Doughty on the way back. It was the sort of opportunity he might have snatched at eagerly only a few days before, and even now, if the camel train had come back promptly, perhaps he might have

---

* Trading caravan.

gone – but in fact, after a few days, there was still no sign of it. The decision, once again, had been taken out of Doughty's hand. Not sorry this time to have been let down, he persuaded an old man whose grandchild he had cured to act as his guide, and set off with him to look for the Moahib Arabs, who were camped nearby, in the relative cool of the mountains.

By now his existence was well known to the wandering bedu, but he was still taking a considerable risk in trying to join up with a tribe where he had neither friends nor direct contacts. Mahanna sent word to vouch for him, but Doughty was relying entirely on the Arabs' code of hospitality to the travelling guest. He was under no compulsion to move on: despite all the invective which he occasionally poured out later about the Arabs and their religion, this faith in their goodwill speaks volumes for his own attitudes.

In fact, the only argument when they finally caught up with the Moahib was over which of the Arabs should have the honour of feeding and entertaining them, and the stranger was quickly found space in the tents of one of the tribesmen. He had started on his second spell of bedu life, a series of wanderings that would take him through the four months of summer until, towards the end of October, he arrived at Ibn Rashid's capital of Hail.

So far, he had relied almost entirely upon the charity of the Arabs with whom he had travelled, profiting from their strict observance of the bedu laws of hospitality. For the next few weeks at least, he would follow a more independent life, almost like one of the lone wandering Arabs who might attach themselves for a spell to a friendly tribe. He lived in his own tent, rode his own stumbling and sickly camel as the group moved from place to place, and, so far as he was able, paid from his shrinking store of reals for whatever food and drink he was given.

It was, despite the intense summer heat and the aches and pains that still troubled him almost continuously, one of the most rewarding periods of his travels. If he had still to suffer the constant curiosity and occasional suspicion of his companions, there was little or no actual violence offered to him. As his strength grew, so did his determination to travel further back into the heart of Arabia: there was still more to see, he was convinced, than the primitive simplicity of life with the bedu.

There were now frequent expeditions setting off to the Red Sea coast, but the idea of going home had lost its attraction. Dreams of gazing on the reality of Hail and undiscovered Kheybar inspired him again; his ill-health was now, perversely, an excuse for delving deeper into the Arab civilization. He was 'too feeble' to struggle to the coast, he declared. And in any case, 'as each breath of air refreshed my spirits, I mused anew of breaking into Arabia'.[28] It was not an ambition that won the universal approval of his companions.

He had only been with the Moahib a few days when their senior sheikh, Tollog, told him as pleasantly as he could that he should leave. The next day some of the tribe were joining the rice merchant he had met earlier, and Doughty should go with them to Wejh. 'It were better for thee to return to thine own people, and not die: depart tomorrow with Abu Sinun, but drink now thy coffee, and speak we no more of this.'[29] Appeals and reproaches alike were fruitless – perhaps the Arabs were tired of his company; perhaps they were genuinely concerned for his welfare, or worried about the possible repercussions for themselves if he were to die. Probably it was a mixture of all three.

But if Doughty had been indecisive before, he showed his determination now. His mind was set on Kheybar, and he was also worried that other tribes might hear that he had been driven out, and treat him similarly. The next morning the main body of the camp moved off. The party going with the rice caravan clearly had their orders: first they tried to persuade him, then to force his camel to move on with them, then to bully him, until finally they raised their sticks against Doughty himself. He sat stoically through the whole performance, stolid as his camel under their threats and blows, refusing to move. Eventually, defeated, they left him alone in the desert, hurrying away in case they themselves were left behind.

At that his camel, instinctively unwilling to be abandoned, tried to follow them, but Doughty managed by brute force to wrench her head in the direction of the departing camp, even though the Arabs were out of sight. She galloped after them, scattering his possessions unheeded behind her in the sand, while he clung on for dear life, peering desperately and short-sightedly around the desert in the hope of catching sight of the group of Arabs. 'A horrible distress it were, to be bewildered in these hideous lavas, like the floor of a furnace in the sun, and without water! I rode with this burden at heart, lest I should see the people no more; my eyesight was never good.'[30]

For the sake of remaining in the desert, Doughty had risked not just the blows of the Arabs, not just the anger of the sheikh, but the very real danger of being lost and abandoned to die of thirst. It was a mark both of his native obstinacy and of his determination to continue with his exploration of Arabia.

When he did catch up with the Arabs, he thought it sensible to keep his distance for a while, until in the evening he took the bull by the horns and made his way to Tollog's campfire. There were no recriminations, and the old man greeted him kindly enough: if Doughty could not be sent away, he seemed to think with native bedu fatalism, he would just have to make his way with the tribe, doctoring as best he could.

Doughty's medical practice was simple, if effective – generally nothing more imaginative than a few drops of croton oil, served up as a laxative with a little sugar. A normal dose might have been a couple of drops, but within a few days he had realized, like Gifford Palgrave before him, that the iron digestions of the nomads required extraordinary treatment. Twice and three times the usual dosage proved little more effective; it was only when they were receiving eight drops, not two, that the purging effects of the oil began to be felt. His first patient, in fact, was Tollog himself: the diary entry for Friday 22 June tells the story. 'To Tollog I gave eight drops of croton oil. This very soon worked; but since he had drunk a large draught of *mereesy*,* his belly swelled up and he was much oppressed . . .' He was apparently suffering from nothing worse than painful indigestion, but the treatment of the sheikh, and the way Tollog boasted of it later around the campfire, was the best advertising Doughty could have had. 'The doses I give you would be death to other persons,'

* Dry milk.

he exclaimed – an observation which gave the Arabs considerable pride in the strength of their constitutions.

With indigestion, Doughty could help them; but they were also facing the very real danger of famine. As the summer wore on, so the shortage of food got worse, until even the Arabs, hardened to long periods of hunger, were spending hours lying lethargically in their tents. 'Almost dead with hunger,' reads the diary entry for 3 August; and a couple of days later, once again, 'famished with hunger'. For Doughty, the experience brought to mind the sufferings of the ancient desert hermits and ascetics of the Bible. His view of them and their inspiration provides some insight into the austere, religious element of his own motivation. 'There fled many wilfully from the troublesome waves of the world, devising in themselves to retrieve the first Adam in their own souls, and coveting a sinless habitation with the elements . . .'[31]

But life with the bedu now was a means to an end: introspective though part of his motive undoubtedly was, there was now a practical reason too for him to persevere in the desert. Kheybar was his obsession, the oasis town itself now a symbol of the unknown Arabia. His copy of Zehme told him that there had been Christian visitors before him in Teyma and even in Hail – but in Kheybar, he firmly believed, he might be the first European.[32] The ruins and inscriptions he had found at Medain Salih and elsewhere on his travels had already justified his original decision to join the Hadj and travel south – but although they had provided new evidence about the Nabataeans, the other peoples of Arabia, and the extent to which they had travelled and traded together, he had still failed to find the new civilization he had originally hoped for. Perhaps the Jews of Kheybar would satisfy that ambition.

But as the summer passed, Doughty seemed to be no closer to making that journey. The Arabs were unwilling to run the risk of taking him to a place which lay so close to the two holy cities, where a non-Muslim and those who accompanied him would be in even more danger; and in any case, the destruction of the date harvest by the clouds of locusts he had seen passing overhead meant that there was little reason for them to make the hazardous journey across country which would be swarming with hostile tribes.

The famine was getting worse, and when some of the sheikhs rode off to meet the Fukara sheikhs at the *kella* near Medain Salih, Doughty thought it wise to go with them and see whether his old companions might welcome him back. The garrison seemed pleased enough to see him, but among the Fukara, even his old companion Zeyd dismissed him curtly. 'Khalil is now out of my hands, and I will no more answer for him; besides, when he was with me, and we were so much friends, Khalil called me *hablus*.'[33] Their quarrel was not forgotten after all. The Fukara were probably angered by Doughty's long stay among a tribe with whom they were not on particularly good terms; and anyway, when food was as scarce as it had become, there was little enough reason to welcome another mouth to feed. Motlog, the sheikh, was even more dismissive than Zeyd, in an exchange noted verbatim in the diary. 'Motlog: Khalil, what is your business here with me? Remove to el Ally and lodge at the kella. I do not receive you to lodge with the Arabs, nor will any receive you. D: Nay, all will receive me. It is the way of the Arabs.' But for all Doughty's defiance, he knew that all the stranger could rely on was the law of hospitality – the three days' grace allowed to any stranger as the *thaif Ullah*, the guest of God, especially when he had shared their food.

> I wondered with a secret horror at the fiend-like malice of these fanatical beduins, with whom no keeping touch nor truth of honourable life, no performance of good offices, might win the least favour from the dreary, inhuman, and for our sins, inveterate dotage of their bloodthirsty religion. But I had eaten of their cheer, and might sleep among wolves.[34]

Travels in Arabia Deserta has many coruscating attacks like this one – the crusty old curmudgeon looking back on his sufferings and forgetting the kindness and honourable treatment he received. It was not a fair or just response: the Arabs, after all, were suffering privations of their own. They had been helping and supporting him for weeks, as he forced his company upon them; and in any case, even this apparently unfriendly meeting ended cordially. Doughty might think of them as wolves, but he could not only sleep but also eat among them: the diary records that 'they cooked a good mess for me with *samn* . . . they gave me of it kindly to take away, lest I should hunger'.

His attitude towards all the Arabs he met shifted with his mood and the incidents of the moment. He was often disappointed, but he always believed that the nomads – 'a merry crew of squalid wretches, iniquitous, fallacious, fanatical' though they were – would treat him well. 'I have never arrived at the nomad *menzils** without a feeling of cheerfulness, but I never entered a desert village without misgiving of heart; looking for Koran contentions, the dull manners of peasants, and a grudging hospitality.'[35]

The bedu were never dull: and in this case, they compromised, as they often did. The *Nasrany* tagged along with Motlog and the Fukara for the next two weeks, but kept at a distance. At night-time he would leave his bags in the sheikh's tent for safekeeping, but he himself would sleep away from the main encampment, alone under the stars.

It was August, still high summer, and the Muslim holy month of Ramadan was fast approaching – which meant more abuse for Doughty from 'the impertinent tongues of Ramathan zealots'.[36] Often, among the more relaxed and less fanatical beduin, he responded with a good-humoured raillery – once, for instance, he disarmed criticism by insisting that the wandering Arabs themselves worshipped nothing so faithfully as sex and tobacco – and his reputation for plain speaking and truthfulness generally stood him in good stead. His constant refusal even to consider a pretended conversion to Islam seems to have won him at least as many friends in the desert as it made him enemies in the towns, and he was assiduous in giving the impression of sympathy for his hosts' religion. 'Although he be a Nasrany, he is a *weled*† very well minded toward the Moṣlemin,' Tollog observed on his behalf when he was under attack from the Fukara.[37]

Doughty's real feelings about the Arabs were complex: T. E. Lawrence observed about *Travels in Arabia Deserta*, 'If there is a bias, it

* Camp sites.
† Young man.

will be against the Arabs, for he liked them so much.'[38] He lacked
the imaginative sympathy to see that he might be taking advantage
of them, and he saw their good qualities – their hardiness, their
generosity and their hospitality – and was angry and disappointed
when they turned from him. But these occasional outbursts of bitterness were kept locked secretly in his heart: for all his belief in honesty,
he was well aware that it was invaluable to be thought of as a friend
of the Muslims.

By now, he was well known among the different tribes who
wandered through the area. Word of the *Nasrany*, the *Frenjy*, who
so confidently claimed the regard and protection of the Ottoman
authorities, had spread from campfire to campfire, and there is no
doubt that Ibn Rashid himself had been given detailed reports about
him. Apart from the account from his representative in Teyma, he
had received Motlog at his palace in Hail, and must have quizzed
him then about the stranger who was travelling with his tribe.

There were still friends to be found among the Fukara, despite
Motlog's warning. Even the unpredictable Zeyd seemed more ami-
cable now Doughty's presence was established again, and other Arabs
were willing, too, to welcome him into their tents as a guest. But
his heart was still firmly set on making the journey to Kheybar, and
he was delighted when, late in August, the tribe left the plain around
the *kella* and set off again for Teyma. A small group of beduin was
going to spend Ramadan in the town, and Doughty decided to join
them. From there, perhaps, he might find companions to take him
on to Kheybar.

Travels in Arabia Deserta describes him looking back with bitterness
on the plain, the *kella*, and the mountains which he had once been
so anxious to see – 'the mawkish mummy-house cliffs, the sordid
kella, and perilous *Moghrareba** of Medain Salih'.[39] Later, he described
his initial stay there as 'sixteen weeks of incessant slavery'.[40] No
doubt after the physically draining weeks of the summer he was
weary of both the place and the company, but there is nothing in

* Moors.

the diaries to suggest that such a contemptuous verdict reflects his view at the time. On the contrary, the cheerful welcome he generally had at the *kella* must often have been a welcome relief from the changeable attitude of the nomads.

Nine years later, in Damascus, he happened to meet Mohammed Aly, the *kellaji* with whom he had such a savage quarrel. Certainly then there was no bitterness about the 'sordid kella' or the 'perilous *Moghrareba*': he greeted him warmly, and loaded him with presents of sugar, tea and tobacco for the rest of the garrison and any other old friends who might happen by the fort where he had spent so much time.

But the move back to Teyma was a statement of intent. Along with the *kella*, the monuments and the plain, he was leaving behind the temptation to wait meekly for another pilgrim caravan to take him home again. With hindsight, and bearing in mind the sufferings that the next few months would bring, perhaps there was something ironic about his enthusiasm as the Arabs rode up into the hills, but he saw this as his final, irrevocable breakthrough into the unknown world of Arabia. 'Now, leaving the Turkish haj-road country, I had Nejd before me, the free High Arabia!'[41]

Doughty revealed himself as an unbeliever almost as soon as they arrived at the outskirts of Teyma. Everyone else was fasting because of Ramadan – 'full of groans and complaining' – but he went straight up to a group of labourers leaving the date plantations to demand a branch of the dates and a cup of water. 'Is not this Khalil the kafir, he that was here before?' asked one, horrified that he should want to break the fast, even though, as a traveller, he was entitled to eat.

But there was a worse threat than mere disapproval facing him. He had been told by passing travellers weeks before that the ancient well in the centre of the town had collapsed, and even that he himself was being blamed for it – but he had no reason to suppose that matters were as serious as they apparently were. The townsmen, he heard now, were convinced that the walls around the well had come crashing down because he had written about them in his notebooks: if he were seen again in the town, they would kill him.

His bedu companions urged him to turn and ride at once back to their main camp. When he had been welcomed to Teyma before, he had been in the company of a respected sheikh, Zeyd; now, with a group of nondescript Arab tribesmen, there was no one of rank to protect him. But the obstinate *Nasrany* was still sitting there calmly, arguing that he would surely be able to make the Teyamena see reason, when they were joined by two townsmen who had apparently ridden out especially to meet him. One of them was a leading Teyma sheikh – and, far from wanting to kill Doughty for having by some black art destroyed the well, he was anxious to persuade him to use his undoubted skills as a *Frenjy* to build it up again.

The sheikh was a well-travelled man, who had visited Damascus and Iraq, and yet he seemed to feel a simple faith in Doughty's skills. Doughty himself certainly welcomed the opportunity: even though he had no experience at all of building wells, he believed he could construct a sound wall that would enhance his reputation among the bedu. Success would immeasurably enhance his prestige; he never considered the possibility that he might be exaggerating his talents.

But for all the confidence he had shown around the campfire, there was a moment's understandable nervousness as he rode in with his two escorts through the narrow alleyways he remembered from his last visit to the town – 'Hasan! Art thou able to defend me if there should meet with us any evil persons?' – but throughout his six-week stay in Teyma he was better accepted than he was in any other Arab town. The nomads' distrust of the townsmen was, it seemed, as deep-seated and ultimately as ill-founded as had been the townsmen's of them. The Teyamena were disturbed by his openly contemptuous attitude towards the fast, but amused, too, at the way the bedu had warned him about their likely intentions towards him. 'It is like the *beduw*! but here, Khalil, thou hast nothing to fear, although there be some dizzy-headed among us like themselves!'[42]

Doughty responded to the challenge of the well with gusto. He envisaged camel loads of square stone blocks being hauled up from the ruins of the old town, curving new ramparts rising proudly upon the foundations of the old, with tie-walls stretching back into the earth behind – a well that should be a suitable memorial to himself in the years to come. The Arabs, though, had no appetite for such grandiose schemes. The walls, after all, had only collapsed around one side of the well: for the time being, they reasoned, the other side could still be used to draw water. The excuse he was given was that the sheikhs were absent in Hail, and that nothing could be done until they returned, but there were those too who wondered whether his enthusiasm might not have exceeded his competence.

> Some would ascertain from me how I composed the stones, that the work should not slide; they enquired 'if I were a mason, or had I any former experience of stone-building?' and because I stood on no rewards, and would be content with a *thelul** saddled, they judged it to be of my insufficiency, and that should little avail them.[43]

Perhaps the Arabs' simple faith in his western skills was less complete than it had appeared. Once the initial queues had died down, and the novelty of the European *hakim* had worn off, his attempts at doctoring, too, were greeted with as little enthusiasm as he had found elsewhere.

For all that, though, he encountered little outright hostility. His hosts were willing enough to give him another chance to study the ruins outside the town that he had glimpsed so hurriedly on his last visit – the surviving stone walls of the old settlement, half buried in the sand, and the wreckage of a group of pillars, presumably from some long-gone pre-Islamic temple. There were no inscriptions there to add to his collection, but in the centre of Teyma he missed the most exciting opportunity he had had so far. One of the stones that had crashed down from the wall of the collapsing well-pit was covered in inscriptions, which he had no chance to copy down. It was an ironic failure: this, later known as the Stone of Teyma, now standing in the Louvre, would have been the finest of his discoveries.[44]

It was Doughty's health, which he so often blamed for interrupting his travelling, that prevented him from copying down this most important set of carvings. Probably he hoped to do the work later at his leisure, but he was interrupted by a sudden and terrifying blindness. It was the most frightening incident of his whole time in Arabia: while he had accepted from the start the danger of violence, or of a

* A camel bred for riding.

lingering and painful death in the desert, the possibility of disease, still less of blindness, seems never to have occurred to him, until one morning he awoke with his eyes sore and swollen.

The Arabs told him on no account to put water near them, but he, trusting to his medical book rather than their advice, sponged them continually. It was the Arabs, and not the self-appointed medical man, who were proved right – a point they did not fail to make to him with an understandable measure of *schadenfreude* as he struggled around, virtually blind, for a week and a half.

> Ten twilight days passed over me, and I thought, 'If the eyes should fail me! – and in this hostile land, so far from any good.' Some of the village, as I went painfully creeping by the ways, and hardly seeing the ground, asked me, 'Where be now thy medicines!' and they said again the old saw, 'Apothecary, heal thyself.'[45]

Others, perhaps more kindly, suggested that he had been struck by a 'looker', someone with malignant powers, who could kill or injure with a glance. The disease, according to Doughty, though, was ophthalmia, something he had noticed was common among the Arabs. Although its effects began to ease after a fortnight of near-blindness, his eyes remained very weak throughout his time in Arabia.

One mark of his popularity among the people of Teyma was the number of offers of marriage he had from the young women there. During his time in the desert Doughty's impeccably correct sympathy for his hostesses brought him a succession of proposals, made more or less directly and more or less seriously. Zeyd's wife Hirfa, according to Doughty at least, had not been displeased when her husband had offered to pass her over to him as his new wife, and since then there had been several other contenders. As he sat in the field just outside Teyma, where the bedu were encamped, and where he had set up his medical 'practice', a number of young widows and unmarried women offered themselves as possible partners. Some were attracted by the prospect of marrying a man who they believed had the confidence of the highest Ottoman government officials; some wanted him to stay with the Arabs, and others suggested that they would accompany him back to his own country.

That journey, though, remained far from his mind. His aim was still to reach Kheybar, and Teyma was nothing but a stage on the way. No one, either among the bedu or among the townsmen, was willing to take him to the town, where the reception from the Ottoman authorities might be hostile – 'Wellah, I tell thee, between us is nothing but the cutting of wezands!' declared one bedu sheikh to him.

At Ibn Rashid's own capital of Hail, though, he calculated, he might well find a companion, and also a recommendation from the Emir himself. That, too, would give him the opportunity to meet the 'mighty prince of beduin blood, who lorded it over the tribes',[46] about whom he had heard so much at Maan and at Petra, before he had even set foot in Arabia.

He had already seen evidence of Ibn Rashid's power in the fearful flight of the Fukara after his first visit to Teyma; he must also have read about Hail and its earlier European visitors as he pored over Zehme's compendium in his tent. According to the people of Teyma, Ibn Rashid himself might prove hostile to the wandering *Nasrany* about whom he had already heard – more to the point, perhaps, he might be displeased with them for sending Doughty on to him. But visiting the legendary desert capital had been one of his earliest motives for travelling into Arabia at all, and once he found a bedu guide in Teyma who offered to take him there, Doughty was anxious to start on the journey deeper into the Arabian heartland.

He rode off out of Teyma with a group of Bishr Arabs, leaving the townspeople and his old Fukara companions behind. It was another gruelling journey – the diary notes successive days of nine hours' travel, seven hours, eight hours, eight and a half hours – and where the Fukara had been generally friendly, this new party of nomads seemed from the start intolerant and threatening.

As they pushed further east, he also noticed that all the tribeswomen they met wore face-masks, only their eyes visible. The easy, relaxed chatter and flirting he had enjoyed with Hirfa and her companions was only a memory. The signs were all ominous: now, he was in another country, the 'jealous and Wahaby Nejd'. He was moving into the harsh reality of the desert and its people.

Several times his new companions had second thoughts, urging him to turn back and rejoin the Fukara rather than travel on eastwards. He was travelling, said one of them, into a country that would not welcome him and his foreign ways.

> 'Khalil, the people where we are going are jealous. Let them not see thee writing, for be sure they will take it amiss; but wouldst thou write, write covertly, and put away these leaves of books. Thou wast hitherto with the beduw, and the beduw have known thee what thou art; but, hearest thou? they are not like goodhearted in yonder villages!'[47]

But the journey east into the highlands was hard enough itself without worrying about the reception he might get at the end of it. He struggled on with his ailing camel, riding fifty miles in a single day, with no break for rest or food. He could not afford to lag behind: there was the constant worry that his newfound companions, anxious that they might be attacked themselves at any moment by robbers, might simply leave him behind in the desert if he failed to keep up.

After ten days' riding they arrived at the little settlement of Mogug, where Doughty's camel simply refused to go any further. In this shabby, tumbledown village he rested for a day and a night, persuading the local sheikh to force one of his companions to wait with him, even though the rest of the party were pressing on without them.

If in one sense he had travelled deeper than ever before into the unknown desert, in another he quickly discovered that he was, as he put it, 'in the world again': the further behind he left the *kella*, the closer he drew to Baghdad and its trade routes. Later, in Hail, he would be astonished to see tin flasks of gunpowder stamped with the manufacturer's name, 'Hall of Dartford'; in Aneyza he bought English cod liver oil in the *suk*. He had read about the ancient trading caravans that once snaked through the desert, and even seen the carvings and inscriptions the traders of long ago had left behind on the rocks; now, centuries later, in the little town of Mogug, he saw German Zündhölzer lighters from Vienna offered to the bedu tribesmen, instead of the flint and steel with which they started their fires and lit their pipes.

It was the end of October, sultry weather with rain and lightning – but at last Doughty was within reach of Hail itself. The villagers of Mogug would do nothing to stop him – if the Emir had any objection to his presence, no doubt he would deal with the matter himself – and in the morning, before he set out on the last stage of his journey, the stranger was given a final breakfast coffee. There was another day's journey, a night spent in the open air in the streets of Gofar, another small village, and then, early in the morning, they arrived at the high turreted walls of the ancient city of Hail.

Doughty was slumped on his camel with tiredness, but his companion insisted that he should walk, rather than ride, through the streets of the town. He pretended that there were low gateways to negotiate, but the real reason was that the sight of a Christian gazing down proudly from his camel might anger the people: far better for both their sakes for Doughty to arrive humbly and on foot. Perhaps it was a wise precaution, but far from arousing the hostility of the townspeople, their arrival passed almost unnoticed. For nearly an hour Doughty sat in the marketplace, deserted by his frightened companion, who no doubt considered that his duty had been fulfilled by bringing him this far. But the men in the town followed the Persian fashion of dyeing their beards with saffron: for once, Doughty's conspicuous colouring did not immediately give him away as a foreigner.

However, inside the castle, alerted to his presence by a courtier whom Doughty had first met months before in the *kella*, Ibn Rashid and his advisers were discussing what they should do with him. For all the exhausted Doughty knew, they could be deciding on his imprisonment, his immediate banishment, or even his death: huddled, starving, against the wall, though, he had thought only of whether he would be given breakfast.

In the short term, at least, he had little to worry about. First, the Emir's steward called him in to eat in the sheikhs' guest hall. It was not an appetizing meal – 'the worst dates of their desert world', he said[48] – but it did at least suggest that he was not to be hauled off at once as a criminal or a spy. Then, a little later, he was summoned in to meet the Nejd ruler himself.

152

He had first heard of Ibn Rashid when he was in Petra and Maan. He had imagined him then as a worthy successor to King David, ruling in his remote kingdom with wisdom and justice – or possibly, less believably, as some kind of Arab Robin Hood, protecting travellers from the depredations of robber chiefs through the exercise of his power. Even Doughty had not been completely immune from the romantic view of the Orient that he so despised.

Since then, though, as he travelled south with the Hadj and then wandered through the desert, a different picture had gradually built up of a powerful and cruel leader, a man who punished wrongdoers swiftly and brutally, a tyrant who had fought his way to the throne over the bodies of his murdered relatives. Doughty had seen the fear of the bedu as their eyes ranged the horizon for his avenging soldiers, and heard the warnings of townsmen and nomads alike that he could expect no mercy from the mighty king. None of this can have prepared him for the man he saw before him, lying on his elbow by the fireside, surrounded by cushions, and staring at him silently in the twilight. The diary describes the scene. '... A square room, stained with ochre, with the floor and also walls handsomely carpeted, where he was couched in the gloom. I saluted him with "Salaam aleyk", and he did not return my salutation . . .'

Mohammed Ibn Rashid wore his hair braided into long side-locks like the bedu, framing a lean, bird-like, yellowish complexion, with the unhealthy look of a man who had struggled through years of sickness and disease. Nine years earlier, while Doughty had been plodding blamelessly away in the depths of the Bodleian Library, Ibn Rashid had been fighting his way to the throne. Since then, with a mixture of generalship and subtle diplomacy – a later traveller observed that he 'preferred politics to fighting, and gold to lead and steel'[49] – he had been gradually extending his influence among the towns of Shammar, while avoiding as best he could direct conflicts with the might of the Ottoman empire or with his rival in Riyadh, Ibn Saud.

The two men, one a ruthless and ambitious ruler with the blood of his family and his rivals on his hands, and the other a scholar and traveller, a man of peace, could hardly have been less likely to appeal to each other. But Doughty blundered on with his greeting.

He should have waited until he was spoken to, and in any case, he should not have presumed, as an unbeliever, to offer Ibn Rashid the Muslim greeting. But the *faux pas* was ignored. 'Sit down,' commanded the Arab Prince, and proceeded to quiz him closely.

Where had he come from? Who had he been with? What did he think of the bedu? Ibn Rashid must have known the answers to most of the questions already, since his spies and agents had met Doughty in the *kella*, in El Ally, in Teyma and in Mogug, but the honest answers he received apparently pleased him. The Emir, like his courtiers, still remembered the visit of William Gifford Palgrave in disguise fifteen years before: one old sheikh leaned towards him, and whispered, 'This is not like him who came hither – thou canst remember, Mohammed in what year – but one that tells all things plainly.'[50]

In 1862 Palgrave had arrived in Hail, like Doughty, professing to be a doctor. But he and his companion were secretly serving two masters, studying the possibility of building French influence for the Emperor, Napoleon III, and reporting to the Jesuits in Damascus about the potential for converting the Arabs to Christianity: they travelled in disguise, pretending to be wandering Syrians. Palgrave, the son of a glittering aristocratic English family, took on the character of the travelling healer Seleem Abou Mahmood El 'Eys (the Silent).

By the time the two impostors left Hail, the Emir, Mohammed's brother Telal, was convinced they were not what they seemed, and there were those in the court who wanted them done away with. Whether or not any detailed knowledge of their secret missions ever leaked out in the city, there is no doubt that the memory of their sustained deception still lingered.

Now, though, Mohammed was clearly doing his best to put Doughty at his ease, at least while he found out more about him and his reasons for being in Nejd. He invited him to see the Arabian antelope, the *wothyhi*, where it roamed in his palace gardens. The diary, scribbled up later in the privacy of his room, notes that Doughty had 'pleasant and easy conversation' with the Prince, although there was clearly a hint of menace from one senior member of his entourage, who 'enquired of me did I hope to see my country again'. But even when the sensitive question of religion came up, Ibn Rashid remained restrained and civil. Instead of using the contemptuous term *Nasrany*, to which Doughty had grown accustomed in the desert, he asked him whether he were *Mesihy*, a follower of the Messiah. It was a small but reassuring gesture: Doughty had made an unusually successful beginning.

But it was still a delicate situation, with Ibn Rashid anxious to know exactly why the stranger had come, and what support, if any, he had from the authorities of the Ottoman empire or from the European nations. Descriptions of him as a spy and an agent of the *Dowla* must have reached the palace, and Doughty's unsure grasp of Arabic did little to improve matters when he was asked a direct question. 'But what could move thee, he said, to take such a journey? I responded suddenly, "*El-elum*, the liberal sciences," but the sense of this plural is, in Nejd and in the Beduin talk, tidings . . .'[51]

He had inadvertently told the nervous Prince that he had come to his country seeking news and information – that he was indeed a spy. His next *faux pas*, a piece of simple bad luck, followed almost immediately. The Emir, interested to see how extensive was Doughty's command of the language, ordered him to read from a huge leather-bound volume of Arabic history kept in the chamber, and pointed at random to a chapter where he should start.

Doughty read the Arabic text obediently: '*The king . . . slew all his brethren and kindred . . .* ' The passage referred to a long-dead ruler, but Ibn Rashid was well aware of his own reputation as a sort of Arabian Richard III, steeped in the blood of his own kinsmen. The cruel coincidence of the passage Doughty was ordered to read sounds almost like a scene from Shakespeare.

Only a few years earlier the ruler who now sat before him had first stabbed his nephew in order to seize control, and then butchered the dead boy's cousins, their slaves and their entire households in an attempt to make himself secure on the throne. The suave Hamud, Mohammed's cousin and heir, the man who was to prove Doughty's friend and protector, had been his cousin's henchman in this bloody night of the long knives.

It was *Sheytan** that I had lighted upon such a bloody text;
the Emir was visibly moved! and with the quick feeling of

---

* The devil; the devil's work.

the Arabs, he knew that I regarded him as a murderous man. 'Not there!' he said hastily, 'but read here! – out of this chapter above,' beating the place with his finger . . . [52]

Doughty's impetuosity, his tendency to speak first and think later, now seems one of his more endearing characteristics, but it brought him a number of tense moments. There were worrying signs of how his own treatment might change – as they left to visit the gardens, for instance, he was handed a piece of paper which had been taken from another Christian who had arrived at the court. No word was said of the unknown man's fate, or why his letter from the Patriarchate of Damascus had been confiscated; a little later he heard of a Christian visitor offering vaccinations who was killed in the desert by the bedu. Perhaps he was the same unfortunate traveller whose letter of introduction had been seized, or perhaps he was another unwanted visitor. Either way, it was a chilling reminder of the way that a Christian or a European could vanish into the dark shadows of this desert court, and be utterly forgotten.

But Mohammed was still treating Doughty gently: perhaps the best way to ferret out what the stranger's intentions were would be to put him at his ease. He escorted him on a tour of the palace grounds, and asked him, as if in simple conversation, where the next stage of his journeying might take him. Doughty, shrewd enough to know that a request to travel to Kheybar might require a degree of diplomatic preparation on his part, told him reassuringly that he was bound for Baghdad, out of Nejd, and out of Arabia – a sensible route, in fact, for a European who wanted to make his way home. With some relief, no doubt, the Emir promised to help him on his way.

The 'narrow, dark, and unswept cell' where Doughty was put up offered little comfort, but it did give him enough privacy to resume his diary, which he had left unwritten for several days, following the advice of his bedu companions. It was written up quietly and, as far as he could, secretly. One of the complaints about Palgrave had been that he 'had written whatsoever he enquired';[53] and in any case, Doughty had not forgotten the rumours that had swept Teyma about the malign effect of his 'writing up' the town well. It was time to bear in mind his early note to himself to be circumspect.

In the court there was intense interest in his medical powers – Mohammed's kinsman and heir, Hamud, for instance, asked him in a whisper whether he had a cure for impotence, while the Emir himself requested a list of the medicaments he carried – but among the people of the town he found the same difficulties he had encountered all along. Within a few days it was clear that few people were willing to hand over money in return for his attention.

Palgrave before him had much the same experience with his doctoring. In his case, the fact that he was travelling in disguise, desperate to establish himself beyond suspicion as a *hakim*, meant that he was better prepared than Doughty – compared with the single, largely unthumbed copy of Taverner, he carried two European medical texts and a couple of Arabic books, as well as a wider variety of medicines and ointments designed to impress potential patients – but even so, he found the Arabs implacable in their refusal to pay unless and until they were cured. Palgrave, too, was more shamefaced about the 'horrid . . . most scandalous imposture . . . unpardonable cheat' of his doctoring; Doughty, for all his refusal to take refuge in a disguise, seemed far more relaxed about pretending to a skill and a learning that he did not possess.

But if it did not bring in money, his deception did win him influential friends. The four reals Hamud eventually gave him for curing the dysentery from which his wife and young son were suffering was little enough, but it was more than Doughty gathered in from any of his other patients – and, more to the point, the Prince's gratitude almost certainly saved his life later in his stay.

For more than a week Doughty was well treated. But his behaviour had done little to assuage the Emir's suspicions: word must have got back, for instance, of his warning to the Emir's kinsmen that British naval vessels were implacable in the fight against slavery. 'As for all who deal in slaves, we are appointed by God to their undoing. We hunt the cursed slave-sail upon all seas, as you hunt the hyena,' he had told them one night over supper.[54] When the remark was passed on to Ibn Rashid himself, it can hardly have reassured him about the friendly intentions of the Europeans in general, or the role of this one in particular.

And Ibn Rashid needed reassurance. When they talked about the opening-up of America, for instance, he asked Doughty pointedly whether the continent did not have inhabitants before the Europeans arrived. Before, Doughty had contemptuously told Arabs who accused him of spying out the land ready for a foreign invasion that there was nothing to spy on and less to covet in the inhospitable sand deserts of Arabia; with the ruler of much of that same despised country, he had to get across the same message rather more tactfully.

To a degree, he succeeded: his accommodation might be shabby and uncomfortable, but the Emir's staff sent him over a breakfast of dates each morning. It was also a mark of official approval that some leading citizen would usually entertain him for a meal later in the day – and if that failed, he could always go to the *Mothif*, the government guesthouse. For the first few days of his time in Hail, at least, he could rely on the powerful protection of the Emir's approval.

But his health had been severely tested by the hard ride from Teyma, and it was some time before he felt fit enough to set off on anything more than the gentlest of strolls through the streets of the town: when he did, it marked a turning-point in his stay. He took a long walk around the town walls, wandering to the surrounding hill-tops and through the ruins of a former suburb, and returned to find the marketplace abuzz with talk of his expedition. He had been seen drawing and making notes, causing new gossip about his intentions. A couple of days later he noted that the men of the town were no longer asking him to eat with them – 'Perhaps some of them little pleased with my free bearing,' he scribbled anxiously in his diary. For several days he recorded little but notes of the food he managed to scrape together – a few dates, or a handful of rice, usually eaten alone in his little hovel.

The Emir had left Hail to inspect the outlying parts of his estates, and with him had gone Doughty's protection. His advisers were already warning him of the dangers posed by the *Nasrany*'s continued presence, while the more hostile Muslims in Hail took their chance to increase the pressure on their unwanted guest. When Ibn Rashid returned, it was to find feeling running high against the unbeliever. He sent for Doughty almost straight away, but any hope that they might return to the earlier easy and friendly relationship was soon dashed: Doughty's greeting was ignored, and the Emir, surrounded by 'malignant young fanatics' who, Doughty was convinced, had lost no opportunity to turn him against his eccentric guest, asked pointedly what he had been doing and what he had seen around the city.

Doughty said he was ill, and spent most of his time stretched out weakly on the floor of his lodging. He had never properly recovered from the trials of the journey into the town, and the lack of food over the last few days was affecting him. But it was the manner of the reply that did the damage: even during the audience before Ibn Rashid, he was almost fainting.

He found it hard to follow the conversation; his mind was wandering, and some of his replies seemed barely to make sense. It looked to the court and the Emir as if the tetchy foreigner was dozing off in the very presence of the ruler. Whether the Prince was genuinely offended or not, it was a good excuse for him to bring the interview to an abrupt end, and he swept angrily away. From that moment, as Doughty lay in his room, spies from the court would frequently burst in upon him, checking to see that he was not secretly writing down information about the town.

And he had more worries on his mind. As it became clear that he could expect little practical help from the Emir in finding a way out of Arabia and back to the coast, so he began to look to his own resources. They were slim indeed, and whether or not he travelled on to Kheybar, he would need to pay companions to travel with him: the few possessions he had would have to be sold. He would simply have to beg or borrow space to sleep in a tent, and hope to hire himself a camel.

One of his patients was prevailed on to give him some six or seven reals for the toothless old beast he had bought among the Fukara – Doughty had little enough faith anyway that the mangy creature would have the strength for the journey; perhaps it was significant that the purchaser had come to him for treatment for his eyes! – and another four or five came from the sale of his tent. It was not much, and it left him entirely dependent on the companions he might find for the journey – but it might just see him to the coast. Certainly, in Hail, his prospects seemed to be deteriorating by the day.

And as word spread that Doughty had lost Ibn Rashid's support, he began to suffer more frequent insults and even occasional attacks. One sheikh from a group of foreign bedu who had travelled to Hail for talks with the Emir was only dissuaded with difficulty from plunging his dagger into the *Nasrany*'s breast, and in another incident even the humble keeper of the Emir's coffee house struck him with a camel stick.

The first attack Doughty deflected by appealing both to his age and to his status as a traveller. 'If thou mayest come even to the years of this beard, thou wilt have learned, young man, not to offer any violence to the guest,' he told the sheikh.[55] No doubt his travelling had aged him, and certainly even as a youth he had always behaved older than his years, but the appeal to the gravitas of age from a man barely thirty-four years old might have caused a smile in any less desperate circumstances.

In the coffee house, though, no one raised an eyebrow at the attack – and in any case, Doughty had no choice but to rely on his wits. Physical resistance could only ever be a last resort. Alone in the desert, he might hit back, or even draw his pistol to outface an attacker, but he had learned from his confrontation with Mohammed Aly in the *kella* that violence in public could only turn against him. Surrounded by Muslims, it would be suicide for an unbeliever to strike out at one of the faithful, even in self-defence.

So when the coffee-house keeper attacked him, he went straight to the Emir. And he had more to complain of: much of the money he had made from selling his possessions had been stolen from its hiding place among his bags. But there was little the Emir or his officers could, or would, do for him. He threatened to dismiss the *kawaji* for his insolence, and made at least some effort to find out who was responsible for the theft of the reals from Doughty's bags, but he was plainly tiring of the *Nasrany* and the trouble he was causing in the town.

There was a brief respite with the arrival of the Hadj caravan on its way from Baghdad to Mecca. Many of the camels were laden with bales of cloth and other supplies that the traders had brought with them; there were butchers' stalls, bakers, and all the tradesmen that Doughty must have remembered from his own journey with the caravan from Damascus a year before. Just before they left he was approached by one of the pilgrims, 'a pale alien's face with a chestnut beard'. At first he could not catch what was said, but then the stranger asked, in a low voice: 'If I speak in the French language, will you understand me?'

The two stood together in the marketplace, surrounded by the chattering Arabs. The stranger was an Italian, who had been travelling in the Middle East for eight years, and who had become a Muslim. His plan was to return north with the Hadj, and wander through the lands east of the river Jordan, before returning home to Italy, 'wiping off the rust of the Mohammedan life', and publishing the story of his travels. Hurriedly, they swapped experiences, but the Hadj was moving on. As the Italian mounted his camel to depart, the two men clasped hands and exchanged names, like two spies in a foreign and hostile country.

Doughty remembered for several years the name the Italian had given him, Francesco Ferrari, although he admitted that he had no way of knowing whether it was the man's true name or one given simply to deflect further questions. Later he passed on the details first to Italian officials in Damascus, and again in Italy, but no one had heard of him. Like the Christian traveller whose letter had been seized in the court, he had simply been swallowed by the vast, mysterious darkness of Arabia. Doughty knew then, and pondered later, that he himself could easily have been lost in just the same way.

But he had little time then to worry about the mysterious Italian. No sooner had the Hadj caravan gone than the Emir's men sought him out. He had already let it be known that he wanted to travel on not to Baghdad but to Kheybar, and the soldiers had found some bedu who would take him along the way.

Once the word was given, his departure was brutal and hurried. If he delayed, they told him, the Emir would have his head cut off. Even Hamud, still grateful for Doughty's treatment of his family, could do nothing to dissuade Ibn Rashid from having him thrown out, although he won him permission from the soldiers to make one last appeal to the Emir himself.

There seemed to be every chance that he was riding like the Christian traveller he had heard of earlier, to a lonely death out in the desert, where no one would ever know what had happened to him. He did not trust the bedu who had been found to accompany him, even though the Emir himself wrote him a safe-conduct pass when he pleaded for it. Mohammed wanted him out of Hail. 'I asked, as the Emir was going, "When shall I depart?" – "At thy pleasure" – "Tomorrow?" – "Nay, today." He had turned the back, and was crossing the *Meshab*.'*[56]

He was to be taken to another tribe some seventy miles south, who would escort him on to Kheybar. That at least was the plan, but Doughty was by now convinced that he would be done away with on the way, safe conduct or no safe conduct – Palgrave, after all, had been given a letter to the authorities in Riyadh which was virtually an invitation to them to put him to death. And yet there was no choice: Doughty asked the captain of the Emir's guard to swear to him that there was no plan to have him murdered, and listened as the officer told the bedu that if anything happened to the *Nasrany*, they would lose their heads.

With that assurance he had to be content, and he shuffled off out of the gate on a hired camel which the Emir, either in a last fit of generosity or, more likely, in his anxiety to see the back of him, had paid for. Ringing in his ears was a warning from one of the bedu who were to be his companions. 'Make haste along with us out of Hail, stand not, nor return upon thy footsteps, for then they will kill thee.'[57]

* Open courtyard.

Chapter Six

oughty, though he had no idea where he was going, had
not the slightest thought of retracing his footsteps. His concern was rather that his newfound companions, having
seen how slightly he was regarded by the leading citizens of Hail,
might simply do away with him in the desert. He had the public
promise of Ibn Rashid's officer that nothing of the sort was intended,
and also his safe-conduct signed by the Emir himself – but different
orders might have been given behind his back. The wide horizons
of the desert, as he well knew, could be a very private place for a
killing.

Doughty walked as the others rode: weary though he was, it was
not worth the risk of causing an argument over who might ride the
camel that had been hired for him. All he had to defend himself was
his native wit and his revolver – and if he ever used the gun, then
the hand of every Arab that he met would be against him. Once he
had fired a shot in anger, he might die violently, or he might struggle
to a lonely and agonizing death in the desert, but he would certainly
never leave Arabia.

The Arabs, though, were interested simply in getting rid of their
unwelcome companion as quickly as they could, with as little risk

to themselves as possible. The Emir's instructions had been to take him to join Kasim Ibn Barak, a bedu sheikh who might have him taken on to Kheybar, and when they arrived at his camp at the end of the fourth day, they simply put down Doughty's bags from their camels and made as if to ride off and leave him. Doughty, bolder in the camp than he might have been alone in the desert, dragged one of the camels to the ground by its beard, insisting that they should deliver the message from Mohammed Ibn Rashid personally. Ibn Barak was at a loss. 'Well, say, Khalil, what shall I do in this case, for wellah, I cannot tell; betwixt us and those of Kheybar and the Dowla there is only debate and cutting of throats . . .'[1] Ibn Barak was as unwilling as Ibn Rashid to have dealings with the Ottoman authorities in Kheybar, and instead he ordered Doughty's two companions to take him on to the sheikh of another tribe who was encamped nearby.

But Doughty's two companions were so desperate to be rid of him that they ignored the sheikh's instructions. Despite their oaths and promises – 'not binding, which was made to a *Nasrany*!' they declared – they left him at the first Arab tent they found, where an old woman and her daughter-in-law were preparing a meal for their menfolk. The *Nasrany*, torn between the dread of outright attack and the terror of abandonment, was being bundled around the desert like an unwelcome and embarrassing parcel.

It could have been a disaster – left alone, with no recommendation, and no one to speak for him. But the poor herdsman whose homestead it was shared what little food he had, and promised that the next day he would take him personally to yet another sheikh, who might be able to help him on his way. Doughty's two companions had used the chop-logic of religion to justify breaking faith with him; this poverty-stricken family was different. 'These were simple, pious, and not formal, praying Arabs, having in their mouths no cavilling questions of religion, but they were full of the godly humanity of the wilderness.'[2] Once again it was on the straightforward human decency of the poor nomads that he was able to rely, rather than on the formal morality of religion. The herdsman, who rejoiced in the name of Thaifullah, or Guest of God, did indeed ride with him for an hour the next day to deliver him to the camp of

Eyada Ibn Ajjueyn, where he introduced him as a skilful doctor. Eyada's tribesman, Ghroceyb, promised to take him on to Kheybar, in return for payment of four reals. Doughty now had less than thirty reals left in his purse, but he had no choice: another four days' travelling would see him finally in the town which had been his obsession for months. And once there, perhaps he would at last be able to scrape together a little money by offering his cures to the people.

It was a strange and unfamiliar journey, partly because of the gloomy weather, with heavy grey cloud where before there had been beating sun, and partly because of the grotesque volcanic landscape. There was nothing but ash and cinders underfoot, beaten down into a firm path by the passage of thousands of camels over the centuries. Around them was a cracked and twisted chaos of ancient lava, and further off, the tortured silhouettes of extinct volcanoes. On his way to the city which he had been so eager to visit for so long, Doughty should have been enthusiastic, even excited, but the atmosphere of the journey was one of overpowering menace.

First, there was Ghroceyb himself. He was on foot, half walking and half running as he spied out the best path for the camel to take. He looked about anxiously, alternating between fervent prayer and nervous glances at his matchlock, which hung from the camel-saddle. It was loaded and primed, ready for use against any attacker, but the anxious Ghroceyb wanted even more protection than the gun could provide. At one point he turned suddenly and caught sight of Doughty jotting down a reading from his aneroid: if the *Nasrany* had knowledge of such wonderful things, he begged, would he not cast a spell to guard them through this dangerous place?

As they descended to the oasis, swarms of flies gathered around them, and the atmosphere grew hotter and more sultry. Even the barren dust beneath them seemed to threaten evil.

> The squalid ground is whitish with crusts of bitter salt-warp . . . and stained with filthy rust: whence their fable, that 'this earth purges herself of the much blood of the Yahud, that was spilt in the conquest of Kheybar' . . . A heavy presentiment of evil lay upon my heart as we rode in this deadly drowned atmosphere.[3]

Now, Doughty was riding into the very heart of the 'Apostle's Country', where he could expect even less tolerance than he had found elsewhere, and where Ibn Rashid's safe-conduct would carry little weight. The people of Kheybar were traditionally at odds with the ruler of Hail.

Night was falling as Doughty and Ghroceyb entered nervously through the town gate: the *Nasrany* was friendless, in a town in which he could expect little mercy. Ghroceyb, worried about an ancient blood-feud, was anxious to be away again by first light, but he found friends to provide an upstairs room and a meal of dates – although their exertions on the journey had left them unable to eat until they had quenched their raging thirst.

Both their hosts and the townsfolk at large were intensely curious about the stranger in Kheybar. Neither Doughty nor Ghroceyb had said anything about his religion, but the Arabs had their suspicions, which were confirmed when his host's son showed him around the town and led him, as if by accident, straight into the courtyard of a mosque. His hasty turning away from the building without offering a prayer was proof enough and, once again, he faced the direct question that he dreaded.

> Abd el-Hady locked his street door; and coming above
> stairs, 'Tell me,' said he, 'art thou a Moslem? And if no,
> I will lay thy things on a cow and send thee to a place of
> safety.' 'Host, I am of the Engleys; my nation, thou mayest
> have heard say, is friendly with the Dowla, and I am of
> them whom ye name the Nasara.'[4]

The scandalous news spread rapidly through the town, and those who were offered medicines for sale muttered darkly that they would soon get them for nothing. At the first sign of trouble Doughty had hidden his pistol under his robe again and, sure enough, a couple of soldiers arrived to bundle him out of the house, ignoring his desperate questions about whether they intended to kill him in the street. He was to be questioned by their commandant, Abdullah Es Siruan, the Ottomans' military ruler in the town.

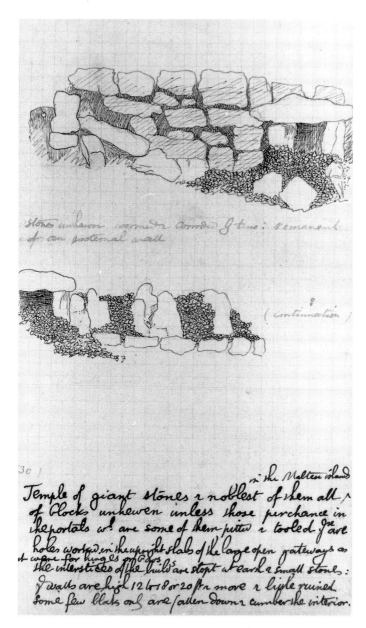

stones unhewn ~~worn in~~ corroded of time: remanent
of an exterual wall

(continuation)

30

in the Maltese island

Temple of giant stones & noblest of them all &
of blocks unhewen unless those perchance in
the portals w.ᵈ are some of them putted & tooled & are
holes worked in the upright slabs of the large open gateways as
it ~~were~~ for hinges on & days the interstices of the build are stopt at each & small stones :
& walls are high 12 to 18 or 20 ftn more & litle ruined
some few blats only are fallen down & cumber the interior.

A page from Doughty's European notebook. His European diaries were
filled with notes and sketches of the places he visited, including this one
from Malta of a ruined temple he called 'noblest of them all'.

Doughty in Damascus. This photograph carries a note on the back in pencil, signed by T.E. Lawrence: 'CMD in Damascus 187–, from a drawing by a French artist, in the possession of Mrs Doughty.'

Above Doughty's sketch of the interior of the *kella* from which he explored the ruins of Medain Salih.

Left Written often on camel-back, hidden beneath his robes as he worked, Doughty's Arabian diaries are a miracle of precision.

Left Doughty's sketch of the first monument at Medain Salih.

Below Doughty was constantly sketching as he travelled. This pencil drawing shows an encampment of the Sehamma tribe.

Bottom Doughty's view of the harsh lava plain of the Harra, across which he travelled. In the foreground are the remains of an antique stone circle.

It was a rowdy and antagonistic meeting, conducted in the street before a crowd that could easily have become a lynch-mob. Doughty's bags were dragged out of the house, and his possessions held up for inspection. At first there was little enough to be listed by the town scribe – a camel bridle, a water bag, bags of dates, a tin of tea, scanty supplies of milk-curds and rice – but as Siruan delved deeper into the bags, so the suspicions grew. Doughty's host shouted out with horror when a comb was pulled out – such a 'perilous instrument' could only be some evil foreign snare for good Muslims, he declared; a bundle of books was to be sent post-haste to the Pasha at Medina; a brass tape-measure caused more anxiety; and then, worst of all from Doughty's point of view, his empty pistol-case was dragged from the bottom of one of the bags.

If there was a pistol-case, then where was the pistol? Doughty, the revolver nestling against his bare chest, said nothing – and one of the crowd shouted that it must have been confiscated in Hail. It was a good enough explanation, and no one thought of searching the *Nasrany* himself; in any case, Siruan was anxious to move on to the real object of his search.

'Have you money with you?' he asked, threatening punishment if the *Nasrany* tried to hide it, and wheedlingly promising reward if he handed it over. Slowly, Doughty opened the tin of tea that had been pulled from his bag. Buried deep inside was his purse, and inside that were six Turkish liras. With those liras, of course, lay all Doughty's hopes of finding a passage back to the coast, but with the baying crowd behind him and the grasping commandant in front, he had no choice but to hand them over, 'for their better keeping', as Siruan said smugly, carefully adding the liras to the official list of Doughty's possessions.

His host of the night before would not have him back in the house unless he abandoned his Christian faith and became a Muslim, so Doughty was sent to lodge with one of the soldiers while his books and papers were sent off for examination in Medina. In the meantime, it was decided, he might practise his medicine and keep his few provisions, but he was little better than a prisoner waiting to hear his sentence.

While Siruan shouted and raged, stirring up the crowd with

bloodthirsty promises to chop off the stranger's head if the Pasha at Medina should order his execution, a quiet, dignified Arab approached Doughty and sat down next to him. This was Mohammed En Nejumy, a prosperous merchant of Kheybar who was to become one of Doughty's closest friends in Arabia.

Over the next few days En Nejumy came to visit him several times at the soldier's lodging where he had been told to stay. Together, lighted on their way after dark with flaming palm-branches, they wandered through the town, visiting the coffee houses, and drinking and talking with Siruan himself – who was more relaxed without a crowd to impress, and told Doughty amiably that he might wander where he liked in Kheybar.

There was a reason behind this change of heart. The massacre of Christians in the Ottoman empire eighteen years before had been followed by the bombardment of Jedda by English ships, and by the execution of the Pasha of Damascus for his part in the killings. That was a powerful curb on the behaviour of the commandant. Doughty had boasted of his important – thought largely imaginary – connections in the Sultan's court, and had reminded anyone who would listen of the close friendship which existed between his own government and that of the Ottoman empire: better by far for Siruan to keep him contented as long as he could do so without prejudicing his own position among the fanatical Muslims of the town.

So the requirement that Doughty should report to him twice a day, like a prisoner surrendering to his bail, was camouflaged as a hearty 'invitation' to coffee; occasionally, too, Siruan entertained him to dinner. Doughty, though, had too much experience of genuine Arab hospitality to be beguiled, and he also had the advantage of being able to discuss Siruan and his conduct with Mohammed En Nejumy. 'Half-humane black hypocrite' was Doughty's description of the commandant, while Mohammed wrote him off contemptuously as 'the son of an ass'.

It was only in En Nejumy's house that he could be sure of a warm welcome, with Mohammed urging him to visit it whenever he wished, and to eat and drink there as if in his own home. Once again, he felt the reassuring warmth of Arab hospitality – though elsewhere in the town it was a very different existence from the one

Doughty remembered among the bedu tents. 'We drank round the soldiers' coffee; yet here was not the cheerful security of the booths of hair,* but town constraint and Turkish tyranny, and the Egyptian plague of vermin . . .'⁵

The Ottoman empire, on whose alleged friendship Doughty relied so heavily for his protection, was here in an even sorrier state than he remembered from Maan – many of the soldiers in this remote station had given up hope of ever being paid, and relied for their food on what little corn they could swindle out of their officers as supposed rations for dead or non-existent camels. The hardship left many of them weak and sick – an ideal opportunity for Doughty to win himself much-needed friends with his medical help. He hurried from house to house, prescribing doses of quinine and rhubarb for soldiers with fever, and simple meat and broth for those who were suffering from sheer famine.

And yet despite Siruan's nervousness about Doughty's possible powerful friends, despite the goodwill engendered by his medicines, the tolerance with which he was treated was extremely fragile. When he was spotted outside the town one morning, burying the notes from which he had discreetly written up his diary, rumours swept through the market.

Depending on the sophistication of the gossip, he was either preparing some malevolent magic spell, or spying out the land ready for some future invasion by the unbelievers. There were warnings of Arab gunmen lying in wait for him behind the clay walls of the plantations, and of shadowy figures preparing to stab him as he walked at night.

Siruan, still anxious about his own fate if the stranger should die, and at the same time rather enjoying the bloodthirsty warnings his position entitled him to issue, forbade him to go beyond the town walls. If he did, he was told, he would be clapped in prison.

And yet, in the coffee houses, all the townsmen declared that they held the highest opinion of him. That, of course, was largely the instinctive Arab dislike of any confrontation – but Mohammed En Nejumy gave him in private another explanation for both the

---

* The nomads' tents.

hostility and the declarations of esteem. '"Knowest thou, that all the Kheyabara tremble for fear of thee?" "And how should they be afraid of one man, who is infirm and poor, and a stranger?" "This is the manner of them, they are like beasts, and have no understanding. They say thou art a magician!"'[6]

Doughty remained under his friend's protection. He was gaining an insight into the people of Kheybar from Mohammed En Nejumy that he had sadly lacked in Hail, and his reliance on him was growing all the time. Despite the strict injunction to stay within the town walls, he was taken each day to work and to pass the time in his orchard. En Nejumy was a man of some standing and considerable popularity in the town, where he was known as Amm Mohammed, or Uncle Mohammed – and with such an escort Doughty could afford to ignore the threats against him.

Together they went to see more inscriptions carved on the rocks in the valley, many of them in Kufic* script, many more in Arabic, and still more with grotesque pictures of wild animals. All of them were transcribed painstakingly into his notebook, but Doughty's real interest had moved on from the inscriptions and the history of ancient Arabia. His hopes of finding a surviving colony of Jews in Kheybar had been dashed. The people of the town were clearly of different descent from those of Hail or from the bedu tribes with which he had travelled – but they were the dark-skinned offspring of African slaves, not Jews.

In Mohammed En Nejumy, though, he had found a kindred spirit who enjoyed sharing information and opinions as much as he did himself, and he was desperate now to pick up every last detail he could about how the Arabs lived, about their beliefs and their attitudes.

In one thing he would not take the advice of his new friend. While Mohammed En Nejumy would disguise his contempt for Siruan, the Ottoman governor, under a display of civility – 'After all,' he said, 'slave, and cursed one, and tyrannical fool, though he be, yet is he not here the officer of the Dowla?' – Doughty's bluntness of speech and manner was turned indiscriminately on the governor and his

* A variation of Arabic from the Iraqi city of Kufa.

friends. Despite the hostile rumours, despite the stories of imminent
attempts on his life, he would not curb his tongue. It was a long time
since he had jotted down his reminder of the need for circumspection.

When Siruan came into the coffee-hall, and everyone else rose
to greet him, Doughty alone would remain sitting stubbornly in his
place. Urged to move aside to allow one of the leading sheikhs of
the town to sit down, he grumbled that the sheikh could find himself
another seat; and when one of the senior military officers took him to
task, he astonished the company with the virulence of his response.

'I have wandered in many lands, many years, and with a swine
such as thou art, I have not met in any place,' he said. To call anyone
a pig – an unclean and disgusting animal – was a bitter insult; to use
the term to a friend of the governor at a public and semi-formal
gathering was asking for trouble. The rest of the people sitting
around, and the officer himself, pretended not to hear – 'The slave
. . . has not the heart of a chicken,' said Mohammed disdainfully
later – but Doughty's enemies could afford to wait. Given time, the
arrogant *Nasrany* would certainly be in need of more friends than
he could find: the time for revenge would come.

After he had been in the town for two weeks, Siruan finally
composed a letter to the Pasha at Medina describing the arrival of
the *Engleysy* and asking what should be done with him. A messenger
was sent to bring back the Pasha's response; and until his return,
Doughty could only wait, with the whole town wondering whether
the word would come back that he should be put to death.

> These were days for me sooner of dying than of life . . .
> the black people meanwhile looked with doubt and evil
> meaning upon the Nasrany, because the Pasha might send
> word to put me to death. Felonous were the Turkish looks
> of the sot Abdullah, whose robber's mind seemed to be
> suspended between his sanguinary fanaticism and the
> dread remembrance of Jidda and Damascus . . . [7]

En Nejumy, who had served in his youth as one of the Sultan's
bashi-bazouk shock troops, took care to carry his sword with him
whenever he walked around the town, and threatened to cut in two
anyone who dared to lay a hand upon his friend. He cared little for

the *Dowla*, he declared – and yet both he and Doughty knew that, if word came back that the stranger was indeed to be executed, one sword would be little use against the whole town.

The general feeling was that the longer the Pasha in Medina took to send back his judgement, the worse it looked for Doughty – and the days stretched into weeks without any sign of the returning messenger. En Nejumy, for all his outward confidence, was concerned that the fanatics in the town might lose patience and take matters into their own hands, and he was making plans to hide his friend up in the mountains, with a supply of milk and dates.

He also extracted a promise from Siruan that he would disregard any order to execute the *Nasrany*. Instead, the commandant said, he would provide him with a camel and let him go, swearing to the Pasha that he had escaped in the night. Jedda and Damascus were still on his mind; after all, he reasoned, the Pasha might be recalled at any time – but if killing Doughty led to international repercussions, it would be upon Siruan's own head that the Sultan in Istanbul might exact his revenge.

When the messenger did arrive, though, late one night, it was only to demand that all Doughty's books and papers be sent for examination at Medina. Siruan, anxious to keep control of the situation, refused him permission to write on his own account to the Pasha, but Amm Mohammed provided him with paper and ink, and promised to arrange for the messenger secretly to carry a letter on his journey back. Mohammed had no doubt about what might influence the authorities in Medina – but Doughty, to his friend's intense frustration, remained obdurate. He would no more trim his words for the Pasha than he had swallowed his anger for the commandant. '"See in writing to the Pasha that thou lift him up with many high-sounding phrases." – "I shall write but plainly, after my conscience." – "Then thou art *mejnun*,* and that conscience is not good, which makes thee afraid to help thyself in a danger."'[8]

Doughty had no illusions about the seriousness of the threat to his life: he had heard several stories of the murder of unbelievers, quite apart from the ominous accounts of the disappearance of Chris-

* Mad.

tians at Hail. He had no wish to be another martyr, and still railed bitterly against the Damascus consul whose lack of concern for him, he believed, lay behind all his troubles.

But his plain speaking was policy as well as principle. So far in his travelling, it was forthrightness that had won him most friends. The reputation he had established as an honest man had stood him in good stead many times, and he decided to rely on it again, painstakingly setting down his whole history in Arabia.

> I wrote with my pencil in English, for Mohammed told me there are interpreters at Medina. I related my coming down with the Haj, from Syria, to visit Medain Salih; and, that I had since lived with the Beduw, till I went, after a year, to Hayil; from whence Ibn Rashid, at my request, had sent me hither. I complained to the Pasha-Governor of this wrongful detention at Kheybar, in spite of my passport from a Waly of Syria; also certain Beduins of the Dowla coming in, who knew me, had witnessed to the truth of all that I said, I demanded therefore that I might proceed upon my journey and be sent forward with sure persons.[9]

It was without explanation or apology, it gave no details of any future plans, and there was an almost arrogant confidence in the demand for his rights. It was hardly the letter of a supplicant, and it contrasted markedly with the anxious, self-justifying and tortuous message which Siruan sent to explain his own inactivity.

There followed more days of tension, with Doughty fearing that every knock at his door might announce the arrival of a warrant for his execution. He tried for a while to find himself more friends in his role as doctor, but even that was a risky enterprise: one soldier died after he had treated his fever with rhubarb, laudanum powder and quinine, leading to accusations that it was the doses which had killed him. Mohammed and his other friends managed to quash those rumours, but he was banned from practising his medicine.

As if that were not enough, word was filtering through with the trading caravans from the north about the war between the Russians and the forces of the Sultan, along with graphic descriptions of the cruelty and deceit of the Christian forces, which were said to have burned Muslim civilians alive, and even blown up crowds of them with explosives.[10] At the same time the soldier with whom Doughty had been sharing a lodging was moved out, leaving him alone, and suspecting a plot to murder him quietly during the night. Any such attempt, he knew, would find plenty of willing volunteers in Kheybar.

His position was becoming desperate, and even En Nejumy's offer to spirit him away into the mountains at the first sign of danger was little consolation. His health was still weak, he had no knowledge of local landmarks, he would have no shelter from the sun, and water only for three or four days: even if he managed to escape capture, he would have little hope of survival on the inhospitable lava-field.

He spent as much time as he could at his friend's house, but when the messenger finally did return from Medina, it was on a day when En Nejumy had left on an unannounced hunting trip. The *Nasrany* was alone at the moment of his greatest danger.

Doughty kept out of the way as best he could through the morning, hiding in En Nejumy's house, while waiting every minute for the feared summons to Siruan's coffee-hall. It was midday before En Nejumy himself returned, and then, despite Doughty's mounting anxiety, he sat and bartered for an hour with a party of merchants who had just arrived in Kheybar, before he set off to find out what the Pasha's message said.

Once again there was no resolution. The Hadj had kept the Pasha and his officials busy, said the letter; once the pilgrims had left, they would examine the books and papers, and return them to Kheybar. But the second part of the message – which Siruan tried to keep from Doughty – was more reassuring: 'In the meanwhile, you are to treat the Engleysy honourably and with hospitality.'

From the messenger himself, who seems to have been as indiscreet as only a trusted bedu envoy could be, he learned that his old friend Mohammed Said Pasha, the leader of the Hadj, had stood by him once again. He had mentioned nothing of the deception by which Doughty had originally joined his caravan twelve months earlier, but told the Medina authorities that he was astonished that the *Nasrany* should be held in captivity in Kheybar. His only crime, he said, was that he was too adventurous in his wanderings.

It was good news so far as it went, and much of the tension that had plagued him ebbed away as word spread that the Pasha had ordered that the *Nasrany* should be well looked after. Now, rather than worrying about possible assassins behind every wall, he could sit at peace by a spring outside the town, watching the dragonflies, the lizards and the darting silver fish. In its way, it was an idyllic life – but, two months after his arrival in the town, he still seemed no closer to being allowed to leave, and the hot season was drawing in. 'My languishing life, which the Nejumy compared to a flickering lamp-wick, was likely, he said, to fail at Kheybar.'

It was on one of his twice-daily visits to Siruan that he saw six starved and weary camels couched outside the governor's door. They could only be the mounts of a group of soldiers from Medina: the Pasha's final verdict must have arrived!

Rather than face Siruan immediately Doughty fled back to En Nejumy's house, but the Pasha's decision reached him soon enough. 'Good news, Khalil! thy books are come again, and the Pasha writes, Send him to Ibn Rashid,' Siruan told him, and the next day he handed him a personal reply from the Pasha himself to Doughty's own secret letter.

Written in uncertain French, it was carefully complimentary about his travels, his efforts to redraw the map of Arabia, and his investigations into the ancient monuments of the region – but it warned of the danger Doughty must face from 'Bédouins téméraires'. For that reason, said the Pasha, it would be best if he were to return at once to Ibn Rashid, and go on from there to continue his travels to his destination.

It was indeed good news – for Siruan. His superiors were deftly passing the embarrassment of the wandering *Nasrany* back to the recalcitrant sheikh from whom he had come: if anything untoward should happen to him there, there could be no blame attached to the Sultan's officers. Siruan, at least, was freed from his troublesome dilemma.

But for Doughty, although he showed no sign of realizing it, the message was little better than the death sentence he had feared. The warning as he left Hail had been unambiguous – death would be the penalty for returning into Ibn Rashid's territory. To make matters worse, when the books and papers were eventually returned from Medina, the safe-conduct Ibn Rashid had given him was missing. Friendly words from the Pasha in Medina would be meaningless in Hail: he would be returning naked, destitute and friendless to a despot who he had been told would kill him on sight.

But the danger seemed to elude him. Buoyed up by the apparent support of the government officials, and flattered by the regard with which he was treated by the soldiers, he demanded stridently that all his possessions should be returned to him – particularly the six liras which Siruan had seized. Over the next few days he challenged the commandant repeatedly, declaring publicly that he would have him sacked – and, a week and a half later, the arrival of another letter from Medina seemed to support him. The governor was to take care of how he treated the *Nasrany*, said the message; he was to restore all his property immediately, and was to report back at once to the Pasha if anything was missing.

But Doughty seems almost deliberately to have been trying to anger and offend the Arabs, insisting first that he was no subject of the Sultan, then describing with glee the military might of the British at Aden, and declaring solemnly when asked what the *Engleys* were good for, 'They are good rulers.' And yet, for all that, he inspired considerable warmth.

Doughty's medicines had saved the life of En Nejumy's daughter when she was suffering from fever, and for that reason alone he would have been glad for him to stay on in Kheybar, working as his salesman, and making a new life for himself among the Arabs. But even apart from that, there is genuine affection in the picture of the schoolmasterly Doughty, pottering amiably about the town. En Nejumy gave the other side to the portrait of the arrogant *Engleysy* insisting on his rights.

> 'Who . . . can imagine any evil of Khalil? for when we go
> out together, he leaves in one house his cloak or his driv-
> ing stick, and in another his *agal*!* He forgets his pipe, or
> his sandals, in other several houses. The strange negli-

* Head-band.

gence of the man! ye would say he is sometimes out of
memory of the things about him . . . But I am sorry that
Khalil is so soon to leave us, for he is a sheikh in questions
of religion, and besides a peaceable man.'[11]

But even leaving was not a simple matter. Doughty's finances
remained in a desperate state. He hired a disreputable soldier named
Eyad – a bedu who now lived as a townsman in Medina, and 'one
who had drunk very nigh the dregs of the mischiefs and vility of
one and the other life' – to take him back to Hail at a cost of five
more of his dwindling store of reals.

Even so, he refused Siruan's offer to provide him with food for
the journey, and even to pay half of Eyad's wages. Doughty would
accept nothing from the man he still saw as his enemy – and very
little either from his closest friend. From Mohammed he would take
no more than a few dates as a leaving present, and he insisted in
return on giving him some of his precious stock of medicines, buying
him a new gun-stock and a tunic, and even trying to repay him in
cash for the food he had given him over the previous weeks. It was
a clumsy gesture, even if it was made with the best of intentions,
and it called forth a most dignified rebuke from the Arab merchant.

'Nay, Khalil, but leave me happy with the remembrance,
and take it not away from me by requiting me! Only this
I desire of thee, that thou sometimes say, *The Lord remember him for good*. Am I not thy abu,* art not thou my son,
be we not brethren? And thou art poor in the midst of a
land which thou hast seen to be all hostile to thee.'[12]

After the usual delays Doughty, Eyad and another young soldier,
Merjan, rode out of Kheybar and back towards the volcanic hills of
the Harra, with Mohammed making his final goodbyes. '"Now God
be with thee, my father Mohammed, and requite thee." – "God
speed thee, Khalil," and he took my hand. Amm Mohammed went
back to his own, we passed further; and the world, and death, and
the inhumanity of religions parted us for ever!'[13]

It was the Arab farewell that he had commented on before –

* Father.

calm, controlled and sincere – but Doughty, in the desert thousands of miles away from his home, was moved by more than his friend's affection. For all his infuriating racial pride, for all his refusal to accept Islam as an expression of religious love, for all his quarrels and disagreements, he instinctively recognized the similarities between many of the ways of the desert and those of the Victorian gentlemanly tradition he had left in England, so far behind him.

Each time Doughty set off on a fresh stage of his journey, he seemed able to summon up fresh optimism: wherever he was going to could only be an improvement on the place that he was leaving. As they left the town, he rejoiced that he was travelling away from 'the pestilent Kheybar *wadian*,* and the intolerable captivity of the Dowla, to a blissful free air on the brow of the Harra'; a little later, when the oasis finally vanished over the horizon, he declared: 'Oh joy! This sun being fairly risen, the abhorred landmarks of Kheybar appeared no more!'

But by the time they first saw the glimmering white tower of Hail, the long and arduous journey had sapped that optimism. Ibn Rashid himself was away on an expedition but, riding through the long, empty market, the three travellers felt a chill of terror as the reality of their predicament hit home. At the end of the street, which was deserted because it was the afternoon prayer time, and because all business had been suspended while the Emir was away, they met first Aneybar, and then small knots of curious townsmen. Aneybar, who had been left in charge by Ibn Rashid, ignored them at first, but the townsmen – among them the malignant old coffee server with whom Doughty had quarrelled on his last visit – predicted cheerfully that this time the foreigner would indeed be put to summary execution.

Doughty was given his old lodgings for the night, and once again he was offered dates and *leban*. But there was no disguising the hostility of the people – and while Aneybar was unwilling to take any action on his own account actually to harm him, he was certainly

* Plural of wadi.

not going to see the Emir's commands flouted so publicly, and in a way which might rouse the anger of the people. His decision, once the travellers had been summoned for an audience, was swift and dramatic. '"Here rest tonight, and in the morning (he shot his one palm from the other) depart! . . . Thou hast heard, Khalil?" and he showed me these three pauses of his malicious wit, on his fingers, "Tomorrow! – The light! – Depart!"'[14]

Nothing could have been clearer. Aneybar was determined that the Pasha's attempt to shift the burden of Doughty's presence from himself to Ibn Rashid should not succeed. Eyad should take him straight back to Kheybar, he declared. Both Eyad and Doughty tried to dissuade him: the camel was too weak for the journey, they said, and in any case, Eyad did not dare to go against the orders of the Pasha. For his part, Doughty declared that any injury that befell him might be avenged either by the *Dowla* or by the British themselves.

But Aneybar was implacable: Doughty must go, and that without delay. He must go, too, to Kheybar – not north to appeal to the Emir himself, not to Baghdad, not east towards the Gulf coast, where Doughty had suggested he might find a ship to India, and not south-east to the province of Kasim, another possible destination that he proposed. It was a sleepless, tormented night; Doughty was helpless in the grip of a political tussle between the rival Arab factions. The irrational optimism that the Pasha's support had given him had drained away as Aneybar berated him, and he could see only disaster ahead. Certainly, he thought, he would be killed if he showed his face again in Kheybar. 'When the morning sun rose, I had as lief that my night had continued for ever. There was no going forward for me, nor going backward, and I was spent with fatigues.'[15] It was a moment of abject hopelessness – but despite that, he stood firm against the beguiling voices of those in the crowd at the town gate who wanted him to convert to Islam there and then, and thus solve all his problems. Aneybar had told him that becoming a Muslim would put everybody on his side; as it was, his determined refusal whipped the bystanders into a frenzy. Only Aneybar's reappearance prevented him from being attacked.

At Doughty's insistence, Aneybar scrawled out a brief safe-conduct to replace the one the Emir had signed, which had been lost in Medina. 'No man to molest this *Nasrany*,' it said curtly, with the signature Aneybar Ibn Rashid beneath it – but even that slight reassurance he refused to give to Doughty himself, handing it over instead to Eyad, his unwilling companion. Doughty, he said, should pay five reals to his companion, and Eyad would not desert him.

There was one final plea to be allowed to travel north towards the Emir's camp and Baghdad. 'If thou compel me to go with Eyad, thou knowest that I cannot but be cast away: treachery, O Aneybar, is punished even in this world! May not a stranger pass by your Prince's country? Be reasonable, that I may depart from you today peaceably and say, The Lord remember thee for good.'[16]

Once again Doughty had hit precisely the wrong note. The accusation of treachery and the warning of retribution to come drove Aneybar to rage. Pulling his sword half out of its scabbard, he stormed that there was no choice, that the unwelcome *Nasrany* should return to the town from which he had come. It was his final word: Kheybar, to which, only a few months earlier, Doughty had begged so fervently to be allowed to go, was now the last destination in the world he would have chosen; but it was to Kheybar that he must now set out again.

Eyad and Merjan were at least open to Doughty about their intentions. Eyad said he had already spent the five reals he had been given, so there was no possibility of returning them; but he did not dare to follow Aneybar's orders and take him back to Kheybar. His plan was to leave him either in Gofar, the first town out of Hail, or with a group of wandering bedu. What was more, he added, emboldened by Doughty's contemptuous treatment at the hands of the Hail authorities, the return journey would be very different from the one they had made before. He would ride, and the *Nasrany* would walk.

Doughty was in no doubt that it was among the wandering bedu that his best hope lay, slim as it was. Apart from the hostility he had encountered personally, he had heard stories of even more blood-curdling threats against him from among the Arabs of the oasis towns: the people of Seleyma, in Ibn Rashid's country, for instance, had sworn to cut him in pieces if he ventured into their village. When they arrived at Gofar, he begged them, if they must desert him, to do so at some encampment rather than in a town – and, for good measure, he slept across the heavy camel-saddles and the bags to make sure they could not leave him in the night.

At first light the three ill-assorted companions set off once more. Again the despised *Nasrany* was on foot, stumbling over the hot gravel on his bare feet – and although they had not actually abandoned him, the Arabs were not prepared to slow their pace. He knew that several days of such efforts would almost certainly kill him: after only a few hours the exertion brought on a violent nosebleed, the blood gushing over his hands as he struggled to catch up. There was little sympathy for his plight, although they did slow down slightly and allow him to stagger along by the camel, supporting himself by gripping onto its saddle.

For four days he struggled along like this, dragging his camel stick through the gravel in the vain hope of leaving some trail he might follow back if they did ride off and leave him. It was a tense, mistrustful time, with the wild-eyed and bloodstained Doughty convinced several times that his companions intended to shoot him. Weak as he was, his response was one of anger rather than fear. Feeling against his chest the reassuring pressure of his secret revolver hanging from its cord, he told the two Arabs that if they drove him to it, he would kill both of them, and take the camel for himself.

He had carefully not mentioned the gun – but the threat itself was vehement enough to make them pause. As they rode on ahead, he was turning over in his mind what chances he would have if he were indeed forced to kill them. It was not a cheerful prospect: in every direction there was nothing but hundreds of miles of desert, peopled with hostile Arabs. The ophthalmia which he had suffered in Hail had left his eyes too weak to tell friend from foe; and being alone, he would be unable to draw enough water for his camel even if he were lucky enough to stumble upon a well. Better by far to hold his peace, while watching his companions all the time: they would take any chance they could either to slip away or even to murder him.

Caught between Ibn Rashid and Kheybar, the two Arabs were

frightened for their own skins, and Doughty's own arrogant bearing must have been a continuing provocation. He wanted to avoid antagonizing them – but at the same time he needed to preserve what he could of the instinctive wariness they felt for him. When challenged, he would not back down – any display of weakness could only add to the damage already done by his treatment at the hands of Aneybar and the Hail authorities.

Watching each other narrowly, they covered around a hundred miles over the painful gravel wastes, until eventually they came up with a small group of Arab tents. This, clearly, was the place where the two Arabs had decided to leave him. But, though Doughty knew that staying here might offer him better hope than clinging on to his unwilling companions, he was not prepared to see them go without speaking his mind. There was, after all, the question of the money he had paid Eyad.

> Eyad said, when we were sitting alone, 'Khalil, we leave
> thee here, and el-Kasim lies behind yonder mountains;
> these are good folk, and they will send thee thither' . . .
> 'Ullah remember your treachery, the *Aarab* will blame
> you who abandon your *rafik*,* also the Pasha will punish
> you; and as you have robbed me of those few reals, he
> may confiscate some of your arrears.'[17]

For all his bitterness and sense of betrayal, it is hard to know how else the two unfortunate Arabs could have acted. They had to escort Doughty away from Hail, but they could not take him back to Kheybar as they had been instructed. Anyway, he did not want them to try. What could they have done for him more than leave him with another group of Arabs who might help him on to Kasim and thus out of Arabia?

But Doughty was not content with hard words, and when the nomads were finally persuaded to allow him to join them, he demonstrated that he had learned something about double-dealing from the stories of treachery he had heard in Hail and elsewhere. The two simple Arabs demanded a document to certify that he had left their

* Companion.

care safely. But the paper he gave them, upon which their lives might depend later if they were questioned by Ibn Rashid or any other authorities about how they had fulfilled their orders, detailed the payment that had been made, and added that Eyad, 'engaged by Aneybar, Ibn Rashid's deputy . . . to carry me again to Kheybar, here treacherously abandons me at Aul, under Sfa, in the Shammar dira'. The two men could not have read the words which might later condemn them: they were happy with their discharge, and only too glad to be finally relieved of the troublesome *Nasrany*. Doughty would never know whether they would ever be called to account with his paper. But as the two Arabs rode off, it was enough to know that he had indeed had the last word.

The Arabs with whom he had been left said they knew another sheikh travelling nearby who would surely take him on to Kasim – it was a feature of Doughty's travelling that each sheikh in the desert was reputed, at least by the Arabs who took Doughty to join him, to be greater and more liberal than the last.

Before they set off to find him, though, Doughty decided to take practical measures to lighten his bags: alone in the desert, he found a lizard's hole, and there buried most of the books he had carried with him around Arabia. He kept his copy of Zehme, his Sprenger, his Bible, his one, still-unthumbed, medical textbook and, he said later, 'several leaves' of a volume of Chaucer. Everything else was buried in the sand, under a big stone which he rolled on top of them, as he prepared himself for what he knew would be his last chance to get out of Arabia.

It was a symbolic moment, a final, determined, Prospero-like casting aside of the books and the learning on which he had relied for years, during his Arabian travels and before. For the remaining months of his journey he continued to garner information about the Arabs, their habits, their beliefs and their history – but his concentration more than ever was on the gathering of first-hand human experience. It was as if he felt that the books had taught him all they could; it was time now to turn to the people around him.

Later he was philosophical about the burial – 'He is a free man

that may carry all his worldly possession upon one of his shoulders,'
he mused in *Travels in Arabia Deserta* – but it was, too, a severely
practical decision. Neither his physical strength nor his rapidly shrinking funds could last much longer: if he could not make his way to
Kasim, and from there to the coast, he was likely to die in Arabia.
His books weighed heavily in his bag, and anyway, they had often
excited suspicion and hostility among the superstitious Arabs: better
by far to be rid of them. Once again he could afford later to be ironic.
'I . . . gave them honourable burial in a thob's hole; heaped in sand,
and laid thereon a great stone. In this or another generation, some
wallowing camel or the streaming winter rain may discover to them
the dark works of the *Nasrany*.'[18]

When they caught up with the sheikh, Ibn Nahal, Doughty's
companions were careful not to introduce him as an unbeliever or
a foreigner. He was, they told the great sheikh's tribesmen, a doctor
from Damascus – but the pretence was idle: as they entered the tent,
the men who sat around recognized him at once as the *Nasrany* about
whom they had been told.

Where the townsmen were malicious, the bedu were fearful. The
great liberal sheikh, like so many others, was keenly aware of the problems that might come from welcoming the *Nasrany* among his tents,
and the effusiveness of his welcome was matched by the determination
with which he ordered that his guest should leave that very night.

Doughty was still being hustled from one unwilling host to
another – and it was a poor Arab, not a great sheikh, who eventually
agreed to take the stranger in until he found someone to accompany
him to Kasim.

The tribesman accepted Doughty into his family and, after a few
days, found a travelling stranger named Hamed, who was prepared
to take him on to Kasim for another five reals. Hamed had called at
the camp to visit his wife and his son, and their departure together
gave Doughty another graphic illustration of the bedu's brief and
unsentimental farewell. Just back from one long journey, and about
to set out on another, Hamed wasted few words.

> To his housewife, he said no more than this: 'Woman, I
> go with the stranger to Boreyda.' She obeyed silently;

and commonly a beduwy in departing bids not his wife farewell: – 'Hearest thou?' said Hamed again, 'follow with these *Aarab* until my coming home!' Then he took their little son in his arms and kissed him.[19]

Apart from being taciturn, Hamed was suspicious of the stranger: Doughty noticed that he would not even drink from the same bowl as an unbeliever. But he stuck loyally by his *rafik*, even though most of the travelling bedu they met by the way seemed to recognize the *Nasrany*, and treated him with more or less hostility.

The first few days of their journey were over the sharp-sided gravel which had caused Doughty such pain earlier, but eventually they reached the rolling sands which showed they had arrived on the borders of Kasim. It was a very real frontier – the furthest boundary of Ibn Rashid's power, beyond which Doughty could not place even the shakiest of reliance upon Aneybar's safe-conduct pass. But it would also be, he was convinced, another view of Arabia – and also a vital step on his way home.

In the province of Shammar, which he had just left, most of the wandering tribes had heard of the mysterious foreigner who carried medicines and asked such probing questions. In Kasim, perhaps, fewer people would have heard of him; on the other hand, he had been warned that it was a hot-bed of Muslim fanaticism, where an unbeliever might expect to arouse even more hostility.

Moreover, Kasim was at the centre of a network of trading routes: Hamed suggested that they might find caravans travelling to Kuwait or Bosra, without going as far as the main town of Boreyda. Either one would be a big step on the way out of Arabia, but if Kasim was a staging-post on the way home, it was one that Doughty now wanted to see. Used by now to his *rafiks* trying to offload him as quickly as they could, he refused to be diverted.

A few hours later Hamed and Doughty stood on a hillside over-looking Boreyda. Doughty was still cheerful, and staggered by the beauty of the town which lay below him.

> And from hence appeared a dream-like spectacle! A great clay town built in this waste sand with enclosing walls and towers and streets and houses! And there beside a

> bluish dark wood of ethel trees, upon high dunes! This is
> Boreyda! And that square minaret, in the town, is of their
> great *mesjid*?* I saw, as it were, a Jerusalem in the desert!
> ... the last upshot sunbeams enlightened the dim clay
> city in glorious manner, and pierced into that dull pageant
> of tamarisk trees.[20]

But Hamed's view of this shimmering mirage of a town was more
pragmatic. As they paused outside the brick-red walls, he warned
Doughty slowly and seriously that it was time to abandon his policy
of openness about his religion. Among these people, more than any
he had met so far, he would have to pray and pretend to be a Muslim.
He should make much of his skills as a doctor, Hamed advised him,
and in that way he might scratch a living in the town; but most
important of all, he should keep his peace. 'Say not, "I am a *Nasrany*",
for then they will utterly hate thee ... Thou hast suffered for this
name of *Nasrany*, and what has that profited thee? Only say now, if
thou canst, "I am a Muslim".'[21]

As evening fell, they entered the town, their camel shuffling
through the silent and deserted streets. The advice was well-meant,
but Doughty was probably constitutionally incapable of following it,
even if he had had the chance; in any case, within a couple of hours
he was brutally exposed as a *Nasrany* and an unbeliever.

Hamed had said his brief goodbyes at the Emir's hostel, leaving
Doughty half asleep on a clay bench, surrounded by porters and
servants. He was startled from his reverie by the sound of a *muezzin*,
and when he asked hurriedly for a place to sleep rather than joining
them in their prayers, there was no doubt about who he was. He
was dragged off protesting into a dark room in the hostel.

His bags, with his pistol stashed away at the bottom, were locked
away; the only weapon he had was his penknife, which he took out
ready to put up a desperate fight for his life. His worst fears, and the
direst warnings of Hamed, seemed to have come true.

It was clear as soon as he was dragged back down the echoing

* Mosque.

corridors to face the town sheikhs that there was no point in dissembling, even if he had wanted to. At least one of them had seen him in Hail, and knew not only that he had been expelled by Ibn Rashid, but also that he had been ordered back to Kheybar. That he should have disobeyed that instruction was in his favour – this was, after all, a town where the people were fiercely protective of their independence of Hail and its Emir. Doughty's indignant independence went down well. '"Did not Aneybar forbid thee going to Kasim?" – "I heard his false words, that ye were enemies, his forbidding I did not hear; how could the slave forbid me to travel, beyond the borders of Ibn Rashid?"'[22]

That delighted the sheikhs who were questioning him; but the rest of the household were less easily won over. Doughty was sent to fetch his papers from his baggage, hurried along by blows and curses from the servants who had been sent with him. They set upon him, ripping the barometer from the cord by which it hung from his neck, snatching his cloak, and rifling through his clothes and his possessions for money – although, luckily, they failed to dig deep enough to find his revolver.

Tired and outnumbered though he was, he put up a stiff resistance, until the captain of the guard arrived in answer to his shouting. He ordered the thieves to return all they had taken, on pain of having their hands cut off. It had been a frightening few moments, and there were dangers still to come, but Doughty's courageous resistance had won him a valuable friend.

The experience had shown at least that there was a rule of law in the town, but it had not taught Doughty any humility; on the contrary, it had reinforced his belief that only a determined and dignified attitude could protect him. When he was taken to Abdullah, the Emir's regent, the next day, he challenged him directly: 'Is it a custom here, that strangers are robbed in the midst of your town? I had eaten of your bread and salt; and your servants set upon me in your yard.'

Abdullah was apologetic – the robbers were beduin, not citizens of Boreyda, he claimed unconvincingly – but he would not have him in the town. His only concession was that the weary traveller might stay for one day to gather his strength before moving on to Aneyza, a couple of hours' journey away. What welcome he might find there was problematical, but the Emir was in no mood for argument.

In the few hours he had to spend there, Doughty jotted down every observation he could about Boreyda, every story he could hear about its rulers and its people. Palgrave had been there in his disguise as a wandering Arab doctor, but little was known about the town, and even its position was wrongly shown on most maps. And if Doughty was interested in Boreyda, the people of the town were also interested in the first undisguised Christian to enter through its ramshackle gates. Even though he was accompanied by the captain of the guard, children and passers-by followed them down the street, jeering and catcalling at the *Nasrany*.

Eventually one of the Emir's swordsmen laid about him with a stick, beating the crowd to send them to their homes, so that he could be led hastily through the back streets to his room – but the reason for Abdullah's anxiety to get Doughty out of the town was obvious. The mob was hammering at his door, screaming for his death. Like Hail, Boreyda would not tolerate an unbeliever in its midst, and his continued presence could only cause trouble and rioting.

If Doughty had hoped for more tolerance in the cosmopolitan centre of Kasim, he was disappointed; on the contrary, the flow of foreign ideas and news which filtered in with the constant stream of trading caravans told against him. The conflict between Russia and the Ottomans was perceived among the Arabs as one between Christian infidels and loyal Muslims: now they had one of the enemies of Islam in their hands, they clamoured to the Emir, why should they not put him to death?

As he had before, Doughty put his trust in the strength of the Sultan himself. He reminded Abdullah, as he had reminded Siruan in Kheybar, of the execution of the Pasha of Damascus after the massacre of Christians there, and of the naval bombardment of Jedda. He was a trusted servant of the *Dowla*, he declared with more passion than accuracy, and if he were harmed, there would be a terrible price to be paid.

By now he was regretting his plea to be allowed to spend the day in Boreyda. Despite Abdullah's command that there should be no more attacks on him, Doughty was ready and anxious well before dawn broke to be on his way. Fanatics might still follow him secretly into the desert to kill him – but at least there he would have a chance to outrun or outmanoeuvre his pursuers.

It was a very different parting from the one at Hail: here in Boreyda the crowd was so unruly and so unpredictable that Doughty had to be spirited away unnoticed by back roads and lonely streets. Abdullah himself came to see the *Nasrany* out of his jurisdiction. He had asked earlier, in a phrase which was to return to haunt Doughty, 'Who will convey the *Nasrany* on his camel to the wadi?' and with him, either volunteer or pressed man, he had brought a guide. He was a poor, elderly Arab who had been paid by the Emir – not an ideal *rafik*, and likely to be of little help if they met enemies on the way. It was a short journey, though, and Doughty had no choice but to trust himself to his new companion.

However, it was an uneasy trust. Whether it was the man's bearing, the way he spoke, or simply a cynicism born of experience, Doughty's suspicions grew through the night that his guide might be playing him some trick. For ten miles they wandered along a track through the drifting sands which separated Boreyda from Aneyza, until they paused in the shade of a tamarisk grove. The town, said the guide carefully, could be reached by sunset.

By midday they had reached a palm wood, with water trickling in a stream. They were in the bed of the great Wadi Er Rummah, one of the massive dry valleys which drain the Arabian peninsula – an ideal place, said Doughty's companion, to wait for the cool of the afternoon.

As he wandered away, supposedly to fetch their straying camel, he turned and told Doughty that the town lay over the next dune, and that he would find men working in a field nearby – and then he was gone. It was only after Doughty, in a panic, had run barefoot to the top of a sand-dune and spotted him riding away as fast as he could that he realized how he had been deceived: Abdullah had ordered his man to take him to the wadi, not to Aneyza itself. The danger that had threatened so many times had finally happened: he was alone in the desert.

He was distraught. 'This was the cruellest fortune which had befallen me in Arabia! to be abandoned here without a chief town, in the midst of fanatical Nejd!'[23] He was an outlaw, with no camel, no provisions, no friends and precious little hope.

Even in this extremity, though, he did his best to be practical. He took the loaded pistol from his camel bag and hung it around his neck again, hidden under his robe. Then he took the maps which he had been at such pains to sketch out during the past few weeks. If they were found among his possessions, in a land so obsessive about foreign spies and so superstitious about the power of writing, they might cost him his life, whether as a magician or as a spy: despite the hard work and the meticulous observation that had gone into creating them, they were torn into small pieces and buried in the sand.

By the field which his treacherous companion had pointed out he found a house, where he asked for water and shelter – but once again he was caught out by the call to prayer. Even though he refused to pray with them, the labourers lent him an ass to carry him the few miles to the town, but it was yet another reminder that there was no possibility of simply avoiding notice in the cheek-by-jowl life of the oasis. The same thing happened in the evening, when he was staying in a small outlying homestead just outside the town: if he would not pretend to be a Muslim, then he would be treated as an outcast.

Forty years later another English traveller in Arabia heard the story of Doughty's exposure from the grandson of Ibrahim, the owner of the homestead. His father, he said, had been one of a group of young men who had berated Doughty as an infidel, and he had passed on the story of his brush with the legendary *Nasrany* traveller. 'Ibrahim, a godly man, had roused him to join in the prayers of his household. The guest explained that he was a Christian, whereupon, "*Nasrany*!" exclaimed the old man, "*Audhu billah*, I take refuge in God!" and would have struck him.'[24]

Ibrahim's son and his friends had crept up to the door of Doughty's room as dawn broke. He had not prayed the night before, they said accusingly, and now he was missing the morning prayers too. Doughty, perhaps, had said his own prayers in his own way, but his reply was still dissembling, if not actually untrue. 'Friends, I prayed,' he told them, only to be exposed when they looked around the bare woodshed where he had slept – and demanded to know where he had performed the ritual washing before his devotions.

In Aneyza the next day Doughty had no opportunity even to try to hide his religion. The first people he met in the street, before he had even arrived at the Emir's *majlis*,* recognized him at once. News of his coming had beaten him to the town, and he was greeted in the street as '*Nasrany*' and '*Khawaja*', or Jew. Pride overcame circumspection, as it always did. 'I am no *khawaja*, but an *Engleysy*,' he replied indignantly.

Doughty's pride in being a Christian and an Englishman is clear – but his unwillingness to deceive even strangers in the street by pretending to be a Muslim is a mark, too, of some respect for them. To Zamil himself, sitting on a seat spread with a Persian carpet in the open air, he was straightforward and dignified. 'I come now from Boreyda, and am a *hakim*, an *Engleysy*, a *Nasrany*. I have these papers with me; and it may please thee to send me to the coast.'[25]

Zamil himself was affable enough; but after the experience of Boreyda his instructions must have had an ominous ring to them. Doughty should go home, he said pleasantly, and return to drink coffee after prayers; but in the meantime he should tell people he was a runaway soldier of the Sultan rather than admit to being a *Nasrany*; and he should keep away from public places.

It was the same counsel as he had heard before, coming with rather more force from the Emir, who had the power to order where he had advised – and yet Doughty remained unable to take it. One of the citizens in the market – 'one of those half-feminine slender figures of the Arabians, with painted eyes, and clad in the Baghdad wise' – plucked him by the sleeve as he made his way home. Where was he from? he was asked – and was he indeed a *Nasrany*? 'Ay,' said Doughty, short and direct, much to the horror of the more obedient Negro servant of the Emir, who replied to every question with the careful formula that Doughty was 'a stranger, one that is going to Kuwait'.

* Court.

But the news that the stranger was a *hakim* who could cure diseases spread almost as quickly as the word that he was an unbeliever – and although there were angry mutterings and threats, not least from the Emir's own uncle, Aly, there were, too, growing demands for his services as a doctor. One of his would-be patients offered him the use of a little open stall in a market side-street, and by mid-afternoon the *Nasrany* was squatting among his potions and ointments, wondering once again, with his irrepressible optimism, whether this time he might not have found a place where he could stay and eke out a living as a healer.

Although he cautiously shut up the doors of his shop when the faithful hurried past on their way to the mosque, he was encouraged not only by word that Zamil, despite the opposition of his uncle, had instructed that no one was to molest 'Haj Khalil', but also by the respect that was accorded to him among the Muslims as a man who had spent time in the Holy City of Jerusalem.

So he clung to his optimism even when well-disposed local people warned him of the dangers he still faced. One of his patients was a prosperous merchant named Abdullah El Kenneyny, who was to become one of his closest friends and most valued protectors in Arabia. He was horrified at the *Nasrany*'s outspokenness, while Doughty himself remained calm and confident.

> 'And art thou,' said he, 'an *Engleysy*? but wherefore tell the people so, in this wild, fanatical country? . . . For are we here in a government country? No, but in a land of the *Aarab*, where the name of a *Nasrany* is an execration . . .' – 'I am this second year in a perilous country, and have no scathe. Thou hast heard the proverb, "Truth may walk through the world unarmed".'[26]

El Kenneyny was astonished: he had always found the English, he said tartly, to be full of policy and deception. But he promised to act as Doughty's friend in Aneyza, to keep an ear to the ground, and warn him if the mood of the people should turn against him. Zamil himself, he said, could be trusted – but even the Emir could not always control the mob.

The rest of the day – 'his one good day in Arabia', as Doughty called it later – was spent in discussions of El Kenneyny's books, and of their different cultures. The Arab was fascinated by the science and discoveries of Europe, by his guest's stories of the Islamic buildings he had found in Spain, and by his learning and accomplishments. About his medical skills Doughty was dismissive – like the wandering Arab tinkers, he said, he was 'better than none when you may not find a better'.

After a night spent on the terrace of a patient's house – more comfortable than the shop floor, and closer to the new friends he had made – Doughty was summoned to breakfast by Zamil. The warm girdle bread, dates and butter were welcome, as was the leg of mutton which the 'gentle, philosophic Emir' sent him later in the day – but best of all was the feeling that, having been entertained to a meal, he might relax at least for a while in the hospitality of Aneyza. It was the sort of easy optimism which Arabia should have beaten out of him by now.

El Kenneyny and Zamil might be friendly, but there were other factions in Aneyza to be considered. Not long after he returned to his shop with the Negro Ali, one of the Emir's servants, a mysterious stranger appeared, keeping his face turned from Doughty so that he could not be recognized. He shouted at Ali that Doughty should leave, and that the shop belonged to him – and when Ali replied that Zamil himself knew about his presence there, the stranger revealed himself as the Emir's fanatical uncle, who had already complained bitterly at his presence in the town.

Doughty left willingly enough – if the shop did indeed belong to Zamil's uncle, he reasoned, then his friends had been at fault in setting him up there. But there was more at stake than the tenancy of a small stall in the market: this violence by such a respected and influential figure at court could only encourage those in the town who wanted to see him sent away or worse.

He sat forlornly out in the street through the afternoon, the shop shuttered and locked against him. Now he had nowhere to hide from the Muslim faithful as they hurried to pray – and there was no doubting the hostility of the passers-by. Zamil was little help: the factions in Aneyza, as El Kenneyny had warned, were clearly too strong for even the Emir to control.

Among friends and enemies alike, though, there were plenty of people in Aneyza wanting the *Nasrany*'s medical attention. Zamil himself had shown him a skin disease he had suffered from for twenty years, and other townsmen were begging for treatment for eye infections, fever and even smallpox. Often they would not deign to speak to an unbeliever, but would describe their symptoms and their needs through an intermediary. Doughty, well aware that every successful cure might add another family to the list of his friends, seldom refused to help.

Some of his patients required little more than good advice. One man, for instance, was loud in his praise when Doughty prescribed a slight reduction in his estimated daily intake of sixty cups of strong black coffee and as many pipes of tobacco. 'Khalil can cure even without medicine!' he exclaimed to anyone who would listen to him – the delight of that sort of cure being, of course, that it cost the patient nothing at all!

Word of his success as a healer filtered back to Boreyda, and messengers arrived one morning offering him payment to return. Short of money though he was, Doughty believed he had found friends and security in Aneyza; he would not even consider returning to the town that had thrown him out so brutally. They could send their sick to Aneyza to be cured if they would, he said, but he would not return at any price. The local people were amazed and gratified at his loyalty to them: the sheikhs of Boreyda would give him at least thirty reals, they clamoured.

> I answered: 'I was in Boreyda, and they drove me from them: also, this Abdullah caused me to be forsaken in the Wady.' (I would not trust myself again in a town, where the worst of all the citizens were the ungracious, usurping sheikhs) . . . 'Neither for thirty mares would I return there. Farewell.'[27]

This, despite the unconcealed hostility of Zamil's uncle and his faction, was Doughty's most relaxing time in Aneyza. El Kenneyny began to introduce him to his friends, among them another prosperous merchant named Abdullah El Bessam, and supper became a daily pleasure, a prelude to an evening of conversation and discussion.

This was the best company in the town; the dinner-tray
was set on a stool (the mess is served upon the floor in
princes' houses in Hail) and we sat half-kneeling about
it. The foreign merchants' meal is more town-like than I
have seen in Arabia; besides boiled mutton on *temmn*,*
Abdullah had his little dishes of carrots fried in butter,
and bowls of custard messes or cured milk . . . [28]

His welcome, though, was less wholehearted than he knew. Forty
years later Harry St John Philby arrived in Aneyza as the trusted
confidant of Ibn Saud, and asked about Doughty. Among those who
remembered the strange *Nasrany* was one of El Bessam's sons, by
then 'a charming, slightly senile old man', named Fahad. He had
been a small boy of eight or nine when Doughty drank coffee in his
father's house.

One of the tasks he had been given by the women of the household, he told Philby, was to mark precisely the place on the commu-
nal dish from which their guest had taken his food. It was from that
dish, once the men had finished, that the women would eat their
separate meal – but, said El Bessam, the food from the spot where
Doughty had eaten, with a bit more on each side just to be sure,
would be fed only to the cats. Hospitality meant that the stranger
must be fed; it did not dictate that decent Muslim women should
share the same food as an unbeliever.

He was remembered kindly enough, though. Earlier, Philby had
met people who remembered him – 'the vaccinator of whom we
used to hear tell' – from their childhoods in Hail, and now he found
that in Aneyza, too, the legend of the strange, red-bearded Christian
persisted. 'Such an one, they thought, must indeed have made his
mark, perhaps in some high diplomatic post . . .'

Doughty's evenings were spent with Bessam, Kenneyny and
other neighbours, smoking the *nargily* pipe while the coffee brewed
upon the fire. However careful the devout were to avoid unnecessary
contact with him, people were openly warm and hospitable. The talk
was of Arabic literature, ancient wars and long-dead heroes, or of
Doughty' s own tales about medicine, Europe and his travels. And

* Wild rice.

if they asked him questions, it was an opportunity for him to quiz these educated and cosmopolitan traders in his turn about the history of the region, to ask for opinions about the whereabouts of towns and cities named in the old geography books, or about the ruins and ancient sites which still fascinated him. They did their best to assuage his curiosity, but even here in Kasim few people could understand why he took an interest in such matters.

From these conversations he also heard the latest tidings of the war between Russia and the Sultan – 'begun and ended in the time of my wandering in the wilderness of Arabia' – and of the support the English fleet had given to the Ottomans.[29] News of the war, brought with the merchants' wares along the trading routes from the north, had whipped up feelings against him in Boreyda – but here Doughty's friends were assiduous in putting around the stories of English support for the Muslims, in the hope that they might convince more people not to mistreat the *Engleysy* who had wandered amongst them.

They were generous, too, or at least as generous as the touchy Doughty would allow. 'He is not poor who hath no need; my poverty is honourable,' he told El Kenneyny and the others who offered him clothes, even money, and he meant it, even though he had barely enough in his purse to get him to the coast. Poverty, indeed, was part of Doughty's self-image as wandering scholar, as *saiehh*, as the pilgrim searching for himself through the deserts of Arabia.

But the anger of the less tolerant faction in the town was still festering behind the goodwill and kindness. Doughty had become expert at deflecting hostility when he was actually confronted: to the astonishment of many of his simpler critics, for instance, he would readily agree to say the first part of the Muslim testimony, 'There is no god but God.' That was a declaration, he reasoned, that need hold no problems for a Christian; it was only the second phrase, 'And Mohammed is the prophet of God,' that made him pause.

He became skilled, too, at declaiming the rounded, sententious religious phrases which might impress his listeners with his devoutness, while blurring the distinctions between their two religions. 'Every creature is a prophet of God,' he told them on one occasion, when challenged to repeat the full testimony. In private he was still capable of damning the Muslim religion in savage phrases but, paradoxically, his exposure to the worst excesses of bigotry was deepening his understanding of the nature of faith itself.

The passive acceptance of Christianity which had been shattered, for Doughty like the rest of his generation, by the implacable advances of science, was being replaced for him by an all-embracing acceptance of religious diversity. It may seem obvious today, but in the nineteenth century it required a leap of imagination to realize that adherence to a particular faith was largely determined by national and racial background. He was a Christian because his family and his people had been Christians; El Kenneyny, on the other hand, 'loved first the God of Mohammed (because he was born in their religion), and then every not-unworthy person as himself'.

To renounce religion would be to renounce race, nationality, family – all the ties which connected a man to civilization – but true godliness meant going beyond the mere strictures and procedures which divided one faith from another. Like the simple bedu in the desert, or like El Kenneyny or Amm Mohammed, the good man could express his love of God most emphatically through his treatment of his fellow men. Love for 'every not-unworthy person' was a fair mark for a man to aim for.

Doughty's experiences in the desert – the biblical sites of Jordan and Syria, the links between the stories of the prophets and the nomadic life he had shared – had done nothing to dent his faith in the primacy of science, his belief in the importance of a spirit of honest enquiry. When he spoke with El Kenneyny about religion, it was to preach the need for a man to stand fast in the faith of his fathers, while maintaining a search for truth through science.

> Nations hold to their religions – 'that is true in their countries which every man saith'; howbeit the verity of the things alleged cannot be made manifest on this side the gate of death. And everyone will stand to his hope, and depart to the Gulf of Eternity in the common faith . . . But let us enter the indestructible temple-building of science, wherein is truth.'[30]

Such an acceptance that the companion of religion must necessarily be uncertainty, and such reliance on the observable truths of scientific study, would have been even more offensive to the fanatic Muslim imams than straightforward, God-fearing Christianity – but here in the desert Doughty was working out a personal faith that would reconcile his doubts with his instinctive religious feelings. It was a faith that would stay with him, growing and developing, for the rest of his life.

But it was enough for the imams and *muttowa*, or religious elders, that the foreigner was a *Nasrany*, an unbeliever in the heart of their city. They were actively whipping up feeling against him. One Friday sermon pointed out meaningfully that the rains which were normally expected at that time of year had not yet arrived – and this at a time when a 'misbelieving stranger' was being entertained in the town. Zamil himself was criticized: the favour shown by 'certain principal persons' towards the *Nasrany*, said the imam, could only provoke the Lord to anger.

The greatest threat of all, though, for unbeliever and faithful alike, was that of smallpox. There was little Doughty could do to treat those who had caught the disease, although he offered to travel to Baghdad to fetch new vaccines. His offer was turned down, either because the townspeople could not agree to unite on the project, or because they felt it might be as blasphemous to show such lack of faith in heavenly providence as to rely on the assistance of an unbeliever. The deaths continued. At the height of the epidemic there were five or six children dying each day, and by the time it was finished, practically every house in the town had suffered a bereavement. Unknown to Doughty, the imams were blaming him for the epidemic. It was God's punishment for his presence there, they said.

Forty years later Harry Philby heard the Arabs' version of Doughty's growing unpopularity. As for the brutality with which he was bundled out of town, they shrugged their shoulders fatalistically – 'the passage of long years had acquitted their consciences'. It had, they said, been impossible to stand against the demands of the religious leaders that such an obvious cause of the scourge of smallpox should be removed.

Philby arrived in Aneyza to an effusive and honourable welcome, as befitted a close adviser of Ibn Saud. But another local worthy was blunt in explaining why his predecessor had been given such short shrift. 'If any be not honoured by the Imam, why – we do not desire him, though he be our own father. Khalil erred in coming as a poor man without recommendation, and if you had come likewise, we should have rejected you . . . Khalil should not have come as he did unless he were prepared to profess the common religion.'[31]

For Doughty, though, there was nothing but uncertainty and anxiety as the hostility of the people gradually became more open. His life, he knew, was in constant danger. 'With the sword also worship they Ullah,' he wrote later.[32] All the time, however, he had the sense that Zamil was watching over him discreetly, from a distance. One of his patients, for instance, a man 'of few words, sharp-set looks, and painted eyes, but the son of a good mother', directed him to an empty lodging near his own where he might stay. From then on he was kept supplied with bread, milk and butter, and his waterskins were regularly filled, all of it without payment. It could only have been from Zamil, Doughty surmised: the sheikh was unwilling to risk the controversy and religious anger that helping an unbeliever openly might stir up, but he was none the less determined that his uninvited and inconvenient guest should be properly looked after.

As had happened in Hail and Kheybar, though, it was Doughty's fascination for the countryside around the town that brought a crisis in Aneyza. In this case it was an expedition with El Kenneyny and some friends to visit a ruined site which did the damage. It yielded little but a few potsherds, but it led to Kenneyny himself being ostracized in the town, while Doughty noticed more and more people refusing to talk to him. There was now open hatred among many of the ordinary people for the stranger in their midst: the unbeliever had been given time to repent, but now there would be no more mercy, they said. The expedition had given the imams the excuse they needed to whip up feeling against the unbeliever.

Almost certainly, the threats were as empty as those Doughty had experienced elsewhere had been – but he took care to vary the route back to his lodging, he kept his revolver hanging at his chest, and he hurried through the darkened streets at night with his cloak wound around his arm, to give himself at least a chance to ward off a blow from a knife.

It was clearly time to move on, if only he could find anyone to escort him from the town. His best plan, he had no doubt, remained to strike out for the Red Sea coast, possibly with some trading caravan heading through the southern volcanic country towards Jedda.

But his money had dwindled still further while he had been in the town, helped by the occasional pilfering from his bags. The delicate ivory tubes in which he kept his vaccines had been stolen almost as soon as he arrived in Aneyza, more than wiping out at a stroke all the slim profits he had made by practising medicine in the twenty months he had spent in Arabia. His watch, which he had hoped to sell for a few reals, followed them. His friends had offered to help him before: he was now, he realized, entirely in their hands.

But there was no doubt that he would have to leave as soon as he could find a caravan that would take him. Children in the street were no longer scolded for shouting after him; sometimes he was stoned as he passed, and piles of rubbish were left outside his door.

One night a thunderous knocking and shouting at his door awoke him. It was too dark to see outside, but he could tell from the shuffling feet and murmuring voices that there were several people standing in the street. From the shadows came the voice of the Emir's uncle, Doughty's bitterest enemy.

Where did he want to go? he asked – and when Doughty replied that he was hoping to travel to Jedda soon with a caravan, the Arab laughed in his face. No, he said; where would Doughty go that very night? His pleas that he needed more time to collect money due from his patients, that he was sick, that he was tired, that he needed to rest until the morning, were all brushed brusquely aside. 'No, thy camel is ready at the corner of the street; and this is thy cameleer: Up! Have out thy things, and that quickly!'[33] And with that, as Doughty pleaded that he had no money, the Emir's uncle punched him in the face. Seeing the half-drawn swords among the crowd, Doughty took the blow passively: resistance, he knew, could only end in his death.

He was to ride to the nearby town of Khubbera, and pay the cameleer two reals for the privilege. The nightmare he had feared had actually happened: he was separated from the friends who he believed might still have seen him to the coast. His expulsion had been well-planned – done in the night to avoid more violence, whether from the *Nasrany*'s friends or from the hostile mob. As he left Aneyza, the darkness so complete that he could not see the ground beneath his camel's feet, he felt deserted and alone.

As they made their silent way on the soft sandy track, the cameleer told Doughty as much as he knew about the night's work. A sudden council of the sheikhs of Aneyza had been faced by a demand from their neighbours in Boreyda – piqued, no doubt, by the impertinent *Nasrany*'s refusal to return at their bidding – that he be sent away at once. Even Zamil, who had wanted to protect him as much as he could, had been unable to resist such a powerful alliance between the sheikhs of Boreyda and the religious leaders of his own town.

The sun was rising as they approached Khubbera. A single watch-tower loomed up over a line of low buildings of dull red clay, and there was no sign of greenness or cultivation. Like his guide in the wadi outside Aneyza, this companion, too – a man, he said, 'of squalid, ape-like visage' – intended to leave his charge some way outside the town. But Doughty was desperate now and, one-to-one in the desert, there was little need for restraint. He drew his pistol out of his bags, and showed it to his unwilling companion. If he would not accompany him, he said, then he would take the camel to the gates of the town with his bags; and if he resisted, then he would shoot the beast there in the desert.

The camel was the man's livelihood: it was an unanswerable argument. And when the half-trained beast refused to go through the narrow gates, Doughty insisted that the cameleer should carry his bags on his shoulders, not just to the square, but to the very doors of the Emir's coffee house. No doubt it was satisfying for once to impose his will on his companion, but it was important, too, that he should be seen to be arriving in the town as a traveller worthy of respect rather than as a penniless supplicant. They might recognize him as the infamous *Nasrany*; they need not guess how weak and vulnerable he was.

Even before they could be summoned in to coffee, Doughty's

cameleer had slunk off to make his way back to Aneyza. Nobody
noticed him go: they were all too intrigued by the stranger. Khubbera
was a town well used to foreign merchants, traders and travellers,
but as he made his way through the crowd in the coffee-hall, he
saw young men whispering together and glancing up at him. They
clearly knew who he was – some even asked straight out if he had
medicines with him, and he heard the Emir mutter under his breath
that he could be sent on to another village – but no one seemed to
want to make a decision about him immediately. The next day would
do.

But as the rest of the gathering stood up to leave, Doughty was
approached by the Emir's blind old father, feeling his way around
the wall towards him. With him was the Emir of the town himself,
who asked whether the *Nasrany* could cure his father's sight. Let him
stay, at least for a few days, and try his skill; after that he could be
sent on to another town, Er Russ, from which he might find a caravan
to Jedda.

Doughty was being bundled from town to town as he had been
from sheikh to sheikh, but his reputation as a healer had at least
bought him a little time – although the tougher line he adopted over
payment for his cures meant it made him few friends among the
townsmen. One man seeking a cure for his deafness stormed off in
anger when all the *muddowy** would prescribe free of charge was the
use of a piece of paper rolled into an ear-trumpet. Others travelled
into town by camel, only to decide to suffer their various illnesses
rather than pay out good money in the hope of a cure.

So his position in the town remained extremely precarious, and
the possibility of another gruelling trip to yet another town, where
a caravan to Jedda might or might not be found, was less than
enticing. The help of his friends in Aneyza still seemed to offer him
the best hope of finding his way to the coast – if only they had not
forgotten him. Doughty had often complained that the Arabs would
make promises one day, only to forget them the next: surely these
friends with whom he had spent so much time would not simply
forsake him!

* Apothecary or doctor.

There were no invitations to coffee in Khubbera, and no friendly words in the street. On the contrary, one layabout made a sort of enthusiastic street-theatre out of the way that the unbeliever's throat might be cut, like that of a sheep or a camel for sacrifice.

> 'Now were a knife brought and put to the wezand of him!
> – which billah may be done lawfully, for the *Muttowa*
> says so; and the Nasrany not confessing, *la ilah ill' Ullah!*
> pronounce, *Bismillah er-rahman, er-rahim* (in the name of
> God the pitiful, the God of the bowels of mercies), and
> cut his gullet; and, *gug-gug-gug*, this kafir's blood would
> gurgle like the blood of a sheep or camel when we carve
> her halse. I will run now and borrow a knife!'[34]

The other bystanders would not let him carry out his threats – but the bloodthirsty glee with which he enacted the death of the unbeliever reflected the jovial hostility of the rest of the people. Only the Emir and his father stood by the stranger, threatening to have anyone who molested him beaten. It was better than no support at all, but the Emir was poor and weak: if Doughty's friends from Aneyza did not do something to help him, then Khubbera might prove to be a bloody end to his travels in Arabia.

Even so, it was with mixed feelings that he answered a knock at his door on his third day in the town to find the smiling, ugly face of the camel-driver who had brought him from Aneyza. Zamil, he said, had summoned the *Nasrany* back to wait for a caravan which was expected to leave for Jedda shortly.

It seemed like good news – but Doughty was reluctant to leave at once. He was halfway through a course of treatment for the old sheikh's eye troubles. Whatever his skill and knowledge as a healer, he had a doctor's sense of duty to the people who trusted in him – and in any case, curing the Emir's old father could only boost his reputation in the town.

It was his patient who decided him: he knew that Doughty's chances of finding a way out of Arabia would be much greater if the promised caravan from Aneyza materialized. His departure might jeopardize the cure he had hoped for at the hands of the *Nasrany*, but he had no hesitation. 'Go, Khalil, and doubt not at all; Go in peace,' he urged him. It was a moment of genuine fellow-feeling and unselfishness.

So Doughty made up several phials of eye-wash to leave behind, and rode off with the messenger. He still saw no reason to trust a man who carried neither letter nor token from his friends in Aneyza – but the resentment that he knew the Arab felt for him might be counterbalanced by his fear of the revolver. It was, after all, only a short journey.

They travelled through the moonlight, with the Arab squatting behind Doughty on the camel. The shadow of the lance he carried with him jogged about on the sandy track as they rode, and Doughty watched it carefully. A sudden movement of that shadow might be his only warning of an attack.

At the villages where they stopped, he deflected hostility with the same mixture of humour, flattery and religiosity that he had used so successfully in the past. An enemy of God? he asked one religious enthusiast – Would you say the same about a camel? Ah, said his questioner pedantically, but a camel is an irrational creature, incapable of any religion. 'Then account me a camel: also, I pray Ullah send thee some of the aches that are in my weary bones; and now leave finding fault in me, who am here to drink coffee.'[35]

It was the sort of impatient, plain man's humour that appealed to the other villagers – and, as Doughty had discovered already, making the Arabs laugh was the best way to avoid dangerous arguments. A touch of sarcasm that might be interpreted as flattery for the butt of his humour made up for the joke – 'I am of too little understanding to attain to thy high things' – and a final religious thought reminded them that he, too, was a worshipper of God, different though their faiths might be. 'The Same who cast me upon these coasts, may esteem an upright life to be a prayer before him.'[36]

Doughty was as comfortable with piously worded sentiments like these as his audience: there was no falseness or hypocrisy in them but, at the same time, they were a very effective part of the soft answer which turned away wrath. Instead of facing bitterness and hostility, he was led off to breakfast and coffee, leaving only a few religious devotees muttering unhappily.

They were still short of Aneyza itself when the Arab stopped

204

the camel, and motioned to Doughty to dismount. Zamil's order, it seemed, had been to leave the Christian at a small shack in a plantation outside the town. There, he would be able to wait in safety for the caravan, while not provoking more unrest in the town itself.

At first it seemed as if the arrangement might mean a welcome rest for the sick and weary Doughty. The next day El Kenneyny arrived to tell him the full story of how news of his expulsion had spread, and how his friends had persuaded Zamil to allow him at least back to the outskirts of the town. He also cashed a bill from Doughty for a few more reals – enough, hopefully, to see him eventually to the coast. His most immediate worries were assuaged: all he need do now was wait for the long-promised caravan.

He spent the nights in a clay-built camel-manger, sleeping under the stars; during the long, hot days he would watch the camel plodding stolidly around the well, and listen to the soft shuffle of its great feet in the sand. Where before he had travelled for miles each day, now he would wander off a couple of times between dawn and dusk to gather sticks for a fire on which he could boil a couple of handfuls of rice; where before he had gazed across the wide desert vista, fixing the presence of whole villages and mountain ranges in his mind, now he stared at the few birds and beetles that inhabited his plantation.

Beyond the plantation there remained the endless, dazzling horizon of the desert; but he might as well have been in a cell.

El Kenneyny had warned him that he might not be able to come out to the plantation because of the unpopularity that would cause him in the town – but even so, Doughty felt lonely and abandoned: 'Their friendship is like the voice of a bird upon the spray; if a rumour frighten her, she will return no more. I had no tidings of Bessam or of Kenneyny!'

Eventually, after three weeks in his open-air prison, he scribbled in Arabic on a slip of paper, 'I am dying with weariness and hunger', and sent it off to El Kenneyny in Aneyza. More than anything else he needed the reassurance that his friends had not deserted him. Perhaps they could arrange for him to move to another garden closer to the town; best of all would be a visit that would break up the long, lonely, idle day, and prove that he was not forgotten.

The day after Doughty's note was sent a serving lad appeared at the plantation with a basket of girdle-cakes and butter, together with a container of buttermilk. He also had a message from his master, telling Doughty that there was every hope that a caravan might be leaving soon. But El Kenneyny himself still kept away. The gifts were some comfort, but they were not what Doughty wanted.

After six long weeks in the plantation the first sign that his long exile might be ending was the gathering in of the strong pack-camels ready for the caravan. The great, slow animals had been put out to graze with the tribesmen around the town, but now they could be seen roaming in the desert around the plantation. The time for his departure was almost at hand.

He was weary and run down, the man who had always been so cautious about his health struggling now even to walk, with his legs covered with painful ulcers following a dog-bite several months before. But if he wanted ever to get out of Arabia, he could not afford to miss this opportunity: his strength, he thought, might hold out long enough for him to finish the gruelling journey – but only just.

> A month! – and I might be come again to European shipping. From hence to the coast may be counted 450 desert miles, a voyage of at least twenty great marches in the uneasy camel saddle, in the midsummer flame of the sun; which is a suffering even to the homeborn Arabs. Also my bodily languor was such now that I might not long sit upright.[37]

If he felt his friends had let him down by failing to visit him, he could hardly complain about the arrangements they were making to set him on his way. El Bessam and El Kenneyny bought a camel to take him to Jedda, where they hoped it might be sold. Instead of Bessam's son, Doughty was to ride with Sleyman, a relative of El Kenneyny's whom he had met already; although the caravan was headed for Mecca, some of the traders would be breaking away from the main body of the riders before reaching the forbidden area where an unbeliever could not travel, and making their way down to Jedda. Doughty could join them.

On the evening before the caravan was due to set off Doughty took his leave of the labourers, and rode slowly down to El Kenneyny's own plantation nearer to the town. There, finally, his friend arrived to greet him, along with Abdullah El Bessam. They were ashamed to have been so overborne by the townspeople that they had deserted him, but nothing more was said of that: it was too late for apologies, forgiveness or recriminations. Instead – a final sign that he was turning his back on nearly two years of wandering through Arabia – Doughty shared out what remained of his medicine chest between them. It was the most valuable gift a man so shorn of possessions could offer.

Then, in the cool of the evening, he clambered painfully up with Sleyman and their bags onto the longsuffering camel, and the two men rode off into the dusk, down the road that had taken Doughty to Khubbera so many weeks before. Then he had been close to despair; now it seemed that his troubles might be almost over.

When they joined up with the butter caravan at its rallying ground a few hours later, they found 170 camels, with some seventy men. It was dark, and bulging goatskins were stacked around, all thickly smeared with date-syrup to stop the liquid butter from seeping out onto the sand. As ever, Doughty's eyes darted around the gathering crowd, his ears alert for any chance conversation: even now, ill, weary and on the point of leaving Arabia for ever, he was hungry for any final titbit, any detail he could scribble down about the place, the people and their history.

He listened carefully as his companions explained how the goatskins would be hung from the camel saddles, how they might get ripped or pierced by thorns on the journey, and how there rode with the caravan a bodger whose job was simply to repair any leaks. Almost unnoticed among the gossip was the ominous news that the entire caravan was going to Mecca. Nobody was turning off to Jedda: Doughty would have to find some other companion to escort him away from the forbidden territory around the two holy cities. It was a worrying prospect, but it was still far enough off to be pushed to the back of his mind. The journey itself was enough to worry about for the present.

At dawn they brewed their final coffee, and eventually set off down the Wadi Rummah, the ribbon of firm sand which runs through the drifting dunes of the Nefud – the great ancient highway of Arabia. Many of the merchants had already heard of the *Nasrany* who was travelling with them: word had spread as far as Kuwait of a wandering Christian three spears' lengths tall, who had used his mystical gifts to find mineral deposits beneath the desert for Mohammed Ibn Rashid. Such were the stories that had spread about him – it was little wonder that the hostility which he met in many of the Arabs was generally mixed with a degree of caution.

If the tedium of his weeks at the plantation had given him an idealized memory of the freedom of travelling under the open skies, he was soon brought back to reality. The *simum*, a hot, dry wind off the desert, was blowing, so that Doughty had to ride with a wet sponge pressed to his face to ease his breathing. The first water they found was brackish and polluted, but there would be no more for miles. They had no choice but to drink it.

As they climbed into the angular rocks and outcrops of the high steppes, the temperature dropped; at times the ground was white with salt, almost like frost. Often there was sharp black gravel crunching beneath the feet of their camels; they had left behind now the soft desert sand, and the clumps of grass at which their camels had snatched as they passed. They had met no wandering Arabs since they left: it was a dead and an unfriendly land.

It was not until four days later, when they had struggled into a more welcoming landscape with clumps of acacia bushes by the wayside, occasional watering holes and flowering cactus, that they met their first bedu. Now, nervously, the camels were kept close together in case of attack; the Arabs would unshoulder their matchlocks as they approached any nomads in the way, and at night they drew the entire caravan into a tight defensive circle, with guards posted against a hostile world.

There were signs of human habitation – cairns and rough stone tombs such as Doughty would have leapt down to investigate earlier in his journeys. Now he sat on his camel, and simply asked the Arabs around him what they were. They professed astonishment that he should not know. 'Works of the kafirs that were in the land before the Moslemin! how, Khalil! Were they not of thy people?'[38] It was a taunt, a joke, that he had heard before: there had been unbelievers in the land before the days of Islam; Doughty was an unbeliever; therefore they were his people. But if the merchants and camel-drivers were uneasy at the thought of sudden raids by fierce tribesmen, the taunts of 'Kafir' were a reminder to Doughty that he had more personal worries. The anxiety that he had pushed to the back of his mind at the start of the journey was now looming larger as each day passed. Every step that brought him closer to Jedda also brought him closer to the point at which the caravan would cross the border into the forbidden lands near to Mecca, and the unbeliever would have to break away. 'The aspect of this country is direful. We were descending to Mecca – now not far off – and I knew not by what adventure I should live or might die on the morrow.'[39]

By now the merchants and camel-drivers were enthusiastically preparing themselves to approach the Holy City. They were carrying out their ritual bathing, stripping off their clothes and wrapping themselves in the *ihram* or pilgrim's robe. As they rode, they shouted their prayers and devotions at the top of their voices – religious ardour that, as Doughty had already seen, could easily flare up into violence. Conspicuous in his ordinary clothes, he could no longer melt into the background, and he attracted constant hostile glances – but he was determined to stay with the caravan as long as he could.

He had been promised that if there were no merchants turning off to Jedda, then Bessam's own servant would travel there with him. Now, though, the servant declared that he would not take the *Nasrany*'s money: as a faithful Muslim, he would continue on the way to the Holy City.

Through a long, miserable night, Doughty checked and re-checked his revolver. As the caravan set off in the morning, he knew it was barely an hour before he would be forced to leave. Perhaps he might be able to find his way to the coast alone, simply by following the traces of dried-up streams – but he knew that the country would be filled with enemies; he had neither food nor water, and his strength was rapidly giving out.

In any other circumstances the green banks of the oasis of Ayn Ez Zeyma, where the tracks diverged, would have been a welcome

sight after the long trek, but now they seemed pregnant with warning. As they approached, Doughty watched a camel miss its footing
just in front of him, and injure its leg. There was nothing to be done
to cure it, and the Arabs leapt to the ground to cut its throat and
hack away joints of meat. The whole grisly operation took only a
few moments – barely long enough for the caravan to move on
200 paces. Doughty was hunched over in his saddle as he watched,
secretively checking his barometer beneath the folds of his cloak. He
scribbled the details into his notebook almost out of habit – 2,780
feet above sea level – but for once his mind was not on the measurements. In a few minutes, he thought, he might suffer the same fate
as the injured camel which now lay, stripped and steaming, at the
side of the track.

The rest of the Aneyza contingent of the caravan had gathered
at a small wayside coffee house a little further up the track. There
was menace in the air as Doughty rode up to join them, though El
Bessam's son Abd Er Rahman drew him on one side, telling him
reassuringly that he had found a distant relative who would take
him to Jedda for just three reals. But there were fierce looks from
the strangers and anxious expressions on the faces of his friends, and
he saw one traveller drawing his *khanjar** from its sheath, muttering,
'He shall be a Moslem!'

A moment later he suddenly rushed at Doughty, the naked blade
in his hand flashing in the sun, and shouted that he would kill the
Nasrany. For now, he was held back by the others, but Abd Er Rahman anxiously warned his father's friend that there was only one
way to be safe: he would have to declare himself a Muslim.

> 'If it please God, I will pass whether they will or no.' –
> 'Eigh, Khalil,' said he in that demiss voice of the Arabs,
> when the tide is turning against them, 'What can I do? I
> must ride after the *kafily*; look, I am left behind.' – He
> mounted without more; and forsook his father's friend
> among murderers.[40]

But if Doughty was stubborn, he was also courageous. After Abd

---

* The curved and edged Arab dagger.

Er Rahman and El Bessam had left, the Arab, whose name was Salem, made another dash at his enemy. Doughty stood stock-still in front of him, staring straight into his eyes and waiting in vain for someone to intervene. His attacker was a Negro, his cheeks slashed with three tribal scars, like many Arabs of African descent. Once, twice, he measured his blow, raising the curved dagger over the *Nasrany*'s chest. For all his fierce looks, he was old and infirm – perhaps Doughty might knock his stroke aside with one arm and then, once wounded, draw his gun with justice on his side.

It was a desperate chance, and one that almost certainly would have ended with Doughty stretched dead on the sand. But he was saved by another member of the party, a member of the Sherif of Mecca's household named Ma'abub, who intervened. The English would take revenge if Doughty were injured, he warned Salem, and the Sherif himself would punish anyone who harmed him. He should not be robbed, and should not be treated violently; instead, they should take him to the Sherif at Taif, who would know what to do.

'I hope it may please the Sherif to hang this Nasrany, or cut off his head! and that he will bestow on me the *thelul*,' muttered Salem. If he could not seize the unbeliever's goods by main force, then he hoped he should get them by the power of the law.

Doughty and Salem were to travel together, the would-be killer and his victim now companions. It was not an easy partnership, although Doughty did his best to reduce the tension between them. 'Well, Salem,' he said, 'I hope we may yet be friends,' and he took some comfort in the fact that the Arab now called him 'Khalil', rather than the more contemptuous 'Nasrany' – but he knew that he was still looking covetously, if secretly, at his bulging saddle-bags and at the camel that carried them.

Other, younger men taunted him with what they believed his fate would be at Taif – either to be hanged, or to have his throat cut. Doughty could do no more, terrifying as the prospect was, than make his way through the present danger; there would be time enough to worry about Taif once he had arrived there safely. For now, he had little to rely on but his ability to make friends, and his revolver, hidden under his stifling robes. Even when he slept, he had to keep his robes wrapped securely about him, so that the gun remained concealed but always ready to hand.

And he remained watchful: when Salem demanded that the *Nasrany* should ride with his companion, Fheyd, he insisted that he would sit at the back, where it was less likely that he could be stabbed unawares in the long night march. He had already, at Salem's insistence, spread out all his goods, including his few remaining reals, so that an inventory could be taken of his possessions – or, as Doughty saw it, so that the would-be thieves could examine what booty they might be able to seize.

It was an odd mixture of hostility and fellow feeling. If anyone sneered at the Christian, Salem would also turn towards him, feeling for his knife and glowering threateningly; passing merchants would look askance on the unbeliever, and curse his father – but at the same time, Fheyd would stop the camel when Doughty was thirsty, and fetch him water, and Salem and the others warned him repeatedly about the danger of sneak thieves in the darkness.

Ironically, it was that warning rather than any sudden outburst of hostility that brought the tension to its perilous climax. Fearing that he was being stalked during the night by a thief who might attack him, he drew the revolver which he had until that moment kept so carefully hidden. Had the supposed thief been a stranger, a bedu tribesman simply looking for booty from the passing caravan, there might have been no repercussions – but as soon as Doughty realized that his supposed assailant was another member of the caravan, he knew that he was in the gravest danger.

When the camels stopped at dawn, Salem demanded to see what he was hiding beneath his robes. A group of about a dozen camel-drivers gathered around them and, with the encouragement of an audience, Salem's anger burst out again. Doughty should either show him the revolver, or prepare to die, he screamed, waving his *khanjar* in his face. The others, too, were fingering their knives, shouting that they should cut the unbeliever in pieces then and there.

He withdrew a few paces on the sand, giving himself more room to face his attackers, and took the gun out of his robes. 'Let none think to take away my pistol,' he said. The old dilemma faced him, but more starkly than ever before: if he saved his life with the gun now, it would only be to die in the desert later. And yet Fheyd was approaching, step for step as Doughty retreated: he had only seconds to make a decision.

It is an image straight from the Victorian pantheon of *Boy's Own* heroes: Gordon of Khartoum, perhaps, in Joy's famous painting; Captain Cook confronted by the South Sea islanders; or any one of a thousand English adventurers facing savages, Spaniards, Frenchmen or other duplicitous foreign hordes.

But Doughty had a different kind of courage. Breaking the spell, he slowly stretched out his hand, turning the revolver so that the butt faced his enemy.

Fheyd snatched it from him, snapping the cord that held it around Doughty's neck as if it were cotton, and he and Salem leapt upon him, snatching his aneroid, his purse and everything else they could find about him. Then they waved the pistol in the air in angry triumph: 'How many Muslims have you killed with this?' demanded Salem, his courage swelling as he realized how completely the unbeliever was in his power, and, as Doughty protested that he had never fired the gun in all his time in Arabia, Salem handed it over to Fheyd to fire off the bullets into the air.

The chambers had been loaded for nearly two years, but there were no misfires: five explosions echoed around the rocks, before Salem shouted ominously, 'Leave one of them!' Clearly he meant to keep that for the *Nasrany* himself.

Sir Richard Burton, or any more conventional Victorian hero, would probably have decided to sell his life dearly and set about the threatening crowd in a final hopeless explosion of violence. Certainly he would never have handed over the pistol in the first place; but Doughty's technique had always been to use his own calm to force his enemies to justify their violence.

It may have been that calm that saved him, the steady-eyed assumption of his status; or it may, he suggested later, have been simple calculating greed on the part of his assailants. 'They now had all. What should my death profit them? This were but one *Nasrany* less, and they would willingly have dismissed me naked from them to go to Jedda, and be sure of their booty.'[41]

Wherever his strength came from, Doughty outfaced his attackers.

213

He stared unflinchingly at the Arab who threatened him, and then turned to the rest of the crowd. The Sherif at Taif would avenge him, he promised. His show of confidence lent credibility to the threat, the muttering crowd began to disperse; and then suddenly, Doughty felt a crashing blow to the back of his neck, and sank unconscious to the ground.

It was Fheyd who had struck him with his camel-stick – for hiding the pistol, he said shortly, when his victim came to his senses. Even now, Doughty was searching for possible allies – seizing a piece of bread from a camel-driver who was eating close by, he stuffed it into his mouth, declaring that there was now the alliance of the bread and salt between them. It was a trick that had served him well in the past: if the cameleer would not help him, at least he could be sure he would not join in any further attack. 'I never found any but Salem a truce-breaker of the bread and salt – and he was of the spirituality,' he noted later, ironically.

Ma'abub, the Sherif's servant who had protected him before, sent to demand the meaning of the shots he had heard, and Doughty, still reeling from the blow to the back of his neck, told how he had been abused and robbed. Salem claimed they had acted out of fear of the *Nasrany*, who was carrying a hidden weapon, but Ma'abub brushed his pleas aside. Salem would have to answer to the Sherif for robbing the traveller, and there were to be no more attacks, he said.

The sand was almost unbearably hot – when Doughty was dismounted, and struggling on his bare feet, he collapsed to his knees every few steps – but the immediate physical violence seemed to have passed. Even so, as the threats and insults continued, he secretly bound a stone in a piece of cloth. It was not much, but it might be all he had to save his life.

By now his strength was almost exhausted, and, despite his awareness of the danger he was in, he was almost falling asleep on his camel. When Salem spoke to him again, he replied with one of the religious expressions which he had found before to be so appealing to the Arabs. '"Thou art not afraid?" – "Is not Ullah in every place?" – "Ay, wellah, Khalil." Such pious words are honeycombs to the Arabs, and their rude hearts are surprised with religion. – "Dreadest

214

thou not to die?" – "I have not so lived, Muslim, that I must fear to die!" [42]

Now, each new step was bringing them perceptibly closer to Taif and civilization. As dawn broke, they joined a road, the first Doughty had seen since he had left behind the green hedges in the outskirts of Damascus some twenty months before; the houses they passed were no longer the rough clay shacks of the oases, but painted and glazed buildings like the ones he had seen in Turkey. He could tell that it was a place where laws were obeyed, and where the authorities of the *Dowla* held sway: whatever new dangers Taif and the Sherif there might hold, there would be no lynch mob to drag him to his death in the desert.

From the next hill-top they saw the town itself, two white palaces dominating the long, low buildings of slate-coloured stone – and within a few minutes Doughty's lingering anxieties about what treatment he might expect were laid to rest. They were met by a Turkish officer, who sent Salem away, still muttering about his hopes of inheriting Doughty's camel once the unbeliever was hanged, as he no doubt would be. His departure was some relief to Doughty – but it was the simple words of one of the Sherif's domestic servants which must have given most reassurance. '"I will bring thee presently," quoth the smiling servitor, "a knife and fork; also the Sherif bids me ask, wouldst thou drink a little tea and sugar?"' [43]

For anyone in Doughty's condition, his clothes in tatters, his hair and beard long and tangled, his eyes bloodshot and his skin sunburned and cracked on his face, the words must have been the stuff of dreams. His camel was led away to be fed and watered, his bags carried up the stairs for him to a room in the Turkish officer's house, and then barbers and servants shaved, washed and dressed him as he sat there unmoving, weak, faint and exhausted. His sufferings were finally over.

Sherif Hasseyn himself welcomed him that evening, quizzing him about his journey, about Hail and Kheybar, and about the attacks he had suffered in the last few days. Hasseyn promised that Salem and Fheyd would be put in irons for their violence; and in the meantime, while Doughty rested and recovered from his exertions, he ordered his officers to see that all the possessions which had been stolen were brought back to him. When he was fit for the journey, he promised, he would be escorted to Jedda, and handed over to the British consul there.

After four days' rest, both for himself and for the longsuffering camel, he did indeed set out for the coast, accompanied this time by a military escort. They retraced Doughty's steps to Ayn Ez Zeyma, where he had first been attacked by Salem. Now, though, they were travelling in safety, if not luxury. After the struggles he had been through, this was a gentle and relaxing journey. 'We were guests of the Night, and of the vast Wilderness. We drew out our victual, dates and cheese and bread, and filled a bowl with clear water of et-Tayif.'[44]

It was after five days that they told him that the next hill-top would show him the end of the journey – and from its vantage point he could make out the tall ships riding at anchor off the harbour at Jedda. Close at hand he took his last look at the woven tents of the nomad Arabs, but now they hurried down the hill towards the town.

And on the next day, Doughty recorded at the end of his book, the angry man who had started his journey in such bitterness at the attitude of the British diplomats of Damascus finished it in the only way possible. 'On the morrow,' he wrote, 'I was called to the open hospitality of the British consulate.'

Chapter Seven

===============

> You have of me Arabia, not seen through the spectacles of scholastical men, but the sounding of the living lips and hearts of the Arabian Arabs . . .
>
> Charles Doughty's private notes

For two years Doughty had stuck by his decision not to take a disguise, not to trick the people among whom he travelled with the pretence of Muslim devotion. He had refused to put on an act – but the hardships of the desert had bred in him a whole new personality. Where Charles Montagu Doughty of Theberton and Cambridge had been shy and reserved, Khalil the eccentric *saiehh* was robust and determined. He might be bullied, but he would not change his direction. Similarly, the bland, unimaginative judgements of the young wanderer in western Europe had given way to the incisive observations of an experienced traveller, and the old querulous anxiety about his health had been forgotten, at least for the time being, as he struggled at the very limits of endurance.

Khalil el Engleysy, Khalil the Englishman, would stay with him for the rest of his life, with his memories of Arabia. Years later, when Doughty was an old man, he had a cabinet in his study containing mementoes of his journey. Carefully arranged inside, alongside the books he had carried around the desert, were a porcupine quill he had picked up by the wayside, his coffee pot, the scales and thermometer on which he had relied for so many of his observations, and a seal inscribed with the name 'Khalil'.[1] That was the name of his travels, and the one by which his future wife would call him throughout their married life.

It was not simply a role that he could slough off easily: for months after he arrived home he would wear Arab dress, and call things by their Arabic names; he complained that meat and European food burned his mouth. Khalil had entered into the marrow of his bones.

Now, though, as he luxuriated in the hospitality of the British embassy, and contrasted it wryly with the offhand dismissal he had received at the hands of Mr Jago in Damascus, it was time to adopt once more the ways of an English gentleman. His adventuring was not over: thin and genuinely ill as he now was, shaking with fever, he was determined to follow through the plan he had spelled out before and take ship to India. But now he could travel as Charles Doughty, moving among his peers: he might expect cooperation and a degree of respect as a gentleman and a scholar.

Those hopes, though, were disappointed. The ship he had taken for Bombay docked briefly at Aden, giving Doughty the idea of inspecting the nearby volcanic island of Perim, which he thought might profitably be compared with the observations he had already made of the Arabian landscape. But the British troops there took one look at the wild-eyed, hollow-cheeked and dishevelled figure before them, and turned him back ignominiously. 'Arrived from Arabia, I was clad as an Arab, and the little cockney adjutant in the camp insulted me before his British troop, and the Commanding Officer would not permit me to visit Perim ... In sum, they had taken me in their imagination for a Russian spy.'[2]

It must have been an easy mistake to make. When he arrived in Bombay, he struggled to the European hospital there, only to be met at the top of the steps by the forbidding figure of the resident surgeon. 'I saw a tall man with a red beard come up the steps on to the verandah; he said, "I want to come into the hospital", and I replied "Only Europeans are admitted"; he then said, "But I am an Englishman, and my name is Doughty."'[3]

His foot was swollen and inflamed, probably from the boils from which he had suffered on his nightmare journey to Jedda, and he had picked up a virulent liver infection from drinking polluted water. Once his racial credentials were satisfactorily established, he was fascinated by the sight through the microscope of the parasites which were troubling him, the doctor said later; if so, it was about the only diversion that Bombay could afford.

Englishman or not, government officials there had seen enough penniless travellers turning up in their comfortable little community and asking for succour, and his appeals for the cashing of a banker's draft and for the loan of books were studiously ignored. Apart from the cash he wanted to borrow some volumes of his beloved Chaucer to while away the hours, and it was the refusal of that help, rather than gratitude for the hospital's treatment, that stayed with him.

> When I requested a loan of a few very ordinary books to amuse my languors it was denied with that supercilious air of suspicion which is intolerable to any forlorn man. Much less when I arrived desperately sick, and having saved only my book of Bankers' cheques about me . . . durst I think of asking such scientific persons to have the humanity to recommend them, but I was obliged to go lie in the wretched hospital till I could send a letter to England . . . [4]

He was angered by his treatment – but even so he offered to prepare a paper for the Bombay Asiatic Society. It was planned as a lengthy offering, setting out in some detail the discoveries he had made in Medain Salih, and comparing them with the stories he had heard earlier. The contrast between the fantastic accounts of the 'famous theatre of a divine judgment' and the crumbling, dusty remains he had found was marked.

> Having got there after great fatigue, I found the Arabs' seven cities, hewn in so many mountains, to be about a hundred funeral chambers, excavated in the sandstone rocks . . . The city appears by the traces remaining of foundations, to have been a cluster of four or five palm villages in clay, each of them surrounded by a wall, a manner ordinary in all the Arabian countries. [5]

He is attempting a judicious detachment, playing down the excitement of his original discoveries. Doughty was already determined to establish his scientific credentials.

When he actually rose to his feet in the society's library on 9 November 1878, though, the few notes he had actually prepared were hurriedly squeezed into a meeting alongside accounts of archaeological finds near Kolhapur, and a report on the local flora of Bombay.[6] Even his name – M. C. Doughty – was wrongly printed in the society's journal.

But this unseemly rush was not entirely the fault of the society. As Doughty lay in the 'wretched hospital', a piece of news had reached him that changed his plans completely. The *Bombay Gazette* announced that the English troopship HMS *Crocodile* was arriving in port, under the command of Captain Frederick Proby Doughty – the same cousin from Martlesham with whom he had rambled through the mountains of Wales so many years before. Small wonder then that, ill as he was, he should have hurried to the port, apologizing to the gentlemen of the Asiatic Society that he found himself, on the point of sailing for England, unable to prepare the detailed paper he had planned.

Doughty found his cousin's ship moored to a buoy in Bombay harbour, a gold Star of India gleaming on her bow as the sailors busily smartened up her white paint. She was due to start the return journey to Portsmouth just two weeks later. Captain Doughty, like most of his family, believed his cousin Charles was lost and probably dead in the deserts of Arabia – and indeed the gaunt and trembling Doughty, limping on his sore foot and stumbling over his words, must have borne little resemblance to the fresh-faced boy the captain remembered from his father's house in Theberton twenty years or more before.

For his part, the ambitious young midshipman whose tales of derring-do had towered over Doughty's childhood now stalked the deck of his own command with the grizzled dignity of a sea-captain who had even further promotion in his sights.

Although *Crocodile* was a veteran of the India troop run, it was Captain Doughty's first voyage out to Bombay: it seemed to be fate that he should have met his long-lost cousin. With Doughty tired, ill and disillusioned, there was no doubt in the mind of either of them what should be done. He would leave hospital, leave Bombay, and sail with his cousin back to England. This time, his travelling really was over.

At 10.45 a.m. on the morning of 22 November, with Doughty's duties at the Asiatic Society hurriedly completed, the *Crocodile* weighed anchor, and he was on his way home. It was the first long sea voyage for a man whose early ambition had been to join the navy and, sick as he was, he took every advantage of it, wandering the ship to watch the sailors at work, and listening to his cousin's tales with the same enthusiasm he had shown as a boy.

There was a fresh breeze across the Arabian Sea, and on 30 November the captain's journal noted: 'Passed close round Aden; it looked particularly well in the morning sun; passed Perim at 8 p.m.'[7] Doughty was getting his last glimpses of the harsh land where he had nearly died and, from the relative comfort of the rail of *Crocodile*, it looked calm and serene. At 6.52 p.m. on 6 December, after steaming steadily up the coast of Arabia, they tied up at Suez. Captain Doughty, at least, had no painful memories to colour his view of the landscape. 'A lovely evening, calm bright and sunny. Never saw barren shores look more lovely; so variegated in their shades.'[8]

But as the voyage progressed, the explorer began to talk. He had tales of his own to tell of the 'barren shores', as Captain Doughty's daughter Marion recalled later.

> Amongst the large company of officers and their wives he had met on board, he was very definite in his preferences. At first bewildered and silenced by the large numbers who sat down together to meals, he gradually selected three or four to whom he was glad to offer tea in the captain's cabin – and it amused my father to note the extreme anxiety shown to be one of those lucky guests![9]

On Christmas Eve the *Crocodile* arrived back in the 'cold, wet, comfortable weather' of Portsmouth, where Captain Doughty's family were waiting to meet him. Doughty was taken straight to Martlesham to share his cousin's hospitality. He was still frail, still mentally tuned to the Arab life he had left behind, and must have been a striking figure in a quiet Suffolk village. Marion Doughty, as she then was, was eight years old; nearly fifty years later she still remembered

> this strange unknown cousin, of whose adventures my father had many stories to tell. My cousin made a great impression on me, young as I was, and I can still see him, as it were yesterday.
>
> Very tall, thin, not in the least bronzed, reddish fair hair and beard, in whitish cotton clothes of some soft Eastern material, a green band often twisted around his waist, sockless, feet thrust into heelless sandals, and using when he went out a green umbrella. This, in December, struck us immensely!
>
> ... As he impressed us children – my brother and myself – so he impressed our elders – his height and dignity of bearing, his extreme courtesy of speech and manner, a quiet shy humour, and an unerring detection of affectation and insincerity.
>
> He spoke seldom, and when he first returned, with some hesitation, as if his native language did not come quite easily to him – but to a child he was not at all alarming, and when out walking had a way of finding interest and using his powers of observation in the dullest surroundings.

But England was not the same place that he had left eight years before; and even the small differences in manners and customs made it less a country in which he could feel at home. Later in his life, when he was asked what was the first change that had struck him on his return, he had no hesitation. 'People helping each other on with their overcoats. When I first went abroad, a man would have resented that as an implication that he was becoming helpless; when I came back, I found it was the polite thing to do.'[10]

Doughty had never felt confident or at ease in society; now, after eight years spent alone in distant lands, he found his own manners and assumptions had become quaint and outdated at home. He had always felt more at home in the past; now, irrevocably, the modern world was yet another foreign country to him.

But Doughty was not prepared to be simply a character, an eccentric. Friendly and easygoing as he was with the family and the children, he believed that the work he had done in Arabia entitled him to some respect among the academic establishment, and he was determined to prove it – the more so because of the lack of support and encouragement he had been offered when he first set off with the Hadj pilgrims.

Getting into print was a matter of some urgency: Doughty already knew that Wilfrid Blunt had arrived in Hail with his wife, Lady Anne, only a few months after he himself had left Arabia, and reports which were filtering through to Paris of a mysterious Englishman travelling through northern Arabia under the name of Khalil were being interpreted as referring to him. Doughty, it seemed, was anonymous, unknown, and in danger of remaining so. And it was not just the Blunts: Sir Richard Burton had been making enquiries about Medain Salih, apparently with a view to setting off on a journey of his own, and the French explorer Charles Huber had also been travelling in the area, with the backing of the Ministry of Public Instruction in Paris. Weak and ill as he was, unless Doughty could get something published quickly, he might lose all the credit for his travelling and his explorations.

Almost his first act when he landed in England had been to write to the Damascus embassy asking anxiously what had happened to the notes, drawings and precious 'squeezes' he had sent from Medain Salih with the returning caravan. He heard back from Mr Jago himself, the consul who had treated him with such disdain – and who still apparently wanted little to do with this inconvenient and inconsiderate traveller. The packages had arrived, Mr Jago told him, and had been locked away unopened in a cupboard. If Mr Doughty wanted, he would be more than welcome to come and collect them for himself. There was also, incidentally, 1,000 piastres[11] waiting in his name, the balance of the money he had lodged with his bankers after his return from Vienna.

No one could tell him what condition the delicate *papier-mâché* 'squeezes' were in and, in a panic, he set off from Martlesham to Damascus to collect them for himself. But Doughty was still completely exhausted, shivering with fever, and weak from his liver infection. Once he had recovered his possessions, he spent much of the year recuperating in Italy and Capri, worrying about how to arrange for the publication of his discoveries, and firing off anxious letters to publishers, museums, learned societies and individual Arabists. It was autumn before he could tell a correspondent, 'It is only in the last week that I have felt a little recovered from the miseries of Arabian travelling.'[12]

The weariness of eight years of travelling did not mean that he settled down: over the next months he moved from lodging to lodging, from Vico Equense on the Gulf of Naples to Capri, Siena, Viareggio, Bagni di Lucca, Florence, Spezzia and Sicily. But it was very different from his old serendipitous wandering across Europe, and still more removed from the physical challenges of Arabia. He was still obliged to stay in the cheaper lodging houses, but these were comfortable towns where the English expatriate community often stretched back for generations, and where there were English schools, newspapers and doctors. Among the churches, the gaily coloured villas, and the vineyards and orchards of Vico Equense, for instance, Doughty's *Baedeker* would have told him, 'visitors of all nationalities are met with. The space is limited, but the district generally is pervaded with an air of peaceful enjoyment.'

They were favourite places for escaping from a northern European winter, places where the expatriates came to find quiet and recuperation, and where many of them became infected with a sort of literary gush. In Capri the doyenne of the English community wrote enthusiastically of the peace of the late 1870s. 'Silence, warm green silence, is around you. You can watch the jessamines and orange blossoms popping and bursting in the sunshine until their scent makes you lean back against the wall and doze in a dream of heady fragrance . . .'[13] At Bagni di Lucca, in Tuscany, there had been several writers and artists before him. Elizabeth Barrett Browning had sung its praises in a letter home soon after she was married.

> We have taken a sort of eagle's nest in the highest of the
> three villages, called Bagni di Lucca, which lie at the heart
> of a hundred mountains, sung to continually by a rushing
> mountain stream. The sound of the river and of the *cicali*
> is all the noise we hear . . . [14]

Doughty was still a sick man and, though never a gusher, he too welcomed the recuperative qualities of the various Italian towns where he lived. He was looking for the peace that would enable him to put in order the disparate impressions of some twenty months' wandering through the desert.

His friend Alois Sprenger, the author of the Arabian geography book he had carried on his travels, arranged for the publication of a series of articles in the prestigious German journal *Globus*, which would at least give him the opportunity to establish that, whoever might have followed him, he had been the first explorer to reach Kheybar, and the first to bring back copies of the Medain Salih inscriptions. Through his correspondence with the magazine's editor, Richard Kiepert, he was also able to keep abreast of the progress of his rivals, Huber and Euting. It was one of these letters from Kiepert that showed how well-founded were his anxieties. 'Huber thought he was the first European to penetrate into this part of Arabia, but has discovered that he was wrong, and that an Englishman, calling himself Khalil had just traversed the very same region. Am I right in believing you are that Khalil?'[15] Among the scientific community in Europe, Kiepert promised, he would correct the growing belief that Khalil was the pseudonym of Wilfrid Blunt. 'Mr Blunt was never nearer to Kheybar than 170 English miles; it is therefore strange to believe that he was that Khalil. But I shall write to the Editor of the *Bulletin*[16] to settle that error.'[17] That was some relief. But the progress of Charles Huber was galling: his travels were admiringly documented in the European academic journals, he was awarded the gold medal of the Paris Geographical Society, he had already arranged the publication of 146 inscriptions. With Euting, he was credited with the 'discovery' of the carved stone monument which Doughty had found in Teyma. His lionization was all in stark contrast to the indifference with which Doughty found himself being treated. And then, in 1884, came news that put those feelings of rivalry into context. 'Did you read the article . . . on the ancient Aramaean monument found at Teyma by Professor Euting of Strasburg, and that your follower Charles Huber, also of Strasburg, and companion of Euting, was murdered by the *Beni Harb* not far from Jedda?'[18] The news must have brought back memories of Doughty's own confrontation in the sand, as he struggled towards Taif. If Huber had fared better than Doughty in terms of the respect of his peers at home, he had paid for it dearly.

Initially there was considerable interest in the inscriptions Doughty had brought back, even though the British Museum, he complained later, turned them down 'rather contemptuously'. His self-confidence blossomed: from Berlin and Paris came tentative offers to arrange publication, and it occurred to him that he might make some much-needed money from his efforts as well as establishing himself as a scholar and explorer.

But Doughty was never much of a negotiator, and he had a weak hand to play. The inscriptions were only copies, and roughly made copies at that; everyone knew that he was desperate to see them published; and in any case, other explorers would be coming back soon with similar material. When the Royal Museum of Berlin asked him to name his price, Doughty fixed on £500; their initial counter-offer was £300, and even that was withdrawn after they had seen some of the 'squeezes'. He turned to Paris, suggesting that the Académie des Inscriptions[19] there might make a similar offer – but the arrangement they eventually proposed was simply that they would publish the material in a single volume, giving Doughty 150 free copies for himself.

It was not a deal that would ease his financial embarrassment, but both Doughty and the Académie knew that he had no real choice, and in 1884 the *Documents Epigraphiques recueillis dans le nord de l'Arabie* appeared in Paris, to almost complete lack of interest. Just thirty-one of the author's copies were sold, giving him a net profit of precisely FF614.85.[20] That was to be the sum total of Doughty's financial profit from his months in Arabia for years to come.

He continued to feel bitter about the lack of interest in the inscriptions that he had taken such trouble and so many risks to gather, and about the lack of money that he made from them. They represented a considerable achievement: the different languages of the various examples he had gathered demonstrated how the various ancient Arabian races had been dispersed over the peninsula, and how the trade routes had linked them together. But for all the excitement with which he had copied them down from the rough rock faces where he had found them, for all his insistence on scholarly accuracy, his interest had never been really engaged by the minutiae of the inscriptions: despite the urgency with which he pressed his claim as their discoverer, the haggling with various museums and learned bodies meant that it took him more than five years to get them into print. The passion which months of travelling through Arabia had inspired was focused on more than a collection of rough carvings.

His attempts to gain recognition at home of his achievements as an explorer were rebuffed even more comprehensively than his efforts to publish the inscriptions. Individual scholars to whom he wrote were impressed, and the articles in *Globus* had excited some interest among Arabists and geographers on the continent, but it was the Royal Geographical Society which held the key to the establishment of a reputation in London.

Late in 1883, nearly five years after his return from the desert, he finally stood before a meeting of the society to which he had appealed in vain from Vienna. He had much to be proud of, and he was not shy of letting his audience know it: 'I can suppose there is no Arabian of the blood who has so wide a witting of his own vast country,' he declared.[21] But the evening was not a success, as Doughty himself realized.

He admitted, less than tactfully, that his grasp of geology might be thought out of date, but went on to tell this learned society airily, 'Once geologist, always geologist.' Warming to his subject, and apparently oblivious to the disapproving glances, he dismissed the criticism that his map might have been improved by more accurate measurements than estimates based on numbers of camel journeys.

> It is the faithful record of nearly two years of incessant
> fatigues and jeopardy. You may know that if I had made
> instrumental observations in such a land they had been
> lost, for I had not returned alive without a miracle. Such
> niceties I count but a poor task of surveyors . . . [22]

Lofty contempt like that was hardly likely to impress an audience of scientists who might all too easily think that the 'surveyors' jibe applied to them. The memory of the evening stayed with Doughty for the rest of his life. He had only recently returned from Italy, and his health had not been good, but he admitted later that he made 'a very poor figure which I am ashamed of'.[23] 'Extraordinary story, remarkable diction. A tall wiry man with a fatigue-worn face . . .' was the terse diary note of one member who attended the meeting.[24]

The chairman of the RGS, Sir Henry Rawlinson, was more outspoken. Sir Henry, a veteran of the Indian army, and of Persia, Afghanistan and Baghdad, was damning about his guest's performance, his paper and his personality. He was an expert in his own right on the deciphering of ancient inscriptions, and not a man to mince his words under any circumstances. Portraits of him at the time show a bristling white moustache, mutton-chop whiskers and bulldog jowls, and even his friends referred to the 'brusquerie' of his manner. In a confidential report he was unyielding in his refusal to countenance the publication of Doughty's account as it stood.

> No doubt the author traversed a large extent of unknown
> country in Central and North-Western Arabia and visited
> many new and interesting sites, but he had none of the
> qualifications necessary to turn his travels to account. He
> had no geographical acquirements; no knowledge of
> instruments; no capacity for useful observation, while
> on the other hand he seems to have to adopt in the
> description of this journey, such an extravagant eccen-
> tricity of style and language as to make his notes not only
> unfitted to the pages of a scientific journal, but almost
> unintelligible to any reader, be he scientific or other-
> wise . . . [25]

At the time the daunting Sir Henry must have been more than a match for a weak and sickly Doughty. But, once in an argument, Doughty too was unwilling to compromise, as one of the society's former secretaries recalled later. 'I tried to act as a peacemaker, but Doughty was difficult to handle. Rawlinson was a fiery old fellow, who used to glower at me across the Council table . . .'[26]

The account of the paper that was finally drawn up by the society's secretary caused considerable acrimony. It concentrated on precisely the romantic orientalist view of Arabia that Doughty despised. He was described as telling his audience, for instance, that at Maan 'I learned . . . that all the next land of wilderness was ruled by one Ibn Rashid, a mighty prince of Beduin blood, who lorded it over the tribes . . . some new David or Robin Hood.'[27]

No doubt the report simply concentrated on those aspects of his address that the writer thought would interest the readers of the *RGS Journal*, but it started a dispute between Doughty and the society that was to last for several years, and would do nothing for his hopes of scientific appreciation.

Doughty had been angered by the original lack of interest of the society in his travels, and later he complained bitterly at the way he was treated both before and after his journey. It was the refusal of RGS backing, he claimed, that had led to his disdainful treatment at the hands of Mr Jago. 'I departed for the perilous Arabian journey without any good word of the London Geographers, the loss of which was the loss of all Consular recommendations at Damascus; for which lack I suffered doubly in that horrible country, and from thence am returned by a miracle.'[28]

He complained that his letters had been ignored, the society's officials had been unwilling to meet him even when he called, and the cantankerous Sir Henry himself had omitted him from a list he had given of Arabian travellers to a later meeting of the society. He had, stormed Doughty, 'the forgetfulness!!? not to mention me, although . . . I saw that he very well remembered me. That was to make me as far as he could pass for no Arabian traveller.'[29] He would not abandon the argument over his paper, and in letter after letter, he defended his style with passion.

> As an English scholar I will never submit to have my language of the best times turned into the misery of today – that were unworthy of me. Some words I should alter myself upon more leisure and better advisement in the revision to make all run more smoothly. It were a dangerous task for others to alter a phrase.[30]

A few months later, still dissatisfied, he was even more forthright:

> I had as soon the good Sherif had hanged me at Taif as
> be made to speak so Middlesex-like . . . Pray let no word
> be altered, or else I retire and must disown it altogether
> as not my work. It is chaste and right English of the best
> time and without a word of Costermongery . . . [31]

In the end, for all the bluster, he did indeed back down in the
face of the immovable rock of Sir Henry's disapproval, and the version
of his paper which was finally printed was the one which had been
recast and re-edited by the society's officers – but paper and publication were the start of a running battle with the Royal Geographical
Society that was to last for years.

There were similar clashes with other learned societies. The
British Association, for instance, had inadvertently left Doughty's
name off its list of life members for two years – an omission which,
he complained, could only lead his friends to conclude that he was
dead. The response of at least one of those friends suggests that his
fears were exaggerated – his former Cambridge examiner, the geologist Dr T. G. Bonney, wrote rather woundingly that he had known
nothing of what had happened to him for years. 'I . . . supposed that
you were residing in peace at Theberton Hall . . . I congratulate you
on your return safe and sound, although you have been "assassin-
ated".'[32] So much, Doughty must have thought, for his hopes of fame
and appreciation. But the association's mistake was a useful stick
with which to beat it for its failure, like the RGS, to reply to his
appeal from Vienna for help in joining the Hadj caravan.

Dr Bonney introduced him to the Geological Society, to which
he presented another paper dealing with the geology of Arabia. No
detailed account exists of the evening, but the records show that
afterwards first one expert and then another was asked to approve
his work for publication – and that it never appeared in the society's
journal.[33] Sir Henry Rawlinson was evidently not alone in his estimate of Doughty's scientific prowess: recognition among the scientific
establishment was proving painfully elusive.

Doughty defended his scholarship with the same vigour with
which he had defended his Christianity in the desert – but in fact he

was less sure than he pretended of his right to appreciation for his achievements. His anxiety for approval, the humility with which he wrote to other scholars asking for their help and advice, and the petulance with which he hit back at real or imagined slights, are all marks of his intellectual insecurity. Arabia had made him more outspoken and determined, but he was also painfully conscious of his limitations. Dr Bonney might treat him as a friend – but he had still awarded him only a second-class degree.

For all his studies at Cambridge, for all his clambering about on the Norwegian glaciers, for all his pernickety exactness over the details of his inscriptions, Doughty was essentially a poet, rather than the scientist and scholar he was striving to be. His experiences had set his imaginative soul on fire. With the inscriptions and carvings, for instance, what fascinated him was not so much the steady accumulation of knowledge, building up into a scholarly epigraphist's overall picture of the distribution of the various Arab peoples of antiquity, but rather the imaginative link which they offered between himself and other travellers who had trodden the same paths over the centuries.

At Medain Salih he had found a grotesquely carved comic mask, grinning from a bearded face, its tongue lolling out contemptuously.

> Seeing this larva,* one might murmur again the words of Isaiah, 'Against whom makest thou a wide mouth, and drawest out the tongue?' I called my companions who mounted after me; and looking on the old stony mocker, they scoffed again, and came down with loud laughter and wondering.[34]

An archaeologist might have drawn one set of conclusions from the carved stone face, an anthropologist another, and a geologist another. They would all have looked at the rock and the carving through the lens of their own scientific specialization. But Doughty, whom no one could accuse of undue levity, sees a centuries-old joke;

* Mask.

he sees the link between the verses of the Bible and the simple Arabs who are his companions. His view of the stone face is imaginative, introspective: like the crudely carved names and slogans he had already found along the trading routes, it is a silent reminder that the present is at one with the past, that he is himself the heir of those who have gone before. It is the conclusion of a poet rather than a scientist.

So, too, is his response to the landscape around Kheybar – a description of which was one of the geographical discoveries he claimed. The details of the scene are faithfully painted, but it is again an essentially subjective description. We smell the rank stench of the soil, feel with Khalil the overpowering atmosphere of menace.

> The vulcanic field is a stony flood which has stiffened; long rolling heads, like horse-manes, of those slaggy waves ride and over-ride the rest: and as they are risen, they stand petrified, many being sharply split lengthwise, and the hollow laps are partly fallen down in vast shells and in ruinous heaps as of massy masonry ... We came though palm groves in a valley bottom ... Foul was the abandoned soil upon either hand, with only a few awry and undergrown stems of palms. The squalid ground is whitish with crusts of bitter salt-warp, and stained with filthy rust ... [35]

The diaries written before he arrived in the Holy Land reveal a conventional, literal-minded character, apparently without passion. It was the experience of Arabia, the accessibility of antiquity, the sense of a gritty reality behind the romantic blethering of the orientalists, that had shaped him. Arabia, one way or another, would continue to inform his writing and his imagination.

Early in 1879, within a few months of his return to England, he had started work on what was to become *Travels in Arabia Deserta* – an account of his own experiences in Arabia, of the clash of two cultures, of an individual's struggle in a hostile society. The desire for recognition as an explorer, and the need to raise what money he could, had driven him to get his inscriptions published as soon as he returned to England, but they were little more than a distraction from his main work. After a few months of what appeared to be an unequal struggle with uninterested publishers, he shrank back into the lonely life of a writer.

Living in Italy as a traveller, moving from lodging to lodging, was still at least as cheap as a settled life might have been in England, and much more congenial. It was not just the weather and the scenery: in an expatriate community he might find manners and customs less changed from those he remembered. He could put on his coat without fear of being helped. But he was not there simply to recuperate, and he had no time now for keeping a diary, still less for the sightseeing he had indulged in on his earlier wanderings through Europe. In his work on *Travels in Arabia Deserta* he had found the interest for which he had been searching before, and his days were filled with work on the diaries and notebooks which were gradually being transformed into his book.

It was a long and painstaking task, but he evidently made steady progress.[36] He worked through the notebooks, picking out the details and fleshing them out from his memory, and by the autumn of 1882 he was writing to his friends that the book was all but complete: Professor Sprenger wrote back to him:

> Your book promises to offer much fuller information than
> could be expected from a single individual ... we shall
> obtain from it a correct notion of the configuration of the
> soil and of the peculiar race of men bred upon it. It is
> extremely rare that a traveller has an eye for all the vari-
> ous phenomena that come under his observation.[37]

Such encouragement from a respected Arabist and geographer such as Sprenger would have delighted Doughty – and yet it is clear that the friendly Sprenger had not even seen the book. *Travels in Arabia Deserta*, for all its wealth of detail and information, is much more than a simple travel narrative, or the geographical treatise he describes. Khalil himself is at the heart of the book; it is his presence and the detailed examination of his reactions to the strange and

frightening world that surrounds him that make the story. His journey becomes almost a pilgrimage.

It is an image which had appealed to other Arabian travellers:
Richard Burton, thrusting exotic sights and daring escapades before
an admiring public some twenty-five years earlier, had called his
own bullish adventure story *Personal Narrative of a Pilgrimage to El
Medinah and Mecca*,[38] while Lady Anne Blunt chose the title *A Pilgrimage to Nejd*[39] for her own almost goggle-eyed depiction of the fantastic
and romantic world into which she and her husband had strayed.[40]
But Doughty was a much more inward-looking character than the
travellers who went before and after him. He was neither Blunt nor
Burton: *Travels in Arabia Deserta* is above all the story of an individual's fight for understanding and for survival – much more *Pilgrim's Progress* than *Pilgrimage to El Medinah and Mecca* or *Pilgrimage
to Nejd*.

But if Doughty believed that his labours were over, he was sadly
disappointed. It was the manner rather than the matter of the book
that put off the publishers to whom he first sent off his massive
600,000-word manuscript in its barely legible scrawl early in 1883.
His studies in the Bodleian had been almost exclusively of ancient
literature, and it was to the style of his 'beloved Master Edmund
Spenser' and 'good old Dan Chaucer' that he had aspired as he wrote.
He had been moved, he wrote later, by his 'dislike of the Victorian
English'.[41]

> In writing the volume Arabia Deserta, my main intention
> . . . was not so much the setting forth of personal wander-
> ings among a people of Biblical interest, as the ideal
> endeavour to continue the older tradition of Chaucer and
> Spenser, resisting to my power the decadence of English
> language: so that while my work should be a mere script
> for Orientalists, it should also be my life's contribution,
> so far, to literature.[42]

But the 'decadence of English language' was the stock-in-trade
of the publishers to whom Doughty was writing. Fashionable as the
subject of Arabia was, attacking 'Victorian English' in dealing with
them was as tactless as denigrating scientific exactitude had been at

the Royal Geographical Society. One after another, they rejected the manuscript. 'Most readers and all reviewers would . . . say that parts of it are not English at all,' wrote one. 'The manuscript ought to be taken in hand, recast, and practically rewritten by a practised literary man.'

When, in 1885, Cambridge University's Pitt Press did agree to bring out an edition of the book, it was out of respect for the information it contained about the Arab world rather than for its literary qualities. Under pressure from Professor William Wright and Professor Robertson Smith, two leading Arabic scholars at the university, they agreed to publish 1,000 copies of the work in two quarto volumes at an estimated cost of £700 – even though their initial calculations suggested they might only sell some 150 of them. But there was a catch: the printing would not go ahead, they announced, unless he would agree to accept the alterations and emendations of Professor Smith.

Doughty, already piqued at the damning criticism of his writing from all sides, was horrified, and his uncompromising response almost led them to cancel the entire arrangement. At one meeting the two academics tried repeatedly to persuade him to abandon some of the more glaring archaisms of his style. One of them later told a colleague about the indignant author's reaction.

> Both were filled with admiration at its wonderful story, but taken aback by the style . . . After two hours strenuous discussion, Doughty quietly said, 'I would prefer that the book be not published than change one word of my English. I value my style much more than my matter.'[43]

Smith himself – although he admitted privately to friends that he found little to admire in Doughty's writing – tried to reassure him that any changes and corrections would be easily borne. But he spelled the plain fact out directly enough: the publishers, he said, were ready to spend money on Arabia, but not on his experiment in English.[44]

Smith, though, had dealt with difficult authors before, in his capacity as editor of the *Encyclopaedia Britannica*, and he did his utmost to bring the two sides together. The final agreement allowed Doughty to accept or refuse his suggestions as he thought fit – but it cut the print run from 1,000 to 500, and put at least some of the financial burden on the author himself. It was clear from the start that Doughty's great work would make him no money: all he could hope for now was simply to see his book in print.[45]

He had sacrificed any possibility of making a profit for himself, and now he had put at risk the very publication of the book on which he had already spent nearly seven years' effort. For his work to be worth such dedication, it had to be accurate, and with the first volume already at the printers, he continued with the detailed revision of what he had written. He fired off letters to archaeologists, scientists, Arabists and travellers all over Europe and beyond to check facts, gather more details about the items he had brought home with him, and ensure that the spelling and translations of the Arabic phrases he used were as authoritative as possible.

The tone of his letters is often humble: truculent as he could be in defence of his writing, he was prepared to acknowledge his limitations when dealing with acknowledged experts. 'My difficulties will often seem to you childish,' he wrote apologetically to Professor M. J. de Goeje, a famous Arabic scholar whom he had first met during his time at Leiden,[46] while to his sometime rival, the traveller Julius Euting, he offered grateful thanks for help with the Arabic of his inscriptions: 'Best thanks for the correction, *Gofeifeh*. I suspected there was a letter wrong. I should be grateful if you could tell me if my sketch map is wrong between el 'Ola and Wejh, and whether you found it satisfactory for the rest . . .'[47]

Of his geographical discoveries[48] and his map, constructed, as he said, 'from the accidental wild talk of Beduins',[49] he was particularly proud. That he was successful in checking and verifying the details of his own observations can be seen from T. E. Lawrence's estimate of the role of the book in his own desert campaign. Sir Henry Rawlinson might query his accuracy; Lawrence, the Arab Bureau and the entire British war effort in Arabia had no such qualms. Many of the Arabs who joined the revolt came from the tribes with whom Doughty had wandered, Lawrence said later: *Travels in Arabia Deserta* 'became a military text-book, and helped to guide us to victory in the East. The Arabs who had allowed Doughty to wander in their

GOD'S FUGITIVE

forbidden provinces were making a good investment for their sons and grandsons.'[50]

But all the defences of Doughty's obscure and idiosyncratic prose have the smell of special pleading. *Travels in Arabia Deserta* is a book that repays study a thousandfold, but no one can claim that it is a straightforward or an easy read: so why did he adopt a way of writing that not only antagonized his publishers, but was also certain to come between him and his readers?

The book that was to be published had to be *his* book, written in his words. He could undoubtedly be cantankerous and obstinate, but his determination in the defence of his style shows him to be a man of courage. As far as he was concerned, the constant attempts to refine his writing style were an attack on the accuracy with which he had sought to reflect the atmosphere of the world through which he had travelled. Arabic words and phrases, archaisms, the rhythms of his sentences, were all part of his overarching concern to present 'the soil of Arabia, smelling of *samn* and camels'.[51]

> As we looked for our Aarab, we were suddenly in sight
> of the slow wavering bulks of camels feeding dispersedly
> under the horizon; the sun nigh setting, they were driven
> in toward the Beduin camp, *menzil*, another hour distant.
> Come to the herdsmen, we alighted and sat down, and
> one of the lads receiving our bowl, ran under his *nagas**
> to milk for us . . . [52]

His writing, above all, is the art of light and shade. To rewrite a passage like that in bland, everyday Victorian English would be to flatten it, to eradicate the delicate tones of the original. Striking out the unfamiliar words and simplifying the construction of the sentences might make the passage superficially easier to understand, but it would dilute the mood of a shimmering desert twilight, and hobble a rhythm that is often Biblical. The two volumes of *Travels in Arabia Deserta*, Doughty observed pointedly years later, were 'only nominally prose'.[53]

He had allowed himself to be browbeaten over his report to the

* Female camels.

Royal Geographical Society, but when it came to his book itself, he was unmovable. This was no mere paper for a London society, but his first effort at a literary work that would live after him. It should represent the truth about his journey as precisely as he could express it; it should present the character and contradictions of Khalil; and, just as important, it should reflect his deepest feelings about the English language itself.

A letter written more than thirty-five years later gives a glimpse of the intensity with which he pored over his revisions in Italy. He was visited as he worked in Alassio by the distinguished orientalist Guy Le Strange,[54] who 'spent a morning with me at my rooms: he among inscriptions, and I busy writing *Arabia Deserta*. I fell asleep many times over my work, never having fully recovered from Arabia, which he good-humouredly did not mind.'[55]

The visit, incidentally, demonstrated more than Doughty's weariness: it was not only publishers and academics who were uneasy with his writing style. Le Strange said later that his companion and fellow orientalist, Laurence Oliphant[56] was so impressed with the work Doughty had done already, but so bemused by its style, that he suggested that he should offer to rewrite it from start to finish.[57] It was a back-handed compliment that might have provoked a sharp response if it had ever reached the author.

But Doughty had more mundane matters on his mind than his running battle over 'chaste and right English of the best time'. From Italy he fired off a series of letters to the Royal Geographical Society in an attempt to end their quarrel, and win himself some practical support. Would they indemnify him against any possible personal loss caused by the tough contract he had signed with the Cambridge University Press? No, they would not.

Would they pay for the services of a 'competent Arabist', who could check Doughty's Arabic as he went? No, they would not. Would the RGS – 'a rich Society, which professes to aid those enterprises, and has no other cause for existing' – offer him a grant of £50 towards the mounting costs of his enterprise? The response to that plea was the same as all the others, and Doughty wrote back angrily, 'If the result of my application had been otherwise, I should have thought it a *miracle* . . . It is evident to me that the lack is not on my part, and the hostility of the RGS I suppose I may ascribe to the personal enmity of some considerable personages . . .'[58]

From petulance, he was slipping into near-paranoia. He was growing increasingly anxious that other accounts of Arabian travels might pre-empt his own book – and also, he claimed, beginning to wonder whether going on with volume two was worth the strain it was putting on his health and his meagre resources.

> The obstacles are so great, the vexations are so many, the
> present terms of the University Press are so onerous, my
> health is so weak, and the ruin of my time so disgusting
> that I begin to doubt if I ought not to wash my hands of
> the task . . . Why should I make such a sacrifice for a few
> persons called Orientalists and geographers nearly
> unknown to me? I am afraid it will be beyond my
> powers.[59]

It has the sound of an angry stamp of the foot rather than a genuine threat; but when Doughty wrote that letter, he was still eighteen long months from finishing his painstaking amendments. For all his optimism of five years earlier, it was the summer of 1887 before the notebooks and diaries, according to Doughty's pencil jottings across them, were all finally revised. On 23 July he was able to write to his friend and fellow Arabist Professor de Goeje, 'I have been working incessantly upon my second vol. of Travels . . . Now, *el-Hamd'illah*,* as the Beduins say, I am at the end, and have only the Index to print off.'[60]

But there had been more even than the publication of *Travels in Arabia Deserta* to fill Doughty's life. As he worked passionately and singlemindedly on checking and revising the book, his personal life had changed radically. The roles of shy, stammering schoolboy, soli-

* Praise be to God!

tary traveller and lonely, unappreciated scholar were all in the past; now he had a new part to play.

Two years before his triumphant letter to de Goeje, he had been spending the winter of 1885 at Alassio, in Italy, where he had met General Sir Montagu McMurdo, a veteran of the Sind campaigns and the Crimean War. The general's father-in-law and commanding officer had been Sir Charles Napier himself, known as the Conqueror of Sind,[61] and it was natural that Doughty, with his own frustrated dreams of serving Queen and country, should seek to make the acquaintance of such an old warrior – the more so as he was a friend of Doughty's Cambridge contact, Professor Robertson Smith.

Compared with the towns Doughty had lived in before, Alassio was little known to the English: the general, retiring there ten years earlier, had been the first foreigner to make his home on the slopes overlooking the straggling line of villas which stretched along the shore below.[62] Now he was a respected member of the community, the terraced garden his wife had planned and set out on the mountainside well known and widely admired – although, to the general's chagrin, the local women appeared to find his cherished stone walls particularly useful for drying their laundry in the sun.

Doughty became a frequent visitor at the Villa Napier, named in honour of Lady McMurdo's illustrious father – and the following spring he proposed to the daughter of the household, Caroline Amelia. At twenty-three, she was nearly twenty years younger than he was – young enough for him to be confident of being able to maintain his position as respected head of the family and the source of wisdom and knowledge. And at the same time his bride-to-be enjoyed family military connections of which any frustrated naval officer might be proud. Later that year he wrote to his friend Le Strange: 'My dear *arooz** is daughter of General Sir Montagu McMurdo, one of the heroes of Scinde . . . Our wedding will be in October, *Inshallah*.'[†63] Her family may not have been impressed at the more practical aspects of the match: Doughty, at forty-two, had weak health, little money and no evident prospects, while Caroline

* Wife.
† God willing.

had no private fortune – but there was no doubting the love the couple felt for each other. In October 1886, back in England, they were married at St John's Church, Fulham.

But not ill health, marriage or bereavement were to be allowed to interfere with *Travels in Arabia Deserta*. For their honeymoon Doughty took his bride and his books off to a little granite cottage overlooking the Helford river in the Glendurgan valley, near Falmouth, in Cornwall. It was a remote, peaceful start to their life together: when Doughty could be persuaded away from his desk, they would watch the women of the village leading strings of donkeys, laden with pilchards, mackerel, lobsters and crabs, along the five-mile track to Falmouth market. Or the two of them might wander through the laurel maze and the famous gardens of Glendurgan House. For Caroline, the exotic plants and trees must have been a reminder of the home and garden she had left behind in Alassio. She longed to travel to the Middle East, to see at least some of the places her new husband had told her so much about, but he, intent on finishing the second volume of his book by Christmas, was immersed in his work. He wrote again to Le Strange. 'I have brought my bride to this Cornish coast, and we are living in a cottage in beautiful grounds, hoping to go on after this to Italy . . . If we go to Syria, will Oliphant answer a letter of enquiries? I hear he never writes?'[64] But Italy was more than a year away, and Syria would have to wait until after *Travels in Arabia Deserta* was published. The deadline of Christmas that Doughty had set himself was pushed back first into the new year, then to the autumn: for now, even in the time not devoted to his writing and revision, he was closeted in his study. A few days later he wrote again to Le Strange to thank him for the gift of a newly translated Arabic classic. 'I have received with the greatest pleasure your beautiful volume of Mukadassi[65] . . . in my little spare time, I have already got far into it . . . I am working again: the second vol. of Arabian travels is half through. *Inshallah* it will be ended in the spring.'[66]

But ten months later he was still exchanging anxious cards with Professor de Goeje in Leiden as he fretted over the Arabic of his index. He and his wife had moved from Glendurgan to rent a little cottage called Beacon Crag, high in the cliffs outside the fishing village of Porthleven on the other side of the Lizard peninsula. Personal worries, even the most serious ones, were kept at bay. One card in September 1887 apologizes for a delay in writing. 'I did not write to thank you by the next post, as my dear wife's confinement filled me with anxieties. She is safe, but our little one is in the churchyard.'[67] Pregnancy was a dangerous adventure for the Victorians, and still-birth a common tragedy. But even so, there seems something disturbingly detached about the businesslike way Doughty pressed ahead with his writing and his studies as his wife of barely twelve months recovered from her ordeal. A few days later he is writing to de Goeje again.

> You have indeed enriched my index, which has become to me the most interesting part of the work. There are a shoal of words . . . which have puzzled everyone that now, to my comfort and astonishment, you have – I am afraid with no little tiresome expenditure of your valuable time – fully made out . . . I thank you for your kind sympathy – my dear wife is getting on well and out of danger.[68]

Even making allowances for the limitations of a postcard and for Doughty's unwillingness to write to a professional and academic colleague about his personal feelings, it seems a cold, controlled note. There is an echo of the young man who watched so dispassionately as the shipwrecked fishermen were plucked from the sea off the coast of Sicily.

Apart from a brief reference in another postcard to de Goeje to a 'slight relapse' later in the same month, which delayed a planned visit to his wife's family in Alassio, there is no more mention of Caroline Doughty's illness or of the couple's dead first child. Doughty had lived a solitary life as a child, and spent much of his adulthood travelling among strangers: the expression of feeling or affection remained almost an impossibility. Emotion upon the page was one thing; real life, it seemed, was more difficult to manage.

It was a long struggle, both for him and for his new wife; but early in 1888, nine years after he had started work, the two volumes of *Travels in Arabia Deserta* appeared from the Pitt Press.

It was never going to be a big-selling book. Quite apart from the demands of Doughty's style, more than 600,000 words of closely-printed text gave ample evidence that this was, in Doughty's own phrase, 'not milk for babes'[69] and, at three guineas a copy, it was an expensive as well as an acquired taste. It was in no sense a book for the casual reader – and the production costs incurred by Doughty's almost obsessive corrections and alterations at every stage meant that his debt to the publishers amounted to nearly £750.

So, at the age of forty-four, the man whose literary ambitions had been forged amongst the ancient texts of the Bodleian Library twenty years before had produced his first work. In a sense he had never been a young man – in his thirties he was already pointing dramatically to his beard as evidence of his great age and venerability; and his travels had filled nine years when he might have been writing – they had been, he wrote later, 'a not wholly welcome life-day's interruption'.[70] It was, though, the stimulus of Arabia that had unlocked his vivid imagination.

There is nothing that gives as close an insight into the interests and the character of Charles Doughty as the 1,200 pages of *Travels in Arabia Deserta*. Whether through concern for his privacy, or because of a misplaced sense of modesty, he burned all his manuscripts of the book itself; but the original notebooks which he carried through Arabia survive, alongside the published volumes themselves.

In those notebooks, often barely legible, are scrawled Doughty's on-the-spot observations and reactions, the measurements made with his thermometer and his aneroid barometer, and his sketches. He disregarded most of the written accounts of his predecessors in Arabia, so it was the notebooks which provided the skeleton for his determinedly accurate and precise account of his travels – the account praised by T. E. Lawrence later as 'a great record of adventure and travel (perhaps the greatest in our language), and the great picture-book of nomad life . . .'[71]

Before everything, Doughty wanted to be truthful, to paint as full and faithful a picture as he could – but this was to be more than a dispassionate portrait of a strange and exotic people. His own remarks make clear that the construction and style of the book had an importance of their own. He wrote later, 'The A. Deserta volumes had necessarily a personal tone. A principal cause of writing them was, besides the interest of the Semitic life in tents, my dislike of the Victorian English, and I wished to show, and thought I might be able to show, that there was something else.'[72]

That 'something else' was to be found, throughout Doughty's life, in the distant past. He was struggling not only to record his travels and discoveries, but also to create a new and original literary style, with its roots in the Bible, Chaucer, Spenser and the sermons he had pored over in the Bodleian – a style which would rediscover 'the old manly English, full of pith and stomach'.[73] That passion for English style, in its turn, was part of his ardent patriotism: it is not just in Khalil's delight in the efforts of the British navy to combat the slave trade, or in his boasts of the efficiency of the British empire, that *Travels in Arabia Deserta* demonstrates its pride in England and its history.

Sometimes, that pride can sound like vulgar bluster – why, Khalil asks, can the western powers not seize Mecca to protect the Christians there? – but, at this stage of his life at least, the real meat of Doughty's patriotism is backward-looking. It is historical, rather than political.

It is not only in the words he chooses, or the rhythms of his sentences that he resembles his long-dead masters. The entire world-view of *Travels in Arabia Deserta* is based upon Doughty's antiquarian reading. For all his contempt for facile orientalism, and however much he shared the reality of their day-to-day life, he saw among the Arabs the jingling world of chivalry he had read about in his youth. Zeyd, for instance, is described 'pricking sheykhly upon the mare to his endeavour, with the long wavering lance upon his virile shoulder'.[74]

Again, he refers to Mohammed Mejelly, the vain sheikh of Kerak, as 'a trembler in the field; better him were to comb his beard delicately in a pedlar's glass with his wives at home, than show his fine skin to flying lead and their speary warfare'.[75] It is an ironic, sideways glance that reflects Chaucer's vituperation as well as his vocabulary.

Other writers, such as Thomas Hardy and G. M. Hopkins, were also reaching out for the terms of vanishing trades and crafts, and for obsolete and dialect words which might express their meaning more precisely, help to create a particular atmosphere, or simply keep elements of the language alive. No one, though, compared with Doughty, working alone, in the completeness with which he melded style, language and meaning.[76]

His words reflect his disenchantment with the life and language of late Victorian England, and the emotional distance from both of the Arab world in which he was travelling. Long-dead expressions could be brought to life as a reassuring link with past generations, much like the rope marks on the stone surrounds of the desert wells: the Arabs' dates, for instance, are 'stived in heavy pokes of camel-hide';[77] their *fenjeyns* or coffee cups are briskly cleaned with a 'rusty clout'.[78] Arabic words, too, are grafted into the narrative, until the *menzils*, *rafiks* and *suks* of Arabia are almost as familiar as English. Sometimes, archaic English and colloquial Arabic are side by side, as when the wife of a wandering tinker 'larded his mess with *wedduk*'.*[79]

But the difference between Doughty and the romantic orientalists for whom he had such contempt was that Doughty was searching for accuracy, not archaism. He was using unusual expressions to give a precise account of a unique and foreign world. The squalid poverty, the harsh treatment of women and the sick, the hours of mind-numbing tedium, are all part of his picture: the aura of medievalism is never allowed to disguise the reality.

Travels in Arabia Deserta is much more than a museum gallery of foreign and obsolete words and expressions. 'Art is that which gratifies in an elevated sort the senses of seeing and hearing,' Doughty noted in his jottings, but his writing is alive not just with the sights and sounds of the desert, but with the smells and textures of nomad life as well. As he describes the agonies of the summer sun, even the *lack* of sound seems to echo in the ears.

> No matins here of birds; not a rock partridge-cock, calling with blithesome chuckle over the extreme waterless desolation. Grave is that giddy heat upon the crown of the head; the ears tingle with a flickering shrillness, a subtle crepitation, it seems, in the glassiness of this sun-stricken nature: the hot sand-blink is in the eyes . . . [80]

* The fat from the camel's hump.

The writing goes beyond the recording of straightforward sensory impressions. The senses seem to swim together in the bewildered confusion of the brain under this constant battering of heat.

That sense of being inside the head of either the narrator or one of the characters is common in *Travels in Arabia Deserta*. It is often hard, for instance, to distinguish between reported and direct speech: whether in the conversations he describes or in the voice of the narrator, Doughty echoes the sounds and rhythms of the speaking voice. Mohammed Aly, for instance, comes back to the *kella* from a trip away to find that his sheep have been stolen.

> Shaking himself from the unwonted wet, he stamped mainly in his trooper's boots, and swore in Pilate's voice, there should not be a head of the sheep go lost, no! nor of the goats neither. Every man should have his own again, and that right soon, by Ullah: and were those robbers any of B. Atieh, Wellah! as ever the haj should be come to Tebuk, he would bind the sheikhs of them to a cannon-mouth![81]

Apart from the notes scribbled in Doughty's own journals, writing played no part in day-to-day life as he wandered with the Arabs: it was a world of listening, not reading. The ancient dramas and sermons in which he had immersed himself at Oxford come as close as literature can to the spoken word – but it was in Arabia, as Anne Treneer points out, that 'Doughty learned to put the sound of a voice into his prose'.

He has, too, a fascination with the telling of tales, as they must have been told around the fire in the nomad encampments. But the anecdotes and diversions from the main story do not detract from the loose structure imposed on the book by Doughty's travels; rather, they are a part of that structure, a way of demonstrating the discursive, communicative world in which Khalil is living.

Each individual tale is handled with subtlety and precision, often with sudden changes of mood. Doughty's friend Amm Mohammed tells the story of a *Solubby*, one of the despised wandering tinkers of the desert, who surprised his wife with her lover. The tale has a fragile Chaucerian joviality as it describes the absurd trap laid for the

246

unfaithful woman, until the last bleak words: 'But when the poor Solubby saw their shameful sin, he caught his spear; and suddenly pierced them both through and killed them.'[82] Doughty is describing a world where human passions and tragedies are the stuff of fireside tales; but his own experiences showed it also to be a world where tempers could flare and violent attacks could come suddenly and unexpectedly.

He appealed instinctively to the past, against what he saw as the corruption of language, manners and morality of his own time, but *Travels in Arabia Deserta* is not backward-looking for its own sake. The achievement of the book lies in the way that language, style, rhythm and structure are all directed towards the one end of accuracy in presenting landscape, characters, mood and atmosphere.

It is at the same time an intense, inward-looking picture of Khalil himself and of his development, and an almost obsessively precise account of the environment and the people among whom he was moving. In a long-past English world Doughty found a way of inter-preting a foreign and almost incomprehensible one.

The reviewers greeted the book with enthusiasm and respect, although they were often bemused by the archaic style which, said *The Times*, 'places his work under a distinct disadvantage'. The reviewer also noted the efforts Doughty had made to capture the timbre of Arabic speech.

> A remarkable book . . . probably the most original narra-tive of travel published since the days of Elizabeth. Mr Doughty is evidently persuaded that the English of today is a degenerate speech, and declines absolutely to clothe his thoughts in it, preferring to revive what he believes to be the pure and manly English of 300 years ago. The fact is that Mr Doughty has lived so much among Semites that unwittingly he has become one himself so far at least as mode of expression goes . . . [83]

The *Spectator*, appearing the next day, was more impressed by Doughty's writing, and by his skill in picking out individuals from the crowds that throng his narrative. If the style was strange, even Elizabethan, it was none the less magnificent for that.

> The opening passages of the book assure us at once of the strong hands of a master of narrative. The English is of leisurely, antique order, with frequent periods of great stateliness . . . It is born of the writer's own personality, and ripened as some of our best English has been, by the leisure and sunshine of the East.[84]

But Sir Richard Burton, in the *Academy* three months later, was more bad tempered, partly as a result of his own wounded *amour propre*. 'Mr Doughty informed me that he has not read what I have written upon Arabia; and this I regret more for his sake than for my own. My "Pilgrimage" would have saved him many an inaccuracy . . .'[85] Geographers, epigraphists and students of Arabic would find the book of the highest importance, he said; it was, 'despite its affectations and eccentricities, its prejudices and misjudgments, right well told'. But Doughty's punctuation was daft, his style archaic, and many of his observations about the Arabs, their history and their country either not original, not interesting, or simply not correct. It is the angry tirade of a man who feels that his territory has been trespassed upon, and that his own pre-eminence has not been respected. Most of all, though, it is Doughty's character, as described in Khalil, that angers him: he has not behaved in the way that a gallant English gentleman should.

> He is stoned by the children, and pushed about and hustled by the very slaves; his beard is plucked, he is pommelled with fist and stick, his life is everywhere in danger, he must go armed, not with the manly sword and dagger, but with a penknife and a secret revolver; and the recital of his indignities at length palls upon the mental palate.[86]

That censure probably says as much about Burton as about Doughty – and yet he has a point. Throughout his travels Doughty demonstrates a most un-Victorian masochism, or at least an acceptance of being in a weak position. Sometimes he turns it to his advantage, almost challenging his adversaries to strike or abuse him; but occasionally there is a sense that he positively enjoys the feeling of vulnerability, almost of martyrdom.

But as to the accuracy of *Travels in Arabia Deserta*, there have been few critics over the years to echo Burton's complaints. Harry St John Philby, who on his own travels met and spoke to several of the characters who figure in Doughty's book, paid his own tribute in a later interview.[87] '*Arabia Deserta* is the finest and most complete description of the old Arabia produced by anyone, his predecessors or his successors. I have studied the book on the spot, and I don't think I have ever been able to detect a flaw or a mistake in it.'

There was appreciation, too, from writers and poets. Although the Blunts had arrived in Hail some six months after Doughty, the lengthy delays in producing *Travels in Arabia Deserta* meant that Lady Anne's *Pilgrimage to Nejd* had been published for seven years by the time Doughty's book saw the light of day – but Wilfrid Scawen Blunt was outspoken in its praise. Barely a month after the first reviews had appeared, he was writing to say that he had finished the book, and found it fascinating; another letter from the then-unknown Robert Bridges echoed his verdict. He had been introduced to the book at his London club, he said.

> I had no desire to spend a month in the desert, but I was soon in the midst saying my *Shuf Tollogs* to myself; jolting on your broken-jawed *naga* and wooden *theluls*, and starving in those desolate places with an enjoyment you can never have known; for which merely to thank you were sufficient excuse for my writing ... It stands out of the flatness of modern literature as Etna from Sicily ... a perfect accomplishment.[88]

But Doughty had to be content with the appreciation of a few devotees. Just as the scientific establishment had refused to honour his discoveries in Arabia, so the literary world at large seemed unmoved by his work. For the time being at least, the 500 copies printed by the Pitt Press remained almost unnoticed by the booksellers.

*   *   *

His relationship with Caroline Amelia, meanwhile, staid and restrained as it must have appeared to an outsider, was happy and contented. When they were apart, she said later, he would write to her every day. And although she burned all his letters after his death, she quoted one passage, written shortly before their wedding. 'I am by nature self-willed, headstrong, and fierce with opponents, but my hectic season in suffering in this world has bridled these faults and in part extinguished them . . .'[89]

In Caroline at least, it seemed, he had found someone to whom he could unburden himself. They both realized that Arabia had been the formative experience of his life so far, and that to share his life she would have to share something of Arabia. With his long-awaited book complete, in February 1888 Doughty took her first to her parents' home in Alassio, and then on the visit to Syria and Palestine she had craved since she had first heard the stories of his travels.

First they stayed in Jerusalem, and then moved on to Beirut, where they lodged for some time with Doughty's former Arabic teacher, Abdu Kahil. Among the old acquaintances whom they met in the city was Mohammed Aly from the *kella* near Medain Salih – Caroline Doughty described years later[90] how 'a small decrepit figure came skirmishing round with cries of "Ah, Khalil, Khalil!"' Perhaps it was as well that the old garrison commander could not see the less than flattering description of him – 'dim with the leprosy of the soul and half-fond'[91] – that his former guest had left for posterity – but their quarrel was forgotten, and he gave Doughty and his wife an ostrich egg as a memento of his stay with the Ottoman garrison.

For several months more they lodged in the village of Aita, high in the Lebanon mountains, using it as a base for visits around the countryside. Amid the Roman and Phoenician ruins of Baalbek, one of his friends said later, the newly married Doughty started a tradition which lasted for the rest of his life. He rose early, and went out while it was still dark 'to greet Mrs Doughty with a mass of the beautiful yellow wild roses of Baalbek, which he knew she longed to see at last with her own eyes; and on all their holiday journeys ... he always went out before dawn on the first morning to greet her at breakfast with the special flowers of the district.'[92]

Touching as the gesture was, though, there was much more to the travelling around Lebanon and Palestine than armfuls of flowers. When his cousin, Captain Frederick Proby Doughty, was about to be married, he had written an account of his life to give to his future wife: Doughty was going a step further. In taking his wife to the Middle East, Doughty was, so far as he could, welcoming her into the most formative experience of his life. For a man who found emotional closeness so difficult, it was an immense expression of trust and affection.

Late in October, hoping for mild autumn weather, they set out on horseback for Tyre, Sidon, Nazareth and Lake Galilee. It was in many ways a journey full of disappointments. Doughty had written from Cornwall to his friend Laurence Oliphant at the adventist colony he had established on the slopes of Mount Carmel, near Haifa, and they had hoped to visit him on their journey; but although they found the colony, with its red-tiled stone houses, looking out across the bay to the white walls and minarets of Acre, Oliphant himself was away in London. Off to the north-east, though, its summit covered with snow, Doughty could point out to his bride the distant summit of Mount Hermon, the brooding peak that had watched his departure with the Hadj twelve years before.

Struggling south along the little-used tracks, Doughty and his wife were lashed with rain for days on end. 'We were not long out before the country, in which there are no roads, became well-nigh impassable, and we were endlessly detained by extraordinary rains which fell till Christmas, from which we at last escaped to Jerusalem.'[93]

The weather brought on a bout of bronchitis, which delayed them for a spell in the little town of Nablus; but through it all Doughty was revelling both in showing his wife the world he had lived in, and in renewing his own acquaintance with Arab culture. The long months of work on *Travels in Arabia Deserta* had not exhausted his interest: some of his purchases, like the ancient alabaster vase and the Egyptian statue he bought in Jerusalem, or the winged Cupid picked up from a peasant in Kerak,[94] sound like simple souvenir-hunting, but he also found time for some serious study.

In Damascus, for instance, he managed to gain admittance to the ancient library in the hall of Saleh El Din's tomb, retrieving a list of the 3,000 ancient manuscripts there to send back to Cambridge University. There was the same curiosity and determination, the same excitement in the face of antiquity, that he had shown amid the ruins of Medain Saleh.

> There remain a great many fragments, some half-burned, which were saved from the destruction of Tamerlane's conquest: no-one is able to see them. Almost no-one, and then only Moslems, read in the so-called public library. I was shown the binding and fragments, and in two or three volumes were leaves of old Latin sermons, written on parchment. The writing did not look older than xiv cent . . . [95]

At the end of March, having made their way back to Beirut by boat, they took a steamer for Italy. Caroline, who had spent hours sketching the streets and markets of Beirut, had been given at least a taste of the life that had shaped her husband; and for Doughty himself, this was a final farewell. He wrote of it as he left with affection and nostalgia. They were, he said,

> leaving this land, as I think nearly all leave it, with a mingled feeling of pleasure and regret. The time to visit with most pleasure is from now onward till May, in the season of greenness and spring flowers, and it is worth making some sacrifice to come hither. We may see some changes after a few years, roads will probably be made ere long, and a railway is about to be begun from Jaffa to Jerusalem: yet the country is too thinly peopled to be made much of in our time.[96]

In a very real sense, Doughty never did leave Arabia: although he was only forty-five years old when he wrote that letter, much of his writing for the rest of his life drew on his experiences there, and it was as an Arabian traveller that he would be honoured in his old age. His grasp of Arabic might slip, but Khalil would travel with him until the day he died.

As he sailed away from Beirut, though, he had the feeling that what he had once described as no more than an interruption to the main business of his life was behind him. Before him was Italy, a life of scholarship and poetry, and the epic poem he had envisaged from his youth.

Chapter Eight

When the printing and publishing of the *Arabia Deserta* volumes was completed, I found little interest was taken in such work at home. I felt therefore I had done therein what was in my power, and as the Arabs say, I might wash my hands of it; and could now turn to what I considered my true life's work with the Muse.

Letter to T. E. Lawrence, 6 November 1920

D oughty and his wife were not returning to England. Instead, after a brief visit to Caroline's parents in Alassio, they moved a few miles further round the Italian coast to take a villa in the little seaside town of Bordighera. The reception of *Travels in Arabia Deserta* had been a disappointment, but Doughty was ready now to turn to a new and challenging project.

He had chosen an idyllic spot in which to begin. 'After almost a month of incessant wet, the days are clear and warm again. From our windows, we see the beautiful coast as far westward as the mountains beyond Cannes,' he told Robert Bridges.[1] And more than that: all the guidebooks commented on the eastern flavour of the orange gardens, the olive plantations and the welcoming groves of ornamental palms of Bordighera itself, huddled on the shore of the Mediterranean. 'Bordighera is far less Italy than Palestine . . . we can imagine, if so inclined, as we wander through the old town and its environs, that we have been transported to the Holy Land.'[2] It was not just the reassuring olives and palm trees: other writers noticed less savoury similarities with the chaotic towns Doughty had known in the Middle East. 'It has the usual narrow streets, rather smelly and not over-clean, here and there arched over, or else buttressed across, so as to weld all the houses more or less into one mass.'[3]

But this was no return to the harshness of life in the Arab world. The climate was mellow, and even if the English community was more recently established than had been the case further south, it was still large enough to fill the pews in the 300-seater Anglican church. For the next nine years the Doughtys stayed on the Riviera, moving from villa to villa during the winter seasons in Bordighera, Ospedaletti and San Remo. There were all the comforts of home to be enjoyed: they could eat as if they were in Theberton. In San Remo, for instance, 'fowl, ducks, geese, guinea fowls, turkeys and pigeons can always be had at moderate prices ... There are several very good grocers' shops at which, during the season, every article procurable in England can be found.'[4] There were English doctors, a chemist, an American dentist. Life was not only cheap; it was also comfortable.

In 1892 Dorothy, the first of their two daughters, was born, and then, in 1894, Frederica, or Freda: the sad memories of Porthleven faded into the past. There could, it seemed, be joy as well as pain in family love. With the children, Doughty found another role to play – that of the Victorian *paterfamilias*, remote but affectionate. Occasionally he would produce verses for them like no others he ever wrote. For Dorothy, for instance, at the age of four:

> Bo-bo! Buongiorno
> Carina,
> Mia bambina,
> piccina,
> Dorothina
> Come tu stai?
> *Bint Khalila,*
> Cosa tu fai?*

Two years later, on Freda's fifth birthday, he wrote home from a visit to London:

At Poppeletti methinks I can see
Your very own little plummypuddy

---

* Good day, darling, my dear little daughter Dorothy. How are you, daughter of Khalil? What are you doing?

With four almonds clear, each one for a year
A piece for Dottle, a piece for Mummum, a piece for Anna
A piece for Rosina
The rest for little you, and none for Babbu ... [5]

Apart from demonstrating that Doughty's poetic and metrical gifts
did not necessarily extend to children's poetry, the verses give a
glimpse of family life – Anna and Rosina, the servants at Ospedaletti,
and the snatches of Arabic that remained part of their day-to-day
conversation. It was a fond and conventionally sentimental Victorian
life, such as Doughty himself had never enjoyed in his childhood.

Both girls remembered years later how their father had been
immersed in research for the epic poem he was writing – and yet
how he tried to involve them, young as they were, in both his studies
and his memories. According to Dorothy:

> Even during the years of intense concentration when he
> was writing his great epic poem *Dawn in Britain*, my father
> never lost his interest and love for the Arabia he had
> known and the Bedouin he had lived with. He told us
> stories about them for as long as I can remember ... My
> father had an extraordinarily wide knowledge, not only
> of the subjects with which he had to do, but of many
> others, seemingly remote from his interests, so that within
> the family, he was nicknamed The Fountainhead. His own
> work was never far from his thoughts, and besides the
> battered old Homer, he always carried in his pocket a
> notebook which he would bring out at any moment to
> add some observation or thought, often a single word.[6]

The outline of what was to become *The Dawn in Britain*, an epic
poem about the coming of Christianity to Britain, and about the
Roman, Celtic and Germanic roots of the British people, had been
in his head since his days at Cambridge, and even while he was
buffeted around Arabia.[7] Among Doughty's personal notes stored at
Gonville and Caius College, Cambridge, is one relating to the gestation of his epic, which was originally to have been called *The Utmost
Isle*.

> After the University degree and learning to read the Teu-
> tonic languages, it was my patriotic aim to give my life
> toward an improvement especially in the knowledge and
> reverent use of the Mother Tongue. In 1888 were pub-
> lished the two Arabian vols. I began then to write a patri-
> otic and religious work, *The Utmost Isle*, which I had been
> turning over in my mind since the year 1865, and even
> during my difficult wandering in Arabia . . .

That long preparation for his epic was clearly a matter of importance to Doughty. The last twelve words are underlined in red, and
the whole passage marked by double lines in the margin. Even for
a man who had just written the thousand pages of *Travels in Arabia
Deserta*, it was a massive enterprise, which would last another sixteen
years. He had been a student in his early twenties when the idea of
the poem had first occurred to him; he was a middle-aged man of
forty-five when he wrote the opening lines; and he would be well
into his sixties before the final volumes were published.

In Bordighera, certainly, it filled his life for much of the day: his
new wife had to amuse herself in Italy much as she had in Cornwall.
Doughty's days at his desk 'begin at 6.30 a.m. and go on to 9 p.m. . . .
except for the hour for letter-writing that I allow myself on Sunday'.[8]
One of the artistic triumphs of Doughty's travels had been the gradual
way in which he had turned towards the real world of experience
in preference to that of his books; now, though, he retreated deliberately back into his study. Quite apart from the loneliness it must
have meant for Caroline, he accepted at the end of his life that this
singlemindedness had ultimately been destructive. 'After more than
forty years consumedly devoted to poetical studies, since the ten or
twelve of Arabia and the *Arabia Deserta* volumes, I recognise they
have produced in me a culpable forgetfulness of almost everything
else . . .'[9]

Apart from family holidays his only travelling now was the twice-
yearly move from villa to villa at the end of each winter and summer
season. Any lingering thoughts he still had about Arabia were put
sternly behind him, not solely because of his family responsibilities,
but also because of his new project.

257

> I continue to live on the Riviera, enjoying the mild winter
> climate . . . Family ties are now against my again wander-
> ing in the East. I busy myself chiefly in the study of what
> can be made out of the ancient Continental and British
> Gauls and Germans, and feed upon Homer and the great
> dramas.[10]

And yet the change from man of action to contemplative scholar
was neither so sudden nor so complete as it appears. Doughty had
never in any case been a buccaneering traveller in the style of Richard
Burton, for example; rather than imposing a plan of action on his life,
he had wandered through Europe and Arabia largely by submitting to
the winds that blew him. That was what had most angered Burton
about *Travels in Arabia Deserta*.

And all the evidence suggests that, dedicated scholar though he
was, Doughty was never really as obsessive about his studies as he
claimed in his old age. Far from complaining of neglect, his daughters
remembered with delight the stories he told them of life among the
Arabs, and the lifelong pleasure he took in flowers and nature. He
was enough in the world for other members of the British community
on the Riviera to know him and what he was studying;[11] his main
complaint about Bordighera was that it was 'quite bare of books
or galleries; and there is almost no scientific conversation',[12] which
suggests that he was at least looking outside his study for inspiration;
and there were family summers spent in Göschenen and on Lake
Geneva in Switzerland, at Dumfries in Scotland, and at Henwick,
near Newbury, in England.

But even when he was out of his study, *The Dawn in Britain*
remained a constant preoccupation. At home in England and Wales,
he learned to cycle so that he could visit various Roman and ancient
British remains, and in Switzerland he explored the mountain passes
around the St Gotthard, so that his stories of marauding bands of
Gaulish tribesmen might rely on his own experience as well as on
the accounts he had read in his study. The landscapes he paints have
the shock of experience: they are more than simple pictures from a
book.

Then failed men's frozen limbs, and faint all hearts;
That hurtling wind seemed full of icy shafts,
And shrieks of fiends. Then, as beside their minds,
Still seeking paths, the people wandered lost,
Thick cloud uprolling, on the mountain's breast
Cumbered all eyes; whilst tread their sliding feet
On perilous shelves, where depths of dread beneath . . . [13]

In the background, too, are the memories of the Ibsen-like scenes
of the Jostedal-Brae report from Doughty's youth; but he is no longer
struggling for simple scientific accuracy. His vision has breadth, as
well as precision: his observations are merely a part of a wider imaginative scheme. He still wants to tell the truth; but it is an imaginative,
poetic truth.

In 1898, with the children now six and four, the Doughtys decided
to leave the Riviera and return to England, living first in Tunbridge
Wells, home to several of their relations. Doughty's constant solici-
tude for his own health now extended to that of his children. 'We
have set up our tent here at Tunbridge Wells and have almost reluc-
tantly given up our home on the Italian Riviera; but we think before
all of the little ones, and their health is best in the fresh but uncomfortable English climate . . .'[14]

He may well have had the children's well-being at heart –
although the judgement that English weather would be better for
them than the sunshine of the Mediterranean coast would have
raised a few eyebrows among contemporary doctors – but the move
to England also fitted in well with his own work. At this stage it was
entitled *The Utmost Isle* – it was only later that he would be persuaded
by an anxious publisher to adopt the more straightforward title of
The Dawn in Britain. Apart from his bicycling tours around the ancient
sites of England, he had also been visiting scholars and academics
at Oxford and elsewhere for advice about the Romans and their
predecessors with the same meticulousness he had shown in preparing *Travels in Arabia Deserta*.

At Illawarra, Beulah Road, Tunbridge Wells, work continued on the great epic. The house still stands, a large, imposing double-fronted villa at the top of a hill. The name has been changed, and the building is now converted, like most of its neighbours, into half a dozen flats, but it still makes its own silent comment on the social standing of the family who moved in at the turn of the century. The poverty the Doughtys endured throughout their lives was very much that of the upper classes – the poverty of respectability, not the poverty of want. They had standards to maintain, but lacked the money to maintain them. Beulah Road would have been a highly respectable, even desirable neighbourhood; but Illawarra, impressive as it looks today, would have been a considerable step down from Theberton Hall, or from the villa in Alassio. The Doughtys faced the debilitating struggle of threadbare gentility, not the grinding hardship of many families, who lacked the means to feed their children. Poverty is a relative concept, and this was the lot of many younger sons.

Doughty's studies did not keep him in his study: there were many energetic excursions around the country. From one trip into Essex he sent a letter and two cards back to his family, describing his explorations around the cathedral of St Albans, the ancient site of Roman Verulam, and Colchester. 'Arrived at 10 am,' he tells Caroline, and 'spent the rest of the morning in the Museum and the afternoon in exploring the river (Colne) to the sea'. The next day, he said, he would spend some time 'at the probably British earthworks at Lexden'.[15]

Just as Doughty the scientist had observed the landscape and topography of Arabia, so Doughty the poet now gazed across the fields outside St Albans. This time, instead of dispassionately jotting down readings and noting the region's geology, he was giving his imagination full play. Perhaps this might be the very place where the defeated Roman garrison, driven from the town, had rested as they made their escape.

> Cold fleeting Ver, mingled with blood, ran down
> All night; and corses of slain steeds and men
> Cumber his sedgy brinks. From Camulodunum,[16]
> Vast field of swollen Britons' carcases;

Foul ravens flit, to sup at Verulam,
Of fallen Romans. Few, 'scaped forth, have round
Them, in that twilight, mounded bank of mould;
Weak fence, in an hill-place. Wounded the most,
In the dank herb they lie, and daze their hearts![17]

He does not shrink from the horror of the bloated corpses and
the scavenging birds, just as he had not shrunk from the poverty
and suffering of Arabia. But while the writer of *Travels in Arabia
Deserta* might delight in the echoes he found of the distant past, here
he can immerse himself in it completely. It is the warp and weft of
the poem: Doughty seems to see the ghosts of the dying Romans
peopling the misty landscape before his eyes.

His vision before had encompassed both the distant sweep of the
Arabian landscape and the particular gnarled, inquisitive faces that
pressed in upon him, and now he saw not only the broad tapestry
of ancient history, but also the individual stitches. In Arabia he had
gazed in fascination on the crudely dug pits in which the Arabs would
attempt to sweat out their smallpox; he had painstakingly learned
how they repaired leaking bags of clarified butter. Now he was turning his mind to the minutiae of life among the Gauls, the British and
the ancient Romans.

Whether he is describing the banquet offered by King Duneda to
his guests – 'Sheep's flesh in the broth, Seethed chine of boar, and
loaves in bascads* white'[18] – or the funeral preparations in Rome for
the exiled Adminius, 'on purple bier borne forth ... Shrill funeral
pipes, then, slow and mournful note'[19] on the way to his lonely
cremation, Doughty winnows out the details that will bring the
ancient history to life.

But finding a publisher for *The Dawn in Britain* was as much of a
struggle as it had been for *Travels in Arabia Deserta*. His first letter, to
the Cambridge University Press in 1905, six years after he had first
settled into his study in Bordighera, was filled with the apparent
brash confidence of a man who saw himself as the true successor of
the giants of early English literature.

* Baskets.

Modern poets' work has fallen into neglect, and perhaps
it may be *merito*. Where is that sincerity, knowledge, and
right inspiration, which is required even in the humblest
work of art? Where is that intimate knowledge of language, without which there can be only deciduous handi-
work? . . . To speak of the present manuscript. This book
is my life's work, a continuation of Chaucer and of
Spenser, such as conceivably they might have written in
the present . . . [20]

But the extravagant claims, mingled with the nervous appeal on
behalf of his 'life's work', bespeak less self-confidence than appears
at first. *Travels in Arabia Deserta* had not been a business success for
its publishers, and there was no reason to suppose that over 30,000
unrhymed lines of poetry in twenty-four cantos would sell any better.
Certainly that was the view of the succession of publishers who saw
Doughty's manuscript, and their continuing rejections plunged him
into the deepest depression. There seemed to be every possibility that
the work which he had been planning throughout his adult life might
remain no more than an unread, scrawled sheaf of papers.

It was a chance encounter that saved him. Doughty was visiting
Duckworth's offices in Henrietta Street, London, in August 1905 with
his precious manuscript, and carrying with him a copy of an article
about *Travels in Arabia Deserta*, which had been written by the critic
Edward Garnett[21] in the *Academy*. Garnett was Duckworth's reader,
and happened to be in the next room. 'On shaking hands with
Doughty I was captivated by his manner, by his curiously abstracted
gaze, and by his sweet and benevolent smiles. He radiated courtesy,
goodness and modesty when he spoke, which was but little.'[22] He
was as impressed by the manuscript as he was by its author, despite
the awesome difficulties of making out Doughty's increasingly crab-
bed and awkward writing. In September 1905 work began on the
printing of the first of six volumes for Duckworth's.

Doughty's relief was immense, and his commitment, as ever, total.
'Whilst the Dawn in Britain is in the press, I feel I shall have to give
my whole soul to it and to nothing else every day from morning till
night till the work is accomplished.'[23]

Illawarra, 2 Beulah Road, Tunbridge Wells. The house to which the Doughtys returned from Italy still stands, though the name has been changed. The poverty the family endured throughout their lives was very much that of the upper classes – the poverty of respectability, not of want. They had standards to maintain, but lacked the money to do so. Beulah Road would have been a highly respectable neighbourhood, but Illawarra, impressive as it looks today, would have been a considerable step down from Theberton, or the villa in Alassio.

D.G. Hogarth, sketched by Augustus John. The distinguished Arabist Hogarth was one of Doughty's closest friends.

T.E. Lawrence (sketched here by Augustus John) was a close friend of Doughty. Apart from encouraging his writing, Lawrence did his best to bring order to the old man's problematical financial affairs.

Merriecroft, Kent: 'The house itself was the rural idyll of which he had always dreamed. "We have moved here from Eastbourne . . . and have now our home here in the beautiful country . . . The House-name, of good augury, which we have taken on, means simply, 'Wild Cherry Croft'." '

Above Portrait of CMD by
Dorothy Doughty: 'His
friends and family
sometimes teased him
because of his ignorance:
Downing College,
Cambridge, for instance,
has a portrait of Doughty
painted by his daughter
Dorothy to mark the award
of his honorary doctorate
by the university. He is
resplendent in the robes of
his newly-installed dignity –
robes which had been
borrowed on his behalf
from the "unknown"
Thomas Hardy at Max Gate,
Dorset.'

Right Doughty as an old
man, sketched some five
years before his death.

1843 · 1926

CHARLES MONTAGU
DOUGHTY

خليل

POET, PATRIOT and EXPLORER

I feared, till on a lintel which those passed
I read, large-writ, in Everlasting Light:
FEAR YE NOT LITTLE FLOCK: and underneath,
HATH NOT JESHUA SAID THAT GOD IS LOVE.
(Words,which abide,a PERFUME,in our hearts.)

C·M·D·

1862·CAROLINE AMELIA 1950
HIS LOVED WIFE.
AND THEIR DAUGHTERS
1892 DOROTHY 1962
189 AND FREDA 197

Doughty's memorial at Golder's Green Crematorium: 'Two names, two languages; two cultures, two personalities . . . Beneath is the three-fold description Doughty would have chosen for himself: "Poet, patriot and explorer". And then, those final lines from *Mansoul*.'

With the first volumes at the printer's, news came of the death of a cousin, and the inheritance of a house at Eastbourne – the first that Doughty, now sixty-two years old, had ever owned. The family lived in it during the winter, and let it for the summer – leaving Doughty free to take his wife, his children and his seemingly endless pages of proofs for correction off into the country for months at a time. While the first were a constant delight, the proofs were a trial and a frustration, as he wrote to Garnett from a holiday house in East Grinstead.

> The tiresome printers are again at a stand, and are sending me nothing. I am daily busy with the rest, to the utmost of my little strength . . . We are here in a friend's cottage, let for a nominal rent for a time in a beautiful neighbour-hood, and enjoying it like children loosed from school . . . The gardener here, after netting his fruit, fires off his gun once a day with a tremendous bang! which terrifies the bird-robbers till that time tomorrow.[24]

The yearning for a country life of his own is clear. But money remained a problem, and the reviews of the initial volumes of *The Dawn in Britain* suggested that attempts to don the mantle of Chaucer and Spenser would do nothing to ease it. There was near unanimity that, however imposing the poetry, few people could be expected actually to *read* the book, despite a sort of uneasy respect in the face of what the *Academy* referred to as 'the most unexpected book of the year'.

> It is to be feared that the first pages, besides giving some idea of the strangeness of the work both in scheme and matter, will do a good deal towards making most readers feel disinclined to go further and discover its potential qualities . . . To predict wide or immediate popularity for his book would be optimism run wild . . . [25]

The Times Literary Supplement was similarly pessimistic. Much of the story, the reviewer said, was 'infinitely wearisome', but it was the style that would damn the poem to obscurity. 'This strong, strange poem . . . might almost be taken for a publication of the Early English Text Society . . . One's first emotion is regretful irritation.'[26]

Doughty's response was indignant, even pompous. He was clearly hurt by the lack of critical respect: the reviews, he complained, were 'unwholesome and ill-natured'. 'To the Writers, the Patriotic art of English Philology must be entirely unknown, as an art on a level with the best efforts in architecture, sculpture, and painting, which it takes a lifetime of effort to learn.'[27]

A modern reader must have some sympathy with the reviewers. The story of the poem is the doomed struggle of the Celtic peoples of Britain and Germany against the invading Romans, and the arrival of Christianity among them. But an epic poem which is three times as long as *Paradise Lost*, covering a spell of some 450 years,[28] needs a tighter structure than Doughty provides. All too often the reader simply loses his way – a loss of direction that is not helped by the strange words, the Anglo-Saxon and the archaisms, or the frequently tortured construction of the individual lines.

> One day when was, on warfare, Cusmon went,
> Hurt Phoebe with a roving shaft, alas,
> Verica . . . [29]

We get there in the end, but it is a long and roundabout journey.

Doughty's world-view is unashamedly from the Middle Ages – in much the same way as he often saw the nomads of *Arabia Deserta* as Spenserian characters in a medieval landscape. We remember Mohammed Mejelly, 'a trembler in the field', combing his beard in a pedlar's glass;[30] there is Zeyd, riding after his missing camel, 'his long shivering horseman's lance upon his shoulder',[31] or even Chanticleer the cockerel riding proudly on top of the highest camel-saddle in the Hadj, white wings outspread.[32] T. E. Lawrence, always one of Doughty's most sympathetic and perceptive critics, observed that the poem was 'like the trace of Doughty's journeys in NW Arabia, with Arabia left out'.[33] And yet, although his evocation of the physical torments of hell, 'everlasting sink of brimstone', would have been immediately recognizable in the fourteenth century, it is, at its best, a personalized view.

Children of stature, purblind, without stay,
There wander, lost, unnumbered multitude.
Thick-flying eagles, which in fiery loft,
With cruel claws and sharp beaks rend their flesh,
Were their old sins; and serpents, where they pass,
Their pithless limbs unfold . . . [34]

If Doughty enjoyed little affection in his early life, he seems at
least to have had little to torture himself with in the way of guilt or
repentance; yet this is a hell where the sharpest torments are those
of personal love turned to hatred. More savage than the ravening
claws and beaks of the imagined eagles are the reproaches of friends,
relatives and loved ones:

Who spouses were, in the earth,
Children, familiars, shoot out burning tongues,
In flaming hell, that bitterly upbraid;
And pierce, with sharp reproach, each other's breasts! [35]

It is in the homely images and the imaginative sympathy with
his characters that the insight of the author of *Travels in Arabia Deserta*
shows through most effectively in *The Dawn in Britain*. The saints
travelling to Britain by sea, for instance, are terrified by the 'hellish
hubbub' of a storm that threatens to overwhelm them.

They deadly dream, and have forgotten Christ,
As spouse forgetteth the new spouse, in sleep. [36]

There is compassion in the image for the emotional frailty of the
suffering missionaries, and a welcome simplicity in the language.
Similarly, when the betrayed, defeated Briton Caradoc appears before
Claudius in Rome, he speaks with a straightforward, restrained
dignity.

'Gods, which made you so great, have cast us down!'
Voice of the captive king, like warlike trump,
Resounds, in marble Rome! Nor Caradoc changed
His countenance; nor his royal looks abased.
And, quoth he, 'Romans! Whilst I viewed from hence,
Your palaces, your gilded temple-roofs,
I marvelled, ye could covet our poor cotes!' [37]

The descriptions of battles, of scything blades and severed heads dangling from war-chariots, often shock; but the writing is at its most powerful when it pictures the periphery of conflict, image mingled with unforgiving reality:

> There fell a sudden rain then, from the gods,
> Which glisters in the sun, like golden hairs;
> And earth upgave sweet savour of her sod
> Mingled with iron stink of sweat and blood . . . [38]

In *Travels in Arabia Deserta* the real importance of Christianity had been as a touchstone for Khalil's Englishness: what was important was that a man should follow the religion of his fathers. In *The Dawn in Britain* there is a delight in early Christianity, and a reverence for Christ and his disciples – but the instinctive sympathy is for the pagan British tribesmen – 'martial Togodumnos', the quiet dignity of Caratacus, or the ominous bravado of the 'blue Britons' as they await destruction at the efficient hands of the legions. What had shocked the readers of the earlier book was the way Doughty had presented a view from inside the nomadic civilization of the Arabs; now he had made the same imaginative leap into the culture of the Gauls and the early British.

There were those who admired the new poem, demanding as it was. Garnett himself declared: 'I regard Doughty as our greatest poet next to Swinburne ... Some good judges rank him with the masters.'[39] To which judgement the kindest response is that it shows how widely opinions can differ. For the most part, even among Doughty's friends and admirers, there was a distinct lack of enthusiasm. Wilfrid Blunt, who had been fervent in his praise for *Travels in Arabia Deserta*, said bleakly that Doughty's poetry was 'the worst, as his prose is the best, of the nineteenth century'.[40]

But if the lack of interest in *The Dawn in Britain* was a setback, it was one for which Doughty must have been prepared. Throughout his life he had habitually made himself vulnerable, set himself up for rejection, the lonely orphan boy repeatedly picking the scab of his isolation. Setting off with the Hadj had been brave, but it had also invited disaster; so had the obstinate and outspoken rejection of Islam in the desert. Now he was trying to challenge the whole tenor of English literature, with books whose very bulk and impenetrability would discourage all but the most dedicated reader.

But he was fortunate in his friends. Garnett, while working with him on the publication of *The Dawn in Britain*, had conceived the idea of an abridged version of *Travels in Arabia Deserta*. Doughty, who had defended his writing so determinedly against the assaults of the Royal Geographical Society, had stoutly resisted such proposals before; now, he seemed almost meek in his acceptance of the implied criticism of the original work. 'Half a million words does indeed seem a terrible length for the modern reader, the subject also being a vast desert-land, which is in the current political horizon, of little importance.'[41] Perhaps ill-health and the long, hard slog of preparing *The Dawn in Britain* for the printers had knocked some of the fight out of him – at the age of sixty-two, he was, he said, 'like the humpless camel, that has no reserves of strength, and my health hangs on a slender fibre'[42] – but he also seemed determined to see that his work should reach a wider audience. To that end, even though he remained chronically short of money – finding £55 to buy out the copyright from the Cambridge University Press would be beyond him 'in these hard times', he told Garnett – he volunteered to forgo his own royalties from the new book.

He was keenly and ironically aware of the burgeoning value to booksellers of *Travels in Arabia Deserta*, which brought him, the author, no financial profit at all. The publication of the abridged version, *Wanderings in Arabia*, so increased interest in the original books that their second-hand price shot up to around £10 in the bookshops, compared with the original published figure of three guineas.

The worst charge that can be levelled at Doughty as he declares his lack of concern is one of pomposity, even though his claims to patriotic disinterestedness about his work may sound self-conscious and overblown to a more sceptical age – 'My position is that of the ant who desires to cast in the mite he has to the good of his nest,' he observed in one letter,[43] while in another, a few years later, he declared grandly: 'That my work might be of some service to my country has always been, and still is, a principle aim of my life.'[44]

But Doughty's work with Garnett on *Wanderings in Arabia* had done more than improve the profits of London's second-hand booksellers. He had never really 'washed his hands' of Arabia, as he put it, and poring over his writings from more than twenty years before had reignited the deepest memories of his travels. With the final volumes of *The Dawn in Britain* barely off the press, Doughty was already returning in his mind to the desert and his sufferings there.

Wanderings in Arabia was now with the printers. But as Doughty wrote to Garnett to ask for proof sheets to check, he added a diffident note in his letter about another project.

> The Arabian legend of the Mountain of Recognition, near Mecca, has always been of great interest to me. Adam and Hawwa, cast out from the Garden, there meet together again, and recognise each other. My small work, equal to perhaps 90 pages of the Dawn in Britain, is in the manner of a sacred drama. It is now roughly finished, and should be ready by the autumn.[45]

The massive epic grandeur of *The Dawn in Britain* had failed to excite the critics, and thus the reading public: perhaps, he thought, the drama might be a way of speaking more directly to the people. The disadvantage was that Doughty had hardly ever watched a play, let alone tried to write one. 'The theatre is a world of which I personally know almost less than nothing. Once or twice only, I have entered an English theatre in forty years. In Italy, I have been three or four times, and even enjoyed what I heard and saw . . .'[46] It shows: as a drama, sacred or otherwise, *Adam Cast Forth* is practically unactable. There is little action or dramatic tension, and there are almost insuperable problems of staging. A single challenging stage direction makes the point: 'Swart night-hours; Cloudy winged creatures enter from above, and those slowly hover forth . . . ' There is a writer's constant distrust of the actors: a chorus regularly describes the action taking place on stage, in case the audience might miss what is going on.

As a poem, however, which is almost certainly how Doughty intended it to be read, it offers not just the considered and avowedly subjective description of his Arabian experiences, but also a synthesis of that suffering with the calmer, fulfilling life he was now enjoying as husband and father.

It is a work, too, that gives something of an insight into Doughty's own state of mind as he wrote it – and a glimpse of his literary background. It is almost impossible to write about Adam and Eve in English without at least some mental reference to Milton – and even though Doughty declares that he had not looked at *Paradise Lost* or *Paradise Regained* since his mid teens some fifty years before, there are occasional interesting echoes that show at the very least how the poems had resonated in the adolescent's mind.

Doughty's Eve, for instance, is puzzled by her own reflection in a pond as she sits in Eden before the Fall.

> Down, at the water's brink, to view more near
> This thing, I kneeled: she kneeled! I gazed upon her.
> I laughed, I spake: she laughed then, but not spake . . .

Eve in *Paradise Lost*, has a similar experience:

> A shape within the watery gleam appeared
> Bending to look at me, I started back,
> It started back . . .

Both characters are surprised to discover that the strange being – their own reflection – is even more attractive than Adam himself. There are enough similarities to suggest either that the passage had a profound effect on the young Doughty – or that he was exaggerating when he claimed to have ignored Milton throughout his adult life. But it is the differences between the two writers that are more significant.

It is hardly surprising that Doughty should set his poem in a much more vividly conceived desert setting than Milton achieved: one, after all, was writing from intense personal experience, the other from a literary tradition. Milton's 'pathless desert' is hardly there at all. It is a mere backdrop, peopled by unlikely lions, serpents and tigers. Anyone who has read *Travels in Arabia Deserta*, on the other hand, will recognize Doughty's agonizing description of how 'spout-eth thick, warm salt living blood / From the man's nostrils', while Eve's sudden presentation of death in the body of her faithful camel is as arresting as anything in Milton, as it lies

> Stiff, lately dead, cold, stretched out, without breath;
> Mongst thicket of these thorns, lo, and wild craigs!
> Eigh me! And is not, Adam, this the death?
> Whereof dark Angel of the punishment spake,
> In day, when the Lord was angry with us.
> My camel is and is not! Fowl we know not,
> Fret, with crude bloody beaks, ah her cold flesh!

The physical shock of the dead camel staggers Eve with the sudden terrifying reality of death: Doughty has transmuted his raw experience of Arabia into a moment of pure poetic understanding. The point is not to suggest that *Adam Cast Forth* is in any sense as great a poem as *Paradise Lost*, but to show how experience and reality inform one poem and not the other. The Arabian memories of the lesser poet came to life as he worked on his 'sacred verse drama', some thirty years after the end of his travelling, and they continued to impassion his writing. It was not for nothing that his Arabic books and his mementoes of his journey sat beside him on his desk as he worked.

But there is another difference which points to a more fundamental divergence between the two poets. In *Paradise Regained* Milton describes mankind's redemption through Christ's resistance to Satan's temptations in the desert. Doughty, meanwhile, insists pedantically on *Adam Cast Forth* as a 'Judaeo-Arabian legend' – a donnish little note at the beginning explains that Eve is properly called Hawwa, 'the name, the same in Hebrew and Arabic (the root signifies *breathe, live*) has come down to us, through the loss of the strong Semitic initial aspirate, as Eva; whence our Eve.'

But the story is about the reacceptance of Adam and Eve into God's grace. Rather than redemption through Christ, Adam sees how mankind is to learn to live with sin and its consequences – working as farmers, and killing each other in wars, with the eventual saving of the righteous. As in *Travels in Arabia Deserta*, there is little place for the New Testament: that was a story that Doughty could deal with enthusiastically in *The Dawn in Britain* as a way of bringing together the Roman and British civilizations, but one from which he shied nervously away in dealing with an avowedly religious subject.

It was hardly a conventional attitude to the Bible: in his sixties Doughty retained the confusion and anxiety about religion that had troubled him all his life.

In his early manhood he had found organized religion unsatisfying, and had escaped from it into the study of science and the observation of nature whenever he could. His daughter recalled that as an old man he was uneasy in church, and much more comfortable alone, outside, with his thoughts. 'When people spoke to him sincerely about their religious views, he always treated them with respect and trust. As a child, I once asked to be let off going to church because he didn't go, and I often think of his answer. He said, "I am always in church".'[47]

The discovery of the world about him, after all, had been much of the impetus behind his journeying around Arabia. But the scientific establishment had failed to appreciate his efforts, and now he was escaping from science into the poetry that he had always felt to be his true home. Just as he had never completely left behind his religion, so he never left behind his scientific habits of detailed observation and investigation; but for the rest of his life, they would be directed solely towards the writing of poetry. Now and in the future, his love of truth would be expressed through symbols and stories, rather than through attempts at scientific discovery.

About his patriotism, though, he had no such reservations. Whether or not he was content for *Adam Cast Forth* to be judged as a poem rather than as a stage play, there is no doubt that Doughty had dramatic ambitions of his own, despite his admitted lack of theatrical experience. His wife recalled later how he could be heard behind the closed door of his study, declaiming to himself the lines that he had written. Publicly, though, he was once again setting himself up for rejection, courting failure. Might not the drama, he suggested, be a suitable field for a national patriotic and literary renaissance? 'A patriotic band of young literary men putting forth every year national dramas might do great good to the Commonwealth, besides gaining honour to themselves; and now seems to be the fit time, when our drowning people is at length being stirred.'[48]

At sixty-five years old, Doughty himself would scarcely make one of a group of 'young literary men', but his patriotic instincts were not in doubt. Neither, it seemed, were his politics, although the romantic high-Toryism which he expressed in public caused wry amusement rather than antagonism among his friends who held more moderate views: 'A bigger man would not read the *Morning Post*,' observed T. E. Lawrence towards the end of Doughty's life.[49]

He remained shy and retiring – he once pointed out to his wife the house where an old school-friend lived, but refused to visit him. 'I think he would much have liked to have met him, but was much too shy and nervous to think of going to call,' she said later.[50] But he would go for regular walks by the sea and over the Downs outside Eastbourne with the Cambridge medieval historian and Chaucer scholar G. G. Coulton, whom he had got to know since he came to the town.

> He was, at first sight, the model of an old-fashioned English gentleman, striking in appearance and imperturbably courteous, even when he had to express the strongest differences of opinion. Once or twice Alfred Ollivant, the novelist, made a third with us; but his rather extreme socialism met Doughty's extreme conservatism without the least personal friction. Doughty, with his characteristic slight turn of the head, but far more definite sidelong turn of the eyes towards the man he was walking with, would blast Socialism and all kinds of Liberalism in a single Elizabethan phrase, but with such impersonal detachment, or even personal cordiality, that Ollivant would appreciate the utterance almost as much as I did.[51]

Doughty's political views, it seemed to his friends, were those of a man who had lost contact with the world, a man who was content to live through his studies, his books and his writing.

> Arabia Deserta had just been rescued from shameful neglect, and republished in a shorter form which took the public by storm. His shaggy red hair and beard, and faroff eyes, were just what one would have expected from his book, and on his table lay two blackletter folios in which he steeped himself from time to time – St Thomas More's English Works and Thomas Cooper's Latin Dictionary of 1565.[52]

Shortly before his death Doughty was visited by the American academic S. C. Chew, who was preparing an article for the *North American Review*. Chew, too, observed the simple, open-hearted naiveté of Doughty's political views.

> In politics, he had adopted an idealistic Toryism, which attributed to other Conservatives a highmindedness and disinterestedness equal to his own. Of more blatant imperialism there is no trace in his thought – but for all his long dwelling in the east, he does not see eye to eye with such opponents of British policy as his fellow traveller in Arabia, Wilfrid Blunt[53] ... All Doughty's life has been a spiritual quest, a ceaseless groping for light through the murkiness of the world ... [54]

The irreconcilable differences in their political outlook did nothing to affect Doughty's regard for Blunt, whom he considered a friend throughout his life. And in the privacy of his Notes an entirely different Doughty emerges – one who could rage and rail against the injustices he saw around him. Many of the thousands of jottings scrawled in the bundles of 'Miscellaneous Word Notes' are simply unintelligible, and it is impossible now to date the ones that can be read – but among them are exclamations of political passion that would have astonished the companions of his walks across the Downs. Under the Latin heading 'Dives', for instance, he notes: 'You great rich men are the Criminals rather. O ye Nimroths![55] ... Who gave you right to enclose the land? The earth is the Lord's. Men are all his heirs . . .' And again, on a sheet headed 'Education': 'Contagion of ill manners, contagion of corrupt speech, leprosy of astute and malicious evil-mindedness – all in a harsh hideous clatter of machines. Men's minds are worn out. We are conquered by machines . . .'

These are clearly half-formed thoughts, scribbled down on the spur of the moment, rather than reflections of a coherent political philosophy – but they do show how Doughty, for all his obsession with the distant past, could also be moved by the anxieties of his own time. Coulton observed that Doughty 'had read sixteenth century English, and thought the thoughts of that time, until he lived very really in that time',[56] but the same concerns with social justice that had moved Dickens, the same awed fascination with the threat of industrialization that gripped Hopkins and Hardy, stirred him too. Although *Travels in Arabia Deserta* had seen the occasional angry outburst about the evils of slavery, and a continuing sympathetic appreciation of the debilitating poverty which afflicted the nomads, there had been little social concern in his writing so far. His fascination had been with the deep, ancient roots of society, rather than with its contemporary outgrowth.

He had always seen himself as a lover of his country, aware of its origins, and concerned above all with its history and its character. Now, though, there were worrying trends in Europe that he could not ignore – trends which he believed challenged him as a patriot to turn his talents to the immediate benefit of his native land.

A few years before, he had broken off his work on *The Dawn in Britain* to publish, at his own expense, a short volume of patriotic verse – twenty-seven pages of blank verse designed to encourage the soldiers fighting in the Boer War to lay down their lives gladly and enthusiastically. Reading them is not an edifying experience: Doughty, the careful, scholarly poet who habitually spent years researching his work, had clearly dashed into print on the basis of a few reports from the popular press about the cheery heroism of the troops and the savagery of their 'brutish enemies'.

Better are these now heroic days
Of battle and long march, in cold and heat,
Sleeps broken, night alarms, in dry and wet . . .
. . . than when we at home
Ignobly oft consumed the idle hours
In treacherous drink and vice of soldiers' life . . . [57]

It is not so much the unconvincing earnestness that jars as the 'we' – the easily assumed sharing of the soldiers' lot.

Brief is his pain who falls without disease
Before his foeman's face . . .
But longs my soul, and burns my heart, and pants
This breast, dear Foster Land! How sweet it were
To fall, to die for thee an hundred deaths!

Death, wounds and glory, one wants to point out, would probably have seemed a far more appealing prospect from the comfort of 2 Beulah Road, Tunbridge Wells, than they did out on the broad karoo. Treacherous drink and other soldiers' vices, on the other hand, might have had their competing attractions to the young men who were actually being picked off by unseen marksmen from across the veld. For all the promise in the front of his slim volume that its profits would go to the Soldiers' Widows and Orphans Fund, Doughty's, shamefully, was the authentic voice of whipped-up warfare, shrieking from safety for the noble taste of someone else's blood.

There is no doubt that his romantic nationalism was affected by the image of conflict far from home and by the idea of a threat to his native land – but it was the immediacy as much as the direction of the challenge that betrayed him. Throughout his life his writing had been based on years of meticulous study, cogitation and research; in this case, like so many of the commentators at home, he was writing from a position of complete ignorance about the reality of the conflict.

There is some explanation in Doughty's determined isolation from contemporary writing: when he cut himself off from any interchange with other writers, he left himself without any standard by which to judge when his own responses were awry. Even Lawrence, usually his most indulgent of readers, criticized his 'uncharitable narrowness of mind'.

> Doughty was a very curious person, who took his politics and feelings about politics direct from the *Morning Post*. He had no personal friends, and no bonds or nerves uniting him to his own generation, or his fellow-men. His hardness of eye closed him up, apart from life. That led to the inhuman arrogance of his work – himself being the meekest and gentlest of men. It takes a saint to judge the whole world wrong: a god to cast it into hell.[58]

But there is no excuse: the crudity of Doughty's attitude is obvious in the contrast with other poets. While he blustered about 'heroic warfare and swift soldier's death', for instance, Thomas Hardy was picturing the cosmic sadness of a young boy thrown into his grave 'uncoffined, just as found'[59] on the other side of the world. Doughty might expect the soldiers to exult in the 'glorious scars' and 'titles of honour' they suffered in battle, but Kipling, for all his faults, could imagine all too clearly how 'each nerve cried out on God that made the misused clay'.[60]

Under Arms finishes with a warning of 'Dire tempest which must fall upon our shores', and of greater wars to come. Doughty was not alone in foreseeing the outbreak of the First World War – H. G. Wells published *The War in the Air* in 1908, while Saki's *When William Came*, just five years later, described a London under German control, with the Kaiser established in Buckingham Palace, and Britain facing generations of occupation. But there is no mistaking the prophetic fervour with which, first in *The Cliffs* in 1909 and then four years later in *The Clouds*, he presented the coming danger, and urged that the government should prepare itself. The threat now was not in far-off South Africa, but here in Europe. In writing about his warnings, he uses the high-flown language and the abundance of capitals that were so often prompted by his patriotic feelings – but the orphan whose mother had died in childbirth could find no stronger way of expressing himself than this:

> The instant danger to our Nation is that which is pointed
> out in *The Cliffs* . . . Personally, I desire to run every risk,
> for that noble Patria and Foster Soil which brought us
> forth, and our fathers, as every man would in the dear
> and sacred defence of his own mother . . . [61]

A cynic might have pointed out again that a literary figure of uncertain health, now comfortably in his sixties, was unlikely to be asked to run many serious risks in defence of either Patria or Foster Soil. He was as safe from the trenches as he had been from the veld. But Doughty, the man who seemed to be living in the sixteenth century, was in no doubt that his duty as both poet and patriot was to warn his countrymen of the growing strength of the Germans. Whatever Lawrence thought, he did have friends – and as he considered how he should address a more public message, he wrote to them in distress.

> Nothing astonished me so much, after being long abroad,
> as the strange want of patriotism that appeared to be in
> all classes of our countrymen . . . There is now no time
> to be lost, or we must otherwise certainly and deservedly
> be overwhelmed, and that perhaps shortly. And through
> our fault, our children will remain to live on unhappily
> and humiliated in a destroyed and perhaps annexed
> England.[62]

Three days later he was returning, Cassandra-like, to the same theme.

> Most Germans are full of worth: their heads are a few
> ambitious, insolent men, building the organised, mighty
> force of their nation's manhood . . . Their fleet, that might
> meet us *tomorrow* with a chance of success, is not Ocean-
> going, as pretended, but a North Sea fleet. The conclusion
> is obvious. Is it not the destruction, bleeding to death, and
> desolation of this island Power which stands in their way?
> If we let our armour rust, will not our dejected descend-
> ants justly condemn us?[63]

The Cliffs and *The Clouds* are both written, like *Adam Cast Forth*, as dramas, and both, like the earlier work, are virtually unactable. Doughty's talents were not dramatic – and, like the vast majority of people of the time, he had no vision of what war would really be like: the Boer War had been fought at a sanitizing distance which had enabled the suffering to be ignored or disguised. In *The Cliffs*, for instance, Doughty wrote blithely of the 'safety camps' in which British forces imprisoned the Boer civilians – 'Wives, maidens, children of their brutish enemies' – institutions now more accurately remembered as concentration camps, which cost the lives of an estimated 26,000 of those 'wives, maidens, children'.

The blind jingoism of *Under Arms* was still unexorcized: *The Cliffs* also includes a horrific scene in which a baby is gladly sacrificed by its smiling mother to 'Sancta Britannia'. The scene is made even more repulsive by the dripping sentimentality that surrounds it, with faux-pastoral elves kindling their cheery fires as women cast on incense in preparation for the killing. A few short years later Wilfred Owen would write with the bitterness of experience about the grotesque enthusiasm with which an ageing generation offered up 'half the seed of Europe, one by one' in the trenches of France;[64] *The Cliffs* shows a jingoistic Doughty sharing in that bloodthirsty militarism, with an apparent longing for death and sacrifice that is mingled with a bitter and unreasoning hatred.

In *The Clouds* German soldiers gorge themselves in the streets on slaughtered farm animals, while English children starve. The Germans laugh as they taunt the defeated English with the loss of their birthright; others, earlier, had dragged out and shot a white-haired old widow, who was mourning her dead children.

The threat Doughty saw to the country he loved had brought about a massive change from the longsuffering of Khalil in the desert, and even his friends and admirers were repulsed by his attacks on the Germans. T. E. Lawrence wrote: 'They give me the creeps. Such fanatic love and hatred ought not to be. Who are we to judge? I don't believe even God can.'[65] And in an article written shortly after Doughty's death, the critic John Middleton Murry added: 'Doughty had come to be unconscious of the distinction between patriotism and Moloch worship ... the man who could make fairies condone that inhuman sacrifice had become estranged from the country he loved: his zeal had eaten him up.'[66]

His defence might be that he was not alone – that he was caught up in a flood of anti-German propaganda that engulfed Britain before the First World War. And in other ways Doughty showed himself a painstaking and perceptive observer. Like H. G. Wells, he was inspired in his prophecies of the technical advances that might be made on the battlefield – death rays, radio waves which could jam telegraph messages, and 'mines no bigger than a fisherman's float' are all part of his imaginary arsenal. But it is in the depiction of the miseries of mass bombardment and the suffering of crowds of refugees in *The Clouds* that he earned the description given him by his publisher as author of the 'Poems that foretold the War'.

> This vast calamity is more than heart may think,
> Wont to think only on a single sorrow!
> We among the last escaped, nor all escaped,
> I fear, that followed us through burning streets,
> When toppled factory chimneys from their base,
> And shot down spires blocked thoroughfares. Gas and water
> Mains, broken were by their fall . . . [67]

Simple domestic destruction on that scale was unknown and largely unimagined in 1912, but Doughty's imagination went further. He described panicking crowds with the weak and the young trampled underfoot, civilians dragged screaming from their houses, and peals of church bells sounding the alarm from village to village. It is prophecy with the note of truth. Most poignantly, though, he envisaged the extent of the potential disaster, his vision ranging from the individuals rescuing what they can from their shattered houses to the vast panorama of destruction that confronted them as they fled.

> Then ran forth citizens from their burning doors,
> Bearing, what things had hastily saved, their hands!
> Easthampton, which this day when rose the Sun,
> A town was of twelve thousand families;
> Prostrate, a mile-wide waste now heap-wise lies,
> Fuming; we, in gusts, her burning smell from hence![68]

And if the plays show the limitations of Doughty's patriotic imagination, in another sense they give a new depth, a new credibility, to his claims of feeling for his fellow-countrymen. They are the work of a man who loves not only the literature and the language of his country, but also the people themselves.

Saki, in his prophecy of doom about a British defeat at the hands of the Germans, seems to place the blame firmly with the shortsighted selfishness of the working classes, 'the grown-up generation of Berts and Sids'. He distrusts art and 'cleverness', and gazes with distaste on the 'Hebraic looking gentlemen, wearing tartan waistcoats of the clans of their adoption' who appear in occupied London. It is chillingly ironic, with hindsight, how determinedly he identifies profiteering Jews with the German conquerors.

Doughty, on the other hand, shows the nation united against the attackers. They may curse the 'malignant, parricide Parliament' whose unpreparedness has left them so open to invasion, but different races, classes, professions and creeds stand shoulder to shoulder. At a time when anti-Semitism – typified in Saki's tales – was practically endemic among a particular class of Englishmen, Doughty takes a different view.

> A band with swart-
> Eyed looks we marked; whose captains leading forth,
> With lifted sabres, turning oft their looks,
> And to the shifting of their soldiers feet,
> Treading then backward; (Jews, born Englishmen)
> Shouted commandment, in strange Hebrew tongue;
> Men faithful to the state in which they dwell,
> Those in whose hearts antique war-fury burns,
> March to do battle at the foster-shore.[69]

The plays are a strange mixture of jingoistic fury, primitive romanticism and clear-eyed realism, which seem to reflect Doughty's own feelings as the actuality of war began to dawn. Once fighting broke out, he could hear the distant rumble of the artillery from the safety of his house in Eastbourne – but it was not only the sound of the guns which reminded him that, at the age of seventy-one, he was once again missing the opportunity to serve his country. First his weak health had kept him out of the navy; now his age prevented him from joining the forces.

And the fighting came close to home: in 1915 came news of the death of Doughty's nephew, Lieutenant-Colonel Dick Doughty-Wylie, who earned a posthumous Victoria Cross for his gallantry in leading his men ashore at the assault on the beaches of Gallipoli. Doughty-Wylie, the son of Doughty's brother Henry, was shot in the head by a sniper after his men had successfully driven the Turks back from Hill 141. 'Shot, so quick, so clean an ending': Doughty himself might have thought wistfully from his study of the supreme sacrifice and the honour that went with it,[70] just as he must have envied his other nephew who, he wrote later in the war, 'commands one of the last-built great Dreadnoughts in the main fleet at home'.[71]

But despite the tight censorship of news about the war, some idea of the horrors being endured only a few miles across the Channel leaked out into the snug homes of Eastbourne. Only five years before, Doughty's letters had been passing on news of his daughters and their pet white rabbit, and speaking indulgently of the two girls as 'almost twelve feet of naughtiness between them'[72] – but now first Dorothy and then Frederica joined the Red Cross, serving as nurse and house orderly in hospitals treating the wounded who had been evacuated from the front. Hundreds of Belgian and British soldiers passed through the two tiny hospitals at Urmston, near Eastbourne, and Hill House, Hampshire, many of them requiring surgery for their wounds. Caroline, too, worked as a volunteer nurse: whatever image Doughty may once have had of the nobility of patriotic sacrifice must have been battered by the stories they had to tell of the shattered bodies returning from France.

Later in the war, at his family home in Theberton, Suffolk, in a grotesque echo of the crash landing of an enemy balloon he had described a few years before in *The Cliffs*, a German Zeppelin was shot down in flames. The moving Bible quotation in the village churchyard that still adorns the memorial to its crew is a lasting rebuke to the savage anti-German feeling which Doughty shared. 'Who art thou that judgeth another man's servant? To his own master he standeth or falleth.'[73]

But he still regretted missing the chance to serve his country in action. Shortly after the end of the war he wrote to his friend D. G. Hogarth, who had played a leading role in organizing the Arab revolt against the Turks. His letter started wistfully: 'Dear Commander Hogarth (let me put this enviable title, which I know is yours by war-service)', and went on to lament that, at the age of seventy-six, and with his health still causing problems, he had been unable to take any active part in the war effort.[74]

As the war progressed, though, Doughty's patriotic fervour seemed to dwindle. He was still proud of the contribution being made by his wife and his daughters, still deeply affected by the thought of the courage and sacrifice of his nephew – but daily life, with its little selfishnesses, continues through the most titanic struggle. There were disturbing stories of suffering and death coming home from the hospitals – but there were more personal, less disinterested factors as well. There seemed to be no prospect of an end to the fighting; and the most ardent patriot might begin to feel, as the years dragged on, that what began as a struggle for national survival had become something of a personal inconvenience.

Scouring London bookshops for Doughty's books nearly eighty years after the end of the First World War, I found a beautifully kept edition of *The Titans*, a long poem he had finished early in 1914. After the prophetic works of *The Cliffs* and *The Clouds*, *The Titans* marks a return to Doughty's epic manner, describing a war waged by the elemental forces of the Titans against mankind and its gods.

Inside this copy, in the hand I had come to recognize so well, was an inscription to his niece, Doughty-Wylie's sister: 'Catherine Frances Doughty, from her affct U.' No more – it was the reserved and dignified dedication of an elderly gentleman.

Stuck inside the front cover, though, was a letter, dated 2 April 1916, and obviously sent with the newly published book. 'The printing was finished in 1914, just before the War broke out, which has delayed its publication,' Doughty explained, before turning to family matters.

'We have hopes that the Zeppelin raid did not come near enough to alarm you all at Theberton,' he wrote. 'Our town electric lights have been turned down at nine . . .' It is a slight letter, and yet, in its way, a sad one. Despite his passionate patriotism, age and infirmity had reduced the war for Doughty from the trial of strength and principle he had envisaged to a question of family anxiety and a certain petulance. There was, it seems, a considerable amount of inconvenience to himself in the power cuts and the reductions in supplies of paper available to publishers.

Despite his pleas of age and infirmity it is hard to resist the thought that he could have done more than send his wife and daughters out to work. But he watched anxiously as the war unfolded without him. 'The horrible war goes on, and seems likely to continue for another eighteen months or more, with its daily massacres of thousands. The sound of the cannonading on the British Front is wafted here. We have heard it day and night for three weeks.'[75]

But, still grumbling over the 'chorus of snarls' with which he complained the reviewers greeted his warnings about the conflict, he settled down to work on his last and, he believed, his greatest poem. The initial sketch for *Mansoul*, which he said dealt with 'the Riddle of our Being', was almost completed in 1916 after two years' work, he told Garnett – but it was another two years before he was able to say that it was finished. 'I am now past the age of activity in our country's service . . . I have not been able to do more than to devote all my days and hours to the book I had sketched out and had in hand when we met in Edenbridge* . . . It is, I think, my best work.'[76]

But the war took scant account of the ambitions of poets. The cost of printing and paper preventing any possibility of publication, and as year followed year, taking him remorselessly through his seventies, his anxiety began to seem desperate as well as petulant. 'That dreadful struggle looks like lasting two or three years more, which is too far for me to look forward to, who have almost completed my 75th year. I write to you, always my best and kindest literary friend, to ask what you think I had better do.'[77]

But not even Garnett could interfere with the course of the First World War. Doughty, and *Mansoul*, simply had to wait.

* Garnett's home in Kent.

Chapter Nine

... Who come now to late evening of his years
By age is not subdued; but aye he seeketh
If so be he, through Reason's reach, might 'scape
From error, and attain to tread the path,
From now henceforth, of Everlasting Truth ...

Mansoul, p. 94

S   ome years before the war started Doughty had received a letter
     that was to change the remaining years of his life. It came from
     an irrepressible young student at Oxford who had been moved
first by his poetry, then by the stories of his travelling, and finally
by the warmth of his reputation in the Middle East. It was a letter
from the young T. E. Lawrence.

It was not an auspicious start to their correspondence. The bubbly
and eager young Lawrence wanted advice about an archaeological
walking tour he was planning in northern Syria, and Doughty's
downbeat counsel must have come like a flood of cold water.

> It is a land of squalor, where a European can find little
> refreshment. Long daily marches on foot a prudent man
> who knows the country would, I think, consider out of
> the question. The populations only know their own
> wretched life, and look upon any European wandering in
> their country with at best a veiled ill-will. The distances
> to be traversed are very great. You would have nothing
> to draw upon but the slight margin of strength which you
> bring with you from Europe. Insufficient food, rest, and
> sleep would soon begin to tell ... I should dissuade a

friend from such a voyage, which is too likely to be most wearisome, hazardous to health, and even disappointing.[1]

The memories of his own sufferings in Arabia were clearly still fresh – but if his advice was dispiriting, it was at least kind of him to offer it to the young tiro. It was the caution of age, experience and good sense offered to youth and enthusiasm – and Lawrence's response was exactly the same as the young Doughty's would have been. His enthusiasm was more than a match for Doughty's flood of realism. The tour – 'my little pleasure trip', as Lawrence described it[2] – went ahead; and a few months later a second letter arrived from Jesus College, Oxford. 'The Crusading Fortresses I found are so intensely interesting that I hope to return to the East for some little time. It struck me that I ought to see you first (having been much scorned by an Arab near Lake Huleh for not knowing you) . . .'[3]

As a letter designed to excite Doughty's interest, it was a masterpiece. Lawrence not only flattered him as a traveller, still remembered among the Arabs, but went on to add that it was Doughty the writer, author of *The Dawn in Britain* and *Travels in Arabia Deserta*, rather than the Arabian explorer that he wished to meet. The old man was still bitterly disappointed with the reception the critics had been giving his work; the appreciation even of an impressionable young student must have been a welcome change.

More than that, though, there was more than an echo of his own youthful determination in the younger man's story. Where the young Doughty had spent his time at the diggings at Hoxne and poring over the books in Oxford's Bodleian Library, Lawrence had become a constant figure at the university's Ashmolean Library, studying the artefacts there, building up his knowledge of archaeology and history, and developing friendships with such leading experts as Leonard Woolley and D. G. Hogarth.[4] Just as Doughty had ignored the warnings of Mr Jago and pressed ahead with his journey to Medain Salih all those years before, so Lawrence had brushed aside his own wise counsels in his hunger to explore the ancient fortresses of Syria.

His journey had taken him over much of the same ground that Doughty had covered before he set off into Arabia – and in

Lawrence's letters home there is the same fascination Doughty had shown for the people he meets and the details of their way of life, and even a similar affectionate nostalgia for the country he had left behind.

> Nothing is more refreshing than to march for an hour up a dusty road, eating the melon in one's arms; it is as pleasant as loitering in a country lane in England ... When I go into a native house the owner salutes me, and I return it, and then he says something to one of his women, and they bring out a thick quilt, which doubled, is laid on the rush mat over the floor as a chair; on that I squat down, and then the host asks me four or five times how my health is ... [5]

It could almost be Doughty himself, describing his welcome among the Fukara nomads so many years before. When Lawrence was not working at the archaeological dig at Carchemish with Hogarth, he would visit the other ancient sites in the region on foot, dressed as an Arab and living with local tribesmen whom he met by the way. Doughty, as he heard these stories, could hardly resent the fact that his original advice had been ignored: here was a glimpse back into the past, his own history brought to life.

Shortly before Christmas Lawrence arrived at Eastbourne for a visit; over the next three and a half years he spent only seven months in England, but his friendship with Doughty was fixed. It was to reignite the embers of Doughty's love affair with Arabia, and it would last until the end of his life.

Through the years of the war Doughty remained in a state of religious and philosophical turmoil. In his early middle age he had behaved like an elderly man, but in his seventies he was still confronting demons that most people abandon with their youth. Even though he seldom crossed the threshold of a church – at least, when a service was being held – he still maintained the outer forms of Christianity with a passion. George Bernard Shaw emphasized the lonely and combative nature of his faith some years later. 'The Church of

England was too subtle and double-dealing for him: he was a home-made sort of Plymouth Brother, I would say.'[6]

What Shaw misses, though, is the intensely religious nature of Doughty's love of his country. The Church of England was an important element of his view of being English, and the war years had only strengthened his instinctive feeling that religion and patriotism were indivisible.

But he remained riven with doubt and self-contradiction. Doughty the patriot might express his anti-German feelings in terms of the purest prejudice, but Khalil the traveller had been aghast at the religious bigotry he had seen and suffered. The poet of *The Dawn in Britain* might have abandoned the scientific observations of the traveller who wrote *Travels in Arabia Deserta*, but the challenge of science to the apparent certainties of religion remained as formidable as ever.

All through his literary career Doughty had stepped aside from that dilemma. It was part of a lifelong pattern of evasion: in his youth he had escaped from ordinary day-to-day life in the very literal sense of leaving England on his travels – the Hadj and the desert a refuge as well as an adventure. The determined Elizabethanism of his style, too, was a way of distancing himself from the everyday language he so disliked and mistrusted; but it was in his subject matter that he most determinedly avoided confrontation. Arabia, ancient history, even the stories of the Old Testament all fascinated him; so, in its different way, did the urgency of his warnings about impending disaster in *The Cliffs* and *The Clouds*. But they were not the subject that gnawed at his innermost thoughts.

That was Christ, and the possibility of redemption – and, more particularly, whether science had destroyed the possibility of an honest and intelligent man finding comfort in religious belief. Had the discoveries and theories of Lyell, Darwin and those who came after them rendered belief in God impossible? That was the challenge that the poem *Mansoul*, or *The Riddle of the World*, was to attempt to meet head-on.

In style, the poem takes Doughty back from his efforts at dramatic writing to the old epic that he knew best. There is, too, the attempted pastoral that rings so false in modern ears, Doughty sitting all too self-consciously at the feet of his 'beloved master, Edmund Spenser'. But the main thrust of its 3,500 lines of blank verse is to describe the narrator's journey through the Underworld along with his companions Minimus, the least of men, and Mansoul, the embodiment of human striving, in the search for enlightenment and wisdom.

The mystical Muse of Britain gives the Narrator a burnished mirror, made long ago by Merlin himself, in which he will be able to see reflected the doings in the world of men. From the world of the dead, he will travel on to see Mansoul's Dream City, set between earth and sky, where he can watch prayers being offered to Heaven. The mission is arduous and hazardous, but searching for Truth is the duty of an honest man: Doughty himself knew from the start how crucial it was for him.

> What of this very old solar Earth-planet, so minute in comparison of the million other Suns? How came it into being? What of man's later world thereon, and each brief human life therein? and what of aught beyond, has long been to me the Question of questions. In such momentous inquiries, hardly any two thoughtful minds can see the same shadows and apparent gleams, since we are indeed all gropers in thick darkness.[7]

Doughty's own description of his poem is so all-embracing as to be almost meaningless, and where he wrestles with such massive abstractions of philosophy, a modern reader may well think his final work has been deservedly neglected. In fact, its subject is described, much more succinctly, within the poem itself:

> What were indeed right paths of a man's feet,
> That, lacking light, wont stumble in World's murk?[8]

Mansoul, like the story of Doughty's own life, is the description of an intelligent, devout man's response to an epoch of elemental change, and when it deals with his own personal emotional and philosophical struggles, this single poem is as revealing of its author's state of mind as anything he wrote.

The tragedies of his own life are faced directly. In the shadowy underworld the narrator embraces his long-dead mother, and gazes bleakly on the myriad tiny graves, 'Framed like unending dove-cote, in derne cliff', where children and babies lie buried – memories, perhaps, of the little stone shelves he had seen carved out of the rocky cave-sides of Medain Salih.

> Where innocents sleep, buds of great Tree of Life,
> Whom Winter's spite had withered from the root,
> Ere might they to a kindly Sun unfold
> Their first frail leaves . . . [9]

It is a reminder of the emotional pain that had been ever-present in his life – the sense of loss left by the death of his parents, and then of his first, stillborn child. His inability until now to give any meaningful expression to his sadness had left it deep within his soul. Old age had brought it painfully to the surface once more.

Also with him, of course, were his forty-two-year-old memories of the 'bald, sunbleached, gaunt untrod mountain rocks' of the desert, and of the hardy, cruel and generous people they bred. Individual lines and images will strike chords with any reader familiar with *Travels in Arabia Deserta* – Khalil's chance discovery of a grave-house in Sinai, for instance, is transmuted into the Narrator's shock as 'Loath charnel breath smote, smother of the grave, on our lives' sense';[10] there are the stone ramparts of the desert wells, 'scored by generations' twisted ropes',[11] and the volcanic lava-fields of the Harra, 'as stiffened were blown seas, / Great rampant folding wave, to sudden stone'.[12] And as for the people of the desert, the 'tented Children of the East', Doughty's last thought of them was of their open-handedness to the forlorn wanderer who might come, like Khalil himself, to their homes.

> Stand goodly open, those black tents of theirs
> Pitcht in inhospitable high wilderness,
> Whose poor indwellers' wont is, to receive
> To shelter and to surety, guestship, fellowship,
> As they too ben God's guest, his fugitive:
> And the forwarded wayfarer, in their wild paths,
> He sends to their scant hearths, to prove their hearts.
> Wherefore, beseech thee, All-Father, for this sake,

Remember them for good: and fill their mouths,
For Want their portion is, from year to year,
With daily bread![13]

It was a benediction as much as a farewell – 'Remember me for good' the very words of his friend and protector Amm Mohammed, as he watched Khalil leave Kheybar. So simple Christianity was no answer to Mansoul's riddles: no faith which condemned as heretics or unbelievers folk who were capable of such straightforward human goodness could satisfy Doughty's instinct for fairness and truth.

Alongside those affectionate memories of a people he had both loved and feared, though, the more recent jingoistic hatreds of the war years also remain – the Kaiser himself is seized by hell's fiends in the underworld as 'a griesly leprosy blots his werewolf's face', while his ordinary soldiers, too, seem irredeemably damned.

Invading impious hordes
Of Hunnish enemies this hell-horror made.
Midst fire and smoke, *Havoc!* yelled their foul throats,
Known hardly from brute-beasts, by mankind voice . . . [14]

The contrast with Britain's own irreproachable war-dead, with their comely looks, their heads crowned with oak-leaves, their stout breasts bared to 'venom, steel and shot', is complete. Human feeling for suffering is choked on the one hand by unreasoning hatred, on the other by gushing sentimentality – even though the hospital work of Doughty's wife and daughters had brought him some taste of the reality, a realization that there were many

. . . mangled with war-wounds
Remain in life, to slowlier die war-deaths.
Or salved their hurts, and saved to live uneath,*
Must live on, mongst their fellows, broken wights.[15]

It was not enough: the flag-waving enthusiasm for death in battle kept breaking through. How Lawrence, for one, must have winced when he read his mentor's cry for the dead: 'Death seemed them joy, for Mother Country's sake!' As they troop into the Heroes' Hall,

* With difficulty.

with its walls of burnished bronze decked out with dented armour, spears and battered shields like some Wagnerian theme park, it is one of Doughty's least attractive moments. As a writer, he was at his best when he was least confident of his attitudes: the brash certainty of his patriotism repeatedly led him to sound harsh and inhuman.

But it was too soon after the fighting for reconciliation, and the wounds for combatants and non-combatants alike were still too raw; Doughty was an old man, thrashing about in anger and confusion, with faith and doubt, suffering and comfort, pulling him this way and that.

Through the three central characters of *Mansoul* he is searching for divine enlightenment, although the advice of the philosophers and 'seekers of right paths' whom the three meet seems bland and platitudinous. Nebo, the pre-Christian god of Wisdom,[16] tells them like some wordy old nanny,

> 'So do to all men
> As thou wouldst be done by them . . .'[17]

while the Persian philosopher Zarathustra wakes from a thousand-year rapture to urge them sonorously a few lines later to 'Walk in the way of truth, eschew dark paths'.

Thus spake Zarathustra: it was barely worth waking up for. It is Socrates who poses the dilemma that had haunted Doughty for years, and it is easy to see something of the poet in the way the aged Greek philosopher is presented. 'Poor of world's good, he lightly esteemeth thereof':[18] it is certainly the way that Doughty would have described himself. Socrates struggles to reach Truth through the power of his own intellect, to find whether he 'through Reason's reach, might 'scape from error'.

It is, he concludes, a hopeless task: no one can tell whether it was God who made Man, or men who made gods.

But that is no answer; and the underground travellers hasten far beneath the sea, until they reach Canaan, and the coast of the Holy Land. Through Merlin's glass they can see Mount Carmel, where Doughty and his new bride had looked in vain for his friend, Laurence Oliphant; and in the distance are the rocky slopes of the Lebanon mountains, with their ancient cedars. Brooding over everything, as it had brooded over Doughty's departure on his own great pilgrimage, was the image of Mount Hermon 'with his snows' exalted crest, leaning to heaven'.[19] Here, amid the lengthening shadows of his own memories, the poet tried to face the problem that science had posed for his entire generation. Had science rendered God obsolete?

All his early training, all his joy in the power of biblical language and Old Testament history, all his passionate love of tradition, came down on one side of the balance; on the other were his reason and his honesty. The temptation was there: earlier in the poem, he has declared that the story of the Creation is now all but forgotten – 'Nor more is that first family of the world named/Men of divine descent'.[20] Now Mansoul himself goes further. In an age of greatly increased knowledge, he says, there is a book available for man's guidance – not the Bible, but the geological history of the world itself, 'a book of truth, which none can contradict'.[21]

But Doughty, and Mansoul, do not stop there. The book is still only partly open: there remains room for Faith, which alone can take men beyond the reach of reason. And, just as importantly, there is room too for virtue, courage, human kindness. On his way to see Mansoul's Dream City the Narrator visits the Anglo-Saxon poet Caedmon, another apparent incarnation of Doughty himself, 'his hoary beard low-hanging on his breast',[22] to hear tales of derring-do in the defence of England.

In the end philosophers and simple shepherds agree: neither Faith nor Reason is enough alone. Men have responsibility for themselves. It is the search for Truth, not the discovery, that is crucial.

> Time past, our fathers' was; this day that is,
> Is ours; the Future, we ourselves beget.
> The sum of all is, there be many paths
> Of human goodness, and the blameless life,
> Wherein a man may walk towards the Gods.[23]

At the end of the poem the Narrator watches the religious ceremonies in the Temple of the Dream City, and is concerned to see a group of 'drooping, shivering souls' standing aside from the rest, and slowly leaving one by one through a curtained door. He never discovers what happens to them; but his final refuge is in religion.

> . . . On a lintel which those passed
> I read large writ, in Everlasting Light
> *Fear not, ye little flock;* and underneath,
> *Hath not Jeshua said that God is Love?*
> (Words which abide, a perfume, in our hearts.)

The conclusion is a comfort, not a resolution of any of the questions Doughty has been asking. *Mansoul* is hardly subtle philosophy, and it seems ironic that a writer who constructs Doughty's towering gothic palaces of sentences, with their twisting, tortuous passageways, and long-forgotten words lovingly built into the brickwork like the decaying shields of ancient heroes, should be at heart such a simple thinker. It is revealing, too, that a man who could so often seem unbending and intolerant in his attitude to other faiths should at the end accept so openly that virtue, godliness, can have many guises. His Father's house did indeed have many mansions.

Doughty's conclusion, for all its lack of subtlety, avoids the simple prescriptions he puts into the mouths of the philosophers in *Mansoul*. And it is more than a lazy *laissez-faire* tolerance: he is as firm in his insistence on personal responsibility ('the Future, we ourselves beget') as he is all-embracing in his acceptance of diversity. There is something of the tone of the quiet-voiced Khalil from four decades earlier, but it is Khalil without his bitter condemnation of religions. The point, though, is not so much the conclusion itself as its effect on Doughty. Love, rather than duty, would comfort him in his final days. As he reached the end of his life, he was struggling towards the comforting serenity of those words: 'Fear not, ye little flock . . . Hath not Jeshua said that God is Love?'

The poem appeared in 1920, after a series of contretemps and angry exchanges with the printers. With paper scarce and printing expensive, it had been sent to be set up by a firm in Ireland. It was not a decision which pleased its author. 'I had a whole year's trouble . . .

with those unfortunate Irish printers – their long delays, broken promises, and slovenly negligence were colossal . . .'[24]

But once again the reaction of the critics to what Doughty firmly believed was the finest poem he had ever written disappointed and angered him. They treated it generally with a bemused respect, but gave little hope that it would attract a wide readership – and, to his unconcealed anger, even had the temerity to question once again his use of lost words and archaisms. The 'scoffers and scorners', he wrote, the 'cavilers of malicious kind . . . should know better, or their own language better, or should have a better ear . . . I do not grumble, but give their temporary ill humours as I think they deserve to the flames.'[25]

Although he was confident that it was his best work, he was still not satisfied with it. He had toiled over it with his customary singlemindedness, and now he set about an ambitious programme of revisions and additions for the second edition. *Travels in Arabia Deserta* and his reputation as a traveller and Arabist, he said, meant little to him.

> It is the *Ars poetica* to which I have been entirely devoted, and I have devoted my life thereto ever since I left Cambridge. My travels, wanderings, and sojournings in other lands have been but incidents therein . . . I am at present busy every hour of every day, preparing a second edition of *Mansoul* . . . [26]

That version, published in 1923, his eightieth year, shows him still striving to make his language more spare and direct, and his annotations to the copy of the second edition now in the Gonville and Caius College library demonstrate that *Mansoul* continued to occupy him for the rest of his life.

When his friend Garnett repeatedly asked for information for a planned biography, he was curt in his reply.

> I can hardly get through my every day's work. I am always absorbed in my work, to which I devote every hour from early morning of every day . . . I pray, don't ask me about biographical matters, in which I take a very small interest.

I am looking always forward, not back. I have not time
now to do more.[27]

His dedication to *Mansoul* was inspired partly by the realization
that, at eighty years old, and with failing health, he had not the
stamina to start on another poem; partly, it was an old man submitting to the constant temptation of tinkering with what he had done.[28]
But it was not just the writer seeking to improve his work; there
were intensely personal motives as well. In his old age Doughty was
well aware that it was in this poem that he was coming closest to
reconciling some of the dilemmas that had haunted him through his
life. He had, he knew only too well, little time left. There was one
hidden, universal grief that the Narrator of *Mansoul* had heard –

that secret sighing of their hearts
Which, each day, drew more nigh their own dark deaths.[29]

His friendship with Lawrence, meanwhile, was putting other
phantoms from the past to rest. Travelling to Damascus from the
Carchemish diggings, Lawrence found one of the sons of El Bessam,
Doughty's friend and protector from the Arabian town of Aneyza.
On an earlier trip he seems to have believed that he had tracked
down the old man himself, and wrote sending 'salaams from old
Bessam of Damascus, who . . . still helps travellers in the desert'.[30]
But Lawrence's enthusiasm had outrun his caution: the father, who
had welcomed Khalil into his house, had died seven years before.
The renewed contact with the son, though, was enough to encourage
Doughty to try to renew his old friendships.

It was not a particularly cheering venture. Many of the Arabs he
had known could not be found, and most of those who could be
traced were long dead – the desert, after all, was not an environment
that encouraged longevity. But when Lawrence went back to Damascus, he was carrying with him a message from Doughty, which
eventually found its way to another member of the Bessam family.
Now, he was a respected elder of the town, but in those far-off days,
Lawrence wrote, he had been one of the small boys who had greeted
the traveller so courteously at the house in Aneyza.[31]

I left your letter, but afterwards returned and found one
of them at home. He was Hajji Mohammed El-Bessam,
the son of Abd-er-Rahman ... Both of them [Hajji
Mohammed and his brother, whom Lawrence had visited
earlier] remember you very vividly, as a 'very tall man
with a beard'; the Arabs, said Hajji Mohammed, called
you a spear-length. He thought that he was too young
for you to remember, although you seem to have vaccinated him or his brother ... [32]

The old memories, of vaccines painstakingly measured out in the
blustery desert wind, of the courtly greetings of the Arabs, of the
discomfort and the danger, came flooding back. Incredibly, old
Motlog, the venerable Fukara sheikh on whose hospitality Doughty
had relied early in his wanderings through the desert, was still alive;
later, said Lawrence, he would do his best to find him and talk to
him too.

Doughty was thrilled, and over the next few months, he arranged
for two solid silver bowls to be sent out to Damascus to be passed
on to the family of El Bessam and also that of Abdullah El Kenneyny,
his other friend and ally from Aneyza.[33] Twenty years later, in 1933,
the writer Christopher Sykes was taken by a friend to visit an old
man in Damascus.

He showed us a treasured possession, a silver bowl
inscribed in English and Arabic. He told us that Khalil had
presented it to his family, and he remembered that when
he was a little boy, Khalil had vaccinated him in Aneyza.
He was Mohammed el-Bessam, the grandson of Doughty's
friend of 55 years before.[34]

Doughty would have been delighted. He did his best to keep
in touch with Lawrence as the war dragged on, but tight military
censorship meant that he knew little of what was going on in Arabia
or of his friend's involvement there. As the Arab revolt swept north
and the names from *Travels in Arabia Deserta* became reference points
in the military campaign, Lawrence was once again following in his
footsteps, though it was several years before he could talk about it.

'We took Medain Salih and El Ally, and further north Tebuk and
Maan, the Beni Sakhr country, and all the pilgrim road up to Damascus, making in arms the return journey of that by which Doughty
had begun his wanderings . . .'[35] *Travels in Arabia Deserta*, Lawrence
said, had become a military textbook for the campaign: at last, in his
way, Doughty was serving his country under arms. David Hogarth,
who had been appointed director of the Arab Bureau in Cairo during
the campaign against the Turks, told him later how crucial the ageing
volumes had been.

> Two coupled and garbled names, for example, evidently
> intended to reveal a move towards Kheybar, puzzled the
> office for hours, until a search through Doughty's book
> brought to light the two negro villages of Hayat and How-
> eyat in the *harra*; and again and again, his was the only
> mention of tribes and sub-tribes . . . Everything about
> Arabia seemed to be in the book, if one only read enough
> of it![36]

But while the war raged, Doughty knew nothing of that. He
described later to Lawrence how anxiously and with how little success he and his family would scan the newspapers anxiously for news
of the fighting across the country he had known so well. 'Readers
only of *The Times* in the Great War, we had nearly no intelligence
given us of forces operating in Arabia, until you reached Maan and
Kerak, and then only meagre notices without details and therefore
hardly intelligible . . .'[37] The very nature of the fighting meant that
he could not know more, at least until it was all over: the Paris Peace
Conference was under way before he managed to reach Lawrence
with a letter. The reply he received was a masterpiece of under-
statement.

> I had made up my mind that I must write to you, and tell
> you that I had been over much of your country, (more
> securely and comfortably, but in somewhat the same
> fashion), meeting many of the people, and sons of the
> people who knew you out there. It has been a wonderful
> experience, and I have got quite a lot to tell . . . [38]

Whether 'securely and comfortably' adequately described the conduct of the guerrilla warfare of the revolt may be questionable – but even to his friend and mentor, Lawrence was unwilling to talk about his own experiences in the desert in any more detail. It was only later, when Doughty had read his literary account in *Seven Pillars of Wisdom*, that a clearer picture emerged. He read of the 'vast War-work' with enthusiasm, no doubt with a degree of envy, but mostly with the deep understanding of a man who recognized not only the country but also the people concerned.

> Now all that fog is dispersed, and I am able to view your vast War-work near at hand, with its almost daily multi-farious terrible and difficult haps, experiences, physical and mental strains, and sufferings and dark chances that must needs be taken in meeting and circumventing enemies, in the anxious leadership of an Armada of discordant elements, as often naturally hostile among themselves, as Arab tribes, until after two years you won through to Damascus, after enduring all that human life can endure to the end.[39]

He had himself spent long periods during and since the war ill in bed – and there was a sad little postscript to his greeting to the returning war hero: 'I trust', he wrote, 'that the long endurance of so many mischiefs may have left no permanent injury to health . . .'[40] It came sincerely enough from a man who had always been anxious about his own constitution – but it seems an oddly prosaic remark to make to a man who had been through Lawrence's experiences.

More than a decade and a half before Doughty's death his great friend Sydney Cockerell, director of Cambridge University's Fitz-william Museum and a man who collected eminent friends like butterflies, had noted in his diary that Doughty was living a quiet and retired life in Eastbourne: 'A tall upright man, with thick red beard and thick greyish hair, 66 years old . . . very serious and self-contained, with a voice laden with sorrow – but a splendid head and fine manners. He lives the life of a hermit at Eastbourne and knows scarcely anyone . . .'[41]

Now, his physical health was failing, just as his reputation was growing. In 1907 his old college of Caius had made him an honorary fellow; the following year he had been awarded the degree of Doctor of Letters by Oxford University; and in 1912 the old dispute with the Royal Geographical Society had been resolved with the presentation to Doughty of the society's Founder's Medal. In return, he presented the society with an antique globe which had been in his family for as long as he could remember.[42] Then, in 1920, his own university of Cambridge followed Oxford's example by conferring its own honorary degree on him, and two years later he was elected an honorary fellow of the British Academy: at last, much delayed as it was, he was getting the recognition from the scientific, literary and academic establishment he had always believed was his due.

He was particularly delighted at the Cambridge honour, and determined to attend the ceremony, despite increasingly frequent fainting fits. His wife wrote to warn the university authorities about his 'very serious attacks of sudden illness: without the slightest warning, he will become unconscious, and remain unconscious for sometimes three days and nights'.[43] On 15 June 1920, however, he took his place at the Senate House: of all the honours he received in the last years of his life, the honorary degree from Cambridge was the one that pleased him the most.

He now made a point, outside the family circle at least, of being known as Doctor Doughty. Alongside his reputation as a writer, his name as a traveller was growing with the increasing interest in Arabia. Wilfrid Blunt had always been frank in his regard for the man who had beaten him to Hail by only a few months. Doughty had, he said, 'the most complete knowledge among Englishmen of Arabian things'.

The other travellers who followed him to Arabia could only agree. Harry St John Philby, not a man to be prodigal with his praise of other people, described him simply as 'the greatest of all Arabian travellers',[44] while Lawrence put Bertram Thomas's ground-breaking crossing of the Empty Quarter into perspective. The great Arabian

travellers were all gone, he wrote in his introduction to Thomas's
book in 1932.

> In my day, there were real Arabian veterans. Upon each
> return from the east, I would repair to Doughty, a looming
> giant, white with eighty years, headed and bearded like
> some renaissance Isaiah. Doughty seemed a past world in
> himself; and after him, I would visit Wilfrid Blunt . . .
> Doughty's voice was a caress, his nature sweetness; Blunt
> was a fire yet flickering over the ashes of old fury . . . [45]

And it was not only Lawrence who would repair to the house at
Eastbourne. For all Doughty's retiring disposition, it began to hold
considerable attractions for people with any interest in either Arabia
or literature. In the summer of 1920 he received an official invitation
to London to meet a group of senior Arabs, including the Emir Feisal,
the fourteen-year-old son of the Sultan of Nejd, and future King of
Saudi Arabia – and when ill health prevented him from making the
trip, the deputation was brought down to Eastbourne instead.

They were escorted by Harry St John Philby, another noted
Arabian traveller, and another admirer of Doughty.

> I thought they would like to see the greatest of all
> explorers in Arabia . . . His personality scarcely came out,
> but he was very gracious. He remembered the Arab ways
> well enough to give us coffee and tea, and entertain us
> in the usual Arab way. And I think his whole appearance
> and the way he spoke, rather a deep quiet voice, really
> made one believe that he was the author of *Arabia Deserta*.
> He was completely suitable to the part.[46]

Later the ageing poet described the visit to Wilfrid Blunt.

> I wish you could have seen the deputation of Nejd Arabs
> from Ibn Saud the Wahabby which Philby lately brought
> to this country. They would have interested and amused
> you. They visited this town among other places, and
> Philby brought them in to take tea with us. I found after
> many years, I could not converse much with them in

Arabic. Amongst other things, they were greatly astonished at the sight of our enormous shire horses . . . [47]

But if Doughty's Arabic was faltering like his physical health, his
memory and his intellect were as bright as ever. It was his chance
to repay at least some of the hospitality he had received from the
Arabs, and he did not let it slip. He had, he told them, hoped to visit
the Emir's grandfather more than forty years before, but had been
delayed in Hail. Feisal and his entourage – who had already been
taken to London Zoo and Selfridge's Roof Garden[48] – were no doubt
as bemused by the occasion as the people of Eastbourne must have
been by their unfamiliar Arab robes and head-dresses.

There were other visitors, too: Cockerell, of course, hurrying
between Cambridge and the homes of all his carefully nurtured eminent friends; Garnett, anxiously asking after the health of the family,
including the two 'girls' who were now, still unmarried, in their
late twenties;[49] Lawrence was always welcome, despite his constant
anxiety to bring yet more friends to introduce to the man he treated
almost like a father – 'Lord Hartington wants to visit, and his brother-
in-law Harold Macmillan would like to accompany him,' said one
letter.[50] The hermit-like existence that Cockerell had noticed when
he first met Doughty was rapidly changing.

Lawrence was also establishing a reputation for himself as a patron
of contemporary artists in Britain, and was constantly anxious to
persuade Doughty to model for portraits and sculptures. The private
reaction of a man who recoiled from the thought of a photograph
of himself appearing in a book[51] to the painting of a portrait for a
gallery may be imagined; but his regard for Lawrence was such that
he submitted graciously to most if not all of his requests. A letter in
1920 seeks to arrange a sitting for the artist Augustus John; a few
months later the portraitist Eric Kennington[52] was presenting Lawrence's letter of introduction, and asking to start work on the painting
which now hangs in the National Portrait Gallery.[53] Other letters
suggested different illustrations of the author for new editions of
Travels in Arabia Deserta; by 1922 Doughty was so inured to his
unaccustomed role as artist's model that he positively welcomed the
sculptor and medallist Theodor Spicer-Simson – 'a pleasant man, and

no doubt a very good artist'[54] – who had been introduced to him by Hogarth.

That newfound complaisance, though, did not imply any new tolerance of criticism. He responded angrily when 'empty-headed present-day young critics who . . . cannot even rightly scan an English verse' claimed to find influences of other modern authors in *Mansoul*. 'A single line of Spenser excepted, it derives *nothing* that I know of, from any former books. It was the devoted work of nine later years of my life . . .'[55] But then, he had always dismissed supposed literary influences with contempt. When *The Cliffs* had come out, Doughty complained that one review he had taken 'but few minutes to glance through' had the temerity to suggest that the play owed something to Hardy's *Dynasts*. Hardy was one of the most famous and lionized poets of his day, but Doughty was at a loss.

> The writer knows to his small malicious satisfaction that
> I had copied something from a book with the strange title
> *Mr Hardy's Dynasts*. Not moving in the Literary World, nor
> reading the Literary Periodicals, I had never heard of the
> book or the author, and remain in my ignorance till now,
> and shall continue to do so . . . [56]

It is almost comic, how determinedly he avoided the contamination of modern life or literature. 'It is better not to read than to read ill. In these times, it were as well not to read,' says one line in his private notes. In another letter some years later he congratulated Garnett on a literary award presented to his son by G. K. Chesterton – but admitted, 'Not having a *Who is Who* by me, I do not know who Mr Chesterton, who delivered the prize, may be.'[57]

Occasionally, without much conviction, he would apologize for this self-imposed isolation. The name of the poet Edward Thomas, for instance, 'among the martyrs of the cruel War' he did think he remembered. 'But, as an invalid, I live too much out of the literary World, whilst almost, I may say, the generations pass, to know what is of late years doing amongst them; but the Divine Muse is eternal, and the same.'[58]

His friends and family sometimes teased him because of his ignorance: Downing College, Cambridge, for instance, has a portrait of

Doughty painted by his daughter Dorothy to mark the award of his
honorary doctorate by the university. He is resplendent in the robes
of his newly installed dignity – robes which had been borrowed on
his behalf from the 'unknown' Thomas Hardy at Max Gate, Dorset.

Hardy himself was almost certainly unaware of the joke, but still
managed to take a suitable revenge on the man who had never heard
either of him or his magnum opus. His wife Florence wrote later to
Cockerell in Cambridge to confirm that Miss Doughty had returned
the robes. 'Also her papa sends his long poem *Mansoul*,' she added.
'T.H. has looked in it, but is not tempted to read it, I regret to say –
but I am sure Dr Doughty is a delightful man . . .'[59]

But for all Doughty's new standing, he still faced the most pressing
financial difficulties. He had never known financial security, and the
war years had been particularly difficult, with the shares on which
he relied for an income yielding poor returns. A couple of years
later he admitted that his financial management had never been
successful. 'My trouble is, I have as good as everything invested in
Rubber shares and Kent coal. The last, bought at high prices, though
geologically sound, are worth nothing, and Rubber yields now
nothing . . .'[60]

Even his precious library had been ransacked during the war
years for books which might prove valuable enough to provide a few
pounds to help feed his family.

Mansoul, he knew, would provide no income worth considering.
Though he could fulminate against the insensitivity and stupidity of
the despised critics, he was reconciled by now to the idea that his
poetry would remain an acquired taste for a few readers: he had no
expectations of big sales. In his letters, at least, he affected a lofty
disdain: *Mansoul*, he said, was the product of a lifetime's study of
the English language: 'I am content to leave it a legacy to a future
generation.'[61] He had, indeed, a perverse pride in the poor sales of
his books. 'All my work has been solely patriotic, without seeking,
and (mainly) without obtaining any personal reward. (*Arabia D, The
Dawn in Britain, The Cliffs, The Clouds*, etc) – fifty years' work in all.'[62]
The note of self-congratulation may be infuriating, but Doughty's

history is some justification: he had indeed stuck to the manner and the style in which he believed so strongly, at the cost of any hope of wealth or popularity.

But there were hopeful signs that, almost despite himself, his books might start to bring him something of an income for the first time in his life. While he was preparing the first edition of *Mansoul* for the printers, Garnett's abridged version of his travels, *Wanderings in Arabia*, was ready for a second printing. In a letter to him Doughty said that it would have been too expensive to reprint the original volumes of *Travels in Arabia Deserta* – although that problem would be overcome before too long – but that the abridgement itself was admirable, with its 'kindly and crystalline Preface'. The book, Garnett was keen to point out, was more than a geographical description of a far-off and inhospitable region of the world; it was a study of the Arabs and of their eccentric visitor as well.

> As he journeys on, this scholar, geologist, archaeologist, philologist, and anti-Mohammedan, we see Arabia as only a genius can reveal it to us; we see, hear, and touch its people as our own most intimate friends . . . It is a great human picture Doughty has drawn for us in *Arabia Deserta*, and not the least testimony to the great art of the writer is that we see him in the Arabians' minds . . . [63]

Garnett was not only trying with his abridgement to inspire interest in a forgotten masterpiece; he was also intent on reassessing the work, and demonstrating the breadth of its appeal. The news of the book's sales was encouraging: perhaps even at this late stage in his life, his writing might begin to show the sort of financial profit he was convinced it merited.

Certainly, T. E. Lawrence had been using his influence to increase interest in Doughty's work. He was among the friends who wrote to congratulate him on *Mansoul*. 'I think I like it better than *Adam* and next to *Arabia Deserta* of your books. Of course, nothing can replace *Arabia* to me, but *Mansoul* is very nearly doing so . . .'[64] But Lawrence, no longer the fresh-faced young student who had begged and scorned Doughty's advice about Middle East travel, was now in a position to do more than reassure him about his writing, though he still flattered the elderly poet shamelessly. 'Did I ever tell you of our lunch with Mr Balfour when the table voted on the best books of travel . . . five for you, and two for Marco Polo?'[65] He had been anxious for some time to arrange a re-issue of *Arabia Deserta*, for which his admiration was entirely genuine.[66] One scheme he had put forward before the start of the Desert Revolt had been for an edition produced cheaply in Cairo for military purposes. That idea had been a victim of the war, but Lawrence was keenly alive to the financial possibilities, and within two years of returning to Britain he was once again trying to harry publishers and Doughty himself into agreeing to a new edition. Second-hand copies were now selling at over £32 each, he said, discussing possible printing arrangements in America, subsidies and subscriptions with a facility that must have been dizzying for the ailing author. But his conclusion was simple enough. 'There is such a large and worthy demand for the book that it seems shameful not to get it out again soon . . .'[67]

Doughty, battered by the collapse of his investments and still rankling at the financial failure of the original *Travels in Arabia Deserta*, was anxious about possible costs, and also about the hard work in which the project must involve him. His second reservation, at least, was justified, as he told Lawrence. 'I completed the last sheet of the *Arabia Deserta* reprint. The long Index has been trying, and has left me temporarily nearly blind from eye-strain . . .'[68] But early in 1921 a new edition appeared under the imprint of the Medici Society of London. Lawrence's Arabian campaign, the introduction he wrote for the book, the growing interest in Arabia and Doughty's own expanding reputation combined to make it an immediate success, and the print-run of 500 copies sold out in less than three months. The price was the staggering sum of nine guineas each, producing a windfall for Doughty of some £300. Among the book's new admirers was Lawrence's own former comrade-in-arms, Feisal Ibn Hussein. If Doughty had ever worried how his old friends in Arabia might react to their portrayal in his book, the response of one of the Arab leaders of the revolt should have reassured him. 'Feisal is having the ordinary edition read to him and is enjoying it very much. He is most tolerant, and would not take offence at what was said about Islam. And in *Travels in Arabia Deserta* there is nothing very bad about Islam.'[69]

The introduction, incisive, appreciative and written by one of the heroes of the day, was certainly one reason for the book's rapid sale – but it was a task that Lawrence undertook unwillingly, despite his regard for Doughty, and when a third edition was in prospect, he had his contribution taken out. Its removal was, he explained, a mark of respect. 'It isn't really possible for you to say why I withdraw my bit [he felt he had acted like a tourist, and scribbled his name on a monument] but you are the monument and it wouldn't be manners to call yourself that!'[70]

The book's success was gratifying, but it was not enough, even though Lawrence promised that it would eventually prove 'a little gold-mine'. There is no doubt that he had played a leading role in bringing *Travels in Arabia Deserta* back before the public and, in doing so, offered at least a hope of financial security in the future. 'If I had been appointed your press agent about 1900 I'd have grown fat on my commission long ago,' he joked with some justification.[71] But Doughty's problems were real and immediate, and not to be solved by 'if onlys': his income, with a wife and two unmarried daughters to support, was less than £100 a year, and the house in Eastbourne was on the point of being sold.[72] Lawrence now made it his business to try to rescue his mentor's finances.

One immediate source of cash, he suggested, might be the sale of Doughty's surviving manuscripts. The original copy of *Travels in Arabia Deserta* had been burned, although *The Dawn in Britain* survived, and there were also the notebooks he had carried around Arabia. But Doughty's pride meant any such sale had to be handled with care and tact: he would have no objection if Lawrence could find a group of subscribers to buy his manuscript for the British Museum, he said, but there must be no suggestion that he was in need, and no approaches made to his personal friends. Lawrence hoped to raise £500, but eventually wrote to say that the anonymous subscribers' final offer on behalf of the museum was £400.

> If I could have used the argument that you really needed the money they would have given the five: it is the price paid for nice feeling ... I have seen five of them. One says he has met you, but he can advance no details, and

I think flatters himself. The others know only your work.[73]

The sale, Lawrence reckoned, should ease Doughty's immediate worries, but the money would not last him much more than a year. Almost at once Sydney Cockerell offered to buy the Arabian notebooks on behalf of the Fitzwilliam Museum. Again, Doughty was anxious that there should be no approach made to his friends, and also worried that the books would disappoint their purchaser.

> What are these poor little shabby and very travel worn notebooks? Besides being hardly legible, they are nearly unintelligible to other eyes. Not having opened them since 1887, I have just been looking through them. There are a good many pages, being the basis of the Arabia D vols. But sometimes there may be mixed with them some private thoughts and a Wanderer's inmost reflections not suitable for other eyes. All this is against them . . . If money were to be given at Cambridge . . . I fear it would come from individuals and possibly something for private friends, which would be painful to me.[74]

It was a month before Doughty finally made up his mind, claiming a bout of illness as his excuse for the delay. Leafing through the 'poor little scribble books' had brought the memories, which were never far from the surface, flooding back again. No doubt he had also taken the opportunity to check what personal secrets they might give away – but it was the news that his two old colleges, Caius and Downing, would make the presentation to the Fitzwilliam that swayed him. Even in the letter that accompanied the package to Cambridge, though, he still sounded diffident. 'They may, I fear and dread, be a disappointment . . . I was hurried away from Damascus upon a sudden, so I had no time at all to provide myself with notebooks. I can only say that bad as they are, they served the purpose, though I am not proud of them.'[75]

Even in his eightieth year this lack of confidence could be one of his most appealing characteristics. J. L. Garvin, the then editor of the *Observer*, invited him to write a review of a book on Arabian history which Hogarth had produced, but the prospect of setting out his 'ignorant criticisms' in a newspaper article filled him with genuine dread. 'I felt shy, never having written a newspaper article before,' he confessed.[76] And yet neither the *Observer* nor its tiro contributor had any cause for dissatisfaction with the article he eventually produced. Based though it was partly on what Hogarth had written and partly on his own memories of more than forty years before, it had an unmistakable air of authority.

> That vast Arabian upland is in a word everywhere a sered wasteful wilderness, full of fear, where every man's hand is ready against other; a lean, wild grit and dust, stiffened with everlasting drought, where running water lacks, and whose sun-stricken face is seamed from of old, here and there, with shallow, dry watercourses ... Town oasis-dwellers often despise the poor Bedouins, as only little better than wild folk, and half-heathen. By those who know them, however, they are found to be good friends, hospitable, humane among themselves, of a quick and civil understanding ... [77]

With the job finished, there was alongside Doughty's uncertainty of his own journalistic capacity a degree of pride in a job well done. He had no expectation of any money, he declared – 'the kind notice in the Observer . . . is much more, I feel, than their possible payment'[78] – but he did arrange to have twenty-five copies of his first newspaper article privately printed for himself and his friends: the one in the Oxford University Library bears the proud note: 'The Bodleian Library, with the author's compliments.' Selling the remaining copies of the work which he had had printed – at the same three-guinea price-tag that the original volumes of *Travels in Arabia Deserta* had commanded, incidentally – was another small way of easing his immediate financial difficulties.

But journalism was never going to solve his problems, and Lawrence was still not satisfied that Doughty's position was secure. Earlier in the year he had written discreetly to Mrs Doughty suggesting the possibility of a government pension. The Prime Minister, Lloyd George, his government within a few months of defeat at the polls, had his own problems – but Lawrence had no hesitation. 'Lloyd

George had better do that much good before he goes,' he said briskly.[79] Persuading Doughty himself to accept such assistance from his country was likely to prove more difficult, but between them, Lawrence and Mrs Doughty managed to overcome his scruples. 'I have not sought reward for my work, but owing to the Great War, the times are difficult. And in this trouble, I may perhaps be allowed to feel I have devoted fifty years of my life to such a slender contribution as I could offer to the honour of my Country . . .'[80]

Lawrence's successes in Arabia had left him a man with friends and influence, and he waged his campaign at the highest level. He assured Doughty that there were at least seven members of the Cabinet who 'would be glad to serve you in any way you wished'.[81] Thomas Hardy, himself three years older than Doughty, but a man of wealth and honours, was also persuaded to write to the Prime Minister on his behalf.

But it was Lawrence's contacts and determination which were decisive, and in October 1922 Doughty received an official letter telling him that he had been awarded an annual pension of £150. Lawrence wrote soon afterwards to congratulate him.

> There were muddles in the giving of it. Normally, a memorial is presented to the Prime Minister signed by influential people, recommending the 'victim' to his attention. It seemed to me that in your case the procedure was unnecessary, since your work put you *hors concours*. So I suggested it to Lloyd George that the pension be awarded just like that – and he agreed to it.[82]

Lawrence's letter has the brash but openhearted tone of a son boasting to his father. Doughty was about the same age as his real father, Thomas Lawrence, with whom his relationship had been complex. He had died in 1919, and Lawrence seems to have leaned on Doughty as a new, idealized figure of authority, a man whom he could respect and serve, and whose social position was one of uncomplicated rectitude.[83] That is very much how the relationship between the two men had developed since their earliest meetings.

Doughty, for instance, was anxious to read Lawrence's account of the revolt and his travels across Arabia with the tribes. He had shared to some extent in the agony of the gestation of *Seven Pillars of Wisdom*: in 1920, for instance, Lawrence described how he had lost the manuscript of the book at Reading railway station a few months before. By this time he had got over the initial shock of the setback, but he remained dismissive. 'It has all been written out again from memory, but I have decided not to publish it – it will be no loss to the world, for it wasn't much good.'[84]

A few months later, slightly disingenuously, he wrote again to suggest that all the campaign records would be kept secret permanently by the government. 'I'm afraid there is no blue-book of the Hejaz war, and probably will never be. We sent some reports back to Egypt, but they were kept secret, and are now buried somewhere among the records.'[85] In fact, as Lawrence well knew, the official ban on reporting the Arab revolt had been dropped as early as 1917. The only reason for not giving Doughty the information he wanted was his own reticence.

But Doughty, in *his* role of doting father-figure, kept on insisting, and in 1924, with considerable misgivings, Lawrence eventually sent him a copy of *Seven Pillars of Wisdom*. Where Doughty, or Khalil, had seemed to absorb pain and suffering, Lawrence appeared positively to welcome it;[86] and the intimations of homosexuality must have been deeply shocking to the old man, as must Lawrence's rejection of his idea of the nobility of death in the service of his country. In his introduction to the edition of the book he sent Doughty Lawrence wrote, 'All the subject provinces of the empire to me were not worth one dead English boy.' It was the difference between the man who had seen death in battle and the one who had simply imagined it.

But none of these differences was spoken between the two men. Doughty simply thanked him for the loan of the book.

> I return the valuable vol. you have entrusted to me, just
> as I received it (its paper cover was rather used and torn).
> I have taken much care of it and not allowed it out of my
> hands. My eyes have served me well for in much I am
> still young, and small print notwithstanding, I have read
> it to the end.[87]

Privately, he was shocked, and told at least one friend that he believed some parts of the book should be suppressed in Lawrence's own interests.[88] Lawrence, for his part, never asked him for more comments on his book. After Doughty's death he wrote to D. G. Hogarth, insisting that it was only Doughty's own determination that had forced him to send it to him at all.

> I'm afraid the *Seven Pillars* was rather a bitter pill for CMD
> to swallow. The tone of it must have shocked him. I did
> not send it till he had twice written to me asking for it.
> I've long suspected Cockerell or Garnett of putting him
> up to ask me: the old man was long insensible to such
> things, and seldom looked at any recent writing. It was a
> pity he ran into mine – but I couldn't decently refuse him
> the sight of it, could I?[89]

But his efforts on Doughty's behalf were immense, and his attitude towards him unfailingly courteous and affectionate. The novelist E. M. Forster, who planned at one stage to edit a collection of Lawrence's letters, commented on the 'consideration and gentleness' of all those addressed to Doughty. He never, for instance, troubled him with his changes of name, with his desperate efforts as Ross, Smith or Shaw to shake off his own legend. He never mentioned the twists and turns of his relationships with the government, or referred even obliquely to the emotional turmoil which he underwent during and after the war.

Ironically, one of his most concrete achievements for Doughty, the securing of a government pension, lasted only a few months. In the autumn of 1923 Doughty heard that a distant cousin had died unexpectedly, leaving him an income of some £2,000 a year. He had no doubt about what he should do. 'Quite a considerable annuity will now come to me. It can I think . . . render me independent of the pension . . . As it is public money, I should I suppose gratefully relinquish it.'[90]

That 'I suppose' suggests a degree of wistful reluctance, but there was never any doubt what he would do. It was, incidentally, a decision that was typical of Doughty – honourable, and unworldly. Neither pension nor annuity would survive him; his wife, most of whose remaining years were passed in considerable financial difficulty, might have taken a different view of his responsibilities.[91]

Lawrence's intervention, and the unexpected annuity, came too late to save the house at Eastbourne. Only a few weeks short of his eightieth birthday Doughty was writing to friends to tell them that he had decided to move out of the town where he had lived for nearly twenty years into a cheaper house just outside the Kent village of Sissinghurst. Holidays in the country had left Doughty more than willing to move there permanently, and Merriecroft, as the new home was called, seems to have provided a welcome haven. With Doughty himself now clearly near to death, the purchase – for the sum of £2,000 – was made in the name of his wife, but the house itself was the rural idyll of which he had always dreamed. 'We have moved here from Eastbourne . . . and have now our home here in the beautiful country . . . The house-name, of good augury, which we have taken on, means simply, "Wild Cherry Croft".'[92]

The house still stands, set back from the main road a couple of miles outside the village. It remains a solid, substantial property, although much of the garden which gave Doughty such pleasure has been sold off. Just inside the front door, the window of what was his study still looks out onto the shady lawns; at the back is the small stable where the family kept the pony that drew their trap on trips into Sissinghurst.

Partly because of Doughty's natural shyness, partly because of his growing weakness, the family had little to do with local people. On one occasion he asked the noted explorer Colonel Robert Cheesman,[93] who lived nearby, to help him identify a dead bird he had found – Cheesman, incidentally, had been told that the old gentleman in Merriecroft knew 'a bit about Arabia' – and on another, a family driving past the house in their Bentley were shocked and horrified to see Doughty out on the lawn, taking tea with two men in Arab dress. It was not the sort of area where unexpected things were supposed to happen.[94]

But even though it may have been forced by circumstances, the move to Merriecroft did as much as anything to bring peace and serenity to the last years of Doughty's life. He could welcome his friends, among them Garnett, Cockerell and, of course, Lawrence, roaring down the quiet country road on his Brough motor-cycle, much to the dismay of the locals; or he could sit inside and watch Caroline, Dorothy and Freda in the garden as he packaged up copies of the new edition of *Mansoul* to send off to friends. 'We have had quite a busy time settling down in this our new home, which is proving the desired "three acres and a cow"; and I see my wife and children looking very happy indeed in this, the long by them desired country life. It is a pretty little Kentish place.'[95]

At Eastbourne he had been anxious to share with his family the delight in nature that had brought him such joy throughout his life. His daughters remembered to the end of their own lives the long cycle rides out into the woods there to hear the song of the nightingales – but here at Merriecroft the birds and flowers were all around them. In *Mansoul*, wrestling with the arguments of Faith and Reason, he had listened to the

> Shrill flickering hum of sheen small glassy wings,
> That lifelings of a day, dance in Sun's beams.
> Hark birds' full-throated song, in breasts so small![96]

Even the birds of the air, he declared there, could perceive a power behind Nature that they could not understand. It may not be subtle theology, but at Merriecroft that vision seemed to come to life. 'A thrush has just hopped in at my window, looked at me for some time, and twinkled his eye when I chirped to him, no doubt expecting, as he was a young grown one, to be fed . . .'[97]

It was a time of calm and serenity. The work on revising *Mansoul* continued, but Doughty had found the peace that had eluded him for so many years. His daughters remembered the affection he shared with Caroline, nearly forty years after their marriage. 'In his last years, he would look for some special flower or bud in the garden and, twinkling, bring it to her hidden behind his back to make her guess what treasure he had found for her – never guessing that she, who did all the gardening, had watched it grow!'[98]

But Doughty was now a very sick man, increasingly prone to sudden fainting fits, suffering from repeated chest and throat infections, and spending lengthy periods in his bed. Villagers interviewed forty years later, though, still remembered him as a shy, quiet-spoken and intensely dignified figure, his long beard now white rather than red, hanging down eight inches or more from his chin. He might be sitting at a table in his garden with the newspaper, walking slowly through the village with his stick and his small, rough-haired dog, or riding in his pony and trap, wrapped up against the cold in rugs and a cloak.

He seldom spoke much, but he was smiling and friendly enough: the memories were respectful, even distant, but still affectionate. When it came, after all his years of both real and imagined ill-health, his end was swift. On Christmas Day Mrs Doughty wrote to tell Cockerell that her husband was lying downstairs in his study, very ill, and getting weaker by the day; on 17 January 1926 he lapsed into unconsciousness, and three days later he died. He was eighty-two years old.

There was to be no death-bed closing of the circle in Doughty's life, no final reconciliation with the religion and the burial vaults of his family – but neither was there any ringing denunciation or self-conscious statement of principle. In death, as in life, there was simply a quiet, determined refusal to be swayed – a small, dignified, private funeral at the Golders Green crematorium in London. It was a decision that would have shocked both the Muslims among whom he had spent such an intense period of his life, and also the more conventional members of the Christian faith. For all the emotional appeal of the ranks of his ancestors lying in St Mary's Church, Martlesham, it was to London, not Suffolk, that his body was taken. In death, as in life, he abhorred the ceremonial of organized religion.

Caroline, Dorothy and Freda were supported by a few of his close friends. Among them was a slight, retiring figure in RAF uniform. At that time, shunning publicity, Lawrence was serving under the name of T. E. Shaw, but when the report of Doughty's funeral appeared in the newspaper, he had himself listed as Colonel Lawrence. It was one final, fitting gesture to the man he had followed to Arabia; the man who had become his second father.

On the memorial in the quiet West Cloister at Golders Green today are both of the poet's names – Charles Montagu Doughty and, in a carefully carved Arabic script, Khalil. Two names, two languages; two cultures, two personalities: Lawrence, with his own tortured history of changed names and abandoned identities, would have understood. Beneath is the three-fold description Doughty would have chosen for himself: 'Poet, patriot, and explorer'. And then, those final lines from *Mansoul*:

> I feared, till on a lintel which those passed
> I read, large-writ, in Everlasting Light;
> Fear not ye little flock; and underneath
> Hath not Jeshua said that God is Love?
> (Words which abide, a perfume in our hearts.)

He admits, in the end, to the fear that plagued him all his life – but in those two final lines there is at last no doubt to be found. They sound like simple, straightforward Christian faith, without hesitation, reservation, or question: which, upon a public monument at least, is precisely what Charles Doughty, God's Fugitive, would have wanted.

AFTERWORD

Alan Bennett, the playwright, once remarked: 'Before they are any-thing else, if they are any good at all, most writers are absurd.'[1] It could almost be a modern epitaph for Charles Doughty.

In a determinedly unheroic age the whole idea of travelling openly as a Christian through the heart of fanatical Arabia seems ridiculous, an invitation to sudden death – 'Like a man walking through England during the war and declaring himself to be a Nazi,' said Wilfred Thesiger.[2] The portentous way in which the thirty-five-year-old traveller would point to his long beard, and declare that his great age entitled him to regard and respect; the plodding flirtations with Zeyd's wife Hirfa and her companions; the mocking regularity with which the nomads sold him the oldest, most toothless and arthritic camels – throughout *Travels in Arabia Deserta*, Doughty teeters on the very edge of ridicule.

At home he put on the armour of a literary Don Quixote, battling for sixteenth-century standards against an uncomprehending world. Or, like Tweedledum and Tweedledee rolled into one, he cast around for slights from the poetic and scientific establishments. It is hard to be dignified when you are as careful of your dignity as Charles Doughty was.

It is easy to sneer. In his Pisan Cantos Ezra Pound asks W. B. Yeats, with whom he spent the winter of 1914 reading the poem:

> did we ever get to the end of Doughty:
> The Dawn in Britain?
> perhaps not ... [3]

Most people, even among the few who have heard of the poem and the fewer still who have opened it, would have to agree – although they might note in passing the irony of the author of the Cantos criticizing anyone for writing unread and unreadable verse.

And yet, there is a thread of pure heroism running through his life. There were no challenges too great for him; those who mock him might ask themselves whether they could have looked with such a steady eye on the knife-wielding Arab who was threatening to kill him, or whether their view of language and literature is based on a knowledge as detailed and hard-won as was Doughty's.

Doughty's apparent absurdity was closely bound up with his creativity: without his stubborn blundering through the desert, for instance, all his thoughts of a life dedicated to the *Ars poetica* (another phrase that might bring a sardonic smile to a modern lip) would have come to nothing. 'Doughty's two years' wandering in untainted places made him the man he is, more than all his careful preparation before and since,' said Lawrence.[4] His obstinate refusal to have anything to do with contemporary writing made it possible to produce a work as many-faceted, as individual, as incapable of being copied, as *Arabia Deserta*.

If it is little-known today, then that is today's loss: in the long run Doughty's work will look after itself. The world which he described has gone – but the book remains, and not just as a memorial to a vanished way of life. As long as people are a proper subject for poetry, Khalil will survive, studied and dissected in his long discomfiture by Doughty with as much precision and sympathy as James Joyce showed in his treatment of Leopold Bloom. *Ulysses*, in its way, is as much a travel book as *Arabia Deserta*, and one which has been ignored and derided in its time. Fashions change.

It is harder to be optimistic about the poems, even *Adam Cast Forth*, *The Dawn in Britain* and *Mansoul*. Their sheer scale presents an obstacle which is compounded by the difficulties of Doughty's style and his language. George Bernard Shaw paid tribute to his craftsmanship, observation and descriptive powers, and demanded that *The Dawn in Britain* should be brought out in a cheap edition for boys. 'They should all be read in childhood ... The fact that Doughty's books are unobtainable ... is a public scandal,' he stormed.[5] Leaving aside the sexism of the attitude that debars girls from any interest in the history of Rome and ancient Britain, it seems to be a view that reveals considerable ignorance of either boys or publishers.

But whatever the challenges of Doughty's work, his life remains

318

relevant today. When sound-bites and instant opinions have become the normal currency of debate, there is value in the story of a man whose work was executed over decades, rather than years, whose vision was immense, and whose sense of time geological.

Doughty could be pompous and self-important, but he walked on serious ground, faced intellectual challenges, wrestled with them, and finally reached his own resolution. The questions which tortured him, about dogma, about individual responsibility, about the nagging continuance of instinctive religious faith in a world where more and more seems to be explained, are questions which concern thinking people still.

And if at times he seems tetchy and argumentative, there remains the reassuring image of him as an old man, twinkling as he took a flower as a gift for his wife. He was a man who chose a hard life for himself, who battled through it, and who ended his days in peace and serenity. That may not be, all in all, a bad epitaph.

NOTES

BIBLIOGRAPHY

INDEX

NOTES

ABBREVIATIONS
HRHRC: Harry Ransom Humanities Research Center at the
         University of Texas at Austin
Leiden: University of Leiden Library
RGS: Royal Geographical Society

FOREWORD

1 Letter to S. C. Cockerell, 14 July
  1944, quoted in V. Meynell (ed.),
  The Best of Friends.
2 Interview with the author,
  London, 12 April 1996.
3 She had fallen in love with a
  young major in the British army,
  Charles Hotham Montagu
  Doughty-Wylie, known to his
  friends as Dick, who was romantic,
  charming, courageous – and
  married. He was also,
  coincidentally, the nephew of
  Charles Montagu Doughty. Her full
  story is told in H. V. F. Winstone,
  Gertrude Bell.
4 Interview with the author.

CHAPTER ONE

1 Letter to S. C. Cockerell, 19 August
  1923, quoted in V. Meynell (ed.),
  Friends of a Lifetime.
2 The 'word-notes', together with
  several of Doughty's books and the
  diaries of his European travels, are
  kept in the Library of Gonville and
  Caius College, Cambridge.
3 *Mansoul*, ii, p. 43.
4 *The Dawn in Britain*, iii, p. 152.
5 Letter to Edward Garnett, 14 June
  1909 (HRHRC).
6 F. P. Doughty's Journal, prepared

  for his wife before their marriage,
  is kept with various other Doughty
  family papers at the Suffolk Record
  Office, Ipswich.
7 Letter from Matthew Arnold, 1848,
  quoted in Oswald R. Adamson
  (ed.), *The Laleham Commonplace
  Book*.
8 Letter from Matthew Arnold, 1863,
  quoted in ibid.
9 Bishop Charles John Abraham, of
  Wellington, New Zealand. The
  story is told in *The Laleham
  Commonplace Book*.
10 Letter to D. G. Hogarth, 7 March
   1927 (Caroline Barron).
11 Ibid., 25 January 1927 (Caroline
   Barron).
12 Ibid., 7 March 1927 (Caroline
   Barron).
13 Revd L. J. Bernays (ed.), *A Manual
   of Family Prayers and Meditations*.
14 Revd L. J. Bernays, *The Church in
   the Schoolroom*.
15 Letter to S. C. Cockerell, 26 March
   1909, quoted in Meynell (ed.),
   Friends of a Lifetime.
16 Letter to E. Garnett, 15 June 1922
   (HRHRC).
17 At 22 St Anne's Villas, Royal
   Crescent, Notting Hill.
18 Letter to R. Kirkpatrick of the
   British Museum staff, *c.* 1912.
   Quoted in Hogarth.
19 Ironically, bearing in mind

Doughty's later interest in Roman Britain, Hoxne was, 130 years afterwards, the scene of the discovery of the largest hoard of Roman coins and treasures ever found in the country.

20 S. C. Cockerell, obituary of C. M. Doughty, *Observer*, 24 January 1926.
21 John Ruskin, 1851, quoted in John Carey, *The Faber Book of Science*.
22 Letter to Charles Darwin, 16 January 1865, quoted in Mrs Lyell, *Sir Charles Lyell*.
23 Information from Gonville and Caius College Archive.
24 Letter to S. C. Cockerell, 25 March 1926, quoted in Hogarth.
25 Dictated to S. C. Cockerell in Gonville and Caius College, Cambridge, 5 August 1922, and quoted in Hogarth.
26 Letter to D. G. Hogarth, 11 January 1927 (Caroline Barron).
27 *The Times*, 26 January 1926.
28 S. C. Cockerell's diary note, quoted in W. J. W. Blunt, *Sydney Carlyle Cockerell*.
29 *Travels in Arabia Deserta*, ii, p. 482.
30 Charles M. Doughty, *On the Jostedal-Brae Glaciers in Norway*.
31 Ibid.
32 Letter to Sir Henry Rawlinson, President of the Royal Geographical Society, 13 September 1875 (RGS). It is worth noting that Doughty was appealing for the society's backing for his travels: he is not likely to have minimized the extent of his contacts with Lyell.
33 Conversation with S. C. Cockerell, 8 February 1921, quoted in Hogarth.
34 Letter to C. M. Doughty, 7 October 1864, quoted in Hogarth.
35 Letter to D. G. Hogarth, 19 August 1913 (Caroline Barron).
36 Letter to S. C. Cockerell, 28 May

1932, quoted in Meynell (ed.), *The Best of Friends*.
37 S. C. Chew, who was working on his article 'The Poetry of C. M. Doughty'.
38 Letter to S. C. Cockerell, 28 December 1919, quoted in Meynell (ed.), *Friends of a Lifetime*.
39 George Sandys, *A Relation of His Journey to the Levant*.

CHAPTER TWO

1 Joseph Justice Scaliger (1540–1609), a Calvinist who became a professor at Leiden in 1593. He produced editions of several classical poets which gave him the reputation of Europe's leading scholar. Later in his life he faced charges of atheism from the Jesuits.
2 Desiderius Erasmus (*c.*1466–1536), the Dutch humanist and scholar and author of *In Praise of Folly*, taught in Paris, Oxford, Cambridge and most of the cultural centres of Europe, after being ordained a priest in 1492. He was strongly critical of the Catholic Church, but also opposed the dogmatism of Martin Luther and the Reformers.
3 For instance, in an interview with Professor S. C. Chew, published in the *North American Review* in December 1925.
4 There were twenty shillings in a pound.
5 Letter to D. G. Hogarth, May 1920, quoted in Hogarth.
6 The Paris Commune, a revolutionary municipal government, was established in March 1871, but was crushed by the French army during 'Bloody Week'.
7 Doughty spent nine years writing *The Dawn in Britain*, which was published in 1906, but his initial studies for the poem started much earlier.

8 *Travels in Arabia Deserta*, i, pp.
420–22. In the diary there is no
mention of the eruption. He may
originally have written down an
account in a letter sent home at
the time.
9 Paride Palmieri, *Eruption of Vesuvius
1872.*
10 *Mansoul*, vi, p. 215.
11 Ibid.
12 Ibid., vi, p. 212.
13 This subject is discussed at some
length in Edward W. Said,
Orientalism.
14 Sir Richard Burton, *Personal
Narrative of a Pilgrimage to
El-Medinah and Mecca.*
15 In Leiden he had made the
acquaintance of one of Europe's
leading Arabists, Professor M. J. de
Goeje – to whom he would later
turn for help with the preparation
of *Travels in Arabia Deserta.*

CHAPTER THREE

1 Letter to D. G. Hogarth, 19 March
1926, from Mrs Caroline Doughty
(Caroline Barron). She says only
one of the letters Doughty wrote
to his brother from his travels
survived.
2 Letter to D. G. Hogarth, 24 October
1902 (Caroline Barron).
3 *The Dawn in Britain*, v, p. 49.
4 Ibid., v, p. 55.
5 Preface to 2nd edition of *Travels in
Arabia Deserta.*
6 *Travels in Arabia Deserta*, i, p. 59.
7 Preface to 2nd edition of *Travels in
Arabia Deserta.*
8 The Nabataeans were incorporated
into the Roman empire in the year
AD106. They were a culturally
advanced people, whose prosperity
was based on their control of the
thriving trade route from India and
the Arabian peninsula.
9 2 Chronicles 26: 11.
10 *Travels in Arabia Deserta*, i, 18; 'Thy
neck is as a tower of ivory; thine

eyes like the fishpools in Heshbon,
by the gate of Bathrabbim' – Song
of Solomon 7: 4.
11 *Travels in Arabia Deserta*, i, p. 20.
12 Ibid., i, p. 174.
13 Ibid., i, p. 24.
14 Ibid., i, p. 52.
15 Ibid., i, p. 68.
16 Ibid., i, p. 62.
17 Ibid., i, p. 75.
18 Ibid., i, p. 12.
19 Sir Edward Creasy, *A History of the
Ottoman Turks* (Richard Bentley,
London, 1854).
20 *Travels in Arabia Deserta*, i, p. 18.
21 Ibid., i, p. 2.
22 *Mansoul*, 1920 edition, p. 73.
23 *Travels in Arabia Deserta*, i, p. 386.
24 C. M. Doughty, *Mitth. der Kais. und
Kon. Geogr. Gesellschaft in Wien*, xix
Band (der neuen Folge ix).
25 *Mansoul*, p. 86.
26 Doughty, *Mitth. der Kais. . . . .*
27 Isaiah, 51: 1: 'Hearken to me, ye
that follow after righteousness, ye
that seek the Lord: look into the
rock whence ye are hewn, and the
hole of the pit whence ye are
digged'; Travels *in Arabia Deserta*, i,
p. 35.
28 Now the biggest town of southern
Jordan, and an important regional
and administrative centre.
29 *Travels in Arabia Deserta*, i, p. 47.
30 Burckhardt, born in Basle in 1784,
reached Petra in 1812 while
travelling in disguise from Syria.
He also visited Mecca. He died in
Cairo at the age of thirty-three
after contracting the plague.
31 Letter to Alois Sprenger, 10
November 1879, quoted in
Hogarth.
32 *Travels in Arabia Deserta*, i, p. 41.
33 Ibid. i, p. 40.
34 Ibid.
35 Ibid., i, p. 48.
36 *Travels in NW Arabia and Nejd.*
37 Ibid.
38 *Travels in Arabia Deserta*, i, p. 35.
39 He had, after all, some five months

before the Hadj caravan set off. He had no idea at this stage of the delays and obstruction he would suffer.

40 *Mitth. der Kais. . . . .*
41 *Travels in Arabia Deserta,* i, p. 17.
42 Ibid., i, p. 45.
43 Ibid., i, p. 1.
44 Letter to Henry Doughty, 13 September 1875, quoted in Hogarth.
45 Sir Henry Rawlinson, introduction to Doughty's RGS paper, November 1883 (RGS).
46 Letter to Royal Geographical Society, 13 September 1875 (RGS).
47 *Mitth. der Kais. . . . .*
48 Ibid.
49 Ibid.
50 *Travels in Arabia Deserta,* ii, p. 153.
51 About £10. Various currencies were in use interchangeably in Arabia. The Turkish lira was worth about 18 English shillings, or just under a pound; the Napoleon about 16 shillings; the real, or Maria Theresa dollar, four shillings; the piastre was worth about a hundredth of a pound. Before Doughty left Medain Salih to start his travels, he bought a camel for six Turkish liras, or just over £5.
52 Letter to unknown recipient, 1 February 1877. A draft of this letter from Medain Salih was found among Doughty's papers, and is quoted in Hogarth.

CHAPTER FOUR

1 *Travels in Arabia Deserta,* i, p. 5.
2 Preface to 1st edition of *Travels in Arabia Deserta.*
3 *Travels in Arabia Deserta,* i, p. 59.
4 Ibid., i, p. 145.
5 Ibid., i, p. 15.
6 Ibid., i, p. 69.
7 Ibid., i, p. 48.
8 About £1.
9 *Travels in Arabia Deserta,* i, p. 52.
10 Ibid., i, p. 71.

11 Letter to unknown recipient, 1 February 1877. A draft of this letter from Medain Salih was found among Doughty's papers, and is quoted in Hogarth.
12 *Travels in Arabia Deserta,* i, p. 106.
13 Ibid., i, p. 108.
14 Ibid.
15 Ibid., i, pp. 113, 117.
16 Ibid., i, p. 112.
17 Ibid., i, p. 123.
18 Ibid., i, p. 103.
19 Letter to unknown recipient, 1 February 1877, quoted in Hogarth.
20 Letter to Miss Amelia Hotham, 2 February 1877, quoted in Hogarth. Miss Hotham died before it could be delivered.
21 *Travels in Arabia Deserta,* i, p. 138.
22 Ibid., i, p. 142.
23 Ibid., i, p. 155.
24 El Ally stood at the ancient crossroads of the north–south incense route and the east–west trade route along the Wadi Hamdh from the Red Sea into central Arabia. Doughty was almost certainly the first European to see these inscriptions, which probably dated from the sixth century BC.
25 Note in diary (Fitzwilliam).
26 Ibid.
27 *Travels in Arabia Deserta,* i, p. 165.
28 Letter to D. G. Hogarth, 28 March 1904 (Caroline Barron).
29 Letter to unknown recipient, 1 February 1877, quoted in Hogarth.
30 14 Napoleons would have been worth just over £11; 80 piastres around 15 shillings.
31 *Travels in Arabia Deserta,* i, p. 213.

CHAPTER FIVE

1 Sir Richard Burton, 'Mr Doughty's Travels'.
2. *Travels in Arabia Deserta,* i, p. 252.
3 Letter to Edward Garnett, 28 September 1907 (HRHRC).

NOTES

4 *Travels in Arabia Deserta*, i, p. 236.
5 Ibid., i, p. 224.
6 Ibid., i, p. 230.
7 Ibid., i, p. 236.
8 Ibid., i, p. 244.
9 Ibid., i, p. 243.
10 Ibid., i, p. 252.
11 Ibid., i, p. 272.
12 Anne Treneer, *Charles Montagu Doughty*.
13 *Travels in Arabia Deserta*, i, p. 257.
14 Ibid., i, p. 299.
15 Letter to D. G. Hogarth, 16 May 1903 (Caroline Barron).
16 *Travels in Arabia Deserta*, i, p. 289.
17 Ibid., i, p. 306.
18 Psalms 109: 23.
19 'Even these of them ye may eat; the locust after his kind, and the bald locust after his kind, and the beetle after his kind, and the grasshopper after his kind' – Leviticus 11: 22.
20 *Travels in Arabia Deserta*, i, p. 323.
21 Ibid., i, p. 354.
22 Ibid., i, p. 351.
23 Ibid., i, p. 355.
24 Ibid., i, p. 362.
25 Ibid., i, p. 377.
26 Ibid., i, p. 383.
27 Ibid.
28 Ibid., i, p. 409.
29 Ibid.
30 Ibid., i, p. 413.
31 Ibid., i, p. 473.
32 A soldier of fortune from Rome, Ludovico di Varthema, claimed to have made his way there in the sixteenth century, and the Italian Carlo Guarmani, whose account of visiting Teyma Doughty saw, also claimed to have reached Kheybar in 1864. It is uncertain whether di Varthema ever actually saw the town, and Doughty's Zehme cast doubt on Guarmani's claim. Doughty certainly believed for many years that the Italian's account of his alleged visit was imaginary. In a letter written some twenty-six years after he returned home, though, he accepted that Guarmani may have been telling the truth – although 'I should not expect an ordinary Italian of the sixties . . . to be quite above a slight bugia.'
33 *Travels in Arabia Deserta*, i, p. 503.
34 Ibid., i, p. 502.
35 Ibid., ii, p. 300.
36 Ibid., i, p. 510.
37 Ibid., i, p. 501.
38 Introduction to 1921 edition of *Travels in Arabia Deserta*. George Bernard Shaw, however, quotes Robert Graves (letter to S. C. Cockerell, 14 July 1944, in Meynell (ed.), *The Best of Friends*) as remarking that *Travels in Arabia Deserta* is written by 'a simple stupid man, a fanatic: all the while he despises the Arabians . . .' But Doughty, simpler and wiser than any of them, realizes that only a racist can give a one-word answer to a question such as 'Do you like Arabs?' He loves some of those he meets, is sorry for some, hates and despises others. His anger is inspired by the strictness of Islam, as it is by that of any organized religion.
39 *Travels in Arabia Deserta*, i, p. 517.
40 *Travels in NW Arabia and Nejd*.
41 *Travels in Arabia Deserta*, i, p. 517.
42 Ibid., i, p. 526.
43 Ibid., i, p. 545.
44 The credit for its discovery went to the French and German explorers Charles Huber and Julius Euting, who Doughty complained later 'wandered in my footsteps years after me' (letter to Royal Geographical Society, March 1886; RGS). Huber first visited Teyma in 1879, two years after Doughty, recognized the stone's value, and returned with Euting four years later. Between them, the two men transported it to Hail, with a view to taking it back to Europe. Huber, though, was killed in the desert by

his bedu guide, while Euting fled
to Jerusalem after getting involved
in an Arab blood feud. The stone
remained in Hail while their
respective governments, each
determined to secure this prize of
orientalism, started trying to
bargain with the Emir. It was the
French who were successful, either
persuading or bribing the Ottoman
authorities to deport the German
agent, and allow the stone to be
shipped to Paris, where it remains.
Instead of a bookful of copied
inscriptions and a collection of
papier-mâché impressions, Doughty
could have claimed the credit for
one of the most significant
archaeological discoveries of his
day.

45 *Travels in Arabia Deserta*, i, p. 547.
46 *Travels in NW Arabia and Nejd*.
47 *Travels in Arabia Deserta*, i, p. 577.
48 Ibid. i, p. 588.
49 Professor Alois Musil, *Northern
   Negd*.
50 *Travels in Arabia Deserta*, i, p. 589.
51 Ibid., i, p. 591.
52 Ibid., i, p. 591.
53 Ibid., i, p. 580.
54 Ibid., i, p. 603.
55 Ibid., ii, p. 39.
56 Ibid., ii, p. 58.
57 Ibid., ii, p. 59.

CHAPTER SIX

1 *Travels in Arabia Deserta*, ii, p. 64.
2 Ibid., ii, p. 67.
3 Ibid., ii, p. 76.
4 Ibid., ii, p. 81.
5 Ibid., ii, p. 85.
6 Ibid., ii, p. 97.
7 Ibid., ii, pp. 128, 134.
8 Ibid., ii, p. 163.
9 Ibid.
10 Russia was sucked into war with
   the Ottoman empire in the
   aftermath of the Balkan revolt of
   1875. It was a conflict of great
   brutality on both sides.

11 *Travels in Arabia Deserta*, ii, p. 203.
12 Ibid., ii, p. 211.
13 Ibid., ii, p. 215.
14 Ibid., ii, pp. 250–1.
15 Ibid., ii, p. 256.
16 Ibid., ii, p. 259.
17 Ibid., ii, p. 272.
18 Ibid., ii, p. 279.
19 Ibid., ii, p. 296.
20 Ibid., ii, p. 314.
21 Ibid.
22 Ibid., ii, p. 316.
23 Ibid., ii, p. 333.
24 Harry St John Philby, *Arabia of the
   Wahhabis*.
25 *Travels in Arabia Deserta*, ii, p. 338.
26 Ibid., ii, p. 342.
27 Ibid., ii, p. 381.
28 Ibid., ii, p. 352.
29 The Royal Navy was deployed to
   protect Constantinople from the
   Russian advance in 1877.
30 *Travels in Arabia Deserta*, ii, p. 381.
31 Philby, *Arabia of the Wahhabis*.
32 *Travels in Arabia Deserta*, ii, p. 376.
33 Ibid., ii, p. 404.
34 Ibid., ii, p. 412.
35 Ibid., ii, p. 415.
36 Ibid.
37 Ibid., ii, p. 452.
38 Ibid., ii, p. 477.
39 Ibid., ii, pp. 477–8.
40 Ibid., ii, p. 486.
41 *Travels in NW Arabia and Nejd*.
42 *Travels in Arabia Deserta*, ii, p. 502.
43 Ibid., ii, p. 506.
44 Ibid., ii, p. 528.

CHAPTER SEVEN

1 Many of the articles which
  Doughty kept in his study are now
  in the library collection at Gonville
  and Caius College, Cambridge.
2 Draft letter to unknown recipient,
  June 1879, preserved among
  Doughty's papers and quoted in
  Hogarth.
3 Letter from W. K. Hatch, FRCS, to
  D. G. Hogarth, 1 January 1927
  (Caroline Barron). Mr Hatch says

he was able to do little for him, and nearly fifty years later Doughty told him he still had the disease, although it did not trouble him.

4 Draft letter to unknown recipient, June 1879, preserved among Doughty's papers and quoted in Hogarth.

5 *Journal of the Bombay Branch of the Royal Asiatic Society*, vol. xiv (1870–80).

6 Ibid.

7 F. P. Doughty, *Captain's Journal*, HMS *Crocodile*, National Maritime Museum.

8 Ibid.

9 Letter from Mrs Marion Doughty Montagu, daughter of Captain Frederick Proby Doughty, to D. G. Hogarth, 3 January 1927 (Caroline Barron).

10 Memoir by G. G. Coulton, *Cambridge Review*, 12 March 1926.

11 About £10.

12 Letter to Professor Alois Sprenger, 22 September 1879, quoted in Hogarth.

13 Mrs Hugh Fraser, *Further Reminiscences of a Diplomatist's Wife.*

14 Meredith B. Raymond and Mary Rose Sullivan (eds.), *Women and Letters: Selected Letters of Elizabeth Barrett Browning and Mary Russell Mitford.*

15 Letter from Richard Kiepert, 4 February 1881 (Caius).

16 Of the Société Géographique de Paris.

17 Letter from Richard Kiepert, 5 July 1881, quoted in Hogarth.

18 Letter from Richard Kiepert, 15 October 1884 (Caius).

19 The Académie des Inscriptions et Belles Lettres was a part of the Paris Institut de France.

20 Letter from C. Klinckseick, 31 January 1885 (Caius).

21 *Travels in NW Arabia and Nejd.*

22 Ibid.

23 Letter to S. C. Cockerell, 31 March 1922, quoted in Hogarth.

24 The diary entry, by the explorer H. O. Forbes, was passed on to S. C. Cockerell. It is quoted in Hogarth.

25 Report from Sir Henry Rawlinson on Doughty's paper, 11 December 1883 (RGS). At least one of the versions which was rejected was prepared from shorthand notes of Doughty's speech, for which he had not apparently prepared a manuscript.

26 Letter from Douglas Freshfield to D. G. Hogarth, 1926. Freshfield had been at school with Doughty at Elstree.

27 *Travels in NW Arabia and Nejd.*

28 Letter to H. W. Bates, RGS secretary, 10 January 1884 (RGS).

29 Ibid.

30 Letter to H. W. Bates, 11 January 1884 (RGS).

31 Letter to H. W. Bates, April 1884 (RGS).

32 Letter to C. M. Doughty, 10 September 1883, quoted in Hogarth.

33 Information from Mr John Thackray, Archivist of the Geological Society.

34 *Travels in Arabia Deserta*, i, p. 168.

35 Ibid., ii, pp. 71–6.

36 Inside the front cover of the first of the notebooks, now kept at Cambridge University's Fitzwilliam Museum, is a note in Doughty's hand: 'Read (again) and compared throughout with the text. 1 week March 1881. All reviewed for the last time 9 June 1881.'

37 Letter from Professor Alois Sprenger to Doughty, 28 July 1882 (Caius).

38 Burton, *Personal Narrative of a Pilgrimage to El-Madinah and Mecca.*

39 Lady Anne Blunt, *A Pilgrimage to Nejd.*

40 Blunt himself was no less goggle-eyed. 'The religion in whose name we travelled was only one of romance,' he declared grandly.

41 Letter to D. G. Hogarth, 19 August 1913 (Caroline Barron).

42 Letter to D. G. Hogarth, 24 October 1902 (Caroline Barron).

43 Letter to *The Times* from Sir William Ridgeway, 28 January 1926.

44 Letter from W. R. Smith to C. M. Doughty, 23 June 1885, quoted in Hogarth.

45 In a letter written many years later (to the writer N. M. Penzer, 21 February 1920; HRHRC) Doughty said that the publishers had seen the book as a 'certain loss' from the start. 'Thus I had and have no pecuniary interest whatever in the result, receiving only when printed the usual six complimentary copies, and later six more, all which, save my own single copy, I distributed to friends and relatives.'

46 Letter to Professor M. J. de Goeje, 23 July 1887 (Caius).

47 Letter to Julius Euting, 1 December 1884 (Caius).

48 Doughty was the first to establish how the main drainage channels of northern Arabia run into the great Wadi Hamdh. He had also made detailed observations of the volcanic scenery and geology around Kheybar.

49 Letter to Professor M. J. de Goeje, 1 December 1891 (Caius).

50 T. E. Lawrence, Introduction to *Travels in Arabia Deserta*, 1921 edition.

51 Preface to first edition of *Travels in Arabia Deserta*.

52 *Travels in Arabia Deserta*, i, p. 215.

53 Letter to E. Garnett, 17 January 1912 (HRIIRC).

54 The orientalist, writer and Middle East scholar Guy Le Strange carried on a lengthy correspondence with Doughty from the 1880s. He died in 1933 in Cambridge, where he had settled after many years travelling and living in the Middle East.

55 Letter to S. C. Cockerell, 31 March 1922, quoted in Hogarth.

56 Laurence Oliphant, journalist, novelist and mystic, was Guy Le Strange's brother-in-law. In the 1880s he established a community of Jewish immigrants in Haifa, where Doughty and his wife went to stay soon after their wedding. He died in London in 1883.

57 Conversation between Guy Le Strange and D. G. Hogarth, March 1927, quoted in Hogarth.

58 Letter to H. W. Bates, RGS secretary, 4 April 1886 (RGS).

59 Letter to H. W. Bates, 20 January 1886 (RGS).

60 Letter to Professor M. J. de Goeje, 23 July 1887, quoted in Hogarth.

61 Sir Charles Napier took control of the northern Indian province of Sind when his force of 2,800 defeated 22,000 men at the Falaili river in February 1843 – enabling *Punch* to immortalize him with the famous pun with which he is supposed to have announced his victory – 'Peccavi; I have sinned.'

62 In 1887 a local physician, Dr Joseph Schneer, dedicated his book about the town, *Alassio, Pearl of the Riviera* to General Sir Montagu McMurdo. Of Lady McMurdo's garden he wrote: 'One can hardly imagine anything more charming than the conjunction of the most magnificent trees, exotic plants and flowers amid rocks and running waters, with prospects, roads, paths, and rustic benches.'

63 Letter from C. M. Doughty to Guy Le Strange, 21 August 1886 (Fitzwilliam).

64 Letter to Guy Le Strange, 19 November 1886 (Fitzwilliam).

65 Mukadassi was the name given to the Arabian traveller and writer Shams ad-din Abu Abdallah Mohammed Ibn Āhmed, whose *Description of the Lands of Islam* was published in AD 985–6. A copy

had been brought to Europe from India by Alois Sprenger, and edited by Professor M. J. de Goeje in 1877. The edition Doughty was reading was almost certainly Le Strange's own translation, which was published in 1886.

66 Letter to Guy Le Strange, 19 November 1886 (Fitzwilliam).

67 Postcard to Professor de Goeje, September 1887 (Leiden).

68 Postcard to Professor de Goeje, 20 September 1887 (Leiden).

69 Preface to first edition of *Travels in Arabia Deserta.*

70 Letter to D. G. Hogarth, 1923, quoted in Hogarth.

71 Introduction to *Travels in Arabia Deserta,* 1921 edition.

72 Letter to D. G. Hogarth, 19 August 1913, quoted in Hogarth.

73 From Doughty's word-notes, quoted by Anne Treneer in *Charles Montagu Doughty.* Much of this chapter is based on her book, one of a few full-length studies of Doughty's writing.

74 *Travels in Arabia Deserta,* i, p. 518.

75 Ibid., i, p. 26.

76 James Milroy, in *The Language of Gerard Manley Hopkins,* notes, 'It would be difficult to exaggerate the revolution in linguistic interests that took place in England in the mid–19th century, or to overemphasize the progress in knowledge of the history and dialects of English that was made during Hopkins' lifetime.' Apart from Hopkins himself, there was an immense growth in academic philology, with W. W. Skeat forming the English Dialect Society in 1873, and work starting on the *Oxford English Dictionary* fifteen years later. There is no evidence that Doughty had any knowledge of this contemporary interest; but it suggests that he was much more a man of his time than he would like to have admitted.

77 *Travels in Arabia Deserta,* i, p. 227.

78 Ibid., i, p. 244.

79 Ibid., ii, p. 10.

80 Ibid., i, p. 323.

81 Ibid., i, p. 197.

82 Ibid., ii, p. 210.

83 *The Times,* 6 April 1888.

84 *Spectator,* 7 April 1888.

85 *Academy,* 28 July 1888.

86 Doughty took no offence at this critical review. Writing some years afterwards (letter to N. M. Penzer, 21 February 1920; HRHRC), he referred to Burton mildly as 'very friendly and pleasant . . . a remarkable and forceful man'.

87 Recorded interview, broadcast by the BBC as part of 'A Disciple of Spenser and Venerable Chaucer', 24 January 1961 (BBC).

88 Robert Bridges to Doughty, 24 August 1888, quoted in Hogarth.

89 Letter to Mrs Caroline Doughty, quoted by her in a letter to D. G. Hogarth, 19 March 1926 (Caroline Barron).

90 She told Anne Treneer, who described the incident in her book.

91 *Travels in Arabia Deserta,* i, p. 91.

92 Memoir on C. M. Doughty by G. G. Coulton in *Cambridge Review,* 12 March 1926.

93 Letter from Doughty to Robert Bridges, 25 February 1889, and quoted in Hogarth.

94 Letter to Professor M. J. de Goeje, 24 March 1889 (Leiden).

95 Letter to de Goeje, 27 May 1888 (Leiden).

96 Letter to Robert Bridges, 25 February 1889, quoted in Hogarth.

CHAPTER EIGHT

1 Letter to Robert Bridges, 10 November 1889, quoted in Hogarth.

2 Frederick Fitzroy Hamilton, *Bordighera and the Western Riviera.*

3 Edward I. Sparks, *The Riviera*.

4 John Congreve, *Visitors' Guide to San Remo*.

5 Both poems were sent to the children from London, where Doughty was staying. They are quoted in Hogarth.

6 Dorothy Doughty, interviewed as part of 'A Disciple of Spenser and Venerable Chaucer', 24 January 1961 (BBC).

7 In the Introduction to a one-volume edition of *The Dawn in Britain* published in 1943 (Jonathan Cape, London), Ruth Robbins says Doughty had been researching into the history of the Druids in the Caius College library as early as 1869.

8 Undated letter from C. M. Doughty, quoted in Hogarth.

9 Letter to D. G. Hogarth, 1922, quoted in Hogarth.

10 Letter to Professor M. J. de Goeje, 1 December 1891 (Leiden).

11 In a letter to D. G. Hogarth of 12 August 1911 Edwyn Bevan says that his brother, Professor A. A. Bevan, met Doughty while he was living at Ospedaletti. He was known then to be working on 'an epic about the Druids'.

12 Letter to Guy Le Strange, 13 August 1891 (Fitzwilliam).

13 *The Dawn in Britain*, i, pp. 113–14.

14 Letter to Mrs Doughty Montagu, 1901, quoted in Hogarth.

15 Letter and two cards to Mrs Doughty, 31 August, 1 September, 3 September 1901; quoted in Hogarth.

16 The river Ver still runs through St Albans. Camulodunum was the Roman name for Colchester, some seventy miles away.

17 *The Dawn in Britain*, xvii, p. 13.

18 Ibid., ix, p. 6.

19 Ibid., x, p. 116.

20 Letter to R. T. Wright, Cambridge University Press, April 1905, quoted in Hogarth.

21 Edward Garnett was one of the leading publisher's readers of his generation. Among other writers whose careers he promoted were D. H. Lawrence, Joseph Conrad and John Galsworthy. He was also a critic and playwright of some standing in his own right.

22 Account given by E. Garnett to D. G. Hogarth.

23 Letter to E. Garnett, 17 November 1905, quoted in Hogarth.

24 Letter to E. Garnett, undated (HRHRC).

25 *Academy*, 5 May 1906.

26 *The Times Literary Supplement*, 20 April 1906.

27 Letter to E. Garnett, 8 April 1906, quoted in Hogarth.

28 The poem covers a period stretching from the sacking of Rome by the Senones Gauls in the fourth century BC to the destruction of Jerusalem by Titus in AD 70.

29 *The Dawn in Britain*, iii, p. 149.

30 *Travels in Arabia Deserta*, i, p. 25.

31 Ibid., i, p. 218.

32 Ibid., i, p. 70.

33 Letter to D. G. Hogarth, 27 August 1927, quoted in David Garnett (ed.), *Selected Letters of T. E. Lawrence*.

34 *The Dawn in Britain*, vii, p. 153.

35 Ibid., vii, p. 156.

36 Ibid., vii, p. 151.

37 Ibid., xxi, p. 6.

38 Ibid., xxiii, p. 4.

39 Letter to S. C. Cockerell, 2 February 1908, quoted in Meynell (ed.), *Friends of a Lifetime*.

40 Letter to S. C. Cockerell, 9 July 1913, quoted in ibid.

41 Letter to E. Garnett, 26 November 1905 (HRHRC).

42 Letter to E. Garnett, 20 November 1905 (HRHRC).

43 To E. Garnett, 1906 (HRHRC).

44 To E. H. Blakeney, 18 May 1916 (HRHRC).

45 Letter to E. Garnett, 2 June 1907 (HRHRC).

46 Letter to E. Garnett, 8 October 1907 (HRHRC).

47 Freda Doughty, interviewed for BBC Radio, 24 January 1961 (BBC). In the privacy of his Notes, stored now at Gonville and Caius College, Cambridge, Doughty was more bleakly outspoken about his lack of faith in organized religion. 'Man's life is as the image, the reflection, which in a moment passeth away from the glass and is gone for ever. We are born in darkness, we live in darkness, we die in darkness. The priests of the several Religions pretend to hold up a little light.'

48 Letter to E. Garnett, 20 June 1909 (HRHRC).

49 Letter to S. C. Cockerell, 27 October 1923; quoted in Garnett (ed.), *Selected Letters of T. E. Lawrence*.

50 Letter to D. G. Hogarth, 11 January 1927 (Caroline Barron).

51 *Cambridge Review*, 12 March 1926. Alfred Ollivant's sentimental novel about a dog, *Owd Bob*, written in 1898, remained popular well into the 1930s.

52 G. G. Coulton, *Fourscore Years*.

53 Wilfrid Scawen Blunt, who had arrived in Hail with his wife Lady Anne just a few months after Doughty left, was passionate in support of the cause of Egyptian nationalism in the 1880s. He was imprisoned in 1888 for his later activities on behalf of the Irish Land League.

54 'The Poetry of C. M. Doughty'.

55 Nimroth, or Nimrod, is mentioned in Genesis 10: 8–10 as 'a mighty one in the earth . . . a mighty hunter before the Lord'.

56 *Cambridge Review*, 12 March 1926.

57 *Under Arms* (London, 1900).

58 Letter to Charlotte Shaw, 4 May 1927, quoted in Jeremy Wilson, *Lawrence of Arabia*.

59 'Drummer Hodge', 1899.

60 'Dirge of Dead Sisters', 1902.

61 Letter to E. Garnett, 5 April 1909 (HRHRC).

62 Ibid.

63 Letter to E. Garnett, 8 April 1909 (HRHRC).

64 Wilfred Owen, 'The Parable of the Old Men and the Young'.

65 Letter to Charlotte Shaw, 10 June 1927, British Library collection.

66 In *The Times Literary Supplement*, 11 February 1926.

67 *The Clouds*, p. 25.

68 Ibid., p. 31.

69 *The Cliffs*, p. 166.

70 He was at least able to offer Doughty-Wylie's family reassurance about the respect that would be accorded to his grave, which fell into Turkish hands after the evacuation from Gallipoli later in 1915. Stories about the barbaric actions of Turks and Germans were commonplace in wartime Britain, but Doughty promised the family that the Muslims would treat the remains of all the fallen soldiers with honour. When the British forces returned at the end of the war, his confidence was amply justified.

Doughty-Wylie's name, incidentally, features in an odd coincidence of Arabian exploration: after his death his widow persuaded his godson to change his name by deed poll to Doughty-Wylie in his memory. The godson's original name was Brian Thesiger: his elder brother Wilfred was to become Arabia's last great explorer.

71 Letter to E. Garnett, 9 June 1918 (HRHRC).

72 Letter to E. Garnett, 1909, quoted in Hogarth.

73 St Paul's Epistle to the Romans, xiv, 4.

74 Letter to D. G. Hogarth,

12 December 1919 (Caroline
Barron).

75 Letter to E. Garnett, 23 July 1916
(HRHRC).

76 Letter to E. Garnett, 9 June 1918
(HRHRC).

77 Ibid.

CHAPTER NINE

1 Letter to T. E. Lawrence, 1909, in
A. W. Lawrence (ed.), *Letters to
T. E. Lawrence.*

2 Letter to C. M. Doughty,
8 February 1909 (Caius).

3 Letter to C. M. Doughty,
30 November 1909 (Caius).

4 The noted archaeologists Woolley
and Hogarth were deputy keeper
and keeper at the Ashmolean. They
both worked at the British Museum
excavations at Carchemish, the
ancient Hittite capital in Syria,
where Lawrence was accepted as
an assistant in 1910.

5 Letter from T. E. Lawrence to his
mother, 2 August 1909, in Garnett
(ed.), *Selected Letters of T. E.
Lawrence.*

6 Letter to S. C. Cockerell, 29 July
1944, quoted in Meynell (ed.), *The
Best of Friends.* Shaw's view of
Doughty was as forceful and as
backhanded as one might expect.
In various letters to Cockerell he
described him as 'a bigoted
parsonage-bred beachcomber who
found his natural place with the
Beduwy as a deserter from
civilisation' and 'an overwhelming
mastercraftsman in epical blank
verse . . .', and observed, 'Doughty
has the epic qualifications –
immense observation and memory
on which he exercises a mania for
description, and a gift of landscape
composition, not in paint but in a
power of versification that gives
you a vision and feeling of
anything from a bluebell to a
thunderstorm.'

7 Letter to E. Garnett, 4 January
1920 (HRHRC).

8 *Mansoul*, p. 3. Except where noted,
references to *Mansoul* are to the
second edition of 1923.

9 Ibid., p. 37.

10 Ibid., p. 35.

11 Ibid., p. 83.

12 Ibid., p. 28.

13 Ibid., p. 81.

14 Ibid., p. 126.

15 Ibid., p. 124.

16 Nebo was a patron deity of
Borsippa, in Babylon. In the
second edition of *Mansoul* Doughty
notes that the name means
'prophet' in Hebrew, Arabic and
Babylonian.

17 *Mansoul*, p. 55.

18 Ibid., p. 94.

19 Ibid., p. 104.

20 Ibid., p. 53.

21 Ibid., p. 121.

22 Ibid., p. 147.

23 *Mansoul*, 1920 edition, p. 168.
These seem to me to be crucial
lines in the poem, but in his
second edition Doughty rewrote
them as follows:
Of man's endeavour,
    seeking righteousness,
Wherein, reborn, a soul
    may fearless walk
Towards the Infinite
    Unknown, in eternal paths.

24 Letter to E. Garnett, 4 January
1920 (HRHRC).

25 Letter to R. B. Townshend,
29 February 1920, quoted in
Hogarth.

26 Letter to E. Garnett, 15 February
1922 (HRHRC).

27 Letter to E. Garnett, 15 June 1922
(HRHRC).

28 He observed in a letter to S. C.
Cockerell on 1 June 1922
(HRHRC) that 'A poetical work can
never be so absolutely finished
that the writer cannot find some
slight improvements.' The
publishers who had to deal with

his constant changes and revisions to his work throughout his life might have been forgiven a wry smile at the comment.

29 *Mansoul*, p. 231.

30 Letter to C. M. Doughty, 24 November 1909 (Caius).

31 *Travels in Arabia Deserta*, ii, p. 352: 'Bessam himself, and his sons, held the towel to them, without the door, whilst they washed their hands. The company returned to their sitting before the hearth; and his elder son sat there already to make us coffee . . .'

32 Letter to C. M. Doughty, 11 December 1911 (Caius).

33 El Kenneyny himself had died soon after Doughty left Arabia. D. G. Hogarth records that his only surviving descendant was an imbecile boy, and the bowl was eventually returned to Doughty. He later presented it to Gonville and Caius College, Cambridge, where it is still kept.

34 Christopher Sykes, in the BBC Radio programme 'A Disciple of Spenser and Venerable Chaucer', broadcast 24 January 1961 (BBC).

35 T. E. Lawrence, Introduction to *Travels in Arabia Deserta*, 1921 edition.

36 Hogarth, *Life of Charles M. Doughty*.

37 Letter to T. E. Lawrence, 20 October 1920, quoted in Hogarth.

38 Letter to C. M. Doughty, Christmas Day 1918 (Caius).

39 Letter to T. E. Lawrence, 16 May 1924, quoted in Hogarth.

40 Ibid.

41 S. C. Cockerell diary entry, 1909; quoted in W. J. W. Blunt, *Sydney Carlyle Cockerell*.

42 Doughty was glad that the quarrel was at an end, but unable to resist having the last word. Writing back to thank the secretary for the award, and for the congratulations of King George V, which had been passed on to him, he added ingenuously: 'I can only use in writing the simplest expressions, having never allowed my mind to be influenced in the slightest degree by any desire of personal reward' (letter to RGS, 28 March 1912; RGS).

43 Letter to S. C. Cockerell, 12 May 1920, quoted in Hogarth.

44 In his *Encyclopaedia Britannica* article on Doughty. His son Kim clearly disagreed: on his father's tomb, in the Muslim cemetery in Beirut, he had engraved the words 'Greatest of Arabian explorers'.

45 Bertram Thomas, *Arabia Felix*.

46 Harry St John Philby, interviewed for the BBC Radio programme 'A Disciple of Spenser and Venerable Chaucer', 24 January 1961 (BBC).

47 Letter to Wilfrid Blunt, 26 June 1920 (Fitzwilliam).

48 Their visit, which also included a call on Philby's son Kim at his Eastbourne prep school, is described in Elizabeth Monroe's *Philby of Arabia*.

49 The two sisters remained unmarried, living together until Dorothy died in 1962, aged seventy. They established reputations for themselves as modellers for Royal Worcester porcelain, Dorothy producing a classic series of American and British birds, while Freda specialized in representations of children. The Queen, visiting the United States in 1954, presented President Eisenhower with a pair of Dorothy Doughty birds. Freda Doughty died in 1972.

50 Letter to C. M. Doughty, 27 September 1923 (Caius).

51 Some years before he had responded tartly to a request for a photograph for D. G. Hogarth's planned book on Arabian exploration (see p. 52).

52 Kennington had won renown as an official British war artist in the

last two years of the war, but his greater claim to fame came with the publication of his illustrations to *Seven Pillars of Wisdom* in 1926.

53 Lawrence, who commissioned the portrait, presented it to the gallery.

54 Letter to D. G. Hogarth, 19 June 1922 (Caroline Barron).

55 Letter to E. Garnett, 19 August 1923 (HRHRC).

56 Letter to E. Garnett, 7 January 1910 (HRHRC).

57 Letter to E. Garnett, 19 August 1923 (HRHRC).

58 Letter to J. W. Haines, 1 January 1924, quoted in Hogarth.

59 Letter to S. C. Cockerell from Florence Hardy, quoted in Meynell (ed.), *Friends of a Lifetime*.

60 Letter to S. C. Cockerell, 5 April 1922, quoted in Hogarth.

61 Letter to T. E. Lawrence, 29 February 1920.

62 Letter to E. Garnett, 16 September 1923 (HRHRC).

63 E. Garnett, Introduction to *Wanderings in Arabia*.

64 Letter to C. M. Doughty, 5 January 1920 (Caius).

65 Ibid.

66 Hogarth, who was involved in the original proposition in his role as director of the Arab Bureau in Cairo, writes about Lawrence's suggestions in his *Life of Charles M. Doughty*.

67 Letter to C. M. Doughty, 7 May 1920 (Caius).

68 Letter to T. E. Lawrence, 21 December 1920, quoted in Hogarth.

69 Letter to C. M. Doughty, 28 January 1921 (Caius).

70 Letter to C. M. Doughty, 18 June 1921 (Caius).

71 Letter to C. M. Doughty, 23 March 1922 (Caius).

72 A moderate professional salary at the time would have been some three or four times this figure.

73 Letter to C. M. Doughty, 23 March 1922 (Caius). David Garnett, in his *Selected Letters of T. E. Lawrence*, queries whether the lion's share of the £400 may not have come from Lawrence himself – although the fact that he failed to reach the target he had set suggests that he raised at least some of the money elsewhere. The manuscript in the museum bears Doughty's pencil note that the 'first recencis' was completed on 8 April 1892, and the second on 4 November 1894 – but the text was radically altered and rewritten before the poem was published in 1906.

74 Letter to S. C. Cockerell, 5 April 1922, quoted in Meynell (ed.), *Friends of a Lifetime*.

75 Letter to S. C. Cockerell, 7 May 1922, quoted in ibid.

76 Letter to D. G. Hogarth, 19 June 1922, quoted in Hogarth.

77 C. M. Doughty, *Hogarth's 'Arabia'*; privately printed (London, 1922).

78 Letter to S. C. Cockerell, 11 May 1922, quoted in Meynell (ed.), *Friends of a Lifetime*.

79 Letter to Mrs Doughty, 3 March 1922 (Caius).

80 Letter to T. E. Lawrence, 5 March 1922, quoted in Hogarth.

81 Letter to C. M. Doughty, 16 November 1922 (Caius).

82 Letter to C. M. Doughty, 6 November 1922 (Caius).

83 Lawrence discovered in childhood that he was illegitimate, although he only told his mother that he knew after his father's death. For over thirty years he had mistakenly believed that Thomas Lawrence was not his natural father: it was only when her husband died that Sarah Lawrence told her son that Thomas was originally a man of property in Ireland, who had abandoned his wife, family and social position to live with her. A full account is in Jeremy Wilson's *Lawrence of Arabia*.

84 Letter to C. M. Doughty,
4 November 1920 (Caius).

85 Letter to C. M. Doughty, 13 June
1921 (Caius). The reports to which
Lawrence refers were included in
the *Arab Bulletin*, which was
produced in Egypt during the war
as information for Military
Intelligence.

86 Later discussions of Lawrence – for
instance, in *A Prince of Our Disorder*
by the professor of psychiatry John
E. Mack, and in a *Sunday Times*
article of 23 June 1968 – suggest
that one result of his capture and
rape by the Turks at Dera'a, in
Syria, was that in the post-war
years he would go off on secret
trips to be whipped and beaten.
The subject is discussed at length
in Wilson's biography. Doughty, of
course, would have known
nothing about it.

87 Letter to T. E. Lawrence, 16 May
1924, quoted in Hogarth.

88 Conversation with S. C. Cockerell,
recorded in Cockerell's diary, and
quoted in Hogarth.

89 Letter to D. G. Hogarth, 19 May
1927, quoted in Garnett (ed.),
Selected Letters of T. E. Lawrence. The
version Lawrence sent was the
so-called 'Oxford edition', printed
for him in proof only in 1922,
which contains much material
omitted from the revised version
published in 1926.

90 Letter to S. C. Cockerell,
22 October 1923, quoted in
Meynell (ed.), *Friends of a Lifetime*.

91 Doughty's friends were constantly
anxious to ease her situation, but
she had the same scruples about
accepting help as her late husband,
as a letter to S. C. Cockerell in
1932 makes clear. Cockerell had
offered to sell Doughty's old copy
of Siegfried Sassoon's *Sonnets and
Verses* on her behalf, but she was
convinced that she was being
offered above the market value.

'On second thoughts and after a
sleepless night, I have decided to
return the cheque and let you get
out of the scrape with the
booksellers! I won't take 1/- more
than the real value of the book . . .
My oldfashioned ideas simply
make it impossible for me to
accept the gift . . .' (letter published
in Meynell (ed.), *The Best of
Friends*). Mrs Doughty died in
1950, aged eighty-eight.

92 Letter to D. G. Garnett, 12 July
1923 (HRHRC).

93 Cheesman (1878–1962), who was
the author of *In Unknown Arabia*
(1926), travelled extensively in
Arabia in the twenties. He spent
much of his life at Cranbrook in
Kent, within a couple of miles of
Merriecroft.

94 Information from Dr Geoffrey
Hattersley-Smith, who moved into
a house close to Merriecroft
shortly after Doughty's death.

95 Letter to S. C. Cockerell, 2 June
1923 (HRHRC).

96 *Mansoul*, p. 113.

97 Undated letter to Freda Doughty,
quoted in Hogarth.

98 Freda Doughty, interviewed for the
BBC Radio programme 'A Disciple
of Spenser and Venerable
Chaucer', 24 January 1961 (BBC).

AFTERWORD

1 In his BBC broadcast, 'Poetry in
Motion'. He was referring to
Doughty's 'unknown'
contemporary, Thomas Hardy.

2 Interview with the author,
London, 12 April 1996.

3 Canto 83. See Hugh Kenner, *The
Pound Era*.

4 Letter to his family, 11 May 1911,
quoted in Jeremy Wilson, *Lawrence
of Arabia*.

5 Letter to S. C. Cockerell,
23 January 1945, published in
Meynell (ed.), *The Best of Friends*.

BIBLIOGRAPHY

Adamson, Oswald, R. (ed.), *The Laleham Commonplace Book* (Ian Allen, Laleham, 1989)

Ageron, C. R., *Modern Algeria*, trans. and ed. Michael Brett (Hurst and Co., London, 1991)

Allen, Mea, *Palgrave of Arabia* (Macmillan, London, 1972)

Assad, Thomas J., *Three Victorian Travellers* (Routledge and Kegan Paul, London, 1972)

Bernays, Revd L. J. (ed.), *A Manual of Family Prayers and Meditations* (London, 1845)

—— *The Church in the Schoolroom* (London, 1851)

Blunt, Lady Anne, *A Pilgrimage to Nejd* (John Murray, London, 1881)

Blunt, W. J. W., *Sydney Carlyle Cockerell* (Hamish Hamilton, London, 1964)

Browning, Iain, *Petra* (Chatto and Windus, London, 1989)

Burckhardt, J. L., *Travels in Syria and the Holy Land* (London, 1822)

Burton, Richard, *Personal Narrative of a Pilgrimage to El-Medinah and Mecca* (Longman's, London, 1855)

Burton, Richard, 'Mr Doughty's Travels', in *Academy* (28 July 1888)

Carey, John, *The Faber Book of Science* (Faber and Faber, London, 1995)

Chew, S. C., 'The Poetry of C. M. Doughty', in *North American Review* (December 1925)

Congreve, John, *Visitors' Guide to San Remo* (Stanford, London, 1882)

Coulton, G. G., 'C. M. Doughty', in *Cambridge Review* (March 1926)

—— *Fourscore Years* (CUP, Cambridge, 1943)

Creasy, Sir Edward S., *A History of the Ottoman Turks* (Richard Bentley, London, 1854)

Davis, Herbert, 'Charles Doughty 1843–1926', Bergen Lecture (Yale University, 1943)

Doughty, C. M., *Adam Cast Forth: A Sacred Drama in Five Songs* (Duckworth, London, 1908)

—— *The Cliffs: A Drama of the Time, in Five Parts* (Duckworth, London, 1909)

—— *The Clouds* (Duckworth, London, 1912)

—— *The Dawn in Britain* (Duckworth, London, 1906); *Selected Passages from 'The Dawn in Britain' of Charles Doughty*, arranged by Barker Fairley (Duckworth, London, 1935); one-volume edition (Jonathan Cape, London, 1943)

—— *'Documents épigraphiques recueillis dans le nord de l'Arabie'*, ed. Ernest Renan, Académie des Inscriptions et de Belles Lettres, Paris, 1884

—— *Hogarth's 'Arabia'* (privately printed, London, 1922)

—— *Mitth. der Kais. und Kon. Geogr. Gesellschaft in Wien*, xix Band (der neuen Folge ix), trans. Mrs Lyn Oualah (1876).

—— *Mansoul, or The Riddle of the World* (Selwyn and Blount, London, 1920); revised edition (Jonathan Cape and the Medici Society, London, 1923)

—— *On the Jostedal-Brae Glaciers in Norway* (Edward Stanford, London, 1866)

—— *Travels in Arabia Deserta* (CUP, Cambridge, 1888); 2nd edition (Jonathan Cape and the Medici Society, London, 1921); 3rd edition, with Introduction by T. E. Lawrence (Jonathan Cape, London, 1933); *Wanderings in Arabia* (Duckworth, London, 1908); Passages from 'Arabia Deserta', selected by Edward Garnett (Jonathan Cape, London 1931)

—— *Travels in NW Arabia and Nejd*, Paper given to Royal Geographical Society (RGS, November 1883)

—— *Under Arms 1900* (privately published, London, 1900)

Doughty, H. M., *Chronicles of Theberton* (London, 1910)

Doughty, Katherine, *The Betts of Wortham in Suffolk* (The Bodley Head, London, 1911)

Fairley, Barker, *Charles M. Doughty, A Critical Study* (Jonathan Cape, London, 1927)

Farwell, Byron, *Burton, A Biography of Sir Richard Francis Burton* (Longman's, London, 1963)

Fraser, Mrs Hugh, *Further Reminiscences of a Diplomatist's Wife* (Hutchinson, London, 1912)

Garnett, David (ed.), *Selected Letters of T. E. Lawrence* (Jonathan Cape, London, 1938)

Gildea, Robert, *Barricades and Borders, Europe 1800–1914* (OUP, Oxford, 1996)

Hamilton, Frederick Fitzroy, *Bordighera and the Western Riviera* (Stanford, London, 1883)

Hogarth, D. G., *Life of Charles M. Doughty* (OUP, London, 1928)

—— *The Penetration of Arabia* (Lawrence and Bullen, London, 1904)

Kenner, Hugh, *The Pound Era* (Faber and Faber, London, 1971)

Lawrence, A. W. (ed.), *Letters to T. E. Lawrence* (Jonathan Cape, London, 1962)

Lawrence, T. E., *Seven Pillars of Wisdom* (Jonathan Cape, London, 1973)

Lobley, J. L., *Mount Vesuvius* (Roper and Drowley, London, 1889)

Lyell, Mrs, *Life, Letters and Journals of Sir Charles Lyell* (London, 1881)

Mack, John E., *A Prince of Our Disorder* (Little, Brown, Boston, 1976)

McCrum, Michael, *Thomas Arnold, Headmaster* (OUP, Oxford, 1989)

Meynell, V. (ed.), *The Best of Friends: Letters to S. C. Cockerell* (Rupert Hart-Davies, London, 1956)

—— *Friends of a Lifetime* (Jonathan Cape, London, 1940)

Milroy, James, *The Language of Gerard Manley Hopkins* (Andre Deutsch, London, 1977)

Monroe, Elizabeth, *Philby of Arabia* (Faber and Faber, London, 1973)

Musil, Professor Alois, *Northern Negd* (American Geographical Society, 1928)

Palgrave, W. G., *Narrative of a Year's Journey Through Central and Eastern Arabia* (Macmillan Ltd, London, 1865)

Palmieri, Paride, *Eruption of Vesuvius 1872*, with notes etc. by Robert Mallet, FRS (London, 1873)

Philby, Harry St John, *Arabia of the Wahhabis* (Constable and Co., London, 1928)

Raymond, Meredith B., and Mary Rose Sullivan, *Women and Letters: Selected Letters of Elizabeth Barratt Browning and Mary Russell Mitford* (Twayne, Boston, Mass., 1987)

Said, Edward W., *Orientalism* (Routledge and Kegan Paul, London, 1978)

Saki (H.H. Munro), *When William Came* (J. Lane, London, 1926)

Sanderson, I. C. M., *A History of Elstree School* (privately published, 1979)

Sandys, George, *Relation of His Journey to the Levant* (1615)

Schneer, Dr Joseph, *Alassio, Pearl of the Riviera* (Trubner and Co., London, 1887)

Sparks, Edward I., *The Riviera* (J. and A. Churchill, London, 1879)

Tabachnik, Stephen Ely, *Charles Doughty* (Twayne Publishers, Boston, 1981)

Taylor, Anne, *Laurence Oliphant* (OUP, Oxford, 1982)

Thesiger, Wilfred, *Arabian Sands* (Longmans, Green, London, 1959)

Thomas, Bertram, *Arabia Felix* (Jonathan Cape, London, 1932)

Treneer, Anne, *Charles Montagu Doughty, A Study of His Prose and Verse* (Jonathan Cape, London, 1935)

Wells, H. G., *The War in the Air* (T. Nelson and Sons, London, 1908)

341

Wheatcroft, Andrew, *The Ottomans* (Viking, London, 1993)
Wilson, Jeremy, *Lawrence of Arabia* (Heinemann, London, 1989)
Winstone, H. V. F., *Gertrude Bell* (Jonathan Cape, London, 1978)

INDEX

Abd Er Rahman 210
Abdu Kahil 81, 250
Abdul Aziz, Sultan 67
Abdul Kadir 83
Abdullah 187, 188, 189, 194
Académie des Inscriptions 226
Academy 263
Adam Cast Forth 268–71, 278, 318
Aga, Mohammed 84, 86, 91
Alexander the Great 57
Algeria 43
Aly, Mohammed 60, 98, 101, 102, 104, 112; confrontation with Doughty 110–11, 160; instructions from Pasha to protect Doughty on journey to Medain Salih 99–100, 106; meeting of in later years 250; relationship with Doughty 112, 113–14, 146; in *Travels in Arabia Deserta* 246
Amadeus, King 47
Aneybar 178–80, 183, 187
Aneyza: Doughty in see Doughty, Charles Montagu: Travels: Arabia
Arabia: Burton's travels in 42–3, 234; Doughty in see Doughty, Charles Montagu: Travels: Arabia; Lawrence in 295–8, 309–10
Arabia Deserta see *Travels in Arabia Deserta*
Arabs: hostility towards Doughty during travels 114, 120, 125, 158–60, 172–3, 180–1, 185, 186–9, 193, 208; poverty of in Sinai 61–2; and Spain 48
Arnold, Mary 11
Arnold, Matthew 8
Arnold, Dr Thomas 7, 8

Bagni di Lucca (Tuscany) 224
bedu 71; characteristics 127; Doughty living with in Arabia see Doughty, Charles Montagu: Travels: Arabia; Doughty's relations with in Holy Land 71, 73; laws of hospitality 139; poverty 125; religion of 127–8; similarities between imagined peoples of Old Testament and 129–30
Bennett, Alan 317
Bernays, Revd Leopold 9–10, 12, 18
Bessam, Abdullah see El Bessam, Abdullah
Betts, Harriet 11
Bishr Arabs 150
Bismarck 30
Blunt, Lady Anne 223, 234, 249
Blunt, Wilfrid Scawen 223, 225, 249, 266, 273, 299, 300
Bodleian Library (Oxford) 25
Boer War 274, 278
Bombay Asiatic Society 219–20
Bonney, Professor Thomas George 23, 230, 231
Bordighera 254, 258
Boreyda 185–9, 194
Bou Saida 45
Bradbury, Professor John Buckley 16, 18, 19
Bridges, Robert 249, 254
British Academy: Doughty elected as honorary fellow of 299
British Association 77; clash with Doughty 230; and Medain Salih expedition 77, 78–9; presentation of paper on Norway by Doughty to 22–3

British Museum 106, 226, 306
Browning, Elizabeth Barrett 224
Buckland, Revd John 7, 8, 9
Burckhardt, Johann Ludwig 63–4, 66
Burton, Sir Richard 223; reaction to
    Travels in Arabia Deserta 120, 248,
    258; travels in Arabia 42–3, 234

Cambridge University 307; awarding
    of honorary degree to Doughty
    299, 303; Doughty at in early
    years 14–15, 16, 17–19, 23
Cambridge University Press 261–2
Capri 224
Carlist movement 50
Carthage 40–1
Castagneto 36
Cavalieri, Signor 36
Cheesman, Colonel Robert 312
Chesterton, G.K. 302
Chew, S.C. 273
Cliffs, The 276, 277, 278, 281, 287, 302
Clouds, The 276, 278, 279–80, 287
Cockerell, Sydney 298–9, 301, 307
Coulton, G.G. 272, 274
Creasy, Sir Edward 59

Dahir, Sheikh 107–8, 109
Damascus 73, 74, 80–3, 252
Darwin, Charles 14, 15
Dawn in Britain, The 256–66, 271, 317,
    318; and CMD's bereavement
    over loss of mother 3–4; change
    in title 259; Christianity in 266;
    depiction of landscapes 258–9;
    lack of enthusiasm for 266, 268;
    memories of Greek travels 52–3;
    CMD's obsession with 16, 258;
    origin of idea for 256–7;
    publication 261–2; research 16,
    256, 259–60; reviews 263–4;
    sympathy in characters 265–6;
    CMD working on 257
de Goeje, Professor M.J. 236, 239,
    241, 242
*Documents Epigraphiques recueillis dans le
    nord de l'Arabie* 226

Doughty, Ann 1
Doughty, Caroline Amelia (*née*
    McMurdo) (wife) 240–1, 242,
    250–1, 252, 257, 281, 313
Doughty, Catherine Frances 282
DOUGHTY, CHARLES MONTAGU
    Early Years: academic record 16, 23;
        birth 2; at Cambridge 14–15, 16,
        17–19, 23; and death of father 5;
        foreign travels with tutor 13;
        inheritance 6, 24; interest in
        geology and natural science 14,
        15, 16–17, 18; living with uncle
        6–7; navy school and failure in
        passing medical test 10, 12–13;
        school holidays 11–12, 14;
        schooling 6, 7–10, 13; stammer 9;
        strength and determination of 9;
        upbringing 4–5, 11, 242
    Personal Life and Characteristics:
        ancestry 1, 4; appearance 222,
        298; awarded honorary degree
        from Cambridge University 299,
        303; change in character after
        Arabian adventures 217; character
        120–1, 156, 222; and children
        255–6, 258, 259; complaining of
        weak health 19, 27–8, 31;
        contacting of Arab friends in later
        years 295–6; courage 47; death
        and funeral 314; desire for
        recognition as an explorer 231,
        232–3; determination 17, 19; in
        Eastbourne 263, 272; emotional
        detachment and self-sufficiency 5,
        14, 34, 40, 44, 242; failing of
        health 299, 313–14; feelings
        about England after return from
        Arabia 222; feelings of peace in
        last years 313; financial problems
        24–5, 303, 306, 308; First World
        War and anti-German sentiments
        277, 278–9, 280–2, 282–3, 287;
        growth of reputation and
        recognition in later years
        299–300; honours bestowed on
        299; ill-health suffered after

Arabian travels 218, 223–4; in Italy 233, 240, 254–5, 257–8; lack of confidence and intellectual insecurity 231, 307–8; in later years 298–9; leaves Italy for England 259; marriage and relationship with wife 240–1, 250–1, 313; memorial 314–15; and mother's death 2, 3–4; move to Merriecroft from Eastbourne in last years 312–13; and patriotism 59, 244, 274, 277, 282, 283, 287; pension 308–9, 311; political views 272–4, 276; portraits of 301–2; recuperation after Arabia 224; relationship with Lawrence see Lawrence, T.E.; and religion 18, 58, 95, 128, 197–8, 271, 286–7, 293, 314; and science 197–8, 287, 292; selling of manuscripts and notebooks 306–7; shyness and desire for privacy 14, 27, 51–2, 272, 312; standard of living in later years 260; stillborn first child 2, 242; in Tunbridge Wells 260; view on imperialism 59–60; visit by son of Sultan of Nejd 300–1

Travels:

– ARABIA 20, 30, 48, 52, 85–216, 261, 271, 296, 317; abandoned in Wadi Er Rummah by guide after departing from Boreyda 189–90, 194; adoption of Arabic name and learning of Arabic 81–2; - in Aneyza 191–7; doctoring 192, 194; forced out of town 200–1; friendship with El Kenneyny 192–3, 194, 199, 205, 207, 295; growing hostility and threats towards 193, 196, 198, 198–200; life in 194–6; and smallpox 198; antipathy towards Islam 41; attack on during journey to Jedah 210–11, 212–14, 226; in Boreyda 185–9, 194; burial of books in desert 183–4; and camels 121–2,

129, 134–5, 317; decision to stay 138; departure from Hail 161–2, 175–6; describing himself as a saiehh 120, 126; doctoring and medical practice 108–9, 114, 128–9, 141–2, 148, 157, 192, 194, 202, 203; drawings and 'squeezes' sent back to Damascus 223; echoing of Bible stories 132–3, 142; at El Ally 106–9, 114, 115, 132; ending of travels in Arabia 215–16; failure of scientific establishment to recognize achievements 225, 226–7, 227–8, 230–1, 249, 271; faltering of determination to stay in 50, 128–9, 132, 133–4, 136; financial profits from 226; and Fukara Arabs 104–5, 121–35, 143–4, 145, 150; failure of vaccinations 125–6, 129; flight from Teyma 131–2, 150; life with 122–3, 124–5; offer of living with from Zeyd 121; relations with Zeyd 133–5, 143, 145; treatment of by 125, 126; women's affection for 123–4; and Hail 139, 140, 150, 151, 152–61, 178–80; hostility and threats towards by Arabs 114, 120, 125, 158–60, 172–3, 180–1, 185, 186–9, 188, 193, 208; ill-health during 138, 139, 140, 158, 159, 206; inscriptions 131, 132, 135, 142, 226–7; journey to Boreyda with Hamed 184–5; journey to Hail with Bishr Arabs 150–2; journey to Jedda 207–16, 218; journey to Kheybar 163–6; in Khubbera 201–4; - in Kheybar 142, 145, 150, 166–78, 232; departure for Hail 177–8; doctoring 169, 173, 176; friendship with En Nejumy 168–70, 171–2, 174, 176–7; inscriptions 170; legends of mysterious Jews in 105, 127; order from Pasha to be well

Doughty, Charles Montagu – *cont.*
looked after 175; relations with
Siruan 166–8, 169, 170–1, 172,
175, 176, 177; suspicion of by
Arabs 169–70; threat to life
172–3, 174; left with group of
bedu after leaving Hail 181–3;
living with Billi Arabs 137–9;
living with Moahib Arabs 139–41,
142–3; maps drawn 113; Medain
Salih expedition see Medain Salih
expedition; mementoes of 217;
motivation and reasons for
117–18, 126–7; notebooks 133,
243; offers of marriage 149;
ophthalmia and weakness of eyes
148–9, 181; plans after Medain
Salih 116–17, 132; refusal to
pretend to be a Muslim 144, 191,
217, 267; relations with Ibn
Rashid see Ibn Rashid,
Mohammed; relations with Said
Pasha see Said Pasha,
Mohammed; suffering and
conditions encountered 137–8;
suffering in heat 133, 137;
techniques in getting out of
trouble 72, 96, 173, 204, 213–14;
and Teyma 130–1, 146–50; visit
to Mabrak En Naga 135–6;
waiting for caravan to Jedda
204–6; in Bombay 218–20; and
British Association see British
Association
– EUROPE 28–41, 55, 224;
detachment 34, 40; and eruption
of Mount Vesuvius 32–6, 40;
France 30–2; Holland and
Belgium 29–30; Italy 32–7; lack
of interest and enthusiasm for 29,
36, 55; Malta 40; notebook on
29, 30, 31, 38; observation of
people met 39; recuperation in
after Arabia 224–5; visiting
Mount Etna in Sicily 37–9;
Greece 52–3; Spain and Portugal
47–51; surveying of glaciers

in Norway 19–23, 76–7
– HOLY LAND 54–74, 76; in
Damascus 73, 74, 80–3; finding of
flint tools in Maan 67–8, 76;
isolation and remoteness felt
72–3; journey to Damascus from
Maan 68–72; journey to
Jerusalem 54; and Maan 62–3,
67, 92, 169; and Petra ruins 63–5,
103; relations with nomad
tribesman 71, 73; return to
Europe 74–5; search for remains
57; shows interest in effect of
politics on people 59; in Sinai
54–5, 56, 57–8, 60–2, 76, 78;
undermining of foundations of
belief 57–8; use of Bible 55, 57;
lack of regard for own personal
safety 50; North Africa 40–6, 47;
notebooks on 51, 52; reasons for
27; sails back to England from
Bombay after Arabian travels
220–2; view of Arabs 46, 58, 121,
143–4, 144–5; visit to Syria and
Palestine with wife 250–2
Writing and Poetry 303–4: *Adam
Cast Forth* 268–71, 278, 318;
article for *Observer* on Hogarth's
book on Arabian history 307–8;
articles on travels in Globus 225,
227; *The Cliffs* 276, 277, 278, 281,
287, 302; *The Clouds* 276, 278,
279–80, 287; *The Dawn in Britain*
see *Dawn in Britain, The*; *Documents
Epigraphiques recueillis dans le nord
de l'Arabie* 226; dramatic
ambitions 271–2; drawing of on
sense of loss 3; influence of
Chaucer and Spenser 25; isolation
from contemporary literature
302–3, 318; Lawrence's attempt
to increase interest in work of
304–5; little social concern in
274; *Mansoul* see *Mansoul*; poor
sales of books 303; shaping of by
Arabian experience 3, 231, 232,
243, 270; style 39–40, 52; *The*

Titans 282; *Travels in Arabia Deserta* see *Travels in Arabia Deserta*; *Under Arms* 274–6, 278; verses written for his children 255–6; *Wanderings in Arabia* 267–8, 304

Doughty, Charles Montagu (father) 2, 5, 6

Doughty, Chester 1

Doughty, Dorothy (daughter) 255, 256, 281, 303

Doughty, Major Ernest Christie 1

Doughty, Frederic Ernest (grandfather) 1

Doughty, Frederica (daughter) 255, 281

Doughty, Frederica (mother) 2, 4

Doughty, Frederick Goodwin (uncle) 5, 6, 7, 12, 24

Doughty, Rear Admiral Frederick Proby (cousin) 1, 4, 251; account of uncle's financial problems and death 5–6; and Doughty 11–12; naval career 10–11, 220

Doughty, George 1

Doughty, Henry (brother) 4, 6, 10, 74, 281

Doughty, Marion 221–2

Doughty-Wylie, Lieutenant-Colonel Dick 281

Duckworth 262

El Ally 106–9, 114, 115, 132

El Bessam, Abdullah 194, 195, 206, 207, 296

El Bessam, Hajji Mohammed 296

El Eswad 89

El Hadj, Emir 99, 106

El Hejr 135

El Kenneyny, Abdullah 192–3, 194, 197, 199, 205, 206, 207, 296

Elstree school 9–10

En Nejumy, Mohammed 168–71, 171–2, 174, 176–7

Ephesus 53, 61

Etna, Mount 37–9

Euting, Professor Julius 225, 236

Eyad 177, 179, 180, 182, 183

Faiz, Sheikh 71–2

Feisal, Emir see Ibn Hussein, Emir Feisal

fellahin 41

Ferrari, Francesco 161

Fheyd 212, 214, 215

First World War 281–2

Fitzwilliam Museum 307

Flint Implements from Hoxne 14

Forster, E.M. 311

Francis, Henry Thomas 16, 17

Fukara Arabs see Doughty, Charles Montagu: Travels: Arabia

Garnett, Edward 263, 294, 301; on *The Dawn in Britain* 266; meeting with Doughty 262; and *Wanderings in Arabia* 267, 268, 304

Garvin, J.L. 307

Geographical Society see Royal Geographical Society

Geological Society 230

Ghroceyb 165, 166

Gilead 70

Globus 225, 227

Goletta 40

Guarmani, Carlo 130

Hail 139, 140, 150, 151, 152–61, 178–80

Hamed 184–5, 186

Hamud 155, 157, 161

Hardinge, Revd Henry 23–4

Hardy, Thomas 244, 276, 302, 303, 309

Hasseyn, Sherif 215–16

Heshbon 56

Hirfa (Zeyd's wife) 122, 123–4, 149, 150, 317

Hogarth, D.G. 282, 285, 297, 311

Hopkins, G.M. 244

Hotham, Amelia 13; Doughty's letter to 105–6, 114–15

Hoxne 14
Huber, Charles 223, 225–6

Ibn Ajjueyn, Eyada 165
Ibn Barak, Kasim 164
Ibn Hussein, Emir Feisal 300, 301, 305
Ibn Nahal 184
Ibn Rashid, Mohammed 66, 145, 164, 178; and Doughty's departure from Hail 161, 162; meetings with Doughty 152–6, 157–8; relations with Doughty 158–9, 160; ruthlessness of 114, 150, 155
Ibn Saud 153, 195
Ibrahim 190
Isabella, Queen 47

Jago, Thomas Sampson 73, 116, 117, 218, 223, 229, 285
Jedda 168
Jerash 57
John, Augustus 301
Joyce, James 318

Kasim 185
Kenneyny, Abdullah see El Kenneyny, Abdullah
Kennington, Eric 301
Kerak 57, 70
Khasneh (Treasure House of the Pharaoh) 64–5
Kheybar: Doughty in see Doughty, Charles Montagu: Travels: Arabia
Khubbera 201–4
Kiepert, Richard 225
Kipling, Rudyard 276

Laleham School 7–8
Lankester, Edwin Ray 16–17
Lawrence, T.E. 272, 299–300, 318; advice given by Doughty to 284–5; in Arabia 295–8, 309–10; attempt to help Doughty's finances 306–7, 308–9; correspondence with Doughty 284–5, 297; on The Dawn in Britain 264; on Doughty's attack

on Germans 278; and Doughty's death 314; on Doughty's narrowness of mind 275–6; friendship with Doughty 286, 295, 301, 309–10, 311; as patron of contemporary artists 301; and Seven Pillars of Wisdom 298, 310–11; Syrian expedition 285–6; and Travels in Arabia Deserta 144–5, 236–7, 243, 304, 305, 306; using influence to increase interest in Doughty's work 304–5
Le Strange, Guy 238, 240, 241
Lejun 56
Lloyd George, David 308–9
Louvain 29, 30
Lyell, Charles 15, 18, 22, 23, 77

Ma'abub 211, 214
Maan 62–3, 67–8, 76, 92, 169
Mabrak En Naga 135–6
McMurdo, General Sir Montagu 240
Mahanna 137, 139
Mahmud 66, 101
Málaga 48–9
Malta 40
Mansoul 35, 283, 287–95, 303, 313, 318; dedication of Doughty to 294, 295; depiction of First World War 290–1; and Doughty's emotional pain at losses during life 3, 289; and eruption of Mount Etna 35; final lines 315; memories of Arabian travels 289–90; memories of Sinai 60; publication 293–4; reaction of critics to 294; reconciling of dilemmas that haunted Doughty 295; religion and science theme 292; response to criticism of influences of modern authors in 25, 302; revealing of Doughty's state of mind 288–9; second edition 38, 294; style 287–8
Martlesham Hall 6, 7
Medain Salih expedition 56, 85–105,

136, 219, 285; agreement with
Zeyd to act as guide 100–1,
102–3; arrival 97–8; artefacts
collected 106; attack on Doughty
by Mohammed Aly 110–11, 160;
conditions 97; dangers faced 89,
100, 116; deaths and suffering on
journey 94–5; departure for 84;
discouragement of by authorities
83; Doughty's obsession with 66,
68, 73, 82; exploration of caves
and monuments 101–2, 103–4,
106; exploration of ruins 112–13,
219; failure to get permission
from Maan to travel to 66–7, 68;
fearful of discovery 85, 88, 89, 90,
96, 97; finding of stone comic
mask 231–2; gathering of bedu
tribesmen 113–14; inscriptions
106, 109, 112–13, 115, 117;
intervention in assault of man
accused of theft 90–1; lack of
interest in by Royal Geographical
Society and British Association
75–9; observations and records
sent back to Damascus 115–16;
Pasha's instructions to
Mohammed Aly to protect
Doughty 99–100, 106
preparations 81–3; reasons for
126–7; refusal of permission to go
with Hadj caravan by Damascus
Wali 73; relationship with
Mohammed Aly 112, 113–14;
sense of isolation 89, 95–6;
supplies taken for 86–7; tedium of
landscape while marching 90;
verdict of by Doughty in *Travels in
Arabia Deserta* 145–6
Medici Society of London 305
Mejelly, Mohammed 244, 264
Menton 31
Merjan 177, 180
Meshaka, Selim 116
Milton, John 269, 270
Moahib Arabs 139–41, 142–3
Mogug 151–2

Mohammed, Amm 197, 246, 290
Motlog 143, 144, 145, 296
Murchison, Sir Rodney 76
Murry, John Middleton 278–9
Muzeyrib 88

Nabataeans 142
Napier, Sir Charles 240
Nigaard glacier (Norway) 21
North Africa 40–6, 47

Observer 307–8
Oliphant, Laurence 238, 241, 251
Ollivant, Alfred 272
Ottoman empire 59, 64, 74, 168, 169;
conflict with Russia 188, 196
Owen, Wilfred 278
Oxford University: awarding of degree
of Doctor of Letters to Doughty
299

Palgrave, William Gifford 141, 154,
156, 157, 162, 188
Palmieri, Professor Paride 32, 34
Paris 30–1
Pest (Hungary) 75
Petra 63–5, 103
Philby, Harry St John 195, 198–9,
249, 299, 300
Pitt Press 235, 242
Pompeii 35–6

Rasmussen, Rasmus 22
Rawlinson, Sir Henry 76, 228, 229,
230
Roberts, Alison 68
Royal Geographical Society 23, 74;
Doughty's dispute with 22,
229–30, 238–9; lack of interest in
Doughty's achievements 227–9;
lack of interest in Medain Salih
expedition 75–9; presentation of
Founder's Medal to Doughty 299
Royal Museum of Berlin 226
Ruskin, John 15
Russia 196; conflict with Ottomans
188, 196

Said Pasha, Mohammed 114, 122,
134; and Doughty's Medain Salih
expedition 83, 84, 85, 93;
instructions to protect Doughty
99–100, 106, 175; relations with
Doughty 60, 118, 174–5
St Mary's Church (Martlesham) 1–2
Saki (H.H. Munro) 276, 280
Salem 210–11, 212, 214, 215
Sandys, George 26
Seven Pillars of Wisdom (Lawrence) 298,
310–11
Shaw, George Bernard 286–7, 318
Shelley, Percy Bysshe 39, 44
Sicily 37
Sinai 54–5, 56, 57–8, 60–2, 76, 78
Siruan, Abdullah Es 166–8, 169,
170–1, 172, 176, 177
Sleyman 206
smallpox 198
Smith, Professor Robertson 235, 240
Socrates 291
Southwell, Henry 24
Spain 47–51; political unrest 47; traces
of Arab world 47–8
Spectator 247–8
Spicer-Simson, Theodor 301–2
Sprenger, Professor Alois 225, 233
Stone of Teyma 148
Sykes, Christopher 296

Taif 215
Teyma 130–1, 146–50
Thaifullah 164–5
Theberton Hall 5, 6, 11, 75
Thiers, Adolphe 30
Thomas, Bertram 299
Thomas, Edward 302
Times, The 247
Times Literary Supplement 263–4
Titans, The 282
Tollog 140, 141
Travels in Arabia Deserta 54, 91, 143,
184, 243–9, 264, 269–70, 274,
318; abridged version of see
Wanderings in Arabia; accuracy
249; achievement 247; agreement

with publishers to print 235–6;
appreciation of from writers and
poets 249; Arabic in 245; Burton's
reaction to 120, 248, 258;
checking and verifying of
observations 236; descriptions of
nomad life 245–7; difficulty in
distinguishing between reported
and direct speech 246; and
importance of Christianity 266;
influence of Chaucer 244; initial
rejection of by publishers 235;
language and style 88, 234–5,
237–8, 243–5, 247; Lawrence on
144–5, 236–7, 243, 304, 305,
306; on Medain Salih expedition
145–6; as a military textbook
236–7, 297; new edition 305–6;
notebooks as source for 87–8,
243; profits made and success
from new edition 305, 306;
publication 242–3; reception 254,
262; reviews 247–8; revisions
238, 239; starting of 232–3;
theme 234; working on 233–4,
241
Treneer, Anne 128, 246
Tuscany 224

Umm Jemal 59
Under Arms 274–6, 278
Utmost Isle, The see *Dawn in Britain, The*

Vesuvius, Mount 32–6, 40
Vico Equense 224
Viennese Geographical Society 78

Wadi Er Rummah 189
Wallin, George Augustus 130
Wanderings in Arabia 267–8, 304
Weled Aly 105
Wells, H.G. 276, 279
Wood, J.T. 53
Woolley, Leonard 285
Wright, Professor William 235

Yeats, W.B. 317

Zamil 191, 192, 193, 194, 198, 199, 201, 203, 205
Zehme, Albrecht 130
Zeyd 104, 116, 118, 119; agreement with Doughty to act as guide at Medain Salih 100–1, 102–3; described in *Travels in Arabia*

Deserta 244, 264; Doughty's dispute with over camel 134–5; offer to Doughty to live with Fukara 121; relations with Doughty 125, 133–5, 143, 145; and wife 123